Patronage and Principle

A Political History of Modern Scotland

AUP titles of related interest

SCOTTISH TEXTILE HISTORY
editors John Butt and Kenneth Ponting

PORTABLE UTOPIA
Glasgow and the United States 1820–1920
Bernard Aspinwall

WILLIAM ELPHINSTONE AND THE KINGDOM OF SCOTLAND
1431–1514
Leslie J Macfarlane

SCOTTISH HANDWRITING 1150–1650
an introduction to the reading of documents
G G Simpson

THE SCOTTISH HISTORICAL REVIEW

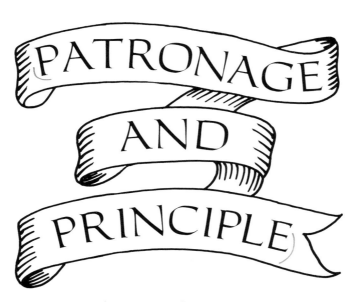

PATRONAGE AND PRINCIPLE

A Political History of Modern Scotland

Michael Fry

ABERDEEN UNIVERSITY PRESS

First published 1987
Aberdeen University Press
A member of the Pergamon Group
© Michael Fry 1987

British Library Cataloguing in Publication Data

Fry, Michael
    Patronage and principle: a political
    history of modern Scotland.
    1. Scotland—Politics and government—19th century
    2. Scotland—Politics and government—20th century
    I. Title
    941.108   DA815

    ISBN 0-08-035063-1

PRINTED IN GREAT BRITAIN
THE UNIVERSITY PRESS
ABERDEEN

To HWR

Contents

Acknowledgements

The work for this book has been done over several years in several places: in Edinburgh, at the National Library of Scotland, the Scottish Record Office and the University Library; in London, at the Institute of Historical Research and the University Library; in Cambridge, at the University Library and at Churchill College. To the staffs of all of them I extend my warmest thanks. John Cooney and Willis Pickard read parts of the typescript, Donald Withrington the whole of it. Their comments and suggestions were most helpful. I am grateful to all my friends for numberless nights passed in Edinburgh, the most convivial of cities, in discussion of Scottish history and politics. They will find that they have contributed a great deal to what I have written.

Introduction

The history which follows has nowhere been narrated in its entirety before.[1] Good general accounts of modern Scotland exist, but politics are granted only a subordinate part in them. That is not surprising: the activity is among the few in which Scots have not excelled, save perhaps after they have emigrated. At home the best of them have more profitably occupied themselves in other spheres, and there has been no Parnell or Lloyd George to enliven the story by his own struggles. Nor has the electoral arena witnessed many great excitements: when not dominated by one party, the country has normally conformed to the pattern in the rest of Britain. In any case, with a legislature 400 miles away, politics could hardly have stood at the centre of national life or even have contributed much to its preservation. Scotland has accordingly produced little in the way of political historiography. Elsewhere it has been the foundation of all other history; here the foundation has usually been laid through social history. But matters have considerably improved in the last twenty years, with a number of valuable monographs. It is surely time to attempt a synthesis.

Beyond bringing together the work of others, however, this volume has an aspiration of its own: to demonstrate that a Scottish political tradition can be disinterred from oblivion and neglect. The objection may be raised that, in the absence of a state, it could scarcely exist—though the man would be foolish who, for example, denied the Poles a political history from 1795 to 1918. There are, of course, many points at which it is difficult to draw a clear line between Scottish and British politics, and I may have erred on the side of being inclusive. But the events could not be given shape unless related to the larger life of the nation.

The view is admittedly tenable that it was in some measure a retrospective invention of Sir Walter Scott, that the ancient patchwork of feudalities had barely coalesced by the end of the seventeenth century before being absorbed into the wider Union. Yet the Union did its share of nation-building too. Amid peace and prosperity, the coalescence continued. The law was codified, national institutions extended their jurisdiction to the whole territory, the

1

conduct of government became, in its corrupt fashion, more systematic. Above all, culture flowered.

The extraordinarily fertile Scottish culture of the great age is inadequately explained on English analogies. It owed just as much to its own Enlightenment (who speaks of an English Enlightenment?) and to the older Calvinist past. From the former it drew its spirit of disinterested inquiry and its cosmopolitanism—it was seldom consciously Scottish, and nationalist hardly at all. From the latter it drew its self-improving energy, its intellectual rigour, its idealism and its democracy. Though by 1832, my real starting point, its highest achievements were behind it, it was assuming a more vulgar and materialistic, though still vigorous, popular form under the influence of new myths of national character held to mark the Scots out from the English. And this bore a late fruit in politics, in the ascendancy of Liberalism. To people often content to use England as a shorthand term for the United Kingdom, politics meant above all, of course, what took place at Westminster. Scottish Liberalism faithfully, almost passively, followed the party leaders there in the great imperial questions. But it was, too, an expression of national values so broad and deep that it could come close to replacing as their vehicle a Church soon hopelessly divided and weakened, and even carry them forward into this century, by which time the culture itself was fragmented and enfeebled. If they were not always taken as of more than provincial significance, the causes and controversies it so copiously produced revealed important facets of Scotland. Indeed, though the old Liberalism was dead by 1930, it may still explain many of such differences as remain between Scottish and English politics. That is why—as well as for the sake of completeness— I have continued this account till the present.

I think it instructive to pursue a continuous narrative, not to be found in histories treating of every conceivable aspect of the nation during particular 'periods'. For the modern era, it is then almost impossible to avoid the First World War as a dividing line. The political narrative is thus deprived of its ending, or else the ending becomes a head without a body, since the effects of the war in public life were not fully seen for some years and took a decade to work out. It is, again, the more difficult to understand the stark contrast of the drained and exhausted post-war polity if this is not directly compared with what went before.

Such continuity was a universal theme of the classical school of political history, in England as elsewhere, and perhaps the essential of its contribution to the growth of nationalism. It may sometimes have gone too far; have attributed ideal properties to national character; have epitomised it as tireless effort in the exercise of determination and will; have preferred to dwell on the high points and pass lightly over sequences of failure. In defence of a similar study of Scotland, I may say that the temptations are largely absent, for the facts of discontinuity and cultural loss have to be accepted. It illustrates rather how an older tradition, though having long followed an unruly path, can all but disappear, in this case to succumb to and be absorbed by the generally undifferentiated mass of a stronger British political culture, so that what was distinctly national became merely regional. Even today, when Scots are much more self-consciously Scottish, they have been unable to resurrect it.

One might contend that the absence of political historiography is at least a minor reason. It makes the Scots incapable of acting in awareness of the past, as the English so often do. When I started my research in the mid 1970s, there were hardly any comprehensive works I could turn to. In most, interest usually petered out after 1707, almost entirely in 1745, in only one of the older studies being sustained till 1843. Not before the *Edinburgh History* of twenty years ago was the story carried coherently forward into the present.[2] That was not itself, however, a political history. If one is to be written with the amplitude which may reasonably be expected, it has to be reconstructed from an enormous range of sources, few of them to any extent concerned with the subject as such.

For it had usually been assumed that Scottish political history was over and done with, even if the assumption has in recent years had to be modified. It can itself be traced back to the great age, to the Edinburgh of the 1820s, when ideas about Scotland were formulated that proved amazingly resilient. One set came from the Whigs, composing their elegant disquisitions in the comfortable splendour of the Signet Library, the other from Scott, scribbling desperately away in Castle Street. Both owed much to Burkean notions of an organic constitution and a living continuity between past and present.[3] But each saw in them different implications for the future of the country.

The Whig view was unionist. It regarded the Union as an act of far-sighted statesmanship which would be logically consummated in Scotland's more or less full assimilation to the rest of Britain. The Scots Whig interpretation of history thus had a peculiar aspect redundant in its English counterpart. There the message of the past was held to lie in the growth of representative institutions, the progress of religious toleration, the advance of knowledge and education. The Scots thought themselves its heirs too, though they did not esteem toleration so much as election by Calvin's God, and were to find equal representation in itself inadequate for a nation also needing institutions. This point was missed by the Scots Whigs. Their unqualified admiration of the English blinded them to all but the blessings of assimilation. They could sincerely believe that in 1707 the history of Scotland had indeed come to a stop. The belief, though now discredited, generally prevailed at the time.

The Tory school also had a peculiar aspect. In England it was concerned with the ascent of the nation into statehood, the rights and privileges of estates and corporations, the strength of the constitution and the law. In Scotland it was besides deeply tinged with nationalism. As Scott wrote, she had since 1707 been left 'under the guardianship of her own institutions to win her silent way to national wealth and consequence'. Inside the Union, therefore, they could still fructify; their destruction was in any event to be deplored. But Scott's veneration of history degenerated among coarser souls into mere nostalgia, into a sentimental wallowing in the lost causes of 1707 and 1745.

We can trace a surprisingly similar frame of mind in some modern views of the Highland clearances and Red Clydeside. In its essential structure, such historical understanding as exists in today's Scotland is erected on the lost or betrayed cause, which may, it is true, have antecedents firm enough for historians to validate the understanding. That generates emotions which console the country for the fact that so much of its serious political activity ran and runs into the sands of indifference and ineptitude. But it also obscures the deeds of those whose causes have not been lost, who have in fact made Scottish history—in this, the Tories are at last getting a revenge.

I do not see how it can fail to be as seriously misleading as the unionism which simply conjures Scotland away. In demonstrating that, I have twice digressed from the continuous narrative. I then deal with the ideologies, socialism and nationalism, which have arisen to rival and eventually to supersede the Liberal one. I have done so because they regard themselves as inheritors and requiters of the lost causes, always assuming that a socialist or nationalist meaning can be read back into them. The making of myths is not necessarily a bad thing. Those made by the Scots of the early nineteenth century helped to distil the complexity of the real world as they sought to advance themselves without sacrificing their identity. In interplay with other forces, the myths did indeed shape history by defining which choices could be perceived as consistent with the national spirit and which not. But the making of myths can also obfuscate reality.

Nationalism, for example, while lively enough in a cultural sense till 1918, hardly existed as a political force, and changed its nature on turning into one. At least till recently, it could not explain what Scots were doing in politics as Scots, for they were surely not pursuing independence. As for socialism, it was all too clearly subject to the general process of Scottish political history, with the idealism of the pioneer days falling victim in the end to centralist conformity. It cannot account for what Scots were doing in politics as workers, since they long shared to a striking extent their rulers' Liberal values. To observe that the Victorian poor led wretched lives, and by our lights unjustly so, is merely banal: it does not prove a 'consciousness' setting them apart from the rest of society.

Moreover, the materialism of the socialist view finds it difficult to reconcile a decline of Scotland with the fact that in the course of this century her people have grown wealthier and happier: for all her problems, she remains among the score or so of the world's leading industrialised countries. The contradiction can only be dealt with by obscure statistical comparisons, in one case, by showing that Sweden has enriched herself faster—on the same reasoning one might argue for the superior socio-political health of South Korea. I suffer no such inhibition in accepting the fact of decline, for history seems to me more than quantification and the comparison of quantities, useful though they may on occasion be.

On the other hand I believe that I have discovered during my studies something better than mere tartanry—to which socialist and nationalist history are anyway not immune. The Labour biography, a surprisingly fecund form, is almost a minor school of kailyard literature. There is persistent devotion to a figure like John Maclean who, in his own eccentric amalgam of the two ideologies, constructed a cause than which none was ever more assuredly lost. But failures are often most affective when deep. And in this miasma of sentimentality, there has been little chance of keeping alive even the memory (let alone any comprehension) of the tradition, liberal and individualistic, but generous and progressive, which had as its crowning achievement the creation of modern Scotland. On the contrary the conventional wisdom, not least that portion of it supplied by Scottish Conservatism, to say nothing of Scottish Liberalism, now views it with hostility.

What Scots were actually doing during its heyday was this: they were obeying the dictates of an ethos which by its nature embraced all classes, which could reconcile national sentiment to the Union, but which, being an idealistic and even a moral force, took relatively little interest in secular political procedures and structures. That was one reason why it did not endure. Yet its aims were not less legitimately Scottish than those of its successor ideologies, of which the accomplishments are in any case meagre. If that is denied, then vast stretches of Scottish history must be blotted out. We must ignore—to give one especially vexing instance—the enormous contribution of the Unionist party, the real bridge between the individualist Scotland of old and the collectivist one of today: a party essentially Liberal, though having ended up through the vagaries of politics as an adjunct of English Conservatism. Thus it is judged irrelevant, even offensive, to the national spirit. Witness the obloquy heaped on Robert Munro, Scottish Secretary 1916–22, for his part in the admittedly misconceived repression which led to the George Square riot. Yet in other respects he was an enlightened man, author of the Scottish Office's one great legislative achievement in the first decades of its existence and to be counted, perhaps above anyone else, among those who have made sure that Glasgow has not suffered the tragedy of Belfast. Here I hope to do him and his like justice.

And since I acknowledge that what they represented is all but dead, I can do so without teleology and prescription. I do not assume that Scotland can only be saved by an Assembly under a Labour administration, as the portal of a participatory socialist paradise. Unlike the materialistic dialectic, my approach admits of no meretricious symmetry and leads to no certain conclusions. At most I can hope to arouse some sympathetic understanding of my subjects, through which a little more intelligence may glimmer into Scottish public life.

Perhaps I should finally declare an interest. My inquiry into politics in Scotland has arisen largely out of the fact that I practise them, and have done so as one of the small and not very valiant band of Tory Home Rulers, about as significant in the affairs of the country in our own day as the Auld Licht Burghers were in theirs. I must leave to others to judge whether my point of view has unduly coloured my account. It is anyway in its basic character an essay, with some judgements speculative. I have aimed to erect an interpretative framework against which others may test their ideas, and if they prove me wrong I shall not repine.

Chapter 1

'Purely Imaginary Abuses'

Among the blessings which Scots felt able to count in contemplating the advance of their nation after the Union was a uniquely beneficent form of government, bequeathed by the events of 1688 and 1707.[1] It offered them peace and progress at home, security and commerce abroad. Moreover, it allowed them to dispense with the distraction of politics. They had, of course, never had a party system with a loyal opposition—instead of Whigs and Tories there had been adherents of the House of Hanover and Jacobites, the latter now extinct. In any case, the Parliament was departed, the Government all but invisible. A factious aristocracy had been tamed by the need to seek favour in London. The bourgeoisie was disfranchised, but did not seem to mind. The mob was apolitical, the peasantry pious and docile. The people were roused only by religious controversy, between those churchmen who wandered on the heights of an untainted Calvinism and those who sank into urbane rationalism; but their disputes assumed no political aspect.[2] The revolutionary thought of the Scottish Enlightenment still left the literati politically quiescent. Where the ferment did flow over into the practical it was channelled with great energy into raising the standard of living through useful sciences.

The demise of the Scottish state was thus little regretted. In its last decades, it had been a constant prey to noble feuding, disruptive of such regular government as might have been possible and held in check only by English bribery. Now, translated to Westminster, the feuds were merely provincial and insignificant. At home, therefore, the rule of law could be extended under a more efficient central administration. Beyond that, London was content to leave well alone, and the Scots to look after themselves. Except in the legislature, the Union remained imperfect. In some other respects it hardly existed, as attested in the Church, the schools and universities, the privileges of the royal burghs, the law and the judiciary, each not only untouched by the Treaty of 1707 but actually guaranteed by it. So the more important institutions shaping the lives of the people were native, and through them Scotland retained a semi-independence: if their vices were at times more prominent than their virtues, they gave her some of the benefits of full statehood without tiresome responsibilities.

Landed property naturally remained the basis of political power, which was diffused through kinship and personal connections. But the Union had also changed much. Outside the subdued aristocracy, groups lacking the chance or need to decamp southwards had won more wealth, broader responsibilities and higher social standing. The country gentlemen were one such, for big holdings of land were by no means monopolised by magnates. Some influence could also be exerted by lawyers, who attended to the affairs of both. If these other groups did not yet outweigh the high nobility, their growing independence had to be respected. The shift in the balance of power further affected the government of Scotland. The problems it presented were not insuperable, but required all the same close attention. It was in particular to the advantage not only of Scotland herself but also of the authorities in London that they should draw the widest possible support from among her peers and MPs. Broadly, it was done by exchanging patronage from above for loyalty from below.

As a matter of fact the peers were often the more easily dealt with. The whole body of them elected sixteen representatives to the Lords. But the choice was almost invariably made from the so-called King's list of official nominees, producing a delegation so servile that some talked of excluding it from the House. A number of the ancient families, such as Hamilton, Minto, Galloway and Selkirk, shared the hope of their English counterparts that aristocracy might be restored as a check on the monarch. They did from time to time challenge the King's list. But the habits of subservience elsewhere in the Scots nobility proved too deep to be easily eradicated.

For the Commons, Scotland had the most narrow and oligarchical franchise of any of the three kingdoms under the Crown. During this period voters in the counties can never have totalled more than 2,500 and those in the burghs perhaps 1,500. The sum of 4,000 compared with a national population of one and a half millions. In relation to that, incidentally, Scotland's forty-five MPs grossly under-represented her.

The electoral system seemed designed for corruption. In the thirty county seats eccentric rules for the suffrage, based on a motley collection of antique laws, restricted it to large landowners, keeping out the lesser gentry and small farmers who often enjoyed it in England.[3] Precise application of the rules was at times confused, but generally they were held to enfranchise feudal superiors rather than proprietors, a distinction important because the superiority could be sold separately from the land. A magnate might parcel his up into a number of smaller ones sufficient to fulfil the qualifications, renting them out to friends and supporters for their lifetimes; or else they might be bought by social climbers from the towns or lawyers who traded and speculated in them. Blocs of votes could be built which were employed in impenetrably obscure and cunning battles for control of the seat. The usual result was to strengthen still more the influence of the most powerful. The composition of the electorate in any county might be quite arbitrary. Its true landed interest could be submerged by the fictitious or 'faggot' votes, cast at the beck and call of one or two noblemen or of outsiders, especially the Government.

In fact, things were not always as bad as they seemed. Nearly all county voters were of a rank and education which rendered them eligible for the increased supply of patronage made available by the Union. They were conscious of their constitutional standing, and not voiceless in the face of abuse. By law each constituency had to fix its electoral register at an annual gathering, the head court. That offered a welcome chance for discussing local and national questions, even for meeting the MP, to a perhaps scattered body of electors. Some made so bold as to instruct him on how to act at Westminster. For many, more especially, the manufacture of faggot votes was a very sore point. In 1778, repeated protests at the head courts led several counties to combine in petitioning Parliament for redress. Legal actions were raised to try and get a judgement against it. But this did not develop into a general movement for reform, since the grievances were mostly personal and amenable to patronage. Nevertheless, seats could always be lost by the disaffection of just a few when the electorates ranged in size from not many more than 200 in the populous counties down to a handful in the smallest. Thus MPs, heads of interests and candidates had to court, sweeten and cajole them far more assiduously than in England.

The burghs, on the other hand, had declined politically, not least because they were no longer a separate estate of the legislature. All those once present in Parliament House were, however, granted a place at Westminster. As they numbered sixty-six, some tiny, they were divided into districts of four or five burghs, only Edinburgh keeping a member to itself. That gave fifteen seats in all. Here the electoral manipulation was less complex but worse. So far from there being any popular franchise, not even the richest and most respected citizens were necessarily represented. The MP was chosen by the corporations on which, as variously defined in the sett (or constitution), membership was confined to certain interests, usually the old merchants' or craftsmen's guilds. Moreover, each council elected its successor, and was naturally inclined to elect itself. Only a minute fraction of the urban population thus enjoyed the franchise. The capital itself had no more than thirty-three councillors, while the total sank as low as nine in the smallest burghs, some of those absentees. Irresponsibility, secrecy, lack of real social standing induced in them a crass venality, which the Government or the other political interests were ever ready to satisfy.

At the same time, the grouping of widely scattered burghs—a typical district contained Lanark, Linlithgow, Peebles and Selkirk—made them difficult to manage. Each might be suborned by a different local landed interest, or by someone more distant. That left a degree of independence at least to the larger burghs. Edinburgh in particular was always minded for the sake of its dignity to exercise a free choice in its parliamentary representation, and required tactful handling to be rendered safe. It was indeed there that a campaign to reform the abuses was started by an advocate, Archibald Fletcher. In 1784 he organised a meeting on the subject of delegates from thirty-three burghs. In 1787 they too petitioned Parliament. The main demand was for an end to self-election by the councils, so as to suppress the flagrant corruption and maladministration in many. But the consequence would have been to grant the right to choose MPs to some larger body of voters. The causes of burgh and parliamentary reform were thus linked. This only made it certain that the Government would concede nothing. Yet it was ever more patently absurd to exclude honest and respectable citizens from control of their local affairs. After 1800 piecemeal changes did proceed, if in a way that left the parliamentary franchise unaltered.

Outside the electorates themselves was one more group enjoying considerable influence. This was the legal establishment, from which sprang many of such reforming impulses as existed. Lawyers were among those who had gained most from the Union, under a separate judiciary retaining its prerogatives practically intact. They formed (with the exception of the clergy, which kept out of politics) the country's only large, trained, professional body. In Edinburgh were hundreds of them, members of the Faculty of Advocates or Writers to the Signet, thronging the central law courts to service the interests of the nobility and landed gentry—who had themselves entered the profession in force and helped to raise its status.

This was convenient for the purposes of government too. Ideas for routine measures were sent as a matter of course to be mulled over at Parliament House in consultation with the parties concerned. If all could agree on the precise form of a Bill there was little trouble in getting it through at Westminster. Legislation as such was rare, however. Strong prejudice existed against changing statutes at all without irrefutable reason, a feeling explicitly embodied in the Treaty of Union's securities for national institutions and private law. Occasional attempts to meddle with them could be ignorant, heavy-handed and unpopular, but Scottish affairs were in general not thought weighty enough to take up much of Parliament's time. That in practice left the initiative to lawyers in codifying, interpreting, indeed reforming the law for the good of society.

Moreover, the Scottish executive, such as it was, consisted of law officers, the Lord Advocate and the subordinate Solicitor General.[4] Though left a fair degree of discretion on the spot, they were responsible to a Minister in London, to the Home Secretary from 1782. Before long their narrow formal powers were stretched, especially during the French wars when more civil together with some military organisation was needed, and when there was sedition to suppress.

Charles Hope of Granton, Lord Advocate 1801–4, gave the Commons the classic exposition of the office in his time. Till 1707, he said, the work of ruling Scotland had been shared among five Ministers. Four had disappeared, leaving the Lord Advocate to discharge their functions alone. He now held 'the whole executive government of Scotland under his particular care'. Despite the Union it was still a different country: 'Its laws, its customs and its manners have undergone no change. In the application of general Acts much local explanation is required and therefore the Lord Advocate must frequently act on his own responsibility.'[5] While the authorities had no wish to extend their powers far, the fact that the limits of legality were so ill-defined could and did lead to arbitrary action by them. Their political purposes came increasingly under attack.

This vestige of a Scottish Government, while in almost every respect minimal, was a key intermediary between the local oligarchies and the sources and resources of power in London. It was so, at least, when conditions were favourable. The view has usually been held that those conditions were established by imperious management of docile MPs through bribes for a greedy electorate. The aim was certainly to get as many ministerial supporters as possible into Parliament, though the results could fall well short of the ambitions. If the methods were corrupt by modern standards, they were taken for granted at the time—not least by opposition elements, which would just as keenly grease palms. Voters, after all, saw it as the duty of their representatives to obtain patronage for them. It reflected their sense of honour and social position. Yet patronage was necessarily a dangerous tool, since Scots could rarely get enough of it: in reality electoral interests might rise and fall because of, or in despite of, the distribution of patronage. It was just one part of the machinery which, at its best, pleased Scotland by providing for her sectional or national interests, while serving the Government's need to keep her quiet and politically conformist. But success depended not so much on the machinery as on the qualities and connections of whoever ran it.

During the first decades of the Union the task was performed by the Secretary of State for Scotland whose office was, however, abolished in 1746 out of misguided political spite. Substitutes for it in the dominance of the house of Argyll and afterwards in the premiership of Bute did not last. When he fell in 1763 there was simply a void, which by Scots was acutely felt. They did not know to whom they should turn in London and had nobody to speak for them there who was not himself prey to the conflict of factions: London for its part neither knew nor cared who were likely to prove its most able or faithful Scottish servants.

What was needed was one man to take control of the machinery. That man was found in Henry Dundas.[6] Regarded as rather an upstart, for he was not a nobleman nor at first even a landowner in his own right, he nevertheless had legal connections exalted enough to give him the job of Solicitor General in 1766, then of Lord Advocate in 1775. He soon displayed talents generally lacking among Scots MPs, for he was shrewd, forceful and diligent, a good speaker and a decisive administrator. His ready address and winning ways, his ability to turn on his charm with the great as to indulge in swinish drinking with the less, meant he was also a perfect fixer of elections. This gave him a chance to aim higher which he very ably exploited. Though rarely scrupling over his methods, he advertised clearly that he was there above all to attend to the interests of a landed class left leaderless by absentee magnates, and to assure their direction of Scottish affairs. All this made him, for example, unusually active in legislation. It even drew him towards reform, notably of the electoral system and in the matter of Catholic emancipation. On the other hand, he was only too prepared to play by the rules of a corrupt age. Time and experience were to bring out his vices: cynicism, gluttony for power, authoritarianism. Since he was never an idealist, his early liberal sympathies did not survive a tempering in the realities of oligarchical government.

After 1779 he enjoyed, as sole Keeper of the Signet, control of Scottish patronage. He soon supplemented it with a generous supply of places and pensions from other sources. Possessed of the wherewithal to satisfy the voters, their families and clients, he built an intricate network of alliances with local political interests. It gave him a huge electoral influence in Scotland. By 1790 it comprehended the great majority of seats. Thus he secured as far as was necessary the country's support for the Ministries in which he served. And he was willing to serve anybody: during the crisis of 1782–3 he was a member of three different Governments, each of different principles. Finally he became an intimate of the younger Pitt, remained a constant lieutenant and reached the pinnacle of his power. A social inferior, and treated as such, he could pose no threat to the ruling circles in the South; at the same time he could deliver north of the border whatever they wanted. So he was safe enough to find favour with the English and potent enough to master the Scots—precisely the combination which both had long sought. He was called the Minister for Scotland, or simply the manager. At his height he was universally popular and respected. Both reflecting and advancing Scotland's integration with the United Kingdom, he was to all, even to opponents, the best national leader since the Union.

At home his achievement was to bring a hitherto ramshackle system to the finest possible pitch of efficiency. It could cope more than adequately not just with recalcitrant individuals but also with the attempt made in the 1780s at a more organised opposition. This was a satellite of the one at Westminster gravitating round Charles James Fox, a sworn foe of the executive power which George III sought in the first part of his reign to enhance, and of which Dundas was a willing tool. In 1783, following the defeat of the experiment in royal government, Fox was able to take office himself in coalition with Lord North, promptly sacking the manager. His rivals then had their chance. Some just disliked him, such as his kinsman, Sir Thomas Dundas, a man of great influence in the northern counties and controller of much Church patronage. Then there was William Adam of Blair Adam, already serving Fox's Whigs as election agent, who wanted to take over the Scottish political machine for himself and them. Others were genuinely intent on reform of Scotland's glaring abuses: their leader, Henry Erskine, was appointed Lord Advocate.[7]

In 1785 the reformers set up a political club in Edinburgh, demurely dubbed the Independent Friends, as a focus for more general support. In fact their chance was past. Scots had not relished the long crisis of 1782–3, with its ministerial shufflings and disruption of the tasks for which they thought government instituted. Careless of the issues, they were painfully surprised at a Scottish administration being changed because somebody thought it could not get on with the one in London. For if Erskine was personable and popular he lacked the electoral skill and influence—which was all that counted at home—of Henry Dundas. He meanwhile had latched on to Pitt, who soon ousted his rivals to become Prime Minister. Winning a large majority at the General Election of 1784, he established himself and his manager in power for the best part of twenty years. They did not, however, sweep Scotland where a mere handful of 'Fox's martyrs' actually lost their seats and perhaps only half of those returned were committed to the new Government. But it was the practice of most to support the Ministry of the day in any event, and

they could be relied on once Pitt proved durable. Certainly Adam's attempts
to build an opposition in Scotland were unprofitable. He had dealings with
seventeen constituencies in the following years, but only five chose MPs
openly hostile to the Prime Minister at the next General Election in 1790.

In 1792 Henry Dundas, now Home Secretary, casually dismissed the
reformers when they tried to get an inquiry on the burghs. He told Parliament:
'The fact is that the abuses are purely imaginary and the Scottish nation does
not feel them to exist.'[8] On the second point he was broadly right. Yet this
brief, weak and fruitless effort did fertilise the seed of a permanent opposition.
To speak of party is premature, but there was in Scotland a perceptible
ideological gap between those holding that the constitutional principles laid
down in 1688 and 1707 needed rescue from executive abuse, and those
content with the cosy, corrupt system which had in practice evolved. It was a
distinction with meaning, a clearer one than any in England—especially as the
rulers of Scotland, increasingly labelled Tories, maintained their monopoly of
power through a lot of nonsense. Still, most Scots who mattered scarcely
questioned the assumption that their constitution was free and happy. The
opposition, for which it was natural to adopt the name of Whig, remained
ineffectual till it acquired some wider base than a political nation so circumscribed could provide.

The manoeuvres there paled in significance before the flood of ideas and
enthusiasms about to be unleashed on Scotland by the French Revolution.[9]
As Henry Cockburn later wrote, it 'was, or was made, the all in all. Everything, not this thing or that thing, but literally everything was soaked in this
one event.'[10] At first many Scots greeted the news from France, for their
political myths inclined them to applaud the fall of tyrants. A gathering of
Whigs in Dundee sent an address to the National Assembly in Paris, welcoming the French to the brotherhood of the free and assuring them that
liberty had done wonders for Scotland. But the spread of confusion and
violence among them during 1790 aroused profound misgivings.

They were reinforced by an outbreak of agitation at home which seemed
to present uncomfortable parallels with that in France. Few ascribed it to
more proximate causes in the decay of the traditional social order. The
agricultural revolution, hastened by the lairds' clearances and enclosures, was
leaving no room for the rising population on the land. Driven off, it either
emigrated or flooded destitute into the towns to seek a livelihood from the
burgeoning new industries. Scotland already had a small proletariat among
the weavers in the West. The 1780s found them in ferment, not just mobbing—
as the lower urban orders always had done to air their grievances—but also
making the first attempts at organising themselves in combinations and
strikes. The tranquil countryside saw the odd grain riot, but disturbance
there arose mainly for religious reasons, from the imposition on parishes of
unwanted ministers by their state or lay patrons. The Kirk's own muted
protests failed to hold the unrest in bounds. The result was a growth of
nonconformity rapid enough to worry the authorities. For though the dissenting Churches were entirely absorbed in otherworldly matters, they won

many members among groups, like the weavers again, taken to be politically radical.

Bourgeois reformers also tried to enlist support in the artisan classes. To that the Government was determined to put a stop. The start of repression came in the summer of 1791 when Pitt issued a proclamation against seditious writings. It solved nothing. Disaffection mounted, going so far as to produce Scotland's first serious political riot for many years, in Edinburgh on the King's birthday, 4 June, 1792. Suddenly the people were inflamed against the authorities, though less by their hardening political dogmas than by their unyielding response to social and economic grievances. Still, a bond of opposition was being formed early between the working and middle classes of Scotland.

It developed with the establishment in the capital of a Society of Friends of the People in July 1792. Unlike its senior counterpart in London it set low subscriptions, founded many branches and aroused lively popular interest. All through that autumn and winter riots flared in Scotland. If the immediate causes were usually non-political, the discontent often passed over into open sympathy for revolutionary ideas. The leading Friends would not follow so far, but by the end of the year they had anyway advanced enough to hold a General Convention in Edinburgh. It was a moderate affair affirming support for the constitution and rejecting the democracy preached by one delegate, a young advocate named Thomas Muir.

The radical leaders were overwhelmingly middle-class, some were even nobles, and all were attached to peaceful reform. But the Government would see them only as wicked Jacobins and fomenters of rebellion among the lower orders. Working through his Lord Advocate and nephew, Robert Dundas of Arniston, the Home Secretary set out to crush them. Early in 1793 he tried to intimidate them by having a few unimportant men prosecuted. Most got off lightly, but enough had been done to persuade the more timorous reformers that the agitation should not go further. Others, undeterred, held a second convention in April 1793. A markedly radical gathering, it provoked Dundas to stronger action. Muir was arrested, charged with sedition and sentenced to fourteen years' transportation by the notorious Lord Braxfield after a blatantly unfair trial. The judge's summing-up was famous for revealing the view of the constitution held by the diehard Tories: 'A government in every country should be just like a corporation; and, in this country, it is made up of the landed interest, who alone have the right to be represented'— a description which, in Scotland, was not even universally accurate.[11]

Such severity served only to revivify the Friends of the People, and in more extreme form. They took to advocating such anarchical innovations as annual Parliaments and manhood suffrage, while their views on how to secure them seemed to equivocate between reform and revolution. A third convention, an all-British one, was summoned to Edinburgh at the end of 1793. The authorities eyed it suspiciously for a few days, then pounced. The meeting was dispersed and three of its organisers were arrested, condemned and transported.

The reforming movement in Scotland now disintegrated. Horrified at the social and political ferment, the Scots Whigs' connection, such as it was, all but dissolved. Some, like Sir Thomas Dundas, went over to full support for the Government. Erskine and Fletcher had in any case steered clear of the Friends of the People for fear of connecting themselves with extremism. Now other moderates were frightened off, while popular support grew uncertain. The remnants were easily mopped up. But Dundas was not yet finished. Under the pretext of a threatened French invasion he sought to strengthen further the Ministry's position, using preparations for war as a spur to patriotic fervour: many radicals, too, including Robert Burns, joined the volunteers that were raised. Dundas then exploited the hysteria he was whipping up to intensify the repression. The Act against Wrongous Imprisonment (1701), equivalent of habeas corpus, was suspended. In the capital a revolutionary plot was discovered (or invented) and the first radical hanged in consequence. There was a general witch-hunt against anyone tainted with dissent—strikes were suppressed, workmen dismissed, tradesmen boycotted, even philanthropy was regarded with mistrust. Erskine himself, though amiable and loyal, did not escape the long reach of the vindictive Tories, who in 1796 deposed him from his post of Dean of the Faculty of Advocates. This concerted campaign brought the agitation to a halt everywhere. There were more riots in 1797 over the raising of a militia, and a secret democratic society, the United Scotsmen, continued in some form till about 1802. But these matters were of little import and in effect the first great political upheaval in modern Scotland was over.

The authorities had confronted and subdued it with surprising speed. The vigour of their reaction is explicable by the passive and loyal nature of the Scotland they had known. Dissidence had sprung from no obvious foundations and within a breathtakingly short time appeared to the conservative to be impelling every class of society towards revolution. The noblemen and bourgeois found the Scottish system irreconcilable with any rational principle, while the impulse among artisans and peasants seems to have been basically social and economic. In neither case would the Government hear of any justification for the protests. Ministers were, of course, genuinely appalled at the prospect of a finicky reformism or a mischievous revolutionary fad creating enough trouble to overthrow Britain's free constitution, which they believed in no degree comparable to the corrupt polity fallen in France. So their response was repression, and if the opposition withstood and survived it, yet more repression. The tactics paid off. The radicals, even moderates among them, were discredited, isolated and crushed. They had never really shaken Scotland's instinctive conformity and obedience. So she was impervious to their influence and indifferent to their fate. Patriotism and persecution easily restored the shaken national consensus.

But despite appearances the Government's position was the weaker for the events of the 1790s. The disaffected were cowed but not in most cases reconciled. Professional men in the burghs, industrial workers or poor farmers, all had the same experience of repression and reforming fervour. Though long cut off from one another they did, when the wars with France ended, begin to find again common grounds of interest and greater support in public opinion. These were the bases of a more coherent opposition. It was to be built up on the underlying social and economic forces issuing in that industrial revolution which brought the deepest transformations Scotland would ever experience. All through society over the next forty years the strains became increasingly evident. They alienated large sections of the nation to an extent that went beyond the comprehension and countervailing powers of the old regime. In the long run the policy of no surrender did the Tories little good. It could only work when the outcome was quick and did not withstand the more persistent reform campaign after 1815.

Meanwhile Dundas continued to consolidate his parliamentary position, for virtually the whole Scottish political nation rallied to the Government in the war years. So sure of himself was the manager that he determined to try and capture every seat in the General Election of 1796. He did not quite succeed, though he contrived to return thirteen peers and possibly forty-three MPs. But this was his apogee. [12]

For the moment, however, dissidence was beaten. Even the respectable Whigs all but gave up and hardly dared show themselves for fear of persecution. The martyred Erskine was still revered by Edinburgh intellectuals of Bar, Church and university. Here—surprisingly, in view of the blight cast on any career by nonconformity—the Whigs attracted some of the ablest young men, notably a group of advocates including Francis Jeffrey, Henry Brougham, Francis Horner and James Loch. Elsewhere a few noble houses, such as Hamilton and Minto, were safe in their territorial fiefs. Adam of Blair Adam, out of Parliament, just held a Scottish electoral interest together with the patronage of the Prince of Wales. But so feeble was the opposition now that for some years its leading figure was an Irish peer, Lord Moira, who served personably as commander-in-chief in Scotland and, better still, formed a local connection by marrying the Countess of Loudoun.

Nobody could have shaken the Tories if it had not been for developments in London. In 1801 Pitt fell and, to Scotland's amazement, Dundas with him. Disgusted by the peace at once concluded with Napoleon, he refrained from politicking for a while. Though undiminished in his countrymen's esteem, he had lost his intimate link with the fount of power and could no longer demand of them a clear-cut commitment for or against the Government. The new Prime Minister, Addington, strained relations in an inept attempt to build its own following in Scotland. This was acutely embarrassing to Lord Advocate Hope, who was Dundas' brother-in-law. He found it prudent to stay out of public view for lengthy periods, before opting gratefully for the Bench. In time a wary working partnership was formed—so long as Dundas was left in control at home, he would tolerate the existence of the Ministry. The limits on his position were all the same revealed in the General Election of 1802. Of thirty-nine friends of the Government returned, perhaps only twenty-six were fully pledged to himself and Pitt. But he was still powerful enough for Addington to sweeten his judgement by elevating him as Viscount Melville afterwards.

Yet public opinion was clearly not to be so easily manipulated now. It was hard to maintain the pretence that inoffensive Whigs were at bottom republican subversives. The lifting of Melville's oppressive weight and the easing of international tension gave them in any case greater security. It found striking expression with the appearance in October 1802 of the *Edinburgh Review*. This was the brilliant, irreverent production of the young Whigs who despaired of succeeding at the Tory Bar. Turning to journalism—Jeffrey was editor and Brougham a prolific contributor—they discovered they could offer a wit and intelligence found in no other periodical of the time. Before long they were widely read in the middle class all over Britain. That raised them, in fortunate contrast to the senior Whigs, to a prominence where they could not be so readily persecuted by the local Tories. Nevertheless they took at first a cautious line, avoiding party controversy.[13]

That happier position persisted even after they showed a decided coolness to the resumption of war in 1803, at a time when the despotism risen in France and the threat of invasion united all in patriotism. Pitt soon returned to office and Melville, with a new Lord Advocate in Sir James Montgomerie, again took control of Scottish affairs. Neither of the great Ministers was as secure as before, however, and both wooed Moira—Pitt for his links with the Whigs at large and Melville for his authority in Scotland. But no arrangement could be found for bringing him into the Cabinet. These were trivialities compared with the blows about to fall on Melville. In 1805 began the proceedings which led to his impeachment for peculation the next summer. Early in 1806, in the depths of this personal crisis, he lost his most potent supporter with the death of Pitt. The Scots Whigs were in raptures at the prospective end of the manager's long reign. But he was acquitted and his power, if weakened, was far from shattered.[14]

Pitt was succeeded by the Ministry of All the Talents. In Scotland it meant the first change of government for twenty-two years, with the main offices filled by Whigs. The Tories wanted Moira as manager, and he pressed his own claims too. But at the insistence of the Whig old guard which had dwelt so long in the wilderness, patronage was entrusted to one of its number, the eccentric ex-Jacobin 'Citizen Maitland', now consenting to use his proper style as Earl of Lauderdale. Erskine came back as Lord Advocate, with John Clerk of Eldin as Solicitor General.

Parliament was dissolved, giving them the chance to challenge Melville's power structure. The new manager was hardly the man to win staid and loyal Scotland, but he was not unskilled at electioneering. The King's list of representative peers was this time his. The long task of building up the party in the Commons was started. Erskine was returned for the Stirling Burghs, Adam—after an absence from the House of twelve years—for Kincardineshire, while the young William Lamb, recently a student at Glasgow and one day to be Prime Minister as Lord Melbourne, secured the Haddington Burghs on Lauderdale's interest. Adam claimed that the Government could count on twenty-three supporters from Scotland, though some turned out mere fairweather friends. In fact the Whigs had actually won no more than six new seats, a performance much worse than in England. The Tories were not decisively broken.

That became clear as the Government quickly began to lose direction.

One supporter wrote of 'an apathy in the conduct of administration which is wonderful.'[15] William Maule, just elected for Forfarshire, noted that 'Ministers are still in the same dormant state respecting Scotland in spite of all Lord Melville's friends are doing to irritate them.'[16] What the hardline Whigs wanted was a purge of those friends from the many positions in Scotland where they were so comfortably ensconced. Plans for it were drawn up, but never executed. Instead, with touching public spirit, Lauderdale and Erskine set out zealously to prove their credentials not as jobbers but as real reformers. In rapid succession they published proposals for the clergy, the poor laws, the tenure of landed property, the test laws and, most important, the legal system. The main purpose here was to re-organise the malfunctioning Court of Session.[17] Its fifteen judges took no care to co-ordinate their rulings. The status under Scots law of such crimes as treason, sedition and combination remained vague during crucial periods of disorder.

Evidently the Government in London would not be long-lived and the plans were hurried along. That was a misjudgement, for they raised major issues, constitutional as well as juridical. The court's form and status were governed by the Treaty of Union. There was serious doubt whether it could be altered simply by subsequent statute or amounted to an unalterable fundamental law. The Ministry had to contend with automatic opposition from diehard Tories—not including, however, the Melville connection, which recognised a need to improve the court but objected to details of the scheme. The same line was taken even by the *Edinburgh Review*. The reform got bogged down, but in any event the Government lasted only a year. The work had to be left to its Tory successor, which by 1811 had thoroughly recast the court's organisation and procedure, doing much to remedy its defects and give it its modern shape.

The resignation of the Ministry of All the Talents had meanwhile marked the end of the senior Whigs' influence. Erskine in particular was discredited by their failures. His disillusion was complete when in 1811 he was ignored in the selection of a new Lord President of the Court of Session, and he retired from public life. In the next year's General Election acid remarks were made at the contrast between the bumbling of the seniors and the zest of the juniors when Brougham, their defeated candidate in the Stirling Burghs, still emerged with credit from the fiasco of a disputed return urged on him by Clerk of Eldin, to whom party management had passed. The future lay ever more clearly with these bold idealists, already pre-eminent, in ability if not yet in numbers, in the key institutions of Bar and university. Unlike their elders, they were not first and foremost concerned to sway the political nation. Their hopes rested instead on the moral training of a new and much broader generation of public opinion. Specifically, this meant rousing and articulating the interest of the middle class in political and economic change. The young Whigs believed that if they could discredit the ideology of privilege, then the system it supported would fall. The theme was taken up by the *Review*. Its rising reputation established cordial contact between the authors and reforming circles in London. This was of little immediate benefit, however. As abroad the struggle against Napoleon and at home patriotic fervour intensified once more, the Scots Whigs had to lie low. Till 1815 overt political activity by them was excluded.

All the same the Government was now less formidable in Scotland than before.[18] True, it had public opinion solidly behind it. Melville's acquittal in 1806 was greeted with jubilation. But the edifice of power was certainly damaged, in part by discord within his own family. His nephew Robert, whom ill-health had obliged to retire as Lord Advocate in 1801, yet remained his closest adviser on patronage and on politics generally. While the Tories were out, he bitterly opposed any compromises, though that could not solve the crisis. Melville was himself more moderate, telling Moira that he had no objection to the Whigs' plans for the country so long as they did not fight his MPs. A second nephew, William, at this point sitting for Sutherland, was being trained to take over detailed management of the interest. But, fearing it might break up in opposition, he tried to strike bargains with Lauderdale, a move endorsed by Melville's son and heir, another Robert. When this came to light, William forfeited entirely the trust which the head of the clan had placed in him, and resigned from Parliament for a while.

Between Melville and his son there was also much misunderstanding. Robert joined the Government which overthrew the Talents in 1807. Henry supported it sulkily, since it would or could not restore him to the Cabinet. The effects of the disunity were seen at the General Election which it soon called. The Tory factions emerged on top, of course, but the Melville interest did no more than maintain itself with about twenty-seven MPs. It found itself unable to attack with any spirit the seats grabbed during the interregnum by the opposition, which held on to perhaps thirteen: by past standards, a remarkable feat. Melville protested that this was because he had not been allowed to recover full control of Scottish patronage, blustering that he would renounce responsibility for it altogether unless he were. It was a deep embarrassment to Robert, who was in effect representing in the Government an interest threatening at any moment to defect. Painfully obvious, too, was Melville's readiness to jettison his son if he could get back into office himself. They came close to an open breach in 1809, though each soon saw that he could hardly dispense with the other. In March 1811 Dundas was still bragging that 'whatever government may think of their own power, they can do nothing in this country but through me.' In May, however, he was dead.

He is not to be placed in the highest rank of statesmen. But two achievements can be credited to him in Scotland. First, he was the father of the Tory party. He had seized the chance of forging her fragmented interests into a stronger wedded to one centre of power or another in London. Then in the 1790s he stirred up a militant conservatism in which to clothe this framework. Thus the Scots Tories became a definable party, with a principle and a machinery for exercising power.

Secondly, he helped to perfect the Union. Not till he took a hand were Scots sure of what they thought a due share of its benefits, especially the spoils of Empire. For twenty years he paid close attention to India, from 1793 to 1801 as president of the Board of Control. The English often bemoaned the favouritism to his countrymen in Indian appointments and concessions, but this was what lured them into the imperial mission. That roused to new heights the British patriotism engendered by the wars. Before long it was as strong as, if not stronger than, the older, specifically Scottish one. Part of Melville's legacy was Scotland's later image of herself as the cultural partner of England in great national tasks. There were even Scots, rather North Britons, anxious to efface any difference between the two. Though he doubtless gave no thought to the ultimate fate of his nation, Melville himself combined the local and imperial in a unique manner. Of all the Scottish leaders of the United Kingdom, he kept the closest links with his country and the warmest interest in its affairs.

After his death, the old unthinking loyalties were eroded and the grip of the ruling oligarchy irresistibly loosened. The other members of the Dundas clan could not match the qualities of their deceased patriarch. Robert, the former Lord Advocate, abandoned politics. There was thus no rival to the succession as manager of his cousin Robert, second Viscount Melville. Sober and conscientious, he lacked his father's earthy geniality as well as his taste and skill for the seamy side of public life, so that control of the constituencies grew weaker. At least, however, he was reconciled with William, who now became MP for Edinburgh. Together they held the family interest together sufficiently to give Melville some weight in London, where he served for fifteen years in Lord Liverpool's Cabinets. Yet they were neither very rich nor extensively landed, and it was habit as much as anything that maintained their position.

They took over in a rapidly changing country where the sentiments which had previously united the people were being dissipated. A hierarchical rural society automatically deferring to the great had married naturally with the aristocratic polity. But now Scotland was firmly set on the path of development into an urban, industrial society where the laird would be an alien. Besides, loyalty was deliberately harnessed to repression during and after the wars. Its victims had no cause to glory in the constitution. Nor did the British patriotism created in those struggles prove a boon to the Tories. When Scots looked at themselves in a wider context they saw they were among the least politically privileged of all. Finally, faith in human brotherhood, propagated by the radicals and lent striking form by Burns, the national poet, became a far more potent rallying cry than affection for the eccentricities of the old Scotland. In the coming unrest the Tories' position steadily deteriorated: people no longer believed a revolution was brewing and began to blame the troubles on failure to reform.

A resurgent radicalism was the basic determinant of the course of Scottish politics from now on. Wartime inflation intensified the sufferings of the workers, who did not await the peace to air their grievances. The Glasgow weavers started agitating over their wages in 1810. The new Corn Law of 1812 brought a burst of resentful rioting, and there were serious urban disturbances the following years. Things became even worse after 1815. The period of high output needed to sustain the war effort was followed by a collapse of prices, wages and employment. Returning soldiers placed further pressure on the labour market, as did the Highlanders arriving in the West in large numbers after the clearances.

Here was a multitude of causes for the radicals to champion, and they found Scotland receptive. Much of the initial stimulus came from the South, especially from correspondence between the weavers in Glasgow and Manchester, and from evangelising tours by leading English radicals such as Major Cartwright. But a native movement soon took root. Just as in the years after 1789, reform societies were established in most Scottish towns, demanding manhood suffrage, annual Parliaments and measures to promote the general social and economic advance of the people.

Before long the Government set once more about repression. A zealous Lord Advocate, Alexander Maconochie, prosecuted without much scruple but also without much sense four of the leading radicals in the State Trials of 1817. They were defended by Whig lawyers, who were able to embarrass him by exposing his rigged evidence. Juries were noticeably reluctant to convict, and none of the accused received a sentence heavier than six months' imprisonment. Altogether, this attempt to show a stern face to disaffection misfired and merely damaged the Government. At the first opportunity, the inept Maconochie was eased out of his post, if only to be replaced by the equally reactionary Sir William Rae.

After a brief economic revival the recession deepened again. In 1819 a wave of riots and demonstrations thoroughly alarmed the Ministry, which brought in the repressive Six Acts. In England the outbreak of proletarian violence culminated in the Peterloo Massacre. Scotland was quieter, but radicals were active and the authorities nervous. In February 1820 they arrested twenty-seven Glasgow men accused of planning an uprising. That failed to quell the unrest. On 1 April posters appeared in the Western towns signed by a committee for organising a provisional government. They called for a general strike and a popular revolt. Troops hurried to Glasgow, where street fighting broke out on 5 April. The same day about fifty men set off from the city to seize the Carron iron-works. Soldiers met them near Falkirk in the so-called Battle of Bonnymuir. A few were killed and the rest taken prisoner: three were eventually hanged. Though a small affair, it frightened Scotland. Never before had this tranquil country emulated England with an armed rebellion of industrial workers. Still, the scale of the trouble was undeniably modest, and its significance lay rather in its wider effect on Scottish politics.[20]

Unlike in the 1790s, the Scots working-class radicals had since 1815 been agitating on their own, with no direct help from society's middle and upper ranks. This isolation, coupled with urban and industrial distress, was at bottom demoralising; it turned some to unreasoning outbreaks of violence or, in sublimated form, to secret societies and conspiracies for insurrection. That stream of activity was, at least as a national movement, crushed in 1820. But there had been all the while another current of proletarian endeavour. Scottish workers had long shown an enthusiasm for social independence, education and self-improvement. At the end of the eighteenth century it found expression through religious dissent and democratic political sentiment. Now it led to a burgeoning of trade unions, craft associations, benefit societies and the like. Here politics, religion and social reform could be freely discussed. Though these bodies were peaceful, a certain militancy among them was not precluded. One purpose of trade unions is after all to organise strikes, and there were some big ones in Scotland at this time—60,000 workers in the West stayed out for a week during the disturbances of 1820. But the alternative forms of action caught on because they were above all constructive: they offered the proletariat the chance to lift itself out of the squalor and hopelessness from which otherwise it could only occasionally emerge to maim, kill and make pathetic attempts at revolution. They were to permit co-operation with the petite bourgeoisie in the burghs, which often shared the working class's radical idealism. They enjoyed the further advantage of largely escaping official attention after 1815. The Government concentrated on those it saw as revolutionary political agitators. It had its hands full with the State Trials and the repression, so that systematic proceedings against all working-class groups were impossible. While militant radicals hanged, trade unionists could organise in peace.

The events of 1820 did not represent a defeat for such people. Indeed, it brought them new strength. Their influence increased steadily—by the middle of the century the impulse for self-help was the distinctive mark of the Scottish proletariat. For the moment their tactic was to emphasise that urgent action on reform would be needed if the violence was not to be repeated on a larger and bloodier scale. Of course, some of their social superiors had once more been incited by the Government to fear and hate the mob. But others, notably the Whigs, agreed with the analysis and the conclusions.

After 1820 the political initiative began to pass them, the advocates of gentle, evolutionary reform. Since the war they had been building up their own constituency among the bourgeoisie and the more enlightened lairds. Their activities were less spectacular than the radicals', but they had made enough quiet progress to convince themselves that reform was possible without revolution. Their purpose remained the preservation of the existing social order, with whatever modifications of the constitution were needed to ensure its survival.

One might say with hindsight that this committed them ultimately to democracy. They did not see things so. They could not conceive of a society where power and influence were not based on landed property. Indeed, they were to some extent a party of the nobility, for the houses of Hamilton, Atholl, Roxburghe, Breadalbane and Minto were all active in the cause of reform after 1815. As patriotic constitutionalists, these found the burgh cliques especially disgusting and were anxious to secure a greater influence for independent gentlemen. The middle-class Whigs agreed. Aristocracy was to them a manifestation of every civilised society. Jeffrey and his circle were if anything anti-democratic. He insisted on a distinction between the right to vote and civil liberty, maintaining that freedom might be guaranteed even by an unreformed Parliament so long as it could meet frequently and criticise without restraint. In any case, he asserted, the Commons did find a place, if not a numerically representative one, for all the elements in British political life.[21]

An important point on which the junior Whigs departed from their seniors was in their attitude to the French Revolution. They tried to pick out its positive aspects, regarding it, despite the atrocities it produced, as the expression of genuine grievances which could find no other outlet. Savage repression, Jeffrey argued, was the worst thinkable response to similar ones in Britain. His strength lay in this open-minded approach to dissent and even rebellion. When proletarian unrest broke out during the French wars, he was the only leading Whig to posit a link between economic distress and the need for reform. He became convinced that more active commitment from his party was needed if the people were not to be lost to British constitutionalism.

In a contest with the ruling class, Jeffrey now reckoned, the people were bound to win. So he urged the Whigs to ally themselves with radical leaders, guiding and restraining their demands, keeping their campaign orderly. He and his friends were thus alert to the chances of widening their base in Scotland after 1815. Within the establishment the possibility of progress was extremely limited. Though many of the ablest at the Scots Bar were Whigs, it was only in 1811 that they started being promoted to the Bench—a concession granted in the Tory package of legal reforms. In Parliament they had recovered from near-annihilation at the turn of the century, but at best could aspire to return only about a dozen members. These, however, pressed valiantly for change. Led by Lord Archibald Hamilton, MP for Lanarkshire, by Thomas Kennedy of Dunure, MP for the Ayr Burghs, and by James Abercromby, who sat for an English seat, they constantly attacked aspects of the Scottish electoral and legal systems and presented many motions for their amendment, all without success. Scotland even possessed one of the few radicals who won their way to the Commons before 1832 in Joseph Hume, MP for the Montrose Burghs; but his interest lay in economic reform.

Whig arguments were not lost on some of the landed gentry, though their position had been strengthened after the war. Suffering from the agricultural recession then, they had demanded and got protective tariffs. These, however, raised prices and clearly cut across the interest of other classes. Radicals concluded that large estates were bad in economic terms as well as in the way they preserved political influence. Instead they argued for a diffusion of the power that went with the ownership of land. A system of smaller farms with a free peasantry would, they claimed, make Scottish rural society more equitable, prosperous and independent-minded. One utopian pamphleteer, Robert Gourlay, wrote of how reform would see 'villages rearing up, and the swoln carcasses of cities falling away and deserted.'[22] Such notions were the origin of the land question which proved so politically contentious for the rest of the century. Gourlay, a touchy laird from Fife, was an example of how certain among the efficient and intelligent Scottish gentry were themselves becoming exasperated at the Government's reactionary attitudes—some also thought they could get along without the Corn Laws. It was in the county elections that liberal opinion was first to make itself felt.

There was only one county completely under liberal sway, and that was Sutherland. The reigning duke, though the wealthiest man in Britain, was thought very advanced by his peers. He believed in parliamentary reform and was a disciple of Adam Smith's political economy, as modified by Malthus. His right-hand man, James Loch, was of impeccable Whig credentials, a Parliament House advocate, a nephew of Adam of Blair Adam, a contributor to the *Edinburgh Review*, an opponent of the conventional landlord interest in his support for free trade and an enthusiast for every type of economic improvement. He too had found the Tory Bar practically closed to him, but turned to estate management rather than politics. The undeveloped tracts of the Sutherland domain in the North gave him scope for action. He set about a long-term programme of opening up communications, introducing new industries and turning moor and mountain over to profitable sheep. The only trouble was that the wretchedly poor, congested population had to be cleared. The benevolent Sutherland and Loch would have regarded any resistance— and there was none to speak of—as quite unreasonable, stemming from primitively conservative people who did not understand what was good for them. In fact they successfully carried through the earliest experiment in social engineering inspired by liberal idealism. After reform, Loch was for twenty years MP for the Wick Burghs.[23]

But the main target of Whig proselytising was the bourgeoisie, which had been staunchly Tory during the war. Even before 1815 its instinctive philanthropy was finding an outlet in public meetings, especially in Edinburgh, on such worthy subjects as slavery, income tax and plans for the North Bridge. Concern was soon aroused afterwards for the most obtrusive Scottish problems of the moment, those caused by the rapid expansion of the towns and cities and the distress of the post-war recession. Thoughts about practical local improvements could be easily led on through a recognition of the appalling state of burgh administration to sympathy for the general aims of reform. Before long the Whigs had the most enlightened, respectable citizens interested in all three.

The Edinburgh Whigs, faced with the insignificant, incompetent and cor- rupt clique in charge of their corporation, were the most vocal. But greater things had been achieved by their counterparts in Glasgow. Its merchant princes, whose already vast wealth waxed fabulous through blockade-busting in Napoleonic Europe, had long won control of the council. They were only kept out of Parliament by the antique arrangement under which they shared a seat with three small burghs. In 1812, however, the popular Kirkman Finlay was elected for the district—the first native Glaswegian MP in more than seventy years. The breaking of the East India Company's statutory monopoly on trade with the Orient was Glasgow's most devout wish. In a tremendous coup he secured Parliament's agreement to it in 1813: one of his ships at once set off from the Clyde to the Ganges. But his liberalism was erratic. He supported the Corn Laws, getting his house attacked by the mob in return, and helped to set up a network of spies to infiltrate radical groups in the West. The Glaswegians' intellectual was James Ewing, the richest man in the city and generous with benefactions. In his pamphlets and lobbying he may have done more even than Finlay to open up the Indian trade. He and a further member of the circle, James Oswald, represented Glasgow in the Commons after 1832. Though these men were by no stretch of the imagination subversive, the Government still contrived to fall out with them. Rae publicly castigated them for having been too lenient over the unrest in the city in 1820.[24]

Dundee was like Edinburgh in having a venal corporation, led by Alexander Riddoch, fighting a rearguard action against mutinous literary men patronised by enlightened lairds, George Kinloch of Kinloch and William Maule, still MP for the neighbouring county.[25] Unlike in the capital, there was also support from a powerful manufacturing interest, in the rapidly expanding textile industry. The quarrel between the two factions was pursued with typical viciousness—Kinloch had actually to flee to France to avoid a charge of sedition. But the reformers won their symbolic battle here, getting a new harbour placed under impartial commissioners rather than the rapacious council. Kinloch was pardoned by George IV during his visit to Scotland in 1822, and became the city's MP after the Reform Act. In many parts of the country, in burghs as obscure and distant as Elgin or Annan, the same battles were being waged.

So the burgh reform movement revived. Hopes for its quick success rose when the discovery of a legal irregularity enabled the burgesses of Montrose to elect an entirely new council in 1818, and Joseph Hume as MP for the district soon afterwards. But the Government found means of stopping similar moves elsewhere. In 1819 Lord Archibald Hamilton succeeded in persuading the Commons to appoint a committee of investigation on the Scots burghs. Its report was unfavourable to the existing regime, but the Government refused to act on it. The reason was, of course, that the councils' special constitutional role made their reform tantamount to parliamentary reform. This objection rendered explicit the common interest of the new civic movement and the political opposition.

Controversy flourished in other spheres: *The Scotsman*, the country's first liberal newspaper, was founded in 1817, soon to be followed by a number of Tory publications.[26] A real newspaper war developed in Scotland with much verbal violence on both sides. The middle classes grew used to partisanship and no longer found attacks on authority shocking. With their growing political maturity, it was absurd for the Government to assert that these honest citizens were the unconscious tools of the mob and that against them the corrupt burgh administrations must at all costs be preserved. Tory intransigence did the Whigs' work of unity for them.

In the aftermath of the Radical War the Whigs felt bound to take some wider initiative. They held their first public meeting for decades in Edinburgh in December 1820. It urged the king to dismiss his Ministers and launched a petition to that effect which collected 17,000 signatures, a remarkable measure of mass support. This was an object to which Jeffrey had long been working. He and his fellow Scots Whigs were at this point ahead of their English colleagues, who were still torn in their relations with the lower orders between fear and friendship. From 1820, Walter Scott reported, the Whig lawyers were in regular contact with the 'democratical party' in Edinburgh.[27] Nearly all these democrats were anxious after the bloodshed of the previous months for a quick and peaceful settlement of their claims, on whatever terms they could get. The Whigs seemed the best associates and leaders, and in their reciprocal sympathy Scotland already had the makings of her Liberal party.

In 1822 Scott reported further that the Whigs were now 'the temporary and nominal heads of the numerous body among the Scottish burghers'. This did not mean that views were entirely consonant in the reforming forces. The proletariat in any case remained disunited, with little class solidarity. Some of the worst violence, such as the mayhem which started up again in the West during the 1820s, was directed not at employers but at fellow workers threatening job security or wage levels. The advanced bourgeois radicals thought enforcement of the laws of political economy the best way of dealing with the trouble. In 1824 Joseph Hume persuaded Parliament to repeal the Combination Acts and thus legalise trade unions, but in the expectation that they would soon die when exposed to market forces. The Whigs had little understanding of social problems and aimed to provide a neutral leadership against the Government, focusing on constitutional grievances. This they managed to do till 1832. But Scott's qualifications had been pertinent: the Whigs, too, worried whether they would be able to keep working-class aspirations in check after reform had been secured, when a substitute would have to be found for this single great unifier of the anti-Tory forces.

For the ruling party repression remained the usual answer to the crises of post-war Scotland, at least to those caused by the proletariat. But the same methods would no longer do with the bourgeoisie. When challenged there, the Tories fell back defensively on the quaint set of statutes governing the constitution. In none of the first few General Elections after 1815 was their hold on the parliamentary representation seriously weakened. Reformers also turned to the law and used ingenious suits to harass the burgh councils. But they seldom won. So confident were the Tories in their mastery of the system that they actually led the way in certain changes. The streamlined Court of Session was their work, and they extended reform here in 1825 and 1830. They instituted juries in civil causes—even appointing Adam of Blair Adam to supervise them—and passed several Acts improving the administration of certain burghs, though the councils' powers were left alone. They were often ready for action if the changes had no direct effect on their control of the political machinery. When they preferred inaction, they took a nationalist stand on the sanctity of Scottish traditions.

But other Tories strove to cure the wider discontents at root. In that they could be keener on social reform than liberals. Keenest of all was Thomas Chalmers, an evangelical minister who in 1819 took charge of a wretchedly poor parish in the East End of Glasgow, convinced he had a remedy for its ills which would set an example to the rest of the country. The Church's influence in the cities was waning. Chalmers sought an answer in demonstrating that it could work there as it always had done in the old rural communities, where the minister and the kirk saw to the people's wants. Social tensions might be resolved if religion instilled its conciliatory moral attitudes in all classes, so that the disaffected would look not to radicalism but to aid from the clergy and their lay assistants. Chalmers hoped, too, that the overwhelming distress of the cities would yield to his treatment by moving the poor to self-help and the rich to spontaneous charity. But the new urban misery and social dissolution proved too much even for his spiritual energy. He made little progress in curing poverty, diffusing morality or winning the masses for conservatism. Yet in his favour it can be said that he saw traditional values had to find new applications for survival.[28]

Of greater impact in the rough-and-tumble of politics was the contribution of an eccentric intellectual, John Wilson. In 1820 he scored a victory for the Tories by winning election to the chair of moral philosophy at Edinburgh University, previously held by Whigs. Inspired romantically by the past, he drew from it the idea of an alliance between the Tory gentry and the oppressed workers against the utilitarian reformers and their business friends—an idea which, when it won general acceptance under Disraeli, saved the Conservative party from the extinction that might have awaited it in an age of mass democracy. Wilson's platform was *Blackwood's Edinburgh Magazine*, where he wrote under the pseudonym of Christopher North. It had been founded in 1817 by William Blackwood as a riposte to the Whigs' dominance of political literature in Scotland—the only attempt so far, the *Quarterly Review* started by Scott in 1807, had failed. Blackwood's greatly discomfited them in matching their sarcasm and wit. The political leader of this younger generation of Tories was John Hope, son of the distinguished Lord Advocate who had served under Addington, and thus related by marriage to Melville. That was doubtless why, despite a poor judgement, he was promoted so quickly, becoming in 1822, at the age of twenty-eight, Solicitor General.

They all helped to bring Scottish Toryism to terms with change, averting for a while its degeneration into an effete ruling caste's dying creed. But it remained ill-at-ease in the emerging system of politics based on competing ideologies, and steadily lost its bearings. The British patriotism promoted by the elder Melville was diluted by the revived nationalism of his son's followers, who had discovered how sacred were the Scottish traditions enshrined in the Union settlement, all the more so for the Tory power they secured. Again, the elder Melville had in some sort, like his master Pitt, always favoured Catholic emancipation. But his heir was one of its most strenuous foes, even if, on the Lord Advocate's reckoning, it would enfranchise only about a dozen individuals in Scotland. The cause was, however, taken up by the younger, progressive Tories given their head in the 1820s by Lord Liverpool. They two recognised that immobilism and privilege, rather than talk of reform, were undermining the nation's faith in the constitution. It could no longer be seriously argued that favours for the servile were the sole guarantee of stability when liberal economics showed what self-sufficiency and thrift might do to create wealth and contentment within the social order. Scotland was anyway becoming less amenable to management, for more stringent public economy since the war had reduced the available patronage. Nor could the Tories maintain their monopoly of it. Admitting to themselves the inevitability of change meant also admitting others to office and influence if, as they now hoped, a common front was to be formed with the Whigs against the extreme reformers.

After 1827 there was no choice but to bow to these necessities. In the spring Liverpool resigned. The succession of Canning promised a more liberal regime, especially over Catholic emancipation. The appalled Melville refused to serve under him. He was followed in his defection by a number of the magnates: Buccleuch, Hopetoun and Lauderdale (this last the ex-Jacobin and manager in the Ministry of All the Talents, who had now become an ultra-reactionary). But the law officers agreed to stay on, Hope indeed aspiring to be manager. Other prominent Tories, such as Sir George Clerk, MP for Midlothian, also decided to support the Government, while Edinburgh town council discussed whether it ought to pander to the new trend by ejecting William Dundas from his seat.

Canning, repudiated by many former colleagues, could only maintain himself with the help of the conservative Whigs, whose leader, Lord Lansdowne, he made Home Secretary. As his manager he had in mind Lord Binning, the Earl of Haddington's mediocre heir. But Abercromby went to the Prime Minister and pressed on him the need to take account of reforming opinion in Scotland. Canning consented to her affairs being directly overseen by Lansdowne, with Abercromby and Kennedy as advisers. This was the decisive break in the management system.

Canning died after five months, to be succeeded by an ostensibly reactionary Government under Wellington and Peel. Though they brought Melville back into the Cabinet, he could not fully restore his power. Nor did his faction gain much from Scotland's outrage when the Ministry was after all converted to Catholic emancipation.[29] Anti-papist feeling was still intense and attested by furious public protests. Whigs supported the measure, but even in failing to sway their countrymen suffered no permanent damage. On the contrary, they won more positions of influence. Jeffrey now became Dean of the Faculty of Advocates and Abercromby was in 1830 appointed Chief Baron of the Exchequer over the head of Rae, who also coveted the post.

With the prospects for reform brightening, the Whigs began to consider more thoroughly what exact shape it ought to take in Scotland. In general approach they were anglicising unionists. They thought complete assimilation of the Scottish to the English political system the best way of preventing a resurgence of management. On those grounds they were quite prepared to destroy the constitution over which the Melvilles had presided, for all its distinctive Scottishness. They were at this stage against having any sort of Minister for Scotland and wanted her affairs to be placed firmly in the hands of the Home Secretary, with the Lord Advocate's post becoming a purely legal one and all other Scottish offices being so far as possible abolished. On the franchise they were, by contrast, conservative. Despite their alliance with democrats, they intended the vote to be given only to the propertied, educated middle classes. The argument then turned into a technical one about where to set the qualifications. If too low, they would encourage dangerous popular pressure on Governments; if too high, they might throw some hitherto safe opinion into the arms of the radicals.

From 1830 matters advanced rapidly. Europe was shaken by a new revolution in France, while at home the death of George IV required a General Election. In Scotland the coincidence inspired unparalleled excitement. The people's demands for reform grew strident and radical Political Unions sprang up everywhere to organise the agitation. The poll gave reformers at least seventeen seats in Scotland, a net gain of four. But only four were returned from the burghs, which remained virtually impervious to popular opinion. In the counties, with their more open franchise, the Whigs' representation had almost doubled in ten years. The election brought them to power. Melville retired and the management system came to an end. Lord Grey, the new Prime Minister, appointed Jeffrey as Lord Advocate and Henry Cockburn as Solicitor General. With Kennedy they immediately constituted themselves a reform committee and within days sent proposals to their chiefs. But the final struggle was to be long and arduous.

Jeffrey entered the Commons at a by-election and brought in his first Reform Bill on 31 March, 1831. It lapsed, however, when the English Bill was defeated that summer and the Ministry had once more to go to the country. Widespread demonstrations, often degenerating into violence, threatened revolution if the Bills were not passed. The Scottish political nation understood the message and for the first time returned a majority of reformers. Jeffrey took the opportunity of challenging the Tories in their stronghold of Edinburgh, standing against a cadet of the Dundas family: the Lord Advocate was defeated in the town council by only three votes. But in Scotland as a whole the Government won twenty-four seats. They included eleven in the burghs where the corporations, venal to the last, yielded to official pressure as well as to the rioters in their streets. Jeffrey, meanwhile returned for the Perth Burghs, introduced his Bill again on 1 July, but it was only to receive the Royal Assent, after many further vicissitudes, more than a year later, on 17 July, 1832.

In Scotland the great Reform Act turned out imperfect.[30] Its authors were obsessed by the fear of going too far towards democracy, so that it contained not just compromises but deliberately conservative elements. Moreover, it passed through Parliament very much in the shadow of the English measure and comparatively little time or attention were devoted to it. Numerous anomalies in its working were to appear.

Scotland was awarded an extra eight seats for a total of fifty-three. Revised qualifications for the franchise increased the electorate sixteen-fold to 65,000 or so. The Whigs believed this struck the right balance between containing the demand for popular representation and defeating the possibility of a revived management system. Otherwise the aims were somewhat inconsistent.

In the burghs the Whigs intended to destroy corruption and cliques for good. They granted the vote to every owner of property worth £10 a year as, usually, to the categories of tenant occupying such property. These provisions actually went further than they would have liked. Since MPs were now to be chosen directly by all voters, they toyed with the idea of pitching the qualifications higher, only to discover that this would make the electorate too low in some places. The new seats were given to the burghs—Edinburgh got an extra one, while Glasgow, with two members, and Aberdeen, Dundee, Greenock, Paisley and Perth, with one apiece, were separately represented for the first time. Yet many of the smaller, more corruptible parliamentary burghs were allowed to retain their status.

In the counties the purpose was to consolidate or, where necessary, to establish the power of the landed gentry. Here too owners of land worth £10 were enfranchised, but the rules for tenants were stricter than in the burghs. Yet the old faggot voters were permitted to keep their suffrages for their lifetimes. There were few changes either in the distribution of the thirty county seats, leaving rural pockets where the Act made no real difference at all. Some of the smallest constituencies—Bute, Peebles, Selkirk, Sutherland—were still separately represented, and there MPs continued to be appointees of the local magnates.

As a national emancipation the Scottish Reform Act of 1832 was not so very impressive. But for all its bad drafting and Whiggish hesitancy it did provide a framework for the expression of a much greater part of the richness and diversity in politics which the country had attained since 1789. The old regime and its institutions, which had once perfectly encompassed the political nation, provided an outlet at the end for only the tiniest part of Scotland's political life and thought. Jeffrey was correct in assessing that frustrated new ideas and movements could destroy British constitutionalism, though his answer, to amend yet also to complement it by enfranchising the respectable, did not provide a permanent solution. In fact he and his friends did destroy the historic Scottish constitution and cared little about doing so. Their conservatism consisted in wanting property to prevail against numbers rather than in wanting to preserve institutions: its basis was an abstract rationalism rather than an attachment to continuity in Scottish history. But institutions were important for Scotland. Her nationhood after 1707 had been sustained, and since 1832 has been sustained, largely through distinctive institutions. The mass public opinion now elevated into a political power was to ask not only for further reform but in time also for the restoration of at least a separate Scottish administration. In the end neither the Whigs' ideals nor their achievements satisfied the nation, though considering what went before they are not to be scorned. The new order owed very little to Scotland's past, but it set the starting point for the whole of the country's modern political development.

Chapter 2

'A Vitiated Establishment'

The Whigs never suspected that they would have as much trouble in running the reformed system as in creating it.[1] In 1832, however, they set to with immense confidence—the Scotch millennium was how Henry Cockburn euphorically described the era he now saw dawning. The Liberal party had won a huge majority in both the parliamentary representation and the popular vote. The Whig administration was the most active in Scotland for thirty years. The new MPs, if not comparing in quality with the best of their English colleagues, were at least a great improvement on the placemen they had ejected.

But the achievement on which the Whigs prided themselves above all was their having secured a momentous constitutional change without violence to the country's underlying social and political structure. To be sure, they would have to appease those radicals who had been enfranchised and maintain their guard against those still without the vote. But over most of Scotland that part of the ruling class which accepted reform stayed firmly in control, and the nation appeared ready to settle down under the new regime. In 1834 Brougham, one of the founders of the *Edinburgh Review* and now Lord Chancellor of England, wrote to Grey, the Prime Minister: 'The whole Scotch people are really attached to you upon principle. They are reformers and improvers, but with a great deal of caution and considerateness, being so according to their habits, both of thinking and acting. Your liberality, therefore, is exactly the kind that suits them, because it is of a really safe and conservative kind, and not rash and heedless.'[2] Complacency was ever a weakness of the Whigs. They did indeed believe that outstanding wrongs would be righted not through the frenetic political activity demanded by radicals, but through moral enlightenment, social reconciliation and economic advance, all of which the more representative constitution was bound in time to foster.

These high-flown notions were of little help in dealing with the pressing problems of the moment, especially the still refractory state of the working class. Whigs generally held that it could best be subdued through strict application of the principles of political economy. In practice they were not so bold. Their hopes of killing off the trade unions had been thwarted, but they feared it might be provocative to impose new restrictions. They thought reform of the Corn Laws could reduce the cost of living, but would not accept the *Edinburgh Review*'s case for total repeal. They saw the need of better means to relieve destitution, but were determined not to have a body of paupers maintained by higher taxes. Meanwhile, some toyed with such impractical schemes as a minimum wage to prevent exploitation of workers. Others believed that the problems of the cities and the Highlands should be solved simply by removing the surplus people through emigration, either abroad or internally, as James Loch, now a Liberal MP, had arranged in Sutherland. For those who remained, great hope was reposed in repairing the deficiencies, all too apparent, of the education system. Undogmatic in religious matters, the Whigs preferred to ignore the tide of agitation inside their own constituency of voters for the restoration of democracy in the Church of Scotland.

The one question to which they felt able to give immediate attention was reform of the burghs.[3] So many had been so badly run for so long that even the old Tory regime had been forced to provide some redress. Just to maintain administration in a state of reasonable efficiency, a number of private Acts, placing such matters as the maintenance of order and public health under so-called police authorities, had been passed for particular burghs since 1800. There the only real residual obligations of the councils were to keep themselves solvent and to elect MPs. Some could not even manage the first—the capital itself went bankrupt in 1833—and the Reform Act had relieved them of the second. The Whigs had a number of changes in mind. A popular franchise for municipal elections was clearly essential. They also contemplated depriving decayed burghs of their charters and abolishing the distinction between royal and non-royal burghs: some of the latter, such as Greenock and Paisley, were by now important towns. In 1833, two years before any corresponding English measures were introduced, the Scottish Ministers started legislating.

But they were shocked at the difficulty of the task. Parliament granted little time for Lord Advocate Jeffrey's measures and he was constantly thwarted by bickering in the committee of Scots burgh MPs to which they were referred. From the muddle three statutes emerged. One permitted more burghs to set up police authorities, in order to allay the fears of the citizenry about the persistent influence of vested interests in the councils. The others, one for the royal burghs and one for the rest, extended the franchise to all £10 householders and provided for triennial elections.

This first practical experience of running a reformed system gave Jeffrey and his colleagues little encouragement. He began to find his position impossibly burdensome. He had averted a political revolution but created a revolution of raised expectations. Scottish Liberals, whose rapacity became notorious, now expected all the patronage previously reserved to Tories to come their way, and importuned him tirelessly. It was as bad with requests for legislation, which were backed by incessant harassment from the MPs. Cockburn wrote of his overworked friend: 'He was left to the mercies of every county, city, parish, public body or person, who had an interest or a fancy to urge.'[4]

Having done their best to assimilate the Scottish to the English political system, the Whigs soon feared that in one respect they had made a profound mistake: while Scotland retained to any extent her own laws and institutions, might it not be preferable to have a proper Scottish Minister? The Lord Advocate was no substitute, especially now that he lacked a phalanx of subservient MPs to use as bargaining counters. In the spring of 1833, when Jeffrey was toiling with burgh reform, Cockburn wrote to Kennedy: 'I am more and more convinced every day, or rather hour, that Scotland can never be managed without some new and responsible person acting, no matter under what name, as Secretary, different from the Advocate, not only because no Lord Advocate can conduct everything, but because, even if he could, he ought not to be allowed or required to do so.'[5] Kennedy had been appointed a junior Lord of the Treasury advising on patronage and elections in Scotland and whipping her MPs. Cockburn's idea was for him to take over general political duties from Jeffrey, but nothing came of this.

It was doubly painful to see the amiable but melancholy Jeffrey, father of the Scottish reform movement, suffering so from these strains. Even in 1831 Cockburn had observed: 'I fear for him in Parliament—nearly sixty years of age, a bad trachea, inexperience and a great reputation are bad foundations for success in the House of Commons.'[6] The difficulties were compounded by his not being in the Cabinet. He had to entrust his business there either to the capricious Brougham, who vaunted himself on familiarity with Scottish affairs but did nothing about them, or to the Home Secretary, Lord Melbourne, who viewed them with languid indifference and was ready only with excuses for inaction. Though assiduous, Jeffrey soon felt thoroughly bored and frustrated. A similar disillusion was overcoming his colleagues. During 1834, all three members of the administration retired from politics, Jeffrey and Cockburn for the Bench, Kennedy into private life. Thus the leading reformers—with the exception of Abercromby, soon to be Speaker of the Commons—deserted the scene.

There followed a brief interlude of Conservative rule, during which the veteran Sir William Rae was again Lord Advocate. The return of the Liberals in 1835 replaced him with John Murray, MP for the Leith Burghs.[7] Another member of the *Review* group, he was not, however, taken very seriously. Inasmuch as the Ministry noticed Scotland, it did so through Fox Maule, newly elected for the Perth Burghs, a young nobleman of rather radical opinions quickly appointed Under-secretary at the Home Office and regularly consulted on Scottish affairs by his principal, Lord John Russell. The Scots Lord of the Treasury, Robert Steuart, MP for the Haddington Burghs, had little influence. It was easier for the distributors of patronage to communicate directly with William Gibson-Craig, imperious boss of the Edinburgh Whigs, or with the Clique, the circle of ruling merchant princes in Glasgow. Under Murray, Scotland was alarmed by renewed working-class agitation and by the crisis in the Kirk that was to end with the Disruption. To the first Murray was hostile, himself leading the prosecution of a group of trade unionists in

1838. On the second he vacillated, unwilling to offend any of the interests involved. He took a passive role, indeed, on most matters. During his tenure of office he got only twenty-two of his fifty-one Bills through. Heavily criticised on all sides, he was not sorry to opt for the Bench when a vacancy occurred in 1839.

Great hopes were reposed in his successor both as Lord Advocate and MP for Leith, Andrew Rutherfurd. Though harsh and overbearing, he was the most successful member of the Scots Bar and for the last two years had been Solicitor General. But he became embroiled in the Church controversy, in which he was too partisan to maintain universally cordial political relations. It left him time for little else, and when he resigned in 1841 Cockburn felt forced to observe: 'He has scarcely fulfilled all the expectations which his reputation excited as a parliamentary debater or manager . . . He has never taken, nor apparently attempted to take, much lead as manager in Scottish affairs.'[8] Cockburn consoled himself with the thought that 'in truth Scotland has produced no eminent House of Commons man since the days of Harry Dundas . . . It was the natural result formerly of their being no popular representation, and it must last till popular representation shall have time to operate.'

The failings went deeper than this glib explanation would suggest. Cockburn was right on the problem of personnel among the Scots Whigs. All the leading commoners were advocates, so that the Bench creamed them off before they could establish themselves politically. In any case they produced no statesman who could stand for Scotland and yet win respect in the United Kingdom as a whole, as Dundas indeed had done. There was thus no coherent Scottish interest in the reformed Parliament, and the Whig oligarchy was less independent of London than its Tory forerunner. Beyond that, the spectacular success of 1832 appeared to have exhausted all the Whigs' ideas and energies, at least in Scotland. Essentially cautious and conservative, they confined themselves at Westminster to tinkering with minor measures when in the later 1830s the country was convulsed by labour troubles and religious strife. Since their anglicising philosophy led them to regard Scottish affairs as peripheral, they made no serious attempt to seek a more effective administration. Altogether, they steadily lost the nation's confidence, with the result that the electoral base which they thought to have secured for themselves was undermined too.

This was also the consequence of strenuous efforts made by the Conservatives to recover from the debacle of 1832.[9] Out of office, with no patronage to offer and unused to dealing with a large electorate, they had then fared disastrously, retaining only one burgh seat and nine counties. But that, a mighty national demonstration to put the haughty Tories down, was not to be repeated on the same scale for several decades. Meanwhile a future for Scottish Conservatism still seemed possible. In the next few years its leaders recognised their residual strengths and began to build on them.

Its loss of influence was clearest in the burghs, which had shifted from being the most reactionary element in Scottish politics to being the most radical. Before 1832 the burgh electors had been a lot of self-interested nonentities with no political base except what the archaic constitution gave them; that was entirely swept away. Moreover, most urban voters remembered that, in the last unreformed Parliament, Tory after Tory had stood up to declare that they should not have the franchise—they thought it took some gall for Conservatives now to solicit their support. Thus, the construction of any popular organisation proved beyond the party's means. Some effort was made to attract new electors in Edinburgh and Glasgow with so-called Conservative Operatives' Associations. Briefly, in 1840, both cities actually had Conservative Lord Provosts. But none of this extended to the parliamentary level. There, though the party did not go down without a fight, it had in the end to write off the burghs.

The situation was quite different in the counties, where the ruling class was still firmly ensconced. It consisted, after all, of the landlords, the natural leaders in every aspect of social and economic life. Rural Scotland did not in any case offer the same fertile ground for partisan controversy as the towns. Agrarian change, under protection from foreign competition, had not depopulated and impoverished it, not at least in the Lowlands. On the contrary, the cultivated area had been expanded, keeping employment steady and enriching many tenants. Voters were much more interested in maintaining a united front of this prosperous farming community than in the political shades of opinion within it.

Most landowners were Tories, though a good number had turned Liberal out of exasperation with the old abuses, which had indeed deprived some of the vote. Yet their political attitudes differed little, for all moved in the same circles and had similar interests. They certainly agreed that gentlemen ought to continue directing the course of county affairs. To be sure, the previous controllers of constituencies were deeply unpopular and met strong resistance if they tried to regain their position, as they increasingly did. But landlords who had used their power sensitively before 1832 and been willing to sacrifice some of it in the cause of wider representation could maintain themselves in public esteem. So the political division in rural Scotland was not a class one, between the newly enfranchised voters and their former rulers. It was instead a retrospective one, between those who had and those who had not supported reform. A sort of two-party system, for and against the diehard Conservatives, developed in the Scottish counties well before it did in England.

A laird of either persuasion could usually depend on his tenants to follow his views in casting their votes. For a Liberal it was rarely necessary to resort to overt pressure—to the Scots his party represented civil liberty, so to comply with his wishes was not regarded as subservience. But that was precisely the reproach thrown at electors who obeyed a Conservative landlord, even though his social interests and relationship with the tenantry were indistinguishable from a Liberal's. The Conservatives definitely had the greater difficulty in defending and expanding their influence. The whole scale of politics had been altered, posing serious problems of adjustment for a party desperate to retain some sway over events. It quickly identified its main obstacle as the 'ten-pounders'—proprietors of the minimum voting qualification, such as smallholders in the countryside and tradesmen or craftsmen in the villages. They could not be subjected to the same control as tenants and they resented what they had felt to be the contempt for them of the opponents of reform. Means had to be found of overcoming their numerical weight in the electorate. The method discovered was the traditional one of creating fictitious votes. The 1832 Act had allowed their existing holders to retain them for their lifetimes, but had been intended to exclude the manufacture of new ones. In reality it did not.

As a result of the Whigs' gratuitous disdain of feudal law, it had been sloppily drafted and offered many loopholes for those experienced in election management.[10] County voters did not have to be resident and wealthy Conservatives from outside a constituency could buy properties within it qualifying them for the franchise. In addition, the new rules for tenants, themselves confused, allowed fictitious votes to be made in more or less the same way as before—it was done by parcelling up the land into suitable tenancies, a cheaper method than the old one of dividing feudal superiorities. Now that elections were no longer closed, but carried out with open nominations and polls on the English pattern, lairds might also exercise an embarrassing scrutiny of voters' preferences. And in their redistribution of seats the Whigs had evinced an honest desire to secure for landed proprietors their due of parliamentary representation, so that small constituencies which they could dominate were deliberately retained. There were two concentrations of Conservative magnates, one in the North-east headed by the Duke of Gordon and the Earl of Aberdeen, the other in the South-east, where Buccleuch was the richest landowner in Scotland and the party's greatest benefactor. Nowhere else did it enjoy such a monopoly of power, but it could rely on a considerable interest in almost every county.

Its inner circle—Buccleuch, Melville and Sir George Clerk—quickly realised the opportunities. In 1833 they sent a memorandum to supporters in Midlothian setting out ways in which votes could be manufactured under the new laws.[11] The practices they recommended spread throughout the land and were notoriously prevalent in the southern counties. They were soon taken up by the Liberals as well, with no greater scruple, though with less efficiency and success. The annual revision of the register, when the qualifications of fresh applicants in each constituency were tested and contested before the local sheriff, turned into the main event of the political year. The registration, rather than the election itself, often decided the representation of the seat, for an MP would usually not bother to stand again if it went against him. Despite the high moral tone of the struggle for reform, it was difficult to see how in this respect the new system was less corrupt than the old.

The Whig Government brought in a Bill to stop the electoral manipulation in 1835, only to see it emasculated in the Lords. It then set up an inquiry to expose the scandals.[12] The report found that, for example, in Selkirkshire there had in 1832 been 280 voters, of whom eighty-six were non-resident. By 1836 the electorate had grown to 552, of whom 288 were non-resident. Needless to say this seat, won by the Liberals in 1832, had been retaken by the Conservatives. In all the numbers on the national county voters' roll swelled from 33,000 immediately after the Reform Act to 48,000 in 1839, an expansion far in excess of the natural rate of increase. Such revelations failed, however, to sway parliamentary opinion decisively.

Still, this legal trickery did keep politics lively. Each of the four elections in the decade after 1832 saw more than twenty contests, a level not reached again till 1868. Quite a lot of seats changed hands, some repeatedly as the fraudulence of one party provoked the other into outdoing it. Wealth and influence were what counted, but that did not necessarily favour the Conservatives—indeed, they often had to rely on the lesser lairds since the local magnates were mostly Whigs. The Conservatives were, however, better organised, and in the later 1830s Sir James Graham was able to monitor regularly the state of the Scottish constituencies. The net effect was that they consolidated and increased their representation. The Liberals held twenty-three seats in every one of those four elections, including nearly all the burghs and three counties. By 1841 a further four had been made secure for them after long struggles over registration. That gave twenty-seven, just half the total, which they could then be certain of winning. On the other hand seven counties consistently elected a Conservative, while another went Liberal only once. The indicators of the Opposition's revival were the nine counties which had voted for reform in 1832 but which by 1841 were safe for the Conservatives, being then uncontested by a Liberal. At this point they were still optimistic and redoubling their efforts—a further seven seats, including three burgh districts, were clearly in contention. After brisk battles the Conservatives did take four of them and might reasonably have hoped to progress further. By their exertions they had pushed their share of the fifty-three seats up from ten in 1832 to fifteen in 1835, to nineteen in 1837 and to twenty-two in 1841.

But the advance need not be ascribed to chicanery alone. There were also issues which the Conservatives were able to exploit. They could appeal to those who thought that enough had been conceded in 1832 and that it was essential to restrain further movement towards democracy. Equally, as firmer advocates of social reform than the Whigs, they gained votes among progressive electors. Their best propagandist, Archibald Alison, writing on a Malthusian theme in 1840, declared: 'No danger need ever be apprehended from measures which better the condition of the poor; it is from their degradation and suffering that a redundancy of numbers, from their comfort and prosperity that a due regulation of population is to be expected.'[13] This interest was bound up with the Conservatives' attitude to religion, for they agreed with Chalmers that the more active social involvement of the established Church was one way of pacifying the people. Here was a marked difference between them and the Liberals: English Whigs were rather anti-clerical and talked much, while as usual doing little, about disestablishment; and even the Scots Whigs had often to look to their dependence on dissenters' votes. The Conservatives were by contrast stern opponents of both dissent and disestablishment, winning over many members of the Kirk who feared for its future. Peel, their new leader, visited Scotland in 1837 and proclaimed: 'I mean to support the national Establishment which connects Protestantism with the state in the three countries' (of the United Kingdom).[14]

There was besides genuine popular dissatisfaction over the feeble performance of the Governments in the 1830s. By 1841 numbers of voters not especially Conservative in sentiment wanted simply to get the Whigs out. Cockburn reported that in the election of that year, when the Conservatives were indeed returned to power at Westminster, 'the Radical and Chartist voters were courted wherever there was a contest by Tories, to whom these votes were almost invariably given; and in return, wherever the struggle was between a Radical and a Whig, the Tory votes almost always strengthened the former.'[15] But this marked the climax of the Conservatives' achievement. Ahead lay the Disruption, in which they chose the wrong side politically, and the Corn Law crisis, which all but wrecked the party. The Scots Conservatives had made a brave attempt to adapt to the new conditions in their country. Against the enmity of most electors, however, it was difficult to sustain enough energy to exploit all the openings offered by the deficiencies of the Reform Act and of the Whig Governments.

As the Liberal coalition was assailed from without, so was it undermined from within. Its pragmatism came under ever more intense assault from various idealistic movements, which won converts even among the respectable. What with Conservative revival in the counties, the Whigs had real reason to fear they might be squeezed out of their ascendancy. From the start of the combined reform agitation they had, of course, been conscious that their and the radicals' aims were not identical. Soon the antagonism came into the open. With an extension of the franchise so limited, many radicals thought it a betrayal.[16] In 1832 they thought about putting up their own parliamentary candidates in many places. But it was a matter of conjecture how strong the forces of reaction would prove in the new conditions, so for now it was as well to preserve the unity of all reformers to ensure victory. As long as they fought together, radicals were pressed to match Whig resources of money and influence. Even in the industrial towns where their strength was concentrated they could not normally win but only sway elections. After helping to eject the respected Whig, James Ewing, from Glasgow in 1835, they merely saw him replaced by a somewhat less cautious man of the same kidney.

Continued disappointment of their hopes made radicals readier to risk a battle with the Whigs. Even so, their tally of MPs never reached double figures, and few were of any ability. Kinloch had revenged himself by taking Dundee in 1832, but died the next year; Sir George Sinclair, returned for his native Caithness, was supporting the Conservatives by 1841; and Andrew Johnston who sat for the St Andrews Burghs was, as a champion of reform in the Church, liable to fall out with dissenters who preferred it to remain tainted. Towards the end of the decade their strength in the Commons was dropping again, largely because of these religious squabbles. The Whigs were able to stage a comeback, marked by the election of Lord William Bentinck for Glasgow in 1837 and of Thomas Macaulay for Edinburgh in 1839, both recently returned from ruling India in the grand style. But this did not take the wind out of the radicals' sails, for they flourished in the lower reaches of Scottish politics. They had a strong sense of civic responsibility and were active in local affairs, constituting a large proportion of the councils in the two big cities. They kept up the pressure for reform, arguing that it should be extended to destroy all the remaining bastions of privilege in the state, the Kirk and in economic life.

Bourgeois radicals were often religious dissenters, so that their Churches claimed an inflated share of political attention in the 1830s. The two main ones were the Original Secession and the Relief; with minor groups they accounted for about one-fifth of the population. They organised themselves politically in the Scottish Central Board of Dissenters, set up in 1834 under Duncan McLaren, an Edinburgh councillor. Their great foe was the Kirk, which they harried as hard as they could: in the capital, where the corporation disposed of the patronage of churches, they strove to reduce the number of clergy and hold down stipends.

Scottish politics were riddled with religious enmity. The radicals were often able to capitalise on it, sometimes to the extent of uniting the country behind them. An example was the controversy over the Maynooth grant during Peel's Ministry of 1841–6. Maynooth, the Catholic theological college near Dublin, had been receiving Government aid for many years. To help appease the Irish, the Prime Minister wanted to raise the grant. Though devised by a Tory, the proposal had much support among Whigs and especially from Macaulay. It was a relatively minor matter, but provoked a dispute of a violence barely comprehensible today. Radicals, who opposed any state endowment of religion, this time won round many who did not disapprove of it in principle by playing on simple anti-papist prejudice: that was enough to persuade the General Assembly of the endowed, established Kirk itself, as well as Conservatives not prepared to compromise in defence of Protestantism. So strong was the feeling in Scotland that only two of her MPs voted with Peel when in 1845 the Commons authorised a higher grant.[17]

Radicalism was not, however, always so narrow and obsessive. It made a special appeal to the business community, which stood square on individualist, *laissez-faire* principles. At the time much central government revenue was raised from an intricate system of tariffs. There were duties on cotton which annoyed manufacturers in Glasgow and duties on flax which annoyed those in Dundee. Radicals saw protectionism as another instance of privilege for vested interests which reform should do away with. From the mid 1830s they took up and shaped the resentment into a mighty campaign which ten years later was to topple a Government.[18]

By far the most unpopular duties were those imposed under the Corn Laws, which kept the price of bread high even in times of plenty. They operated on a complicated sliding scale that only allowed cheap foreign wheat to be imported when there was a shortage of the domestic crop, the object being to maintain a satisfactory return for British farmers. Scottish agriculture was highly efficient, so neither landlords nor tenants felt much need of protection. Thus in Scotland there were few defenders of the laws as they stood. Indeed, almost the whole country believed they ought to be drastically amended, if not abrogated entirely. In England, by contrast, they were strongly supported in the landed class. That deepened the Scots' resentment at aristocratic privilege in general, but did not produce the same clear conflict between city and county as in the South.

Scottish politicians responded to the pressure. The Whigs favoured replacing the sliding scale by a small fixed duty, while the radicals wanted total repeal. Before the fall of the Whig Cabinet in 1841, its Scottish members, Macaulay and the Earl of Minto, were already arguing for changes in the laws, and in that year some were made. But Scotland alone could exert no decisive influence. It took the rapid growth of the Anti-Corn Law League in Britain as a whole to focus public and political protest.

The league was founded in 1839 in Manchester, the centre of Liberal economic thought, by Richard Cobden and John Bright, who went on to conduct with great energy and skill a national campaign for repeal. The Scots radicals formed close links with them (in fact McLaren was to marry Bright's sister) and campaigned with equal vigour. One of the strongest advocates of reform, George Hope of Fenton Barns, was himself a model farmer in East Lothian. Petitions to Parliament were repeatedly sent from the Scottish cities, and Cockburn was impressed enough to note a public meeting in Glasgow where 'principles of commercial freedom were expounded by our greatest merchants of all political sects'[19]—there even the leader of the Conservatives, Sir James Campbell, favoured repeal. Christianity was inevitably brought into it. A convention of dissenting ministers organised by McLaren declared the Corn Laws 'alike opposed to the principles of religion and the precepts of morality.'[20]

But the Scots MPs were on the whole unwilling to commit themselves fully to the cause. Moderate reformers such as Macaulay were embarrassed in their efforts by the extremism of the radicals.[21] To his questions of how the lost revenue was to be recouped and how repeal could in any case be carried against the powerful English aristocracy he received no clear reply. He urged the league to join with those who wanted amendment rather than repeal, because by standing out for the latter when it was not politically possible they would antagonise everybody without getting anywhere. The league in Scotland was, however, disinclined to compromise when it had the people so solidly behind it. In return for his reproaches Macaulay was taken to task at a protest meeting by McLaren for 'being against the enlightened opinion of the middle class'.[22] After 1842 the campaign in England began to slacken somewhat, but it reached a new pitch of intensity in Scotland, largely as a result of the tour undertaken there by Cobden and Bright at the end of the year. They aroused vast popular enthusiasm and were delighted to find all classes in favour of reform. As time went on the Whigs began to throw in their lot with the repealers—by 1845 both Macaulay and Rutherfurd were finding it expedient to appear on the league's platforms.

Overshadowing everything now was the Irish famine. But the distress occasioned by the failure of the potato crop in the autumn of 1845 was not confined to Ireland. It also assumed grave proportions in the West Highlands, though the crisis was manageable compared with the Irish one. The population at risk was less than 200,000 and the landlords' generosity combined with reasonably efficient state aid brought the region through without mass starvation.[23]

As the year advanced and Ireland's miseries grew intolerable, it was from Scotland that a move came which helped to force the Government's hand. Russell, Liberal leader in the Commons who was visiting the country that winter, wanted to get rid of his party's commitment to a fixed duty. Now, he decided, the moment had come. After consultations with Rutherfurd and Minto he published at the end of November his Edinburgh Letter, declaring that through procrastination the Government was failing the country: this was a time for drastic measures when there was no alternative but to repeal the Corn Laws.

Peel had already made up his mind that something would have to be done. The shift in the Liberal position created a formidable coalition against protectionism to which it was safest to make concessions. Early in December he tried to persuade the Cabinet to recall Parliament with a view to suspending the laws. He failed and promptly resigned. Russell was then asked to form a Government but had to give up after a fortnight. Peel returned with the express intention of introducing a measure for repeal. He did so successfully, but this led to a revolt in his party and to his downfall in the middle of 1846.

Scotland's part in his victory was to have remained so steadfastly against tariffs throughout: she was one constituency on which repealers could count in building up an overwhelming opposition to the Corn Laws. It was the first occasion under the reformed system on which she performed what was to be her most important contribution to imperial politics for the rest of the century, by undemandingly providing a solid bloc of votes to a great Liberal cause. For the Liberals at home, however, the outcome was no triumph at all. Rather it exacerbated their bitter internal disputes. Whigs and radicals had often annoyed each other, but managed to retain a commitment to basic reforming Liberalism. The rifts now opened up—over Maynooth, the Corn Laws and the Disruption—amounted to little less than a breach, as was to be evidenced in the 1847 election.

The Corn Law agitation was mainly a middle-class affair. Workers wanted cheap bread and so had an interest in repeal. But they took little direct part in a campaign led by merchants and manufacturers, who were not seen as friends of the working man—with good reason, for in Scotland radical employers fought the trade unions hard and opposed factory legislation. There was thus an incentive for workers to act independently. And this reflected another growing divergence within the old reformist coalition, between those who had won the vote and those who as yet had not. It was natural for the energies of the bourgeois radicals to be no longer so single-mindedly concentrated on parliamentary reform, but directed at seeking advantage for their class in other fields. For the workers, on the other hand, the franchise remained at the forefront of political debate: they regarded the Reform Act as a highly unsatisfactory half-measure, a mere preparation for universal manhood suffrage.

To begin with the trade unions were the focus of working-class activity.[24] But they were still feeble and disunited. They had indeed been illegal till recently, so that no-one had had much chance to gain experience in industrial organisation. They flourished only in good times when workers could pay subscriptions, and were correspondingly vulnerable in depressions when they were most needed. They were severely constrained in their methods of defending members, since strikes often failed. Their main weapon lay in restricting entry to a trade, so the unions' activity—and violence—was above all aimed at that. Nor could they co-operate easily, since each was confined to a single occupation, often in a single town, without wider links. In 1831 came a response to this weakness with the establishment in the West of a federal Association for the Protection of Labour, but any effect it might have had was neutralised by subsequent events.

Trade unionism produced the first big social crisis of the post-reform era in the labour troubles of 1837. A recession during the winter of 1836 soon prompted action by workers to prevent reductions in pay and intimidate the blacklegs whom employers brought in to undercut wages. Conditions worsened till in April 1837 the Glasgow cotton spinners went on strike: this set off a chain reaction which had all the city's skilled trades out by the summer. Troops were sent there in July after violent demonstrations. At the end of the month a blackleg was murdered. The leaders of the cotton spinners' union were at once arrested on suspicion of having incited the crime. The evidence was, however, unconvincing and the Whig law officers were at first reluctant to prosecute. When the accused were nevertheless brought to trial in 1838 the case against them was found not proven except on the count of conspiracy. Yet sentences of seven years' transportation were passed: this provoked a great outcry and the hapless Lord Advocate Murray was savaged in Parliament. But there was also a revulsion against these events. Bourgeois radicals were disgusted to find that the proletariat had not eschewed habits of violence and for a time turned away from co-operation with it, even on general political matters. Many workers also thought things had gone too far and became scared of militancy. Unions went into a decline, with a number collapsing in the next year or two, from which they did not recover for more than a decade.

It was thus left to groups of a more directly political nature to continue the fight for the interests of the working class. They were also very disunited, indeed none of them had more than a purely local base. They were founded on the Political Unions set up to organise agitation on the Reform Bill, which in turn were descendants of the local radical societies that had arisen in the 1790s and after the Napoleonic Wars—this alone was enough to make the bourgeoisie suspicious of them. The penalties of fragmentation were appreciated, however, and in 1836 a co-ordinating National Radical Association of Scotland was established under John Taylor, a Glasgow journalist.

The next step was prompted by developments in England. Radical circles in London and Birmingham produced in 1838 the People's Charter, the document listing six points for political reform which gave its name to the subsequent Chartist movement. This contained two factions. The more moderate, centred on Birmingham and led by Charles Attwood, favoured peaceful action through petitions and propaganda, an approach which came to be known as 'moral force'. The other, under a wild Irishman, Feargus O'Connor, advocated violence if the demands were not met—this was called the 'physical force' school.[25]

The Chartists found a ready audience in Scotland.[25] In the course of 1838 both Attwood and O'Connor visited the country and built up their own groups of disciples. Attwood was the first to arrive on a campaign for a national petition to Parliament in favour of the Charter. He addressed a demonstration of 100,000 on Glasgow Green in May and was received with tremendous enthusiasm. Thence his associates went on evangelising tours of the manufacturing districts, winning widespread allegiance from the local radical organisations and especially from the prosperous artisans of Edinburgh. Scottish leaders of the moral force school appeared, notably John Fraser in the capital and the Rev Patrick Brewster, an eccentric minister at Paisley Abbey. O'Connor undertook his own tour of Scotland later in the summer, gaining the support of Taylor and generally of workers in the West, where poverty was more oppressive and where a taste for violence had developed.

Perhaps in reaction to the defeat of the labour agitation the previous year, moral force was clearly making the stronger appeal among the eighty or so Chartist groups which had been formed in Scotland by the end of 1838. A power struggle ensued between the two factions. The Scots had been invited to send delegates to a National Convention to be held in London with the purpose of submitting Attwood's petition to Parliament, and both sides were anxious that men of their own persuasion should represent the country there. To make explicit the fact that they had the upper hand in Scotland, the moderates summoned in December 1838 a meeting on Calton Hill in Edinburgh which duly voted overwhelmingly in favour of moral force. This aroused the hostility of the Western Chartists, and the dispute between the two groups grew sharper: instead of isolating the physical forcers, the moderates had only split the movement. They suffered a great psychological defeat when in the subsequent election for the convention Brewster was beaten by Taylor in the Lanarkshire district. All the same the victorious candidates were in the majority moral forcers.

But when they arrived in London at the beginning of 1839 they found that they were in their turn in a minority to the large number of militants elected from England. The proceedings of the convention were exceedingly confused and the Scots soon became disillusioned. It was not long before they started to drift home again, one of them, Villiers Sankey from Edinburgh, leaving with the words: 'The people of Scotland are too calm, too prudent and too humane to peril this cause upon bloodshed.'[26] These reservations were justified, for the convention turned out a woeful failure. Parliament greeted its petition with contempt, and in July 1839 its leaders were arrested. For the moment that put an end to Chartism in England, while in Scotland it discredited the advocates of physical force. But the moral force faction did not feel itself defeated—it accepted that more than one effort would be needed to persuade the ruling class of its arguments.

With the way forward unclear, the Scottish Chartists went on to hold their own convention in the autumn of 1839. It was inconclusive, the delegates being pre-occupied with either supporting or thwarting Fraser's efforts to impose himself as a national leader. There were endless disputes about physical and moral force, but they reflected more than anything the personal differences among the contenders for power within the movement: these were never resolved. Finally the convention fell back on the formula 'peaceably if we may, forcibly if we must.' Still, in the absence of resolute central guidance the threat of violence was remote, and moral force remained in effect the only option.

After this experiment with a national organisation, working-class activity in Scotland reverted to its localised basis. The moderates persevered in their work and Scottish Chartism continued to develop, though now independently of its English parent. The local associations flourished as the focal points of a wide range of communal action. All over Scotland there grew out of them co-operative societies, temperance and land leagues, pressure groups for factory regulation and other social reforms, Chartist schools, even Chartist churches. For the first time a proletarian Press appeared, of which the main organs were the *True Scotsman*, representing the moral force group in Edinburgh, and the *Scottish Patriot*, published in Glasgow and taking a more militant line. But the general emphasis was on non-violence, respectability and idealism: a philosophy of social redemption through self-help. There was no common programme and little co-ordinated work among the individual associations. They preferred to go their own way rather than submit to central direction. Indeed, this was hardly necessary for the requirements of Scottish Chartism.

Thus the doctrinal disputes lost their importance. The only remaining disagreement of substance between militants and moderates lay in their attitudes to non-Chartist bodies. The former believed that the Charter must be placed above all else and that no co-operation with others was permissible. The latter could not see why they should refuse to work with anyone in favour of further reform. They were, for example, often active in the network of Complete Suffrage Societies recently set up by bourgeois radicals, of which the leader in Scotland was Joseph Hume, after 1841 again MP for the Montrose Burghs.

The squabbles were, however, largely irrelevant to the fruitful developments in Scotland in the years round 1840. This happy phase was brought to an end by a fresh intervention from O'Connor, with whom the Scots retained links even though disagreeing with his views. He attended their second convention early in 1842 and all but put an end to Scottish Chartism by the disruption he caused with a violent attack on participation in the suffrage societies. Those he assailed simply moved over into them. The remnant soon declined: the local Chartist groups dissolved in apathy, the newspapers closed down and no money could be raised for anything. There was a flicker of activity in 1848, Europe's year of revolutions, which flared into mass demonstrations in Edinburgh and Glasgow. But this was without consequence.

The strength of the movement in Scotland had always lain in peaceful methods, in a catholic spirit and in a long-term outlook stressing that progress could only be gradual and was best secured by the quiet work of building up loyalty to radical principles in the working class. Scottish Chartism did not need and would not tolerate dictation from outside, unyielding dogma or revolutionary fervour. Though moribund within a few years, it was still an achievement, for it showed that workers could break free from the bonds of social control in the existing polity and keep up a sustained effort on their own. It left two legacies. One was in the activists whom it introduced to political work and sent on into other movements. The second was in fostering sober habits, self-respect and self-confidence in the Scots working class. They were reflected in the rapid growth of various voluntary organisations which strengthened its claim to civic responsibility. Ironically, this made it easier for Liberalism to retain the loyalty of the proletariat even when the Liberal party was itself not very progressive, for it inspired in workers the same commitment to ethical ideals as was taking root in the middle class. Chartism was not the only force working towards these ends, but it was in this period the most significant.

The moralistic, rather apolitical character of Scottish Chartism reflected the temper and preoccupations of the nation as a whole. Public life was pervaded by religion. This was underlined by the fact that the Church of Scotland claimed and in many respects held a more independent and important position than the Church of England.[27] The Kirk had never recognised royal supremacy, regarding itself as the equal in the spiritual sphere of the state in the temporal. In the sixteenth century Andrew Melville had declared: 'Thair is twa Kings and twa Kingdomes in Scotland'.[28] The existence of a secular kingdom was obvious enough, but he went on: 'Thair is Chryst Jesus the King and his Kingdome the Kirk, whase subject King James the Saxt is'. The doctrine was not merely theoretical. Even in the 1830s the ecclesiastical constitution was of more practical relevance to most Scots than the political constitution. Westminster was far away and devoted itself to remote, imperial events; the Kirk was the ubiquitous equivalent of today's welfare state. It had almost exclusive control of education from school to university; it supervised poor relief; it still asserted its jurisdiction over the moral conduct of the populace, if no longer through the repentance stool.

But in an age of rapid social change the Church had failed to modernise itself. Its unit of administration was the parish, where the minister was supposed to carry out in person its various responsibilities: it continued to act as if Scotland were the placid, rural society of a century before. With industrialisation, however, the country parishes were emptying. Vast agglomerations of human beings were gathering in the grimy towns and cities of the central belt, where in the struggle for subsistence religion played little part. Chalmers' experiment in Glasgow had not been followed up and the Church was out of touch with these people, largely because not enough new parishes had been established to serve them. Thus the Kirk's welfare system was breaking down: schools were too few and the destitute had to fend for themselves. As always in such circumstances, there was a general cry that the moral character of the populace was deteriorating. Certainly the working class was turning to novel creeds, to the dissenting sects and to radicalism, while the Irish immigrants who made up a great part of the new proletariat in the West remained intensely loyal to Catholicism.

But the Church's hold was weakening even in the conservative rural areas, where dissent also flourished. The problem here was not the loss of a religious spirit but a dour and dogged adherence to purest presbyterianism. And the big issue was patronage, the right of the state or of laymen to appoint ministers. This sat uncomfortably with the theoretical democracy of presbyterian Church government. Patronage had long been the subject of controversy. Instituted under the erastian Stuarts, it had been abolished in the religious settlement of 1690. The Treaty of Union expressly protected that settlement, but in 1712 Parliament restored patronage in one of its few Acts passed in clear contravention of popular sentiment in Scotland. That it had the right to do so was never, despite a tacit compliance, conceded by the Kirk. In practical terms there remained confusion over the law, for in addition to the patron's nomination a presentee (as the candidate for a living was known) still required an ill-defined 'call' from the congregation. This had produced many disputes between patrons and people. They invariably ended with the patron imposing his will, if necessary getting the minister into his church by force, a proceeding named 'intrusion'. The only course open to a dissatisfied flock was secession from the Kirk, and intrusion was the biggest single cause of dissent.

Patrons naturally appointed men whose personal opinions were in no-way disturbing to them. This had led to the Church being dominated by a party designated as Moderate. The typical Moderate minister was described by Cockburn thus:

> Speaking generally, he was a Tory in politics and in religion not in the Scotch sense religious. But his Toryism had very little purely political in it. It began . . . by an early obsequiousness to an expectant patron, probably as tutor in his family, or in that of some of his friends. After obtaining the living, in which the people were seldom thought of, and never consulted, he naturally subsided into an admiration of the system to which he owed his bread, and into a general sympathy with the opinions and objects of the lairds, and into a fixed horror of Dissenters . . . Thus his Toryism was not that of direct principle or party, but a mere passive devotion to the gentry.[29]

Even before the Reform Act inevitably shook the cosy paternalism of Scottish society, the Moderates were being challenged by the rise inside the Kirk of the evangelical movement, a phenomenon with parallels in the emergence of English Methodism and Tractarianism.

Scottish evangelism was, however, a matter less of doctrine than of concern about the social position of the Church. By the 1830s it was obviously failing in its mission, either to minister to the needs of the people or to hold them in the fear of the Lord. As a remedy the evangelicals first wanted to displace the Moderates and fill the Kirk with men zealous for the regeneration of society through the Gospel. Secondly, they saw the need for many new places of worship in the urban areas so that Christianity could be applied to their problems. Thirdly, they thought it of vital importance to get rid of the abuses which turned people away from religion. Unlike the English Methodists they did not feel they had to secede in order to accomplish these aims. On the contrary, they emphasised that only an established Church could be provided with the means to spread the faith among people who would otherwise not receive it. In the 1820s an evangelical party arose in the General Assembly under the Rev Andrew Thomson of Edinburgh. After his death in 1831 the leadership was assumed by Chalmers, then Professor of Divinity at Edinburgh University, who in 1832 was elected Moderator.[30] To him fell much of the burden of guiding the Kirk through the storms that beset it after the Reform Act.[31]

The evangelicals' convictions did not make them especially progressive in politics. Chalmers, indeed, called radicalism 'an aspect of infidelity and irreligion',[32] a sign that the lower orders were not receiving sufficient spiritual sustenance. But most Kirk members, disregarding its conservative views, must have voted Liberal in 1832. This was because they expected the Whigs to carry reform into the ecclesiastical sphere, and in particular to give them the right to elect their ministers in exactly the same way as they now elected their MPs. The English Whigs had, however, no reason to be grateful to their own reactionary national Church and were starting to turn their thoughts towards its separation from the state. A fortiori they were not especially interested in moves to strengthen the established Churches in the other countries of the United Kingdom. Chalmers himself felt moved to point out that 'some may be counting on the last glorious triumph of liberality' (which was how he chose to regard the Reform Act) 'as a step towards the overthrow of religious Establishments'.[33] If the Kirk was to escape this fate, the work of modernisation was now more necessary and urgent than ever.

In the first of their aims, the enlargement of their own influence, the evangelicals soon succeeded—they constituted a majority in the General Assembly of 1834. They at once set out in pursuit of their other aims. Desiring to strengthen the Kirk's presence in the towns and cities they asked the Government for a grant of £10,000 towards Church extension, that is to say for the building of new places of worship.[34] Desiring also to strengthen the presence of the towns and cities in the Kirk, they passed the Chapels Act.[35] This dealt with the problem of so-called chapels-of-ease, subordinate churches erected inside existing large parishes, where the minister did not have the right to be elected to any of the courts of the Church, to presbyteries, synods or the General Assembly itself. The Act granted him such rights—and since these ministers were usually of an evangelical persuasion, that faction's dominance was in effect secured for the future. Finally, the Assembly passed the Veto Act.[36] This was meant to get rid once and for all of intrusion—but not to abolish patronage, which the evangelicals could still assent to so long as it was not abusively exercised. The Act stated that if the congregation, or rather the majority of heads of families in a parish, objected to a presentee, then the local presbytery, which nominally adjudicated, was bound to accept the objection and seek a new candidate. The congregational veto was the ground on which the evangelicals stood and fought in the coming confrontation.

Having set off so confidently, they quickly found that the political situation after reform raised considerable difficulties. Though the Conservative Government which came in under Peel in 1834 was kindly disposed towards them—a reference to the need for Church extension in Scotland was included in the King's speech—the quick return of the Whigs put paid to hopes of a grant. The problem was that the Reform Act had given the vote to many radical dissenters. The Kirk and its rivals were engaged in a vicious struggle for the allegiance of the lower classes. Dissent flourished most in places where the parish system had broken down; conversely a revival of the system seemed likely to undermine the position the dissenting Churches had won for themselves. Their members were in the main Liberal voters, so the Whigs could not afford to offend them. In 1835 Melbourne, the new Prime Minister, offered only an inquiry on Church extension, and in the end no money was forthcoming.[37]

Despite this disappointment, the Kirk now enjoyed a few years of unity, progress and expansion. In the absence of Government aid the extension programme was financed from voluntary contributions and more than 200 churches were built.[38] The Veto Act appeared to be having the desired effect. The Conservatives were friendly, and for fear of conflict patrons were inclined to select presentees agreeable to their parishes. Even Whigs were becoming more amenable—Fox Maule, whose position at the Home Office put him in charge of state patronage in Scotland, supported the evangelicals and used his powers to secure livings for them.[39] There was general relief and satisfaction over the outcome of what seemed to have been a brief crisis after 1832, though it was recognised that much still needed to be done.

But the new regime in the Kirk found a formidable foe in one individual, John Hope, Dean of the Faculty of Advocates. This was the ambitious and unscrupulous man who had started so promisingly as Solicitor General in the 1820s and had seen the whole Tory power structure swept away. As the country's leading lawyer he was still in a position to resist these subversive reforms in the Church. To him the Veto Act was an infringement of the property rights which the Patronage Act had established for the old ruling class, property being held to include the absolute right of a patron to appoint his chosen man.[40] That class had already lost much, and Hope resolved to salvage what he could. He was to play a major part in bringing not only the new regime in the Kirk, but the Kirk itself, to destruction.

The Veto Act had caused one little local difficulty at Auchterarder.[41] The patron was the Earl of Kinnoul, who at the end of 1834 presented to the parish a certain Robert Young. Well qualified, he was after all the subsequent troubles to be for many years an admirable minister there. But he was the nephew of the Earl's factor—and such were the antagonisms introduced now in rural Scotland that this was enough to set the congregation against him. Almost unanimously they objected to his appointment, and the presbytery, following the terms of the Veto Act, turned him down also. During the many months of negotiation and litigation that followed, Hope heard of the case and decided he could use it to resolve what he saw as the plain incompatibility of the Veto and Patronage Acts. By November 1837 it had reached the Court of Session.[42]

The case attracted little public attention at first. But before long it became clear that, if the Kirk lost, its independence would be fatally compromised. Hope, 'screaming and sweating' as Cockburn described him,[43] led for the pursuers, claiming that the Church of Scotland was bound just like any other subject to obey the will of Parliament; if the Veto Act offended against the Patronage Act, the latter must be decisive. Rutherfurd, defending, argued for the co-equality of Church and State; many of the Kirk's laws and institutions predated any parliamentary regulation and Scots law had always assumed for it an absolute power over its own doctrine and discipline. In the middle of 1838 came the judgement: Young was to be instated at Auchterarder, the Veto Act was *ultra vires*, the Kirk possessed only those rights conferred on it by the statute and was required in their interpretation to follow the rulings of the civil courts. The Church quickly appealed to the House of Lords, but there its argument was even more decisively rejected.

This thunderbolt instantly made explicit the problem of its social position. If it had to wait for the sluggish state to rectify abuse, how could it hold the people of an industrial society to religion and how modernise its institutions to accommodate them? The Scots at large were outraged: few of them cared about the technicalities of the Veto Act but they detested intrusion. To them the Kirk now seemed thirled to the Moderate doctrine which denied the people any rights at all. There was a natural tendency among the evangelicals towards greater intransigence, while others in the General Assembly were for plain repeal of the Veto Act. The majority paused to pass a declaration of spiritual independence, harking back to Melville's view of the status of the Church and asserting that it must be the sole arbiter on all matters which it did not freely yield to the judgement of the secular authorities; but then decided to attempt a compromise. The task was entrusted to Chalmers as head of a Non-intrusion Committee. He was not a defender of the Veto Act at all costs, but thought it possible to bring in parliamentary legislation as a substitute—even though this might be construed as a tacit concession on the point of spiritual independence. He certainly hoped that the Whigs, in compensation for having let the Kirk down over the extension programme, would be willing to offer something on patronage. In the summer of 1839 Chalmers and his committee set off for London to negotiate with the Government.

The initiative was worse than useless. Chalmers got on so badly with Melbourne that their encounter destroyed the chance of the Whigs ever doing anything. The churchman found the politician cynical and frivolous; he found his Scottish guest vulgarly fanatical and was intensely suspicious of his Conservative connections. The Prime Minister was only just maintaining himself in power, needed to appease the radicals, thought it impertinent to question the Lords' judgement and disliked popular election. So, while undertaking that in state patronage the Veto Act would be observed and hinting vaguely at wider legislation, his basic tactic was to stall. Getting little change from the Whigs, Chalmers contacted Tory leaders too. It was even less likely that they would prove sympathetic, for while they were all for strengthening the Kirk through extension, their misgivings on the democratic cause of non-intrusion were greater than Melbourne's. Having achieved nothing, Chalmers and his committee returned embittered and with hardening attitudes. This episode greatly diminished the prospects of success for all subsequent efforts at compromise.

The issue first emerged into the electoral arena in the spring of 1840, when there was a by-election in Perthshire.[44] The Conservatives had only recaptured the county in 1837, and it could not be regarded as safe. Their new candidate was something of a non-intrusionist, but his Liberal challenger was more of one. The former gained the support of radical voters and held the seat with an increased majority. The result encouraged his party in Scotland in the belief that it could find a solution to the Church question, which it sought in a toned-down version of the Veto Act. In May 1840 the Earl of Aberdeen introduced a Bill which still permitted a congregation to object to a presentee, but stipulated that the reasons should be stated and that the presbytery should judge them. To this, the presbyterial veto, he could not win over Chalmers, who pointed out that, since the measure would not allow straight disapproval of a presentee as a valid ground of objection, intrusion would still be possible—in any case there was no provision to stop the Court of Session overruling the presbytery. This showed a devious side of Chalmers which others found increasingly exasperating: he had certainly moved from his original moderate line in the London talks, for his reservations meant he was standing out for the veto pure and simple as embodied in the 1834 Act. Guided by him the General Assembly voted against Aberdeen's Bill.[45]

The Church's truculence might have been forgivable after all these rebuffs. But it was dangerous, for it isolated the non-intrusionists from potential political support in the coming climax of the struggle. They had a majority in the General Assembly and wide sympathy in public opinion, but that did not necessarily count for much in dealing with Parliament. Cockburn had shrewdly assessed matters after the Lords' judgement:

> This exclusive addiction of (the Church's) religious members to their religious objects and tenets has had one result which is highly satisfactory. It has made it clear that no political party can be comfortable in using the Church as a political ally. It won't work with the Radicals, who are attached to the Dissenters. It is at fierce war with the Whigs, who won't drain the public purse and persecute other sects to please it, and it has now thrown off the Tories who support patronage and attempt to make the Church surrender its spiritual mastery.[46]

Since Maule and Rutherfurd could not influence the Whig leaders, the breach with Aberdeen, who had felt obliged to withdraw his Bill, was especially ill-advised. A man so powerful in his party was not to be affronted: the non-intrusionists had excluded the chance of its applying itself urgently to the problem once it regained power. That seemed certain, for only the Queen's personal preference was sustaining the Whigs in office. When an election was held in 1841, Peel made clear his hostility to non-intrusion. With the Kirk having alienated all other factions, the question hardly anywhere affected the outcome decisively, though it may well have stopped the Conservatives matching in Scotland their majority in England.

The conflict now proceeded to its tragic end amid the mutual incomprehension of churchmen and politicians. The confused legal history of patronage versus the call in fact gave neither side a watertight case. Parliament asserted the (purely English) doctrine of its own absolute sovereignty. The non-intrusionists stood on ancient Scottish constitutional principle, ignoring the dilution of it that had taken place since the Union. In their agitated mood, they could not understand why Parliament should want to usurp rights it had never, or at least never very clearly, possessed. The case was an arguable one, but their posturing did not help it. From London they looked like theocratic madmen, trying to subvert the social order for the sake of their obscure principles. The Government insisted that the Kirk must do what it must, but that the authority of the state was not to be questioned.

Since Aberdeen's Bill further attempts to legislate had been made by the Duke of Argyll[47] and by Sir George Sinclair.[48] But they failed because of the impatience in London with the extreme positions being taken in Scotland. These were polarised by a series of legal actions arising out of the Veto Act which invariably went against the non-intrusionists. The most vicious dispute was in the Marnoch case, which ended with two ministers claiming the living of this small parish in Moray and two factions in the local presbytery pretending to arbitrate.[49] The General Assembly, after several years of comparative unity of purpose, itself split in trying to pass judgement.

The non-intrusionists were still the largest faction there but did not feel they could expect much from Peel's new Government, which relied on Hope's advice. The Prime Minister might actually have legislated, though he was not prepared to till tempers had cooled and the Kirk had had time to reflect on the peril of its position: the possibility of renouncing its connection with the state was already being openly canvassed. Yet many shrank from that. They were behind the formation of the so-called Middle Party, basically non-intrusionist but wanting above all to avoid destroying the ecclesiastical constitution and so ready to forego the Church's furthest pretensions.[50] This convinced Peel that the extremists were overplaying their hand. He was wrong, for the 1842 General Assembly, where the Middle Party appeared in force, was also in the majority the most militant so far. For the first time it demanded complete abolition of patronage. Its most defiant deed was to vote an uncompromising statement of spiritual independence, the Claim of Right. This asserted that

> all and whatsoever Acts of the Parliament of Great Britain, passed without the consent of this Church and nation, in alteration of or derogation to the . . . government, discipline, rights and privileges of this Church (which were not allowed to be treated of by the Commissioners for settling the terms of the

union between the two kingdoms, but were secured by antecedent stipulation . . .
inserted in the Treaty of Union, as an unalterable and fundamental condition
thereof, and so reserved from the cognizance and power of the federal legislature
created by the said treaty) as also all and whatsoever sentences of courts in
contravention of the same government, discipline, rights and privileges are and
shall be, in themselves, void and null and of no legal force or effect.[51]

That was unmistakably clear. Yet still the Government, convinced that
firmness would win, refused to believe the old Kirk might ruin itself. In fact
it moved rapidly to its doom. In January 1843 Sir James Graham, now
Home Secretary, replied to the Claim of Right.[52] He wrote that spiritual
independence in the evangelical sense would create an irresponsible Church,
as the sole judge of what fell within the spiritual. But experience proved the
limits of the spiritual and civil could not be exactly defined, so that the courts
must decide. This was the Government's last word. Final, desperate efforts
at a compromise finished with the motion put by Fox Maule to the Commons
in March 1843 for a committee on the Claim of Right. The Scots MPs voted
in favour of it by twenty-five to twelve, with ten former defenders of patronage
abstaining; the division was on party lines except that one Conservative went
with the majority and two Liberals with the minority. But in the whole House
it was defeated by 211 to 76.[53]

Meanwhile the evangelicals had suffered a further humiliation, which made
them schismatics rather than disestablishers. After another legal action, the
Stewarton case, the Chapels Act had been declared *ultra vires*.[54] This meant
that all those mainly evangelical ministers from chapels-of-ease who had sat
in the courts of the Church for a decade were disfranchised: the evangelical
majority in the General Assembly evaporated. A vote in favour of severing
the connection with the state, till now available as a last resort, became
impossible. The Middle Party still held, and many others balked. The Kirk
would have to split.

And so the Disruption took place on 18 May, 1843, the day appointed for
the opening of the General Assembly. The non-intrusionists did not await its
proceedings. The retiring Moderator, Dr David Welsh, instead of following
standard form and handing over to his successor, read a statement that the
Kirk could no longer fulfil its functions. He then led his faction out of the
Assembly hall, St Andrew's Church in George Street, and down Hanover
Street amid solemn crowds to an austere meeting place prepared at Canon-
mills. Chalmers was at once elected Moderator of the General Assembly of
the Free Church of Scotland. 'Though we quit the Establishment,' he
declared, 'we go out on the Establishment principle; we quit a vitiated Establishment, but would rejoice in returning to a pure one. We are the advocates
for a national recognition and national support of religion—and we are not
Voluntaries.'[55]

The Disruption was the greatest disaster that Scottish presbyterianism ever
suffered.[56] It took out of the Kirk 450 of the 1,300 ministers, including a
disproportionate share of the most able and active, with 40 per cent of
communicants. Earlier secessions had been local, and the sects that emerged

from them content to remain modest in size and activity. But the Free Church, though its strength lay in the towns and in the Highlands, aimed to rival the Kirk in every parish in Scotland. By 1847 it had 700 places of worship and 500 schools, with its own provision for higher education in New College. The 1851 religious census put its membership at 500,000 against 800,000 for the Establishment, while dissenters and Catholics each numbered just under 300,000. Instead of an undisputed national Church, Scotland now had three forms of presbyterianism, with the established one enjoying the allegiance of only a minority. She thus possessed no longer a single institution which could represent the character, the conscience, the soul of the nation, and no touchstone for the process of social and political renewal that was bound to continue.

So the Disruption turned out also the most important event in the whole of Scotland's nineteenth-century history, overshadowing even the Reform Act in its repercussions. A great national institution, indeed the most essential of all, was broken up and a fundamental element of Scottish identity destroyed. It had survived the Union largely because of the Kirk. The political remnants of the old Scotland were decrepit, but that did not matter so much when the Church offered something of a surrogate in its civil roles. After 1843 they could no longer be fulfilled—the minister, once an administrator, an arm of the state, a prop of the social order, was now just a pastor and preacher. His supervision of local affairs could not continue and his duties were taken over by others. Thus the Kirk ceased to play a central part in the country's life, becoming a mere denomination instead of being fully established at all levels. This was a matter of supreme importance since after 1832 Scotland was failing to emerge as an effective political community. In many ways the only guarantee of her distinctive character lay in her survival as a religious community. In reality her society became increasingly secular. The middle and working classes were to raise themselves into independent, sectional, centrifugal forces as their common Scottish inheritance of presbyterianism dissolved.

The process was aided by the sectarian disputes which now spilled over into every public question. Since no denomination was strong enough to defeat the rest, they brought only bitterness and frustration. They deeply corrupted political life in Scotland, introducing a petty and malicious impotence which precluded any serious search for solutions in accord with her traditions. There was instead a general return to religious conservatism, in others as well as in the Free Church. That showed itself in extreme moral attitudes, often on such incidental matters as temperance and sabbatarianism. They blunted the genuine charity of the old Establishment, for ministers now saw sin behind all problems and sought to cure them by rooting it out. To the average Scot, Christianity too often presented itself in the guise of hectoring preachers who made Sundays dreary and tried to stop him drinking. So none of the new forms of presbyterianism ever became a Church of the people as the undivided Kirk had been. Its mistake had been to treat the state as essentially a constitutional power with only an indirect interest in society's spiritual or physical health, which it held to be properly the concern of religion. The successor Churches took the same view. They were blind to the state's acquisition, now inevitable, of the decisive influence in social affairs, which increasingly it exercised without reference to them. Thus, obsessed with their own disputes, they closed their eyes to the realities of Scottish society, secularisation and rapid economic growth, offering little practical guidance to a nation in the thralls of profound change. The equality of Church and state could no longer be taken seriously.

For the moment, however, the Church of Scotland was not utterly ruined. Its structure was intact and new ministers were quickly found to replace those who had left. It remained most popular in the rural areas, especially the North-east and South-west, and weakest in the towns. It also still enjoyed solid support from the ruling class, and Peel's Government did what it could to help. Heartened by the loyalty of most Kirk members, it believed it could strengthen the rump and foil the seceders. In 1843 Aberdeen re-introduced his Bill for the presbyterial veto, this time successfully, and the next year a measure recognising the Chapels Act was passed. Before long parishioners of the Kirk had hardly less freedom in their choice of minister than others. It was thus equipped to fight a rearguard action against its enemies.

As for the dissenting sects, they went into relative decline: their rural congregations shrank with the drift of population to the towns, where they had to compete against the Free Church for those disaffected from the Establishment. But their resulting insecurity made them even more aggressive in defence of their interests, and they soon took steps to safeguard themselves. In 1847 the two biggest of their denominations, the United Seccession and the Relief, merged into one United Presbyterian Church. It also set up a political arm, the Central Board for Vindicating the Rights of Dissenters.

The Free Church was certainly the most vigorous of all. It had at once been disappointed in one great expectation, that the Kirk would simply collapse, leaving the seceders as the *de facto* Church of Scotland with which the Government would be obliged to come to terms. Instead it grew proud and arrogant in its sectarianism. It maintained that it was still the true Kirk, asserting the duty of the state to support it with the rights it claimed for itself and intending to stay separate from the state till they were conceded. To emphasise its title to the inheritance of Knox and Melville, it deliberately kept everything so far as possible as it always had been. Patronage was of course at an end, but there were no alterations in doctrine or liturgy. The only major change was one forced on it, for it now had to find its own sources of finance. Chalmers was anxious to stress its distinctiveness from the dissenting sects, among which each congregation provided for itself out of voluntary contributions. He devised a method whereby a levy on every parish was paid into a central fund and then shared out according to need. The Free Church's adherents showed such enthusiastic generosity that it was soon on a sound financial footing.

Many were wealthy bourgeois who now seized through the secession the power which, because of patronage, would always have been denied them in the old Kirk. In the Free Church eldership they found a means of pressing their claims for recognition—they appointed the ministers, paid their stipends, directed their pastoral activity and listened critically to the preaching that set the tone of public debate. Thus the country's most confident and articulate class could provide leadership free from aristocratic interference.

By the Disruption it was set passionately at odds with the traditional ruling class. The Free Church even had the satisfaction of being persecuted. Government moves against it were abetted by the landlords, many of whom denied it the sites it was seeking all over the country for new places of worship. Among them Sutherland, hitherto regarded as a progressive, and the normally amiable Buccleuch were especially guilty. Stories of poor, honest Christians having to hear the Gospel on snowy, windswept hillsides invited comparisons with the Covenanters and aroused public outrage. Fox Maule, a seceder, brought in a Bill to stop the obstruction but withdrew it when the Government offered a committee of inquiry in 1846. Its report condemned the lairds' intransigence, and that was enough to make them give way without legislation.

But the Disruption and its aftermath still produced in the bourgeoisie a political reaction quite as powerful as the one which, for different reasons, was taking place in the working class. To be sure, it committed the overwhelming majority of Free Church members to the Liberal camp. But their Liberalism was not at all like that of the complacently pragmatic Whigs. It was defiantly set on absolute devotion to moral principle and intense hatred of privilege in any form. The Whigs, who had taken an unhelpful and vacillating line throughout, were thoroughly discomfited by it.

Such developments might quickly have consolidated the dominion in Scotland of these rising bourgeoise forces. But they were neutralised by a consequence of the Disruption of a different order. For, as a less harmonious and unified country, Scotland was rapidly provincialised. Formerly the balance and co-operation of her institutions had helped to preserve her semi-independence; now the two most important, the Church and the law, had come into open, bitter conflict. Established religion was in effect overthrown and with it the only possible source of a native reforming impulse. So London necessarily became the centre of Scottish affairs. Parliament would guide all change from now on. It legislated on a wide range of issues—welfare of the poor, education, factories, public health—which once would have been direct responsibilities of the Kirk or at least matters of concern to it. Better social conditions resulted from that, but an accelerating anglicisation of Scottish society as well.

The first example came in the reform of the Poor Law, the need for which had been clamant even before 1843.[57] Scotland had had such a law since medieval times, but rapid economic growth made it inadequate. It could not cope with poverty on the modern scale, for relief was administered through parishes of the Kirk which, as we have seen, were not numerous enough in the expanding cities. Nor could it cope with poverty of the modern type, that arising from low wages or unemployment, since the old law excluded people without sustenance yet fit for work. In any case the benefits paid were small, the flow of funds being dependent on sporadic collections, donations and legacies. Kirk sessions were permitted when short of money to charge a local rate, but rarely did so because of its unpopularity.

A debate about the deficiencies had long been going on. Chalmers was one of the most active in it. He disapproved of rates to finance relief, holding that forced levies had an ill effect both on the givers, whose charitable instincts were thereby suppressed, and on the recipients, whose urge to self-help would be blunted. But this was regarded as a rather glib view. More influential was the work of another Conservative, Dr William Alison, who roused public awareness of the problems by bringing out in 1840 a widely read pamphlet which asserted that poverty was getting worse, that the parish system was breaking down and that moral education was no answer. In response, a Royal Commission on the subject was set up in January 1843 under Lord Melville, the former manager. By the time of his report, the Disruption had made it obvious that a Poor Law administered through the Kirk alone could not survive, and his proposals were turned into legislation by the Conservative Lord Advocate, Duncan McNeill.

He set up a central board, nominated by the Government and sitting in Edinburgh, to supervise relief over the whole of Scotland. That really did no more than put the existing system under an authority other than the Church; the remaining changes were meagre compared to the magnitude of the problems. For the central board still had to work through local agencies—each parish was given a subordinate board of its own and an inspector. The capital's bureaucrats were liberal in outlook, tried to set minimum standards of benefit and gradually improve them, so that parishes would be forced to levy rates. But they could not act without the consent of the electors, who often refused to support the idle. Moreover, a test case in 1849 confirmed that not only the able-bodied but also their families were still ineligble for relief. Though by the end of the decade Scottish expenditure on the poor had doubled, it fell far short of an adequate response to the terrible extent of destitution.

Meanwhile, another indispensable prop of semi-independence was surrendered in the economic field. Governments hardly ever intervened in an almost entirely free economy, where activity was normally financed by Scotland's own banks. They were not subject to any legislation and had successfully resisted attempts at it, notably in 1826. In England the reforms introduced then were sensible enough, for her provincial banks issued notes of only local validity and often failed. But the standing and practice of Scottish banks were quite different. Their notes were so widely accepted and trusted that they had replaced gold.

All the same, Scottish banking was remodelled on the English system by an Act of 1845.[58] It had three effects. First, it preserved, if only after a battle, the Scots' right to their own notes, but in return limited the fiduciary issue, not backed by gold, to its current level of £3 million, a figure from which the issue of any bank that failed would be subtracted. Secondly, issues beyond that would in future have to be covered by gold. This onerous rule purported to deal with a problem—excessive creation of paper money—which in Scotland did not exist. In fact the circulation of notes had fallen from nearly £5 million in 1825, while banking capital had doubled to £10 million. Finally, the foundation of new note-issuing banks was forbidden. The vigorous expansion of the Scottish banking industry came to an abrupt halt, to be replaced by a fossilised cartel.

These restrictions by a Ministry otherwise attached to free trade were never adequately justified. Graham was reminded to his embarrassment of his own words some years earlier on 'the fatal connection between the Government and the single chartered bank which facilitates the prodigality of Ministers and invests an irresponsible body with the most delicate and important function of state, the control of circulation.'[59] That comment went to the heart of the difference between the English system, which financed government, and the Scottish, which financed industry. The danger of instability and inflation in Scotland was thus much less, especially on account of the fierce competition and sound practice among banks. But Peel, who had taken years to work out a satisfactory English regime of regulation, would accept no Scottish deviation. The commercial classes' strong resistance to the Bill found some support in both Houses of Parliament. But there was naturally no help from the Conservatives, while the Whigs were split: Abercromby, now Lord Dunfermline, campaigned for the measure, Hume was strangely indifferent and only lesser figures were ready to put up a fight against it. In the end it went through with little trouble.

Altogether Peel's Government of 1841–6, so beneficial to the development of Britain as a whole, was quite the opposite in Scotland. It was stubborn and prevaricating in dealing with her problems, but above all ignorant of them. For a Conservative Ministry, it was remarkably cavalier with national institutions. The results of the Disruption were certainly more than it had bargained for. If it could have realised how important the Kirk was to the social order and how determined the evangelicals were to preserve that position, it surely would have decided on concession. Granting the congregational veto would not have been a major defeat, for no Government was ever going to fall on a Scottish Church question. Graham later admitted that he should have been more accommodating. But by the end—and this was true of both sides—winning the argument had become more important than doing the best. The Conservatives were left without a strategy in Scotland. They could no longer hope to use the Kirk as a vehicle for their own social reforms. Their only base was the landlords, now the object of greater public execration than ever before. The old patriarchal society had rested on two pillars, the Church and the Tory gentry, both after 1843 in effect cut off from the mainstream of national life. The Conservatives, much more isolated than in England, went into irreversible decline.

The Disruption added an extra gloss of bitterness to the already formidable political struggles of the 1840s, and the country was in a state of high excitement when the Corn Law crisis brought the Government down in the summer of 1846. Peel had carried most of his Cabinet with him on repeal, though not the bulk of his party, which in England was visibly reduced to a parlous state. In Scotland it was also largely protectionist, if not fanatically so, but above all loyal to him. At a stretch it could accept the rest of the nation's objections to the Corn Laws. So in a sense the Scottish Conservatives did not split, at least not immediately.[60] Nearly every one of note followed the line of Buccleuch, their acknowledged head, in voting for repeal but then continuing to take the Tory whip. They thus gravitated to the moderate wing of the official party which greatly regretted the schism and hoped for a quick reunion. At home they were now no more than a pressure group for the promotion of landlords' interests, on which they could unite whether there were Corn Laws or not. But their loyalty to Peel had little point after he and his faction in effect seceded.

In any case Buccleuch had been unable to stop a small circle supporting Derby and Disraeli, the new Tory leaders at Westminster, in their diehard opposition to repeal. It was organised in the Scottish Protective Society under the Dukes of Gordon and Montrose and the Earl of Eglinton. Buccleuch tried to keep them quiet but they carried on arguing for the old tariff system long after its restoration had become politically impossible. They succeeded only in preserving the reactionary image of Conservatism.

Nor could Buccleuch prevent the gradual shift away of those who agreed with Peel. They included most of the party's talent, Aberdeen and all the rising men of the younger generation—Argyll, Dalhousie, Lord Lincoln, MP for the Falkirk Burghs, and Lord Elcho, MP for East Lothian—as well as most other Commons members. Though resisting Russell's blandishments to go straight over to the Liberals, they grew hopeless as Scottish Conservatism showed no signs of revival. At length it occurred to them that the better part of valour might to be bolster the shaken Whigs, equally out of sympathy with the new forces in Scottish politics and equally resolved to maintain the social order against them. Those Conservatives were in the end indeed to conclude that for such purposes the more flexible Liberalism was the better instrument.

After Peel's fall the Liberals had come in under Russell. He appointed Minto, Macaulay and Maule to his Cabinet, while Rutherfurd again became Lord Advocate and James Gibson-Craig was made Scottish Lord of the Treasury. Some had from time to time shown sympathy for radical causes, while both Maule and Rutherfurd had gone into the Free Church. Such a collection of Ministers, as widely representative as the Whigs thought they could safely make it, ought to have been attractive to Scotland. But little could be done to appease the passions aroused there.

That showed itself at once. Macaulay's elevation meant a by-election in Edinburgh. An aloof and unpopular member, he had upheld the principle of established Churches and favoured concessions to Irish Catholics, opinions with which he offended almost every section of his constituency.[61] In Scotland ministerial by-elections were rarely contested, yet this time a committee was formed to oppose him with a candidate in one Sir Culling Eardley Smith, a leading English dissenter. Cockburn commented acidly:

> Folly was the only bond that united Sir Culling's supporters ... His committee contained Established Churchmen and wild Voluntaries, intense Tories and declamatory Radicals, who agreed in nothing except in holding their peculiar

religion the scriptural, and therefore the only safe criterion of fitness for public duty.[62]

He was easily beaten, yet the fact that such a strange coalition could be cobbled together gave grounds for concern. The Whig establishment's reluctance to become entangled in religious politics was well-meaning, but its various antagonists now seemed more united in their wish to teach it a lesson that they were divided by hatred of each other.

Macaulay was eventually made the scapegoat. He was trounced in the General Election of 1847 by his enemies' simple expedient of winning the Free Church's support through presenting a member of it, Charles Cowan, as their candidate against him. This sensation was greeted with glee and gloating by every radical in Scotland. But it was only the most signal feature of a much wider swing, for the Whig committees which had usually run burgh elections since 1832 were everywhere in disarray and vulnerable to new populist coalitions, such as that in the capital, uniting dissenters and Free Churchmen. They captured both of the Glasgow seats, Aberdeen, Dundee and seven burgh districts, narrowly failing to take two more. In the new Parliament radicals and associates thus doubled their representation to about a dozen.

Yet there was no universal triumph for the anti-establishment forces. The Whigs were tenacious and still held more than twenty seats. This was in part because so few contests took place, for the dissolution of parties meant few could be afforded. On the one hand, the radicals still suffered great handicaps in electoral organisation and simply were not able to fight most of the seats. On the other, the gravely weakened position of the old ruling class meant it was in no state to continue the offensive it had mounted in the counties after 1832. There was thus a striking lack of competition between Liberals and Conservatives, who stood against each other in only six constituencies, of which the former gained three and the latter one. Altogether, then, they had respectively thirty-three and twenty MPs in the new House of Commons.

This election was long remembered for the defeat of Macaulay. He was one of the most eminent public figures in the whole United Kingdom, and the impertinent malice of Edinburgh could hardly be credited elsewhere. His fall was taken as the ruination of the spirit of disinterested pursuit of the public good which the Whigs had claimed to introduce into politics. Now radicalism was rampant, the landed interest in decline, the workers recalcitrant, the Kirk shattered and the political system in confusion. All the hopes and dreams that the Whigs had entertained in 1832 seemed to have proved themselves illusory.

Chapter 3

'Violent and Exclusive Partisans'

The events of the 1830s and 1840s amounted to a Scottish Revolution, qualified by the destruction they wrought in an ancient polity to stand with almost any other of the national revolutions in Europe during the previous fifty years. The radical forces released in it looked for a Scotch millennium of their own, quite different from the Whigs', in which all privilege would be swept away. Yet privilege often resided in the institutions, some crumbling, some still fairly strong, which were the tangible evidence of Scottish nationhood. The radicals, usually nationalists too, could not resolve the paradox. Instead they lost themselves in querulous carping that merely served to tire the country and bring to the fore once again its tendencies towards passivity and conformism. They obscured the ultimate answer, the building of new institutions.

Scotland was thus uneasily poised between a dead historic constitution and an unborn new one. Full assimilation was prevented by the vigour of her presbyterian values, which kept her Scottish despite the disappearance of their concrete expressions. The Union was nevertheless strengthened, sometimes in unintended and unwelcome ways, but also by the Whigs' consciously anglicising policies. Now they too faced acute dilemmas, however. They had sought in 1832 to legitimise an existing social order in a proper political constitution. Since much of the order had been overthrown, the task was losing its point, except as a check to radical aspirations. The actual result was to make the Whigs, inside the truncated Scottish polity, a substitute for the effete conservative forces of Kirk and gentry, which had once run a remarkably similar system for the detested Tories. This was no Scotch millennium, but again something akin to a one-party state, with the predictable consequence of stagnant oligarchical government resting on patronage. On that foundation the Liberal Party in its turn established a supremacy which was to last till the next century.

The virtual unanimity of the country's original welcome for the Whigs had, however, long been dissipated. Though almost exclusively entrusted with the conduct of affairs and ruthlessly partisan in promoting official interests, they had henceforth constantly to exert themselves to bolster their shaken position.

One means of doing so was to restore their links with the landed class. They had always had its welfare at heart, and had been rewarded in 1832 by seeing it converted to an extent unmatched in its English counterpart by the moral and political arguments for reform. This was not a revolt against the ways of a hierarchical rural society—the gentry had simply decided that continuance in Tory obstinacy pointed the shortest route to revolution. While the Whigs afterwards lost ground to the Conservatives, these were now reduced to a core of immobilist noblemen, a condition from which they never really recovered. Landlords ready to accept free trade had as much in common with Liberalism as with Conservatism, and were anxious not to be left in dangerous and unnecessary isolation on the side of reaction. The time was ripe for a fresh approach from the Whigs.[1]

It came initially in the agrarian reforms undertaken by Rutherfurd during his second term of office, 1846–51. They were quite unlike all subsequent ones, which were intended rather to diminish the power of the lairds. His main wish was to relieve them of inconveniences imposed by archaic Scots laws. In 1846 he made it easier to use land as collateral for finance and abolished some of the costly formalities of inheritance. Then he turned to the vexed question of entail, by means of which a man could fix the line of succession to his land in perpetuity. The existing statute dated from times when families had to be protected from forfeiture or rapacious neighbours. In some form it now covered about half of Scotland, and for modern conditions was absurdly restrictive. Rutherfurd's Act of 1848 permitted heirs to disentail their estates and dispose of them at will. This let the less prosperous landowners get rid of the burden on their families and made for a freer flow of capital into efficient agriculture. Whatever Rutherfurd's purpose, it also ensured that the connection of landed property and hereditary aristocracy would not continue into the indefinite future. As the new rich bought out the effete gentry, it extended Liberalism in the counties.

But it was too early for the Whigs to renew attack on the rural constituencies lost since 1832.[2] After Derby briefly took office and called a General Election in 1852, a Liberal contested only, without success, the Conservatives' remaining burgh district of Falkirk, and none of the counties they held. Inside this opposition bloc of twenty seats, orthodox Conservatism seemed to regain the upper hand. Peelites had held half the total in 1847. Now two of them retired and were quietly replaced by Derbyites in Argyll and Perthshire, while in the one clash of the factions, which took place in Ayrshire, the Peelite lost. Still, the shift was of little significance, for doctrine hardly mattered so long as the beleaguered remnant of the old landlord interest could retain its grip on the constituencies left to it. Its weakness was revealed by the fact that, during this interlude, Derby could not even get his Lord Advocate, John Inglis, into Parliament.

In any case the Whigs' reconciliation with wider circles of the ruling class was only a sideshow to the real task of pacifying Scotland. It did not touch the burghs, where the bourgeoisie was sensing its power. There turbulence continued. Despite the success in 1847 of a populist alliance between dissenters and Free Churchmen, they soon fell to quarrelling, mainly over the latter's refusal to renounce the principle of Establishment. This went furthest in Edinburgh, where the municipal poll of 1851 was fought on a new pattern with three sets of candidates: Conservative-Church of Scotland, Whig-Free Church and radical dissenters. The last did well enough to get McLaren chosen Lord Provost. That conflict in the city was repeated at the General Election. Anxious to avenge their previous humiliation and to make amends to Macaulay, the Whigs renominated him. The radicals would not support Cowan again, putting forward McLaren instead. With two other Free Churchmen standing, one a Conservative, a lively campaign gave a narrow victory to Macaulay and Cowan. In other seats the populist alliance held. It took the Ayr Burghs and helped the radicals returned for Glasgow in 1847 to beat off a Whig, Lord Melgund. He had so far sat for Greenock, but abandoned it without a fight to Andrew Murray Dunlop, author of the Claim of Right and the most eminent Free Church layman, who had also come to believe that his sect's future lay in league with the dissenters. The number of radical and dissenting MPs was raised to more than a dozen, concentrated in the burghs. They still, however, formed only a minority of the thirty-three Liberal members.

The Whigs now agreed to serve under a Peelite Prime Minister, Aberdeen. He was the only senior British politician acquainted with the intricacies and enmities of Scottish affairs. He was also a kindly, tolerant man who greatly disliked the Parliament House regime. Briefly it was in danger. Aberdeen wrote to Russell:

> Your Scotch Whigs are really too bad. I am unwilling to recognise the necessity of delivering Scotland into the hands of these violent and exclusive partisans; and I think they might be improved by seeing a gentleman of more liberal feelings introduced among them. If this Scotch spirit were to prevail no government could exist.[3]

The gentleman he had in mind was apparently his fellow-Peelite, Lord Elcho, the energetic and strong-minded heir to the Earl of Wemyss who, if always a champion of aristocracy, defined its duty as the improvement of the people's education and welfare. Made Scottish Lord of the Treasury, he exploited his position ably, not just to superintend the MPs but to legislate and to push through administrative innovations. Even so, the regime was able to withstand the Prime Minister's august disapproval. There was scope for initiative elsewhere while Rutherfurd's recent successor as Lord Advocate and MP for Leith, James Moncreiff, was feeling his way. But as a political manager of conciliatory instincts, he saw eye to eye with Elcho on most matters. The latter was to declare their co-operation exemplary: 'No change of system was required so long as the Lord Advocate and the Scottish Lord worked cordially together.'[4]

Moncreiff soon emerged as a key figure in attempts to soothe the country's religious passions.[5] Scion of a distinguished family of landowning clerics and lawyers, he was himself an evangelical who, with others of his kin, had gone into the Free Church. Now that Scotland had three forms of presbyterianism, however, too close an identification by the Government with any one of them would inevitably arouse the ire of the rest, so it had to tread warily. For the moment the dissenters, riddled with radicalism, were beyond the pale. In their attitude to the Kirk the Whigs remained as ambivalent as before. Their first impulse was to uphold Establishments of any kind. But the Church of Scotland had retreated into stunned dependence on the Conservatives, receiving from them favours which the Whigs could not hope to match.

Moncreiff helped to lead the Whigs to the conclusion, already suggested by events in the capital, that they had to woo the seceders. These, while in no sense constituting a political party, were certainly a political force. Many constituencies contained a substantial body of them likely to react strongly if their religious interests were threatened. In the 1850s they formed the largest group on Edinburgh town council and they had solid electoral strongholds in Aberdeen and Greenock. The newspaper of the Free Church, *The Witness*, told readers to vote only for candidates who adhered to it. Yet despite its firm sense of cohesion it also felt vulnerable. It was a minority sect which thus could not dispense with external political support. It had no security, as the Kirk had, in an entrenched constitutional position and lacked the dissenters' experience in the arts of self-defence.

In politics it was torn in two, even in three directions. Its extreme ecclesiastical reactionaries actually tended to vote Conservative, following Chalmers' own convictions. But these were few and its real dilemma lay between accepting the patronage of the Whigs and joining with the radicals against the Establishments in Church and state. Electoral history showed that a populist alliance of the latter kind could defeat them and administer at least a local shock to the system—in Macaulay's case it had been much more than a local shock. Yet the radical dissenters were a peevish crew, particularly sensitive to the seceders' claim that they remained the true Kirk. On the other hand, the Free Church was bound to be somewhat suspicious of Whig approaches. It had noted the anti-clerical streak in English Whiggism before the Disruption and had afterwards suffered greatly at the hands of the landlords, to whom Scottish Whiggism was now showing such conspicuous favour. At the same time the Free Church was surprisingly strong in Parliament House, while at Westminster leading Scots Whigs such as Fox Maule and the Marquess of Breadalbane took up its causes. In all they could offer protection it was unlikely to find elsewhere. Unfortunately for both, the combination of powerful patrons with the Church of the rising bourgeoisie did not always prove unbeatable.

This was illustrated during one of the most bitter Scottish controversies of these years, arising from the dislocation of the education system in 1843.[6] Till then it had been almost a monopoly of the Kirk, which at least aimed to run a school in every parish, and held great sway in the five universities. The result was in its way a model of democratic excellence—not as perfect as Scottish myths suppose, but still among the finest in Europe.

The disputes after the Disruption exposed the depths of sectarian animosity to which the Scots could sink. The Kirk itself was largely to blame through its efforts to retain the privileges it had enjoyed while still a national institution, loss of which would indeed open the way to formal disestablishment. Thus, to vex the seceders, it tried to revive the obsolete test, the legal requirement that schoolmasters should be members of it, and many were dismissed. Nominally the test was applicable to university teachers too, though they proved harder to dislodge. The educational monopoly was anyway promptly dismantled because the Free Church set out to found its own network of schools and colleges. Others—dissenters, charities, even Chartists—were also building schools. So education was expanded after 1843 though it was still not being extended sufficiently to the poor in industrial districts.

The Government's concerns were with the scope which the Kirk—which even now ran the largest number of schools—had to abuse its position and perhaps deter pupils from entering them; and with the regulation of standards among so many voluntary bodies, some always short of money. The first difficulty might have been answered if the Free Church had been able to fulfil its ambition to construct its own national system of education. But the burden of providing places of worship everywhere was too heavy to allow that. Many seceders concluded that a national system, safe from the Church of Scotland's influence and capable of meeting their and the country's needs, could only be operated by the state. They sponsored an association to promote it in 1850. Meanwhile, dissenters clamoured for the schools to be secularised and supported solely by voluntary contributions, while the Kirk argued for everything to be left as it was. Such utter disagreement meant the Government felt forced to intervene anyway. As early as 1847 Rutherfurd carried an Act granting some public aid to all schools of a defined standard. This was the first step towards the Whigs' acceptance of the seceders' more modest aim.

Moncreiff hoped to bring in something to reconcile all interests. His Bill of 1854 followed in administrative arrangements the precedent of the Poor Law—the parochial system was to continue, with a central Scottish Education Board above it. This was to distribute the finance and regulate its disbursement by the parishes, with a view to seeing that they pursued no sectarian bias. Religious instruction would be offered but was not to be compulsory, and the schoomasters' test would be abolished. The compromise won the support of a large majority of Scots MPs on second reading. But because its inspiration came from the Free Church it annoyed the minorities, the Conservative adherents of the Kirk and the voluntarist radicals. They persuaded the High Churchmen and dissenters among the English members to oppose it, so that it was narrowly defeated in the whole House. Several measures on the same lines were voted down in the next few years, though Moncreiff did get rid of the schoolmasters' test in 1861. Eventually in 1864, having failed over a decade to reach agreement, either in Parliament or in Scotland at large, on a national system, he referred the questions to a Royal Commission under Argyll. They were still unsolved when Moncreiff left office five years later.

With the universities he was more fortunate. Tests were a difficulty here too, but he was able to abolish them as early as 1853. There was, despite the legal position, wide recognition of the absurdity of excluding half the population from high academic appointments on sectarian grounds. He also turned to a general reform, in which he was again successful, at least indirectly. Because of political circumstance, however, the measure he had planned was passed under the Conservative Ministry of 1858–9 by its Lord Advocate, John Inglis. There had been much criticism of the standard of university education, thought too low to enable Scots to compete with the products of Oxford and Cambridge. It was an anglicising Act, seeking to introduce into higher education in Scotland, traditionally based on a broad humanistic curriculum, something of the specialisation usual in England. Many had grave doubts about it, though it did foster a system of scientific and technological training far finer than anything in the South. In general the Scottish universities remained, compared to their English counterparts, both distinctive and distinguished. Some hoped they could assume the moral and intellectual leadership of society which other institutions had perforce given up.

If the hope proved vain, this was at least a genuine attempt to improve and adapt institutions in a Scotland otherwise paralysed by the passions aroused in the Disruption. They ruined the Whigs' wider plans. The most ambitious was to reconcile the Kirk and the seceders. The prospect brightened under Aberdeen, who had worked hard to avert the calamity of 1843. Moves were made at the Free Church General Assembly of 1853 for a petition to Parliament begging reconsideration of the Claim of Right. But the Rev Robert Candlish, the outstanding figure since the death of Chalmers in 1847, had them quietly smothered.

An alternative was to bring together the seceders and dissenters.[7] In this the main aim was the creation of a body of presbyterians as large as the Kirk, of which the status would thus surely become indefensible. Perhaps the way could then be opened for the work of 1843, and even of the earlier secessions, to be undone. In the light of what Peel had conceded after the Disruption, it might be possible to restore one Church of Scotland with a degree of spiritual independence acceptable to everybody. Whig attempts to secure religious peace by these means were premature, but did anticipate the actual development in the twentieth century.

The idea emerged in the correspondence of Fox Maule, now Lord Panmure, during 1854, though whatever plan of action lay behind it was at once ruined by the education controversy. In 1857 it was taken up again by Sir George Sinclair, another who had once tried for a compromise on non-intrusion. He organised a convention of ministers and laymen from both sides. It devised a scheme of union, the Sinclair Resolutions. These were endorsed by the principal politicians among the seceders. The influence of Parliament House came into play through Sir Henry Moncreiff, brother of the Lord Advocate, who was a guiding influence on the later negotiations. The impetus among laymen was clear. Only the clergy held back.

There was no response from that quarter for some years, till Sinclair privately lobbied the Rev John Cairns, acknowledged leader of the United Presbyterians. In 1863 they made a formal approach to the Free Church. Talks started in earnest, producing the next year's Articles of Agreement for ratification by presbyteries on each side. Commitment from dissenters was more general for, whatever the Whigs' designs, the project would in the first instance obviously strengthen enemies of the Establishment. They insisted that the new Church should be a voluntary one, renouncing any connection with the state.

This was accepted by some prominent seceders, notably by Murray Dunlop and by their rising star, the Rev Robert Rainy, principal of New College. But they underestimated the rigour of ecclesiastical conservatism among certain of their own brethren. The struggles since 1843 had made these even more fervent in the cause of a national Kirk maintained by the state in the freedom it chose for itself. They were not concerned about the Free Church's *de facto* position of dissent. Voluntarism, they said, would lead to the horror of a secular state. The Rev James Begg, an impetuous demagogue, mobilised the opposition and confronted Rainy in the General Assembly of 1867 with a sizable minority, especially strong in the Highlands, which would brook no compromise. So, though by 1871 most Free Church presbyteries had approved the articles, persistence threatened a fresh schism among the seceders themselves. That could not be contemplated, and the project had to be dropped in 1873.

Despite coming so close to success, it backfired in the end on the Whigs who had promoted it from behind the scenes. A decade of collaboration among the clergy and laity of the two Churches made them realise to what extent their interests were congruent. In the next great ecclesiastical controversy to sweep Scotland, over disestablishment of the Kirk, the seceders and dissenters stood together—this time they found themselves opposed to the Whigs. That was of great effect in uniting radicals of all shades in the more popular Liberalism which emerged from the 1868 Reform Act, and thus in isolating the ruling clique.

The episode represented a major defeat for the Whig policy of conciliation—there was little else that could safely be offered by way of blandishment to the bourgeois radicals.[8] Though these too called themselves Liberals, they had in fact become the strongest opposition to Whiggism now that the Conservative party had irretrievably decayed. But their unyielding dogmatism on every question inhibited their exploitation of the role. Most often they were merely troublesome and divisive. They never cared about alienating anyone not in complete agreement with them. In all circumstances they relied only on those already committed by ideology or sectariansim and trusted to moral bombast to overcome hostility or indifference elsewhere. Mid-Victorian radicalism in Scotland turned out a failure, with few concrete achievements to its credit.

What radicals aimed at was the universal enforcement of the voluntary principle, a policy which arose from their association with religious dissent. The principle was formulated out of its experiences during the previous one hundred years, when it had shown it could organise and finance its own churches and charities, spurning the security offered by state-endowed religion. Now, radicals argued, everyone else should do the same. By extension of the principle they came together with English radicalism in demanding exactly equal rights for all citizens and promotion among them of the maximum degree of self-sufficiency through *laissez-faire* economics and a wider franchise. In other respects they differed from their southern colleagues. Naturally they had their own national causes: they strongly favoured the autonomy of local institutions within a severely circumscribed state apparatus and joined in calls for reform of Scottish government. But the greatest difference lay in the Scots' bigoted pursuit of sectarian interests. Their overriding purpose was disestablishment of the Kirk, and they violently opposed any moves which might be construed as strengthening it or its allies the landlords. They even attacked the Free Church for avowing that it would one day return to a purified Establishment. Real or imagined slights on dissenters roused them to fury. They lacked the more generous and more secular outlook of many English radicals.

This narrow-mindedness meant they often wasted their political opportunities. For example they rejected the idea of setting up an organisation which could rival Parliament House in its electoral manipulations—they held the independence of each constituency to be sacred and election managers' tampering with it to be immoral. That was not the only reason why they long failed to make an impact in the counties especially. They did realise that their progress was being impeded by the Scottish landed class with its connections in London and its easy access to civil and military office. So they welcomed anything that might thwart the gentry: free trade, curtailment of ministerial patronage and pacifism in foreign policy.

Radicals showed, too, some concern for land questions.[9] These had grown more important since the 1820s, when people started to discuss whether large estates or independent smallholdings were preferable, in political and social as well as in economic terms. The tenantry, a class suffering many disabilities and unrepresented in Parliament, was for both reasons inclined to radicalism. The obvious way to make its influence felt was by lowering voting qualifications in the counties. But because rural Scotland was so feudal, tenants could not always afford to express their sentiments; obsequiousness rankled, yet was often necessary if a family wished to retain its lease. Radicals were torn between the wish to train the people to manly independence and the fear that a large new group of tenant voters would be too easily manipulated by the landlords. So they could not commit themselves wholeheartedly to a wider county franchise and left an important source of potential support untapped.

Nor was a firm alliance cemented between the bourgeois radicals and the proletariat in Scotland. One might have thought that the former's voluntary principle would have agreed with the latter's instinct for self-help. The basis for unity existed in the Complete Suffrage Societies, drawing membership from both classes, which survived from the 1840s. The Scottish ones were not especially active, but they stuck to the demand of a vote for all adult males. This made them more thoroughgoing than their English counterparts, which had fallen under the sway of Liberal leaders such as Bright favouring some more moderate reform. The Scots were thus neutralised: the movement as a whole took notice only of the English and accepted their limited programme as representative of working-class aspirations everywhere.

In any case the bourgeois radicals, stern and factious, were never really friends of the people. They saw social problems as the consequence of vice, above all of the lower orders' addiction to drink, and were more devoted to temperance than to any other non-religious cause.[10] The temperance movement was one of Scotland's gifts to the world. Founded in 1829 by a Greenock man, John Dunlop, it had spread quickly, largely through the talents in propaganda of William Collins, founder of the publishing house. By 1838 it had been possible to set up a Total Abstinence Union for the whole of Scotland.

But decades of campaigning had failed to quench the Scots' taste for alcohol, so now radicals turned to the law. Their only major legislative success during these years, the Forbes Mackenzie Act of 1852, brought in Scotland's first licensing restrictions. It was meant to help the workers rid themselves of their degrading habits, making them more self-reliant and politically effective. In fact they detested it, especially as it was enforced by magistrates whom they could not elect. But the bourgeois radicals wanted to go much further. Their next aim was a statute establishing local option, the right of particular areas to vote themselves dry. If national prohibition was impracticable, that was a way of setting up islands of abstinence as examples to the rest of the country. It would satisfy not only the radicals' attachment to local autonomy, but even their nationalism. Drink was a serious problem in Scotland because of the huge consumption of whisky, which the English had not yet learned to appreciate. Thus there seemed good reason for special Scottish legislation. Soon most Scots MPs, supported by the Churches, were pledged to local option. To their indignation, the English majority in the Commons refused to be persuaded—indeed, there was no legislation till the next century.

When bourgeois radicals tried otherwise to help the workers, it was usually by inviting them to become honorary members of the middle class. McLaren and his circle organised in the 1850s a Scottish Freehold Association which encouraged people to buy property that would qualify them for the vote, giving the urban artisans a stake in society and creating a free peasantry in the countryside.[11] But others did believe that the answer to persistent unrest over the suffrage was simply to lower the qualifications. At a conference in 1856 the association adopted as its policy a universal forty shilling franchise, which would bring Scottish arrangements into line with the English ones— the existing distinctions were besides offensive to the radicals' nationalism. But they rarely agreed on anything, and did not long stay united on this demand either. It was not quite representative of opinion among them, for some worried about the effect it might have on the counties. Scots of moderate views certainly thought it too extreme, and Moncreiff at once repudiated it. Parliament's feeling was that Scotland, being poorer than England, could only expect a more restricted suffrage. In the end the radicals opposed a new Reform Bill—introduced by Disraeli in 1859 during a brief spell of Conservative rule to perplex the dithering Liberal party—on the quibbling grounds that it did not meet all their claims.

So these radical exertions on the workers' behalf in fact gave them little satisfaction. And without greater commitment to their aspirations in the political nation, they had few means of asserting themselves.[12] Chartism had collapsed, though in Scotland, because of the large moral force element, that collapse was not so complete as in England. A few Chartist societies did struggle on—as late as the General Election of 1857 one put up a candidate at Paisley. More often Chartists stood in burgh elections in the industrial districts, and a Glasgow activist, James Moir, even managed to get on to the corporation. Distinctive working-class politics never died, but equally did not rise above local or individual efforts without wider consequence. Yet Chartism had given the Scottish proletariat a new self-confidence, as well as leaders who went on into the other, usually non-political movements which had sprung to life in the 1840s. As things stood, the only realistic aims were non-political. The main one was the improvement of industrial conditions.

These, rather than the abstractions preached by bourgeois radicals, were in workers' experience the real cause of social misery. Though disfranchised, they could still mount pressure for the extension of trade union rights and for the regulation of employers' freedom where this was injurious to personal welfare or the public interest. That was the opposite of egalitarianism as understood by the radicals. They held that morality rather than legislation was the answer to economic distress, and that the measures demanded would do no more than make of the workers another privileged class. Here again their dogmatism alienated potential support.

In any case the unions were able to revive after their decline since the 1830s. They gained enough strength to direct a number of disputes—in 1856 the miners went on strike all over the Western counties, in 1858 they came out again for four months and in 1860 troops had to be sent to cow them. So far, however, there had been little co-operation among unions. That now started up with the formation of trades councils in Edinburgh in 1853 and in Glasgow in 1858. Once it had been proved they could work, they were soon tempted into politics—in 1861 the Glasgow trades council declared itself in favour of universal manhood suffrage.[13]

In staking their claims to be admitted to civic responsibility, some workers moved in the opposite direction, towards giving proof of their orderly and patriotic instincts. They did so notably in 1859, when there was serious danger of a general war in Europe as a result of Napoleon III's adventures in Italy. Just as in the 1790s, the Government called for the raising of volunteer forces. In Scotland the response was astounding, with recruitment running at about twice the British average.[14] From Glasgow it was patronisingly reported that 'the social tone of the artisans had been much improved by their becoming volunteers and they had become more loyal and regular.'

Soldiering had long been a relatively respectable pursuit among the Scots, unlike in England, where it attracted only the dregs of society. Even so, their image of themselves as a fighting race was inflated. In fact their membership of the forces was disproportionately small, doubtless because of the strong pacifist element in the Liberal ethos. Yet in a curious way volunteering was to prove compatible with radicalism. Some corps dressed in Garibaldian uniforms, redolent of romance and liberty. Later they donned kilts and paraded behind pipers, so that the movement assimilated the cult of the

Highland soldier, symbol of the Scottish tradition of unflinching courage and stern morality. Spreading through the diaspora, it inspired the formation of tartan-clad regiments in such unlikely places as Calcutta. It was built into the Scots' nostalgic picture of home and fired their enthusiasm for Empire. In Scotland, too, its ideals were disseminated, not least through the wildly successful youth movement, the Boys' Brigade, founded in 1883 by a Glaswegian Free Churchman, William Alexander Smith. So by a bizarre reversal, Liberal politics and religion began to find expression in a Liberal militarism. Different values infiltrated the Scottish consciousness, perversely borrowing their conventions from that pillar of a conservative social order, the army. Among the people the foundations were gradually laid of a new Liberalism which tamed the anarchic tendencies of their national character, tempering moral absolutes with discipline. It also paved the way for an intensified British nationalism, reflected above all in imperialist sentiment. That was to become a major force in Scottish politics.

The burgeoning of voluntary activity was a distinctive mark of Victorian Britain, and especially strong in Scotland. It was equally a sign of how deeply radical values had struck root there. Of political importance for the future, it for the moment paradoxically helped to allay the discontents. It was a surrogate for power among electors excluded from the oligarchy, and a surrogate for the vote among those still without it.

The religious and ethical intensity of Scottish radicalism, readily given a patriotic imprint, made it almost a national movement. Yet it remained politically impotent. The Whig response to the bourgeois radicals was to conciliate them if possible. When that failed, as it most often did, they were easily resisted. Indeed, the Whigs were able to make quite serious efforts to suppress the radical element in Scotland's parliamentary representation. They never succeeded, but they did constrict its influence. Certainly radicals extracted few concessions of substance, for they rarely rose to the task of transforming their obsessions into issues on which the nation could unite, being constantly diverted by their internecine ferocity. In the end a Scotland where more and more people were doing things for themselves was self-evidently one where her decrepit state apparatus was ceasing to matter. But for now the Parliament House Whigs stayed in control of it.

Nor did the radicals assume the leadership of the voteless masses. So towards them, too, the Whigs were left free to act with friendly paternalism rather than hostility: their views on popular education were enlightened, and they opposed radical temperance legislation on the grounds that the lower orders would be raised through gradual training in moral and social responsibility rather than by a ban on their pleasures. Admittedly this offered the workers no more than a long-term chance of political advancement. So while they shared Liberal values, they also kept their distance and pursued their own aims. Increasingly those aims were set in a British context, for the Scottish labour movement was too divided and immature to be anything better than an adjunct of the English one. Again, the Whigs were left undisturbed in their Scottish hegemony.

That lasted till the moment came for a wider reform in the United Kingdom.

So Scotland's own leaders did much to exclude the possibility that the nation or any part of it might, like the Irish, become strong enough in its dissidence to force its claims from time to time on Westminster. Meanwhile, the Parliament House Whigs could pursue with some success their own objects. They knew what they wanted—the overwhelming dominance of a decidedly conservative Liberalism and close integration with the English political system, itself in its more aristocratic character a bulwark against rapid change. Within the narrow compass of the Scottish political system they also had, given the lack of serious local competition, the means to achieve what they wanted. After the upheavals, they were able to restore a degree of stability.[15]

Whig rule was not without its virtues. It had in fact done a good deal for Scotland. It had liberated her from an indefensible electoral system and from an obscurantist loyalty to tradition, so from the strictly political obstacles to personal liberty and social development. Approximately uniform rights were now established everywhere in Britain. While the Union thus became more complete, the English refrained from using it to impose on Scotland: they left the consequences of the Disruption, for example, to be worked out by the Scots themselves. Nor were there any blatant challenges to national feeling like the established Churches in Wales and Ireland or the English administration in Dublin Castle. Scotland was altogether unaware of nestling as an obscure little nation in the bosom of a world power, regarding herself not as politically subject but rather as the cultural partner of her great neighbour country. Her politics could develop much in line with politics there, further diminishing the risk of a rupture. When Scots thought about public affairs they did so in the context of the United Kingdom. Elections in mid century were decided in that context or else on local issues, and rarely on those of a national Scottish character.

Where relations were not harmonious it was less because of England's imperialism than of successive London Governments' indifference to and neglect of the Scots—only in that sense did she dominate the Union to their disadvantage. Problems without parallel in the South indeed occurred, but English politicians did not understand them or did not know that they existed. But then Scottish politicians could not solve them either. They had created a system which left little room for separate consideration of their national questions. They were all the same very pleased with it. And they dismissed those who called for changes as Tories conspiring in the name of the old regime or as radical trouble-makers.

Yet the constitution was decidedly the more defective for one result of reform. This was the loss of a Minister for Scotland, which the management system had always in practice provided. The Whigs had hoped in 1832 to give the Home Secretary real, and not just nominal, control of Scottish affairs. But that did not happen. His responsibilities covered an island where six out of seven inhabitants were after all English. He had many demanding duties and was happy to delegate the minor ones, among which he counted those in Scotland. Ready to hand for this purpose was the office of Lord Advocate. Even under the old dispensation he had been the constant adviser of the manager, who corresponded with him regularly and relied on his counsel.

Now that the responsible Minister was simply not interested in Scotland, it was natural for the Lord Advocate to exercise his functions.

So the effective headship of the Scottish executive was transferred from one office to another, and its status was thereby greatly diminished. The Lord Advocate was mainly concerned with the minutiae of administration and legal procedure: directing investigations and prosecutions, giving advice to government departments on the law, dispensing patronage, dealing with Home Office papers on Scotland and acting as spokesman for the Ministry in correspondence with the public. He was burdened with a great deal of rather trivial routine in a way that the Melvilles, for example, had not been. Thus he remained essentially a law officer with no leeway for political leadership of the country, no opportunity to build up personal influence and little independence from London. Within these limitations Moncreiff was a reasonably active, reforming Lord Advocate, but otherwise the post was usually entrusted to politically unambitious dullards lacking any interest in distinctive Scottish policies.

Many Scots objected to all this. Not only did they find it offensive that nobody except Edinburgh advocates could advance to the head of the administration, but they also felt that chances of taking the political initiative were being missed. Yet successive Governments, following the hardly impartial advice of Parliament House itself, refused to contemplate changes in the arrangements. They argued that Scottish politics consisted only in legislation which the Lord Advocate, a legal official, was well fitted to conduct. He was anyway formally responsible to the Home Secretary, and the fact that the latter seldom had to step in proved London's satisfaction that Scotland had no political life worthy of a separate structure.

The executive branch of government also included some special Scottish agencies, however. A few of the country's peculiar interests or institutions were recognised by Westminster as having no counterpart in England and were placed under the control of *ad hoc* administrative boards.[16] There were now three of them: the Board of Manufactures, established in 1726 to aid the growth of industry; the Fishery Board, dating from 1808; and the Board of Supervision, set up in 1845 to oversee the workings of the new Poor Law. During the next decades the system was extended: in 1863 the Board of Supervision was given charge of public health in general, and repeated attempts, eventually successful in 1872, were made to establish a board for education. These bodies contained eminent laymen supposed to represent the public interest, though in practice the work was carried out by professional specialists who could do as they liked. Nominally Home Secretary answered for them in Parliament, but the MPs felt entirely shut out from the operations of this embryonic Scottish civil service.

The position of the Scots members at Westminster was altogether unsatisfactory. In proportion to her population Scotland remained grossly under-represented: in 1832 she was given fifty-three MPs out of 658 when she ought to have had nearly ninety. The new generation of members showed more energy than the old, but failed to make up in quality what it lacked in quantity. This lack of political weight had tiresome results. Little time was set aside for Scottish debates, which usually had to wait till other business was finished in the small hours of the morning. Scottish Bills were often abandoned to make room for measures which the Government thought more important. That cavalier attitude was naturally not shared by the Lord Advocate to whom, rather than to the Home Secretary, the MPs were forced to turn when they wanted something done. Even during the session he was, however, often absent in Edinburgh. Scottish Lords of the Treasury had no administrative power unless, like Elcho, they sought it. Every other one, however, acted rather as election manager and whip—in the latter capacity he was more concerned with pressing the Ministry's views on the Scots members than the reverse.

Extended discussion of Scottish measures visibly bored the English MPs and, if anything, roused hostility to useful reforms. So the Scots almost gave up trying to debate their affairs in the House and instead did their business in private meetings. There they would try to come to an understanding on the general outline of a measure, persuade the Lord Advocate to work it up into a Bill and then rush it through with as little discussion as possible whenever the Government could be induced to grudge an hour or two. But the eagerness for speed made them too accommodating to English prejudices and ignorant amendments. The process was anyway fouled by the factiousness of the Scots even, or especially, on minor issues. The Ministry easily wearied of their obscure disputes and would crumple before the least opposition. Laws were either not carried at all or passed with inadequate scrutiny.

The frustration made a political career unattractive to the most able Scots. The seats were frequently offered to outsiders—a returning nabob, a retired military gentleman, a scion of the peerage or an English party stalwart unable to find a constituency at home. The universal conventionality was thus reinforced. Scotland's best spokesmen came from the Lords, and the great age of the independent Commons member largely passed her by. For almost the whole period from 1846 to 1874 Britain was ruled by Liberals of various hues, including a solid and indispensable bloc of Scots. They remained, however, pliable and reticent before Westminster politicians, so that Liberal dependence on them went unnoticed and unrewarded.

Nor did pressure rise up from the constituencies. Scotland was a small country where most still lived in bucolic naivety or urban degradation, and where the franchise was anyway more restricted than in England. She also lacked the natural leadership provided there, even in the towns, by aristocrats, for her own were usually absentees. It is true that in Aberdeenshire, Argyll, Sutherland and the immense Buccleuch domains of the south the MPs were in effect nominated by the respective magnates. But otherwise the county representation was determined by lesser landowners making their own accommodations. Since they were themselves not especially powerful, they were open to the influence of the Parliament House Whigs. These indeed took the view that leadership was best kept in the hands of enlightened, well-born men susceptible to their control. They tried to ensure that such people occupied the key positions everywhere in Scotland and, except in a few burghs, they succeeded. In the burghs the Liberal elite might look by English standards alarmingly democratic, consisting of lawyers, ministers, merchants, bankers and newspaper editors, though in the minor districts with admixtures of lairds from the surrounding county. They nonetheless felt themselves entitled to make the essential choices for the electorate, which usually could do little but acquiesce. They were also anxious to avoid the trouble and expense of a contest. This was where Parliament House could again step in, by getting agreement to a candidate from the local worthies well before the poll. The point was that those without an established social standing were never found in such company. In practice the system was just as socially exclusive as England's except that the exclusion started operating at a lower level.

It was still remarkable how control was exercised without recourse to the methods common in England and Ireland. There, a parliamentary committee reported in 1870,

> the borough elections are often extremely corrupt. In Scotland, it is stated, without contradiction, that bribery is almost unknown. This is attributed in a great measure to the superior education of the Scotch people; and partly to the fact that, the constituencies being comparatively new, there exists no corrupt class, long familiar with the traditions of bribery.[17]

Yet the control was just as real as elsewhere. All that the reform of 1832 turned out to have done was to produce a change of personnel in the oligarchy. The new one was no less committed to the established order than the old, if more open to pressure and more willing to concede a few gradualist reforms when agitators proved awkward enough. Without either a wider franchise or a thorough reform of Scottish government—neither of which London would grant for the moment—the dissident Liberals were quite unable to shift the Whigs from power.

These thus had a vested interest in inertia. Though the Whig constitution did not exactly encourage initiative, the Scots showed themselves bad at taking advantage of their enfranchisement. Nothing much replaced the old Tory polity but a somewhat imprecise confidence that liberation had been achieved, that the country was advancing and that all would be well once everyone had recognised the profound rightness and goodness of Liberal principle. The real distinguishing feature of Liberal government was that it won the country's strong, enduring loyalty, as Tory government, at least in its latter days, had failed to do.

How was this? Governments at the time knew nothing of psephology. They had no idea why they were in and others out, and so made no attempt to gear their promises and policies to those sections of the electorate which might vote for them. Instead they couched their appeal in terms of general principle. Among Liberals, and above all with Gladstone, this developed into a tone of high moral earnestness. He seemed to assume that Scots voted Liberal simply because they were more moral than others—'Scotland has always done battle for the right,' he proclaimed at the end of his life.[18]

It was a judgement with which most Scots heartily concurred. Their politics were about right and wrong. As one said:

> I am a Liberal because I am a Scotchman. As a matter of personal constitution, the claim of the past, the authority of the present, and the sacred continuity of both, so press upon my imagination as almost to make me a Conservative. But in the history of my own country I find something deeper than the thin stream of its Conservative tradition. I find there in every age a passion for the ideal, and a sense of the obligation of men who deal with public affairs to build upon nothing less than the principles of right.[19]

These attitudes were determined by the Scots' presbyterian religion. Its most important aspects were a democratic tradition in Church government and a stress on correct moral conduct, interpreted in the middle class as respectability. Thus Scots voters rejected Conservatism because it had resisted reform and fought a rearguard action afterwards, so that it was still coloured by immoral privilege and snobbery. But they regarded the rising radical movements with suspicion because they looked so unrespectable, and viewed industrial workers with contempt, both for their religion—if they had none or, even worse, were Irish Catholic immigrants—and for their social degradation. Scottish Liberalism espoused an idealistic conception of the rights of man, yet became in practice a conservative force, hidebound by existing social forms and ignoring the problems of the country's development.

But the attitudes also had a constructive side. Whig ideas of what constituted liberty and progress may have been shallow, indeed hypocritical. Yet there is no doubt that the people identified their own Scottish values with them. That sustained in the body politic a cohesion which might have been lost in the earlier upheavals, and without which Scotland could soon have become an English province. Those values survived in the national psychology rather than in practical action, for after the Disruption independent policy became almost impossible. If it existed at all, it was devised and executed by the administrative boards behind closed doors. They blithely spent the greater part of the money raised from the electorate without exciting in it any obvious desire to learn what was being done, how or why.

In strictly political terms, Scottish Liberalism remained remarkably nebulous. It sprang from a society still homogeneous, but bound together by its moral, religious and philosophical convictions rather than its political activity. For most Scots the fact that Liberal governors now presided over a Liberal nation was perfectly sufficient. A proper ethical spirit in public affairs was assured and mere policy became unimportant. Rather, it might expose the contradictions. Contending proposals would each be justified by an appeal from their advocates to the Liberal values which all held dear. Then, to give way on detail was literally immoral. The party was so secure that in intractable cases it could have dissensions argued out within its own ranks—there were as many double Liberal candidatures of men representing various factions or sects as there were contests between Liberals and Conservatives. But nobody

wanted schism, for that might start the slide towards the horrendous alternatives, reaction or revolution.

So Scots came to no united view of what Liberalism meant for the everyday
organisation of society. Instead small groups of them were locked in bitter
conflict round a range of minor issues. One can excuse Scotland for being
new to representative government and unused to the interplay of men and
ideas, above all to the notion that public business might be conducted by
compromising among them. The only respect in which the Liberal ethos
produced in her the characteristics of a mature democracy was in the probity
of public life, at least in the burghs. But the moralising generalities shrouded
a vacuum at its centre, where other countries had practical politicians and
constructive politics.

In the later 1840s the reforming impetus slackened, and for nearly twenty
years legislative energies were directed towards the limited aim of repairing
the damage left by the Disruption. With the odd exception, such as the
universities, other big issues were neglected. They were aired in pulpits and
public meetings, but a consensus on them could not be reached. Without it
Westminster declined to act. The Whigs did not care to tackle the problems
on their own, and anyway lacked interest in Scottish solutions for them. All
had perforce to assent to their cautious line in public policy. They, while
retaining the Liberal party's progressive credentials, stifled its internal progressive impulses. At the price of a few minor accommodations and conciliatory gestures, their hold on Scotland went unchallenged during the middle
decades of the century.

The General Elections of 1847 and 1852 had given little comfort to the
Whigs' hopes of restoring stability. In fact it was restored soonest of all in
the electoral field, where their own influence could be exercised most firmly
and rival forces largely shut out. After an inept performance, especially
in the Crimean War, Aberdeen's coalition was forced from office in 1855.
Palmerston, his successor, took a robust approach to foreign policy while
adopting a conservative stance at home. Behind this strong new leader almost
the whole of the Scottish political establishment united.[20] To his support in
the Whig nobility he was able to add that of the most powerful Peelite
magnates, Aberdeen and Argyll, who stood by him when their English colleagues declined to serve under him. He also meant to maintain the position
of the Whigs in Parliament House, whose leader, Moncrieff, had worked with
him while he was Home Secretary; they remained among his most loyal
adherents. Palmerston attracted as well men of good reformist—even radical—credentials, such as Panmure and Viscount Duncan, MP for Forfarshire, now appointed Scottish Lord of the Treasury.

He was able to appeal powerfully to the electorate at large. His aggressive
defence of British interests endeared him to it, nowhere more so than in
Scotland. He was helped by a renewed burst of economic growth which
induced a general mood of complacent optimism. To Scots electors there
seemed little further point in the feuding of the last decade, which might only
give openings to the forces they feared most. Occasionally it even let the
Tories back in, and certainly did nothing to discourage proletarian unrest—

though prosperity now also quietened the workers. The vast majority of Scots Liberals was therefore ready to rally to Palmerston, seeking safety in his unusually vigorous form of consensus government and leaving only the extreme radicals and the most reactionary Conservatives immune to his allure. Whether the Scots liked it or not, that meant rallying to the Parliament House regime as well. It was able to re-establish Scotland's Liberal party on a broader base than ever before.

The attraction of broad Liberalism was quickly proved. In 1856 Macaulay accepted a peerage, causing a by-election in Edinburgh. The Whigs chose as their candidate Adam Black, a moderate Free Churchman bound to antagonise the radicals. The latter also bid for the seceders' vote again by nominating one of them. A bitter campaign resulted in a runaway victory for Black. Something similar happened a few months later in Glasgow on the resignation of one of its radical MPs—a Whig easily won the ensuing contest.

The Government repeated the performance on a national scale in 1857 when Palmerston, after losing a crucial vote in the Commons, called a General Election. This turned out his greatest triumph. In Scotland it produced a great strengthening of the Whig party hierarchy under its broad Liberal colours. Many new candidates personally pledged to Palmerston came forward and worked closely with Parliament House against the other factions. These were routed in almost every seat then attacked. Whigs and their associates, who had numbered about twenty in the parliaments of 1847 and 1852, now added half-a-dozen or so to that total, thus winning a bare majority of Scottish seats. The Conservatives suffered most. They had to fight only four contests but lost three, including that in the Falkirk district, their last outpost in the burghs. Two further Liberal gains were made with no effort at all, simply through shifts of allegiance among the magnates. In Argyll the Duke, still a Conservative in 1852, selected for his—as usual—unopposed nominee a supporter of the Government. Aberdeen, now urging the Peelites to rejoin Palmerston's coalition, made a personal contribution by seeing to the return of his son for the Ministry in his own shire. The Conservatives, left with only fifteen seats, were especially humiliated at conceding half the counties to the Liberals. On the other side, radicals were caught in a dilemma. While piqued that the Government would concede them nothing, they could not hope to prevail against popular devotion to Palmerston unless they made at least a formal obeisance to him. Those who did so hung on. The rest lost— such was the fate of Alexander Hastie, a Glasgow MP for the last ten years, and of new radical candidates in Edinburgh, Dundee and Paisley. In Britain as a whole twenty-five anti-Palmerstonian radicals were elected, but none came from Scotland.

Despite the magnitude of his victory Palmerston was not long in office. A year later important sections of the parliamentary groups on which he depended—though not the Scots Whigs—had turned against him. With the Liberals all at odds, the Conservatives came in. Disraeli now made his attempt to pass a new Reform Bill, the defeat of which precipitated a fresh General Election in 1859. It was a quiet affair that left the party strengths in Scotland hardly changed. Though few contests took place, Liberal control was consolidated with the gain of another county from the Conservatives. But the antagonism of Whigs and radicals still smouldered. The latter had abandoned their attempts on Edinburgh and instead were undermining Moncreiff in his seat at Leith, since 1832 a pocket burgh of Parliament House. Faced with the real chance of defeat, he withdrew and stood in the capital, where Cowan was retiring. A radical did take Leith, but the Lord Advocate and Adam Black were returned unopposed for Edinburgh, which for the first time in a decade thus had an entirely Whiggish representation. In the United Kingdom as a whole the Liberal factions won a good majority over the Conservatives. They combined once again, and this union was to prove permanent. The year of 1859 marks, if any one does, the formation of the classical Liberal party, extending on a much greater scale the broad Liberalism already established among the Scots.[21]

But in Scotland herself the harmony was artificial—it resulted from the suppression rather than from the resolution of her conflicts. The voters had little chance to exercise their judgement: only fourteen seats were fought in 1857 and only eight in 1859. So far broad Liberalism had meant political atrophy north of the border. It was, however, rudely disturbed by the events of 1865. Palmerston called an election in which the suffrage became the main issue. Three Ministers—Russell, Gladstone and Bright—were already strongly in favour of extending it. In their view it was clear that the 1832 settlement could no longer be regarded as satisfactory or final and that the various fruitless attempts at amendment should be brought to an end with one sweeping measure.

Liberal election management was this time in the hands of W P Adam, the able young MP for Clackmannan and Kinross, sprung from the house of Blair Adam which had helped to found Scottish Whiggism. He started the organisational work that would transform his party into a modern one. Though even in such a relatively excited atmosphere only seventeen seats were at stake, the vigorous campaign saw it take another leap forward. That was aided by a revision of the county voters' roll carried out under Moncreiff. Conservative electioneering had almost ceased, but the registers were still so cluttered with faggot voters—many long dead or rid of their qualifications— that the task of purging the roll in any seat or of creating enough new voters to win had been too expensive to contemplate. This was a real obstacle to faster Liberal progress. The clearance had startling results. Of the 58,000 names on the registers, 21,000 were struck off. Then 14,000 were added, reflecting the fact that many entitled to vote had not bothered to enter their names because of the infrequency of contests. The new total of 51,000 was only about the same as in 1841, but more genuine.[22] So in the following election the Conservatives did well to take back marginal Ayrshire as well as Aberdeenshire, free to return to its normal allegiance after the death of the Earl of Aberdeen. Elsewhere they were helpless before the Liberal onslaught, being reduced to just eleven seats.

The radicals made gains, yet still accounted for only about a dozen of the forty-two Liberal MPs. The first tenant farmer to stand in Scotland, George Hope of Fenton Barns, was their candidate in East Lothian, though he had no chance in a constituency dominated by landlords. Resentment against them in five other counties, once all bastions of Conservatism, brought startling victories for dissenters or land reformers, however. The Whigs, too, were beaten by the Edinburgh radicals, after Black took the fatal step of opposing a wider franchise. Even Moncreiff forfeited the support of many Free Churchmen who would normally have voted for him through half-hearted reform of the annuity tax, a hated local levy for the financing of Kirk stipends. Against them were McLaren and a younger radical, John Miller of Leithen. After a furious campaign, McLaren headed the poll. The Lord Advocate retained enough respect to hold his seat but Black was put out. Altogether reformers did well at the polls and the Liberals won a large majority. Five months later Palmerston, the chief remaining barrier to change, was dead: and the floodgates of reform were opened.[23]

He left a Ministry under Russell determined to bring in a broader suffrage. The vast majority of Scots MPs supported it. The hopes of the voteless classes were raised and a widespread yet orderly agitation began. This wakened fears in some quarters, however, and before long even radicals were toning down their demands. They asked for an increase in Scotland's representation to sixty-eight seats, while McLaren now wanted no more than £6 franchise so as to grant the vote to industrious artisans. Trying to reconcile the conflicting views, Gladstone, Liberal leader in the Commons, offered Scotland an extra seven seats for a total of sixty, together with a qualification of £7 in the burghs and £14 in the counties. The latter proposal brought fierce opposition from the anti-radical fringes of the coalition, from aristocrats such as Elcho and capitalists such as Samuel Laing, MP for the Wick Burghs. The Bill's second reading was carried by one vote. Eventual defeat was certain. Derby and Disraeli then accepted the challenge of forming a minority Tory Government.[24]

But now it was too late to draw back from reform. Workers felt that for the first time in twenty years they had a chance to influence Parliament. Reformers in Glasgow had established an organisation which soon produced enough affiliates elsewhere to permit a Scottish National Reform League advocating universal manhood suffrage to be set up under the presidency of James Moir.[25] By mid 1867 it had fifty branches and 5,000 members, drawn both from Liberal electors and from unenfranchised workers. The purposes of the two groups were not, however, identical. To Liberals the campaign was a means of driving the Conservatives from office and getting their own Government back. Most workers were strongly Liberal in sentiment, but they saw reform as a step towards the long-term aim of forcing the ruling class to pay more heed to social and industrial problems. Some union leaders now hoped to get the suffrage far enough extended to allow the direct representation of labour in Parliament. So they were willing to co-operate with the Liberal party because it seemed likely to give them the better deal there. But in pursuing their larger aspirations they had little reason to prefer a capitalist Liberalism over an aristocratic Conservatism. They remained ready to associate with politicians of any party promoting legislation favourable to working-class interests.

The dilemmas were intensified at this point by one of the most bizarre alliances in Scottish political history, between the arch-conservative Elcho and Alexander MacDonald, leader of the National Miners' Association.[26] Elcho wanted to maintain the aristocratic constitution but show workers that their aims could be promoted by it. A means of doing so came when unions started agitating in the 1860s for repeal of the Masters and Servants Act (1823). It blatantly discriminated against the working class: where trade disputes involved a breach of contract, it made an employer's lock-out a civil offence but an employee's participation in a strike a criminal one. MacDonald, though prominent in the campaign, was a moderate opposed to industrial conflict. That commended him to Elcho, who entered into cordial relations with him and Glasgow trades council. In Parliament he browbeat the Ministry for its reluctance to change the law and told MacDonald he would 'show up these liberal-minded radicals in their dealings with labour'. His efforts secured in 1866 a measure providing for equal liability as between employers and workmen.

To Elcho this vindicated his argument that political reform was not a precondition of social reform. But it also brought out the latent clash of interests inside the reform league which was to lead to virtual schism between its Liberal and trade unionist wings. As they tried for a common policy they encountered the problem of Elcho. The Liberals had fought him in East Lothian before and, since he had opposed their Reform Bill, wanted to do so again with the help of the league. But some unions would have none of it, refusing to come out against a man who upheld their interests so sturdily. Moreover, if the league was to be merely a political front organisation they could no longer co-operate wholeheartedly with it, especially as its Liberal members, following their leaders in Parliament, were abandoning the demand for universal manhood suffrage. Still, the dissidents were themselves divided over how far to carry on supporting the Liberals—Glasgow trades council was forced to give up political activity because of the passions thus aroused. By the latter part of 1867 the Scottish reform movement was in the utmost confusion. But it was saved when Disraeli decided that he had to take up reform himself to stay in office. The Liberal wing of the reform league then became the main channel for the agitation to amend his plans, while the labour leaders appealed vainly for a wider franchise than either of the two parties would grant.

Disraeli knew that Scotland would have to be handled with subtlety.[27] Though anti-Conservative, her MPs were a group he might hope to dissuade from outright opposition to him. So he too promised her sixty seats and lower voting qualifications, extending the scope for radical gains. But he also proposed a redistribution offering better prospects to his own party. He wanted to cut Glasgow into two constituencies, North and South, in place of the two-member single seat; a Conservative victory in one was conceivable. He then planned to remove eleven towns from the counties and put them in old or new burgh districts. This would have secured the landed interest in its remaining fastnesses and might have restored it in some marginal constituencies such as Ayrshire and Lanarkshire. Both of these, together with

Aberdeenshire, were to be divided in two, doubling Conservative chances of winning seats there.

But the Liberals saw through all this and forced the amendment of his Bill. Some subterfuges then disappeared, while the Liberals inserted new provisions favouring themselves. For example, they united the counties of Selkirk and Peebles but removed from them a new constituency of Border Burghs, creating one Liberal and one Conservative seat where there had been two Conservative before. Even then the Liberals were tempted to vote the Bill down. Here was Disraeli's chance to win over the Scots radicals. He impressed on them that if his measure failed they could not expect another early chance to break the Whig hold on Scotland. Withstanding great pressure from Gladstone, they helped to carry the Bill.

In its enacted form it continued, however, to reflect Disraeli's ambivalent approach. The redistribution divided the three counties and created two university seats, which were expected to go Conservative. But then it gave an extra one each to Dundee and Glasgow, the latter thus becoming a three-member single constituency: these were free gifts to the Liberals. In the burghs the suffrage was, with radical approval, granted to all householders and £10 lodgers. But in the counties special provision was made to protect the now rather precarious position of the Scottish landed class. Owners of land worth £5 a year got the vote, but for tenants the qualification was fixed at a rental of £14 a year, compared with £12 in England. This meant that only about four per cent of the rural population was enfranchised, against 10 per cent of the burgh population.

Disraeli no doubt hoped that the following election would repeat the pattern of 1832, with the party which had carried the Bill sweeping the polls.[28] In Scotland the Conservatives could hardly expect to make large gains—they were contesting just twenty seats, though that was more than in any election for three decades. But they did not reckon with the disaster that ensued. The reform league had won popular loyalty by organising the agitation and now gave unreserved support to the Liberals. As a result they scored a great triumph, winning fifty-two of sixty constituencies and even taking some, such as Midlothian and Perthshire, where they had been weak. The Conservatives did manage to regain Bute and pick up the two county seats in Gallo-way: these were the only instances in which the votes of the lesser tenantry strengthened the hand of landlords able to exert an influence on it. Almost everywhere else the Conservatives were thrashed.

The Whigs too were put on the defensive. Edinburgh was abandoned. Moncreiff declined to stand again, seeking a haven in one of the university constituencies and leaving McLaren and Miller to be returned unopposed. Laing lost the Wick Burghs and in the Stirling Burghs the young Henry Campbell-Bannerman turned out a Whig. But altogether the radicals, with about fifteen MPs in the new Parliament, achieved no overwhelming success. In Glasgow the Whigs managed to persuade them not to endanger the Liberal party's hold by splitting its vote. The two sitting members were retained and the radicals were allocated only the third seat, where their victorious candidate was George Anderson, a social reformer and republican.

Though no proletarian, he was the sole Liberal to present himself as first and foremost a workers' representative. In Glasgow the sheer numbers of new electors meant their interests could not be neglected, yet the support for Anderson showed they could still be fitted in with the mainstream of Liberalism. Advocates of an independent labour line failed completely. MacDonald had wanted to stand in the Kilmarnock Burghs but, because he attacked the Liberals for refusing to adopt universal manhood suffrage, the reform league would not endorse him. Thus deprived of financial aid, he had to withdraw. The only gesture he and his friends could make was to appeal to new electors in East Lothian to vote for Elcho against his Liberal opponent—Elcho was in fact returned.

So there was much in the pattern of Scottish politics that remained familiar. Yet significant new trends were emerging. Though the reform of 1832 had produced independent electorates in some burghs, most constituencies were still controlled by a few powerful people attached to one of the factions in London. There was no means of preventing their repudiation of an allegiance, but in practice the national leaders had through them a reasonable degree of influence with both MPs and voters. In the last decade or two, however, the system had decayed through the fragmentation of parties and a loss of contact between the people and a largely absentee aristocracy. The process was hastened after the reform of 1868, which created an electorate whose size made it impossible to manipulate along the old lines in all but a few seats. A Commons inquiry in 1870 found that

> in England tenants generally vote in accordance with the wishes or known opinions of their landlords. In Scotland they have in some recent instances voted almost in a body against their landlords. This has been attributed partly to the nature of relations between landlord and tenant in Scotland, which are usually of a more strictly commercial character than in England, partly to the fact that the Scottish tenant farmers take a very warm interest in certain public questions in which they consider that their own and their landlords' interests are not identical.[29]

The solution which followed was to replace liaison within the oligarchy by a national electoral organisation under professional workers: and in fact 1868 marks the start of the development of the modern political party. The Scottish Conservatives had set up the year before a National Constitutional Association to co-ordinate their work and extend it to the local level—a Glasgow Workingmen's Conservative Association was founded in 1869. The Liberals, more hostile to central direction, were somewhat slow to follow. But Adam was working doggedly to the same end. When his party left office in 1866 he tried, if often vainly, to keep the Scots Liberal MPs together as a disciplined body. He fostered links between London and the constituencies, attempted to raise funds and sketched out an electoral strategy. The party's performance in 1868 was a signal success for him. He did especially well in organising the burghs, though the counties, resentful of outside interference, were much more difficult—the Dukes of Argyll and Sutherland refused him all co-operation.

Tighter links with London were being forged nevertheless, and these also had their advantages for Scotland. Gladstone, the new Prime Minister, and other reformist leaders of the Liberal Party were—out of genuine democratic idealism rather than electoral calculation—anxious to involve the country beyond the metropolis more closely in the political process. So along with Scotland's greater emancipation came a greater frequency of Scottish debates and measures. It was possible to reach a fairly quick settlement of the education and patronage questions, which had dragged on for years. Great difficulties still had to be overcome, and Gladstone in particular remained most unwilling to countenance the constitutional changes which were the essence of the problem in Scotland. But she was relatively well placed to secure further reforms through her unqualified loyalty to Liberalism and her long list of grievances.

Demands for the re-organisation of Scottish government now grew stronger.[30] They had been heard as long ago as the 1850s, when for the first time considerable sections of the political nation became disturbed about the difficulties of passing Scottish legislation and the anglicising policies of the Whigs. Their worries resulted in 1853 in the formation of the National Association for the Vindication of Scottish Rights. Its character and aims will be described more fully below (see Chapter 9), but can be briefly summed up thus: it objected to Scotland's under-representation in Parliament, to the lack of public spending there, to the exclusive right of lawyers to form her administration and to the neglect of her business in the Commons. In general it declared that the Treaty of Union was not being observed because the English showed scant regard for her laws and religion. The association dissolved after a year or two, though the MPs made sporadic attempts to arouse concern at Westminster for the questions it raised. These failed, partly because they did not catch the imagination of the Scottish electorate, partly because the Whig Government was so cautious and self-satisfied, partly because London tended to deride such ideas as survivals of infantile nationalism. But after 1868 the resistance to reform had to deal with the novel presence of a mass electorate. As parties began to search for means of rallying its support, the position of the Lord Advocate as head of the Scottish administration was fatally undermined.

It had already been proved weak at crucial points in the past. In the delicate political conditions of the 1830s Fox Maule had had more influence than Murray, while in the prelude to the Disruption Sir James Graham had taken direct control of Government policy—the only time in four decades when a Home Secretary had shown the interest in Scotland that the Whigs had originally expected of him. After the Second Reform Act, Governments needed not a law officer or two to keep an eye on legislation, but a proper administrative machinery for turning promises into measures. In 1869 Gladstone received an appeal from forty Scots MPs setting forth a catalogue of deficiencies in the government of their country and asking if it were possible to resurrect the office of Scottish Secretary. He was against the expense of new public departments, so the inquiry he set up under the Earl of Cam-perdown—the former Viscount Duncan—was given a limited remit.[31] It was asked only to examine the case for a Scottish Under-secretaryship at the Home Office, the post which had once in effect been occupied by Maule.

McLaren's evidence provided a telling critique of the existing system.

> There is a feeling among many who have no connection with Edinburgh, that Edinburgh and its lawyers rule everything, and there is a strong feeling of jealousy on the part of many. At present no man, let his talents be what they may, can ever be Minister for Scotland unless he becomes not merely a lawyer, but a successful lawyer, and gets to the head of his profession. Then he may retain office for a long term of years, thus stopping all promotion.

McLaren was clearly influenced in these remarks by his antagonism to Moncreiff. The latter in his own evidence rejected the terms of McLaren's argument. There was no such thing as a Minister for Scotland, he asserted, except it were the Home Secretary, to whom the Lord Advocate was only a legal adviser. The criticism was thus misdirected, and a remedy was to be sought inside the Home Office rather than by attacking the law officers. Ingeniously playing the nationalist card, Moncreiff rejected the alternative of setting up a separate political structure for Scotland, on the grounds that it would have to be based in London.

> In Scotland itself I believe the groundwork of opinion is favourable to the present system. It would certainly be unfavourable to anything that had a tendency to denationalise the conduct of Scottish business . . . If it were once supposed that there was an intention to centralise Scottish administration in London, that which is a quiet groundwork of feeling would probably become strongly developed.

The report of the Camperdown inquiry was far from radical. It did indeed propose the appointment of a Scottish Under-secretary, though it favoured the Lord Advocate retaining his full powers. It recommended further that the two should act as joint advisers to the Home Secretary, the former on political and the latter on legal questions. In addition, it asked that Minister to pay closer attention to Scottish matters in future.

The Government did not respond to these modest proposals, and they failed to arouse much interest among Scots voters. Gladstone was not pre-pared to give Scotland priority of any kind. In 1872, confronted with a motion for the establishment of a Commons select committee on her affairs, he said:

> I wish to remind the Scottish and Irish members of that part of the United Kingdom which has hardly been mentioned in the debate tonight—namely, that portion called England. Now I have not one word to say against the bringing forward of the grievances of Scotland. But the grievances of Scotland are not more real to Scottish members than the grievances of England are real to English members . . . I should object to handing over under any circumstances to the

representatives of one country the manipulation of measures brought before the House having reference to the interests of that country.[32]

For the moment nothing could be done, yet it is difficult today to fault the reformers' arguments—indeed, Gladstone himself was converted to them within a decade.

Their soundness was illustrated, to take only the worst of many examples, by the efforts to set up a national education system in Scotland. The earlier attempts foundered, as we have seen, on sectarian squabbles. Moncreiff tried to break the deadlock by establishing Argyll's Royal Commission in 1864. Its investigations, lasting three years, exposed the defects which had arisen since 1843, with the largest number of schools run by the unpopular Kirk and the rest by a variety of voluntary interests. The commission proposed that these individual authorities should be phased out and replaced by a central Education Board. This was to supervise the activities of a second administrative tier consisting of a board in every parish elected by ratepayers to manage the school or schools there. The most controversial suggestion was that the precise type of religious instruction given in each school should be settled by the parish board acting on its popular mandate, with the safeguard of a conscience clause for dissenters.

Moncreiff immediately set out to translate these plans into law, but was constantly frustrated. Gladstone once postponed his legislation to make room for a measure on the retirement of English bishops. In 1869, when Moncreiff at last seemed to be making progress with the sixth Education Bill he had presented in the previous fifteen years, it was abandoned in the Lords on the final day of the session. Even he was then driven to ask Gladstone for more time to be given to his business. He got a non-committal reply and could only react with fatalistic exasperation. Soon afterwards he resigned.

Moncreiff had been a conciliator, though no less for that a faithful servant of Scottish interests as he saw them. His successor George Young was very different. Autocratic in temperament, he had while Solicitor General alarmed the country with his centralising enthusiasms. His aim was assimilation of Scots to English law and abolition of the Court of Session. But first he resolved to get a schools measure through, though he had to accept the failure of the seventh in 1871. His own subsequent proposals bore the stamp of his preconceptions. In contrast to Moncreiff, who wanted a central board based in Scotland, Young decided that it should be a committee of the Privy Council and sit in London. Once set up it pursued an anglicising policy not reversed till it was taken under the Scottish Office in 1885. But while the eighth Bill was being passed in 1872 objections rested on the settling of religious instruction by the parish boards. Young refused to compromise, assessing that sectarianism need no longer prejudice the reform. Since most Scots were presbyterians, the content of religious teaching was not at issue—only on Church government did they differ. Apart from doctrinaire voluntaries and Kirk leaders with a vested interest, all accepted the principle of national education.

The 1872 Act proved a success.[33] The Church of Scotland's schools were handed over without demur to the state, together with most of those run by other sects. Education was already good in Scotland and there were enough schools to enforce compulsory attendance everywhere—a position reached in England only in 1880. The main defect concerned the Catholics. They had no hope of a majority on any parish board and so could not institute their own religious instruction. They continued to run a voluntary system of schools, which was hard to maintain because of their poverty. The problem was not rectified till 1918.

Gladstone's government of Scotland was in other respects unfruitful, disappointing the general hopes of wide-ranging reform. The radicals' chief concern in this Parliament was the land. Protests swelled over the tenantry's disabilities after the outrageous eviction in 1873 of George Hope for his temerity in having stood for Parliament as a Liberal—especially since his landlord had briefly been, in 1832, the last of Melville's nominees to sit in the Commons for Edinburgh. Young's response was limited. He granted tenants some minor reliefs, but failed to get through a Bill to abolish feudal tenure. The poorer and still voteless farmers gave strong support to the radicals, who finally convinced themselves that rural Scotland was independent enough to defy the gentry, so that the decline of its political power could be sealed by an extension of the county franchise. A campaign for this led by Sir George Trevelyan, MP for the Border Burghs, achieved its aim in 1884.

In the burghs the radicals were even more clearly in the ascendant, and the 1874 election was to bring them further victories. The direct representation of labour in Parliament might have threatened them, but the limits of the latest reform excluded it. In fact there seemed to be no great difference between their interests and those of the enfranchised artisans—temperance, disestablishment, self-help, moral and social regeneration. Scottish radicalism retained its essential religious character, though since the rapprochement of the Free and United Presbyterian Churches it was no longer so narrowly sectarian. It had revived as the old populist coalition writ large, and soon found an outstanding leader in Charles Cameron, a young newspaper editor elected for Glasgow in 1874. But he, like other Scots radical MPs, was a professional man with few contacts in the working class.

This was a penalty of the Scottish constitution. It offered little outlet to the energies of the bourgeoisie, which had thus not come to grips with the political problem of the workers. There was indeed hostility to systematic efforts at improving their lot—in Scotland that had been left to Elcho, an eccentric aristocrat. At the same time, proletarian organisations remained too weak to force a change of mind.

Scots radicals compared unfavourably in their response to these questions with their English counterparts. In Birmingham, for example, Joseph Chamberlain, a businessman with a good understanding of working-class aspirations, took care to bring the unions into his schemes of social and economic improvement. It was true that Glasgow had started to copy them. But the corporation's philosophy was authoritarian: the thought of co-operating with the unions never occurred to it. In Edinburgh, McLaren was very hostile to them, especially in their attempts to secure reform in the law of picketing, made legal in 1874. He detested the idea that workers might be given statutory privileges in pursuing their disputes, just as he had always detested statutory privileges for the Kirk and the landlords.

So there was every incentive for the Scottish labour movement to remain independent. Its organisations were extended and new trades councils were set up in Aberdeen, Dundee and Greenock. There were plans for a national confederation of them all, and one was briefly formed in 1872. In addition, those in Edinburgh and Glasgow contested municipal and school board elections. But they had no success, for most workers held that unions ought to stick to industrial affairs and ignored their recommendations on how to vote. Only in Edinburgh did labour leaders dare to think more ambitiously. Angered by McLaren's uncompromising attitudes, they formed with other sympathisers an Advanced Liberal Association to oppose him in the next General Election. Surprisingly, this also won the support of John Miller, the city's second MP. In 1874 McLaren actually stood in tandem with a Whig, easily defeating Miller.

In Scotland it turned out, despite the initial hopes of 1868, that workers could only win representation in Parliament by finding middle-class candidates to espouse their interests. These were rare. But the potential here for social unrest was neutralised by the decline of labour independence in the later 1870s. A long recession impoverished the proletariat and crippled the unions. The Liberals did in 1877 set up a Working Men's Electoral Union, but it was more concerned with consolidating the influence of the party machine over them than with articulating their grievances to it. At the end of the decade Gladstone, now the hero of democrats, accepted the offer of a Scottish seat. His campaigns took the country by storm and attached the working class more firmly to the Liberals than at any time since 1832.

One thing that the creation of a mass electorate did do, though, was to ruin the position of the Whigs. After 1868 they lost their ability to direct Scotland's political impulses into safe, acceptable channels. Parliament House and the nobility no longer loomed so large in the life of the nation and could not provide a sufficient power base for government. Dissidents now accorded them little respect—rather than spend time trying to persuade the Lord Advocate they preferred to raise their demands directly in the Commons or with Ministers in London.

The insecure governing circles weakened themselves still further by becoming more rigid and intransigent. Young, for example, while holding all the prejudices of his king, acted when Lord Advocate as a Scots Whig ought never to have acted. Forsaking compromise, he tried to browbeat his opponents, which made him unpopular and them more determined. In the end he could only complete Moncreiff's programme and was quite unable to address himself to his wider aims. Gladstone suffered substantial losses in Scotland in the 1874 election and Young was ejected from his seat in the Wigtown Burghs.[34]

The bases of Whig policy—anglicisation and the maintenance of social and political balance under a Liberal elite—had really become irrelevant. Franchise reform meant that the equality of the ruling class and the populace within the constitution could not endure. That made the Whigs' position anyway untenable in the long run. Moreover, anglicisation was increasingly unacceptable to the Scots: this at a time when Young wanted to push it towards its ultimate conclusion. Originally formulated in 1832 to prevent Scotland from slipping back into the Tory dark ages, the policy was inapplicable when there was not the least chance of government ever again falling into the hands of a corrupt aristocratic clique. It was true that the local character of Scottish politics was breaking down as the political system was centralised. But enough people were coming to see that a unified structure for the United Kingdom would not work while Scotland remained in any way distinct, and they were unwilling to pay the price of sacrificing her distinctiveness to make it work.

Chapter 4

'The Dictates of Justice'

During the last quarter of the nineteenth century it rapidly became clear that Scotland's political and social achievements were not measuring up to her expectations and myths. A truly liberal society was to be built on the independence of the individual. Yet on the one hand the middle class, main protagonist of the ideal, still found itself frustrated by a network of privilege which flouted every egalitarian principle. And on the other hand there was now in the grim industrial districts an abased mass workforce for which the ideal was of little practical relevance anyway. That truly liberal society was also to rest on a progressive political system. Yet Scotland's hindered rather than helped the rise of new men with new ideas. Though the bourgeoisie had been admitted to full civil rights half a century before, it had so far failed to displace the Whig nobility and legal establishment in the government of the country. The extension of the vote in 1868 to a much wider stratum of the population ought to have altered profoundly the balance of forces in Scotland. For twenty years afterwards, however, it was reflected only imperfectly in her political life.

Frustration was the key motif of Scottish politics in this period. It produced a series of ferocious attacks on existing institutions. Passions were brought to a height by the fervour Gladstone aroused in his Midlothian campaigns. There followed a determined offensive against the position of the Kirk. The land question was inflamed and the Highlands broke out in revolt. The first serious Home Rule movement was born and a separate Scottish organ of administration was secured. Economic depression made workers begin to doubt the value to them of the prevailing political system. The Whigs were driven to the point of schism and finally, over the Irish question, the Liberal party was cleft in two. It had always been able to adapt to new impulses and accommodate them in its capacious bosom. This time the struggle to maintain the national consensus was the most desperate yet. And in the end significant sections of opinion were lost to it for ever.

One surprising challenge came from the old opposition, when the moribund Conservative party sought to rediscover a role.[1] Besides triumphing in England at the General Election of 1874 it did astoundingly well in Scotland, taking eleven extra seats for a total of nineteen, the only major gains in more than thirty years. They were not confined to the rural backwaters either. In fact the votes were won in the burghs rather than in the counties. One of the three members returned for Glasgow was a Conservative, who thus broke the Liberal monopoly over the city which had lasted since 1832. In all Disraeli's party notched up an impressive list of victories in the West. But it also laboured under persistent weaknesses. It chose to fight one-half of the Scottish constituencies, compared with only one-third at the previous election. There it overreached itself. In a number of Liberal strongholds on the East coast, where no Conservative had stood for years, it fared disastrously.

An important reason for the advance was the performance of Gladstone's outgoing Ministry which, apart from any other faults, had shown only neglect and procrastination in Scottish affairs. But the Conservatives had been making efforts of their own. In 1867 they were the first to set up a political organisation for the whole of Scotland, the National Constitutional Association. From 1868 a committee began to encourage and co-ordinate electoral activities which, after the party's collapse in the 1850s, had almost ceased. Significant also was the start during these years of a long-term accretion of strength in the industrial West. The region's bourgeoisie wavered in its loyalty to the Liberals, a development quickened as the latent power of the newly enfranchised classes was exerted. But even they were not to be completely discounted as barren ground for the Conservatives, who had already found enough support among Glasgow working men to set up a special association for them in 1869. Disraeli's ideas of paternalistic social reform were clearly more attractive to some than the rigours of Liberal *laissez-faire* and individualism.

On a visit in 1874 he urged Scotland to 'leave off mumbling the dry bones of political economy and munching the remainder biscuit of an effete Liberalism'.[2] Little in the way of a positive alternative could be expected, however, from the Conservatives' discredited Scottish leaders, the Duke of Buccleuch in the South and the Duke of Richmond and Gordon in the North. Disraeli himself had to promote a programme of social legislation and try to strengthen the party structure.

Almost immediately on taking office his Lord Advocate, Edward Gordon, brought forward a measure to abolish patronage in the Church of Scotland. It granted the power of electing ministers to the congregations and acknowledged the Kirk's exclusive authority in this matter. To Free Churchmen and dissenters it was a piece of breathtaking shamelessness which coolly conceded all the principles so bitterly disputed in the prelude to the Disruption. It had a partly political aim. The established Church was the only Conservative-minded institution in Scotland with any considerable support. But a large part of the populace, remembering the events of 1843, refused all contact with it. Uncomprehending English politicians thought the objections merely technical and saw no harm in removing their statutory basis, though they were soon to think better of this complacency. Legal measures re-organised the sheriff courts and, in the Appellate Jurisdiction Act (1876), answered a long-standing grievance by guaranteeing Scotland a place among the judges of the House of Lords. Gordon himself became the first Scots Lord of Appeal. Social legislation included Acts on housing for artisans, on public works and public health, and on a further relaxation of entail.[3]

Conservative party organisation came under the scrutiny of a committee chaired by an MP, Sir James Fergusson, a Scot who had been forced to go to England to find a Tory seat. Investigations all over Scotland uncovered a number of complaints among local activists: they were saddled with poor candidates, they could not shake off their association with the unpopular landlords (even though these were often absentees who ignored politics at home), they got little attention from the party chiefs in London and yet could secure effective assistance only from them.

By way of remedy the committee urged a more modern approach on the party, with professional agents taking over the role of the lairds in electioneering. It also exhorted the gentry to popularise itself and called on the Government to press forward with Scottish legislation. After so many measures had been proposed and then dropped by the Liberals, the Conservatives had the chance to draw a contrast with a solid record of achievement.

But in fact the latter years of the Ministry saw the initial legislative eagerness dissipated. The next Lord Advocate, William Watson, a diffident man of no obvious views or ambitions in politics, was greatly criticised by Scots MPs for inactivity. In an attempt to mend matters the Government closed the Lord Advocate's separate quarters in London and moved him into the Home Office. A Bill was introduced to implement the Camperdown proposals, but it lapsed when the Scottish Liberal MPs declined to support it.[4]

The real weakness of the offensive, however, was the extent to which it still relied on landlords. Disraeli, deceived by his experience of England, failed to appreciate the strength of feeling against them in Scotland. His committee was dominated by rural interests and concluded that one way to electoral success was more active use by Conservatives of their social position. This might have been objectionable to most Scots in itself, but it anyway missed the point that with the advent of a mass electorate the magnates' day was passing.

Disraeli's initiative never overcame the suspicion that his party stood for aristocratic reaction. None of the Scots Conservatives, apart from Elcho, followed their leader's line in aiming at a league with the workers against the bourgeois Liberals. They could not rival Liberalism in its penetration of the social fabric of urban Scotland, in the Press, the business community, the dissenting Churches. In the West they made some progress, but it was mainly among mining and shipping interests, notoriously hostile to workers' demands. As for organisation, the National Constitutional Association turned out ineffectual. Not till 1882 was it superseded by a National Union— thirteen years after the foundation of the English one. Disraeli also exacerbated religious questions, in which a numerous body of dissenters was ranged irreconcilably against the Kirk and thus against its Conservative sympathisers. For all his efforts, he finished with fewer Scottish seats in 1880 than he had won in 1868.

The governing party in Scotland was also shaking off the complacency induced by its long dominance. In the late 1870s the Conservatives were openly competing with it for working-class support and this demanded of Liberals a less equivocal redefinition of policy than they were used to making. Gladstone's ostensible retirement from public life in 1875 removed the man who, for all the contradictions in his own attitudes, had at least been able to hold the party together. His prospective replacements were W E Forster, a radical who had nonetheless aroused the enmity of English nonconformity, and Lord Hartington, an uncontroversial Whig. Scottish Liberalism had already had the opportunity of testing their views. In 1874 Sir George Trevelyan, radical MP for the Border Burghs, introduced a Bill for the extension of the county franchise in Scotland, a measure with wide popular support there. Forster both spoke and voted for it, while Hartington made clear his distaste. So when the opinions of Liberal MPs on a new leader were canvassed, a clear majority of Scots favoured Forster. He was not chosen for, unlike his opponent, he had too many enemies in England. Though a radicals' takeover of Liberalism was thereby averted—and perhaps a party split with it—the Scots among them now had a colourless leadership in London for which they felt no particular esteem, and their independent demands and activities grew apace.[5]

Internal dissension and Conservative success also set the Liberals thinking about a tighter organisation, which had hardly been necessary so far.[6] By 1877 their Scots chief whip, W P Adam, had established two regional associations. One, based in Edinburgh, served the East and North and soon fell under the control of the capital's Whigs. The other, operating from Glasgow, covered the West and quickly came to be dominated by the local radicals. The Liberal rift was thus to some extent institutionalised. Only with difficulty could the factiousness be held in bounds, even by the national party leader who now appeared and whose ability and social standing put him above all the bickering. The young Earl of Rosebery was a petulant and over-sensitive character, but highly intelligent and, as an aristocrat with radical sympathies, he neatly bestrode Liberalism's two wings. Though he failed to end the conflicts in Scotland, he did eventually manage to effect an uncomfortable union of the party organisations in one Scottish Liberal Association (SLA).

Still, something more exciting was needed to cure the Liberal malady. The move hit upon by Rosebery and Adam—of inviting Gladstone to stand in Midlothian—was brilliant. From the party's standpoint this heroic, moralising figure was the perfect one to rekindle fading ideals. And Midlothian, though won by a Liberal in 1868, had till then been a fief of the Duke of Buccleuch, as effete an exemplar of landlordism as any radical could wish to assail: his son, Lord Dalkeith, regained the seat in 1874. For Gladstone too the chance was welcome. From retirement he had watched with mounting moral horror the unfolding of Conservative policy. Despite himself, he had come back into politics with violent denunciations of it. Now he felt it time to re-enter Parliament. Midlothian, at best a marginal Liberal seat, provided him with a dramatic backcloth where he could present himself as the champion of truth battling against great odds. In January 1879 Gladstone became the county's candidate, and later in the year he began the momentous campaign to woo his new constituents.[7]

Gladstone dubbed the Midlothian campaign a 'festival of freedom'.[8] And he consciously intended it as a celebration of the moral and political heights to which Liberal man could aspire. When he set off for Scotland in November 1879, the General Election was still some months away. But so tremendous was the task of enlightenment he saw before him that no start was early enough. He took on himself the labour, as no statesman ever had, of giving mass audiences an entire insight into the morality of government, which he believed so basely betrayed by Disraeli. Edinburgh shook with excitement as his arrival drew near, and Liberals gathered from all over Scotland to give him a hero's welcome. The progress began, continued and ended in triumph. Every meeting was attended with almost mindless adulation, every telling point cheered to the echo, every restated moral principle given jubilant affirmation.

Gladstone's presentation was dramatic and stylised. He portrayed Disraeli's Government as typical of the depraved side of man, the enemy of everything true, good, moral and Christian. In his discourses Gladstone stalked the workings of this spirit through finance, administration, foreign policy—all the fields of public duty it had corrupted. From the ten major speeches of the two-week campaign there emerges a precise and coherent Liberal alternative, which crystallises the ethos of Scottish democracy in the nineteenth century.

The state was seen as a deliberative body in which electors performed their duty with juridical gravity. Gladstone claimed that through the ballot box the voter became personally responsible for the actions of government, including its sins. This, he believed, naturally aroused the common man's social concern and critical interest, and no political problem should be thought too complex or difficult for him. Once the citizen was involved, there was no need for the Government to cajole or bully—at some point the popular will would emerge clearly and the ruler's task was then to obey it.

There were a few thoughts for Scotland too. At Dalkeith, Gladstone said that if any portion of the United Kingdom was

> desirous and able to arrange its affairs that, by taking the local part or some local part of its transactions off the hands of Parliament, it can liberate or strengthen Parliament for imperial concerns, I say I will not only accord a reluctant assent, but will give a zealous support to any such scheme . . . The Parliament is overweighted. The Parliament is overwhelmed. If we can take off its shoulders that superfluous weight by the constitution of secondary and subordinate authorities. I am not going to be frightened out of a wise measure of that kind by being told that I am condescending to the prejudices of Home Rulers . . . I will consent to give to Ireland no principle, nothing that is not upon equal terms offered to Scotland and to the different portions of the United Kingdom.

We cannot say how easily Gladstone's audiences took up his forbidding framework of earnest technicality, though we know that printed copies of the speeches sold in large numbers. It must have been the immediate tone and atmosphere which enthralled people, because now the arguments seem frankly turgid and laborious. But they were presented with all the melodrama and sentimentality beloved of the age, and it may be that the exercise rested critically on a few moments when a flash of feeling, however cloying and top-heavy to us, must have illumined immeasurably the relentless moralising analysis of the rest. Among the commands which, for example, Gladstone delivered to his constituents was one never to

> suffer the appeals to national pride to blind you to the dictates of justice . . .
> Remember the rights of the savage, as we call him. Remember that the happiness
> of his humble home, remember that the sanctity of life in the hill villages of
> Afghanistan, among the winter snows, is as inviolable in the eyes of Almighty
> God as can be your own.[10]

But what did the campaign achieve for all those Scots who cheered so wildly? It brought a triumph for the Liberals at the 1880 election, when they won nearly two-thirds of the vote and fifty-three of the sixty seats (though the margin of Gladstone's own victory in Midlothian was unimpressive). The campaign was not, of course, specifically for Scotland's sake and Gladstone meant his words to carry equal weight everywhere in Britain. While he referred to Scottish questions, it was only in illustration of his general themes. He remained in fact a metropolitan politician ignorant of and unsympathetic towards many of Scotland's problems. His contact with them came on by-ways through Rosebery and Parliament House, hardly representative of the country as a whole. Gladstone's identification of misgovernment with Tory government diverted his attention from the institutional failings which lay at the heart of Scotland's complaints. He conceived of the British political system as a unity. In his view, the Scots might have their legitimate grievances, but so did many other minorities. Unless Scottish opinion itself could make a decisive choice for some reform, he was not prepared to grant the complaints any special priority. So from him Scotland gained high moral inspiration rather than practical improvements.

Rosebery wrote to Gladstone in 1880:

> I always thought the stimulus and inspiration which Liberalism required must
> come from you and that the proper tripod for you was Scotland; and if Scotland
> then Midlothian. The intensity required . . . was only to be found in Scotland
> and yourself.[11]

But Midlothian's intensity solved very little. It may have dispelled disillusion and given the Scottish people a vindication of their ideals. But the new spirit did not by itself make their national problems easier to unravel. It outraged the Whigs and gave the radicals excessive hopes of what the Government might concede to them. The ordinary Scots Liberal voter, in principle moderate and in practice prepared to follow wherever Gladstone might lead, was easily overborne by these other two groups. There was a febrile intransigence about public debate in the Scotland of the 1880s which made reasonable answers harder to find. Midlothian set a tone which was struck again and again during the decade. On occasion the high moral passion did secure useful reforms. But at other times it made rather for obstinate difficulties.

Scotland's great, burning issue through most of this period of discord was the Church.[12] Presbyterianism remained the wellspring of national life and many Scots held their politics to be merely a secular version of it. That, till the 1874 Patronage Act threw all into confusion, made for a relatively simple pattern. A majority in the three main Churches probably voted Liberal, but each was associated with a different political allegiance, just as each took a different view of the proper relations of Church and state. The Church of Scotland formed the Establishment, secured but constrained by statute, and containing a large proportion of Conservatives. The Free Church was for an Establishment, but not at the cost of spiritual freedom; this ingenious stand on ecclesiastical questions, halfway between reaction and reform, had once made it an ally of the Whigs, who occupied an analogous position in politics. Finally, the United Presbyterians were against all Establishments, and strongly radical.

The Kirk had been recovering from the calamity of the Disruption, but saw a need to popularise itself in a country where most citizens were now dissenters. In 1869 it asked the Liberal Ministry to abolish patronage. But the Free Church protested and Gladstone, unwilling to offend such a staunch supporter, would not respond. Disraeli felt no obligation to pander to Scots Liberals. 'The Scotch shall have no favours from me until they return more Tory members,' he confided to his secretary.[13] On the contrary he had every reason to try and strengthen one of the few Conservative forces in Scotland. His Act was bitterly resented. The seceders of 1843 had sacrificed all for liberty, and now the Kirk was to win it at no cost whatever. The measure also threatened the other Churches' cohesion, for it answered the main conscientious objection of presbyterians who scorned a Kirk subordinate to the state.

The first result was the radicalisation of the Free Church. In its General Assembly of 1875 Principal Rainy carried a motion in favour of disestablishing the Kirk. Thus the Free Church turned away from the teaching it had consistently proclaimed since 1843: in effect it gave up hope of restoring a purified Establishment and logically declared itself to be a dissenting Church like the rest. There was great resistance to this move. But with other dissenters Rainy now began a campaign to liberate the Kirk, as he saw it, from state trammels and thus to secure equal spiritual, legal and economic status for all presbyterian Churches.

This was a legislative matter for which political support was needed, and under Rainy the liberationists started lobbying Liberal leaders. The issue was raised in Midlothian but Gladstone remained cautious. He said the Scots should consider and agree about it among themselves—meanwhile he would stay neutral. He shared with his colleagues a healthy reluctance to take sides in Scotland's spiteful religious quarrels. An exception was Joseph Chamberlain, the rising star of radicalism, who was already conducting a liberationist campaign in England and who, after McLaren's retiral in 1881, became the most effective champion of Scottish dissent in the Commons. But well before that the question was assuming a dangerous aspect by providing a further point of internal contention in the Liberal party. The Whigs parted from their old friends in the Free Church and stood firm for the Kirk; radicals agitated even more loudly for disestablishment.

After Gladstone's return to power in 1880 the latter intensified their activities, setting up pressure groups and holding public meetings all over the country. Parliament was presented with, but rejected, a disestablishment motion in 1882 and a Bill in 1884. This provoked a counter-attack. The Conservative peer, Balfour of Burleigh, led a Church defence organisation with a network of local branches and urged people to vote against liberationist politicians. Since all were Liberals, that could be construed as a plot to subvert the ruling party. But Liberal Kirk members were not deterred from following his advice, though they eventually set up their own association and found a leader in Robert Finlay, MP for the Inverness Burghs.

Local Liberal divisions erupted at the national level when a group of liberationists broke with the SLA in 1885 to form the National Liberal Federation of Scotland.[14] Its aim was to make disestablishment part of the Liberal programme for the coming election. This naturally exacerbated the dispute, but Gladstone himself, still unsure of the true state of public opinion, declined to intervene. In November he simply reiterated that the party had a common programme which did not include immediate disestablishment. The NLFS took the unprecedented step of denouncing him and decided to present its own candidates at the polls. But to a man of Gladstone's standing the attack was a pinprick. His judgement was borne out by the results of the election, where liberationist Liberals made no great breakthrough.

Gladstone averted a full party split over disestablishment. The Church defence movement only became schismatic after Scotland was presented with the question of Irish Home Rule. When Gladstone came out for it in 1886 many Whiggish members of the Church of Scotland, whose drift away from Liberalism had been halted by his stand on the Kirk, now felt forced to desert. This left liberationists predominant among Gladstonian Liberals, and the Scottish party committed itself to disestablishment in 1887. Charles Cameron repeatedly put motions in favour of it to the Commons and won growing support from the Scots MPs. By 1889 he had a majority of them with him. Gladstone then stated that to his satisfaction Scotland had declared for Church liberation, only to provoke a furious new campaign. The lay organisations on both sides were revived amid bitter sectarianism. But this time the liberationist attack was blunted. The Free Church actually divided. Those who still clung to the doctrine that Establishment was right in principle, if defiled in practice, gave up hope of making their view prevail and left to form their own Free Presbyterian Church in 1892.

The last chance for disestablishment came with the Liberals' return to power the same year. Cameron hopefully introduced a Bill in May 1893. But the resignation of Gladstone in 1894 put paid to these plans, since his successor Rosebery took a dim view of them. In any case he and his Ministers were quite incapable of opening a Scottish controversy as grave as the Irish one that was exhausting them. Cameron tried again in March 1895, but in three months the Government had fallen. The Conservatives' subsequent ten years of office killed the liberationist movement. When the Liberals returned the Churches were seeking reconciliation rather than strife. The Free Church and the United Presbyterians had come together in the United Free Church in 1900. Soon they were making friendly overtures to the Kirk itself about reunion, which was eventually effected in 1929.

The Liberal leadership's espousal of disestablishment was probably a mistake. People began to lose interest in it during the later stages of the campaign, when it engaged mainly dissenting clerics and radical fanatics, whose unbending determination to despoil the Church of Scotland repelled many ordinary voters. In 1886, and more especially after Gladstone's conversion in 1889, it divorced from the party numerous Kirk members who were basically also good, honest Liberals.

The appearance of unwonted unity among them created by the Midlothian campaign was thus indeed deceptive. It no more than subdued the increasingly acrimonious internal bickering of the late 1870s. There was in particular much dispute between the Eastern and Western Liberal associations at that time. The Whiggish officials in Edinburgh confined themselves to electoral organisation and did not seek to influence the policy stance of local parties. They disliked the attempts of the Western association to foist its ideas on everyone else. It was a primary aim of the Glasgow radicals to co-ordinate rank-and-file opinion and put pressure for reforms on the parliamentary party. For maximum impact they preferred a single Liberal organisation in Scotland. Despite the unfavourable omens this was what they achieved in 1881 when the two associations joined in Rosebery's SLA. The marriage was uneasy. In fact, with the opposition safely routed in the election of the previous year, Whig and radical feuds restarted almost immediately, only through new channels.

The two sides found a range of issues on which to differ. The Whigs claimed to be defenders of established religion, moral consistency, law and order, property rights and governmental experience against the radicals' irresponsible attacks. But the substance of the matter was that radical weight in the party, aided by the widened franchise, was waxing every year, and the Whigs were being forced from their paramountcy. Conscious of this shift in Liberalism, they were increasingly alienated from the leadership and ever closer in fundamentals to the Conservatives. A few went so far as defection, but they were for once ahead of their time. Most Whigs believed Gladstone was the only man who could hold the Liberals together and swamp the radicals in a wider grouping. From this belief he derived his position as linchpin of the party: a position which also endowed him with the ability to wreck the Liberal coalition by his personal decision in 1886 to promote Home Rule for Ireland.

Already, however, Gladstone had in effect secured ultimate radical victory in the Scottish party by his 1884 Reform Act, which granted the franchise to all male householders. At a stroke he swept away the delicate safeguards and compromises of the 1868 Act—the distinction in qualifications between burghs and counties, as well as between Scottish and English counties. For the first time there was a uniform popular suffrage throughout the United Kingdom. In addition, the constituencies were redistributed so as to reflect more closely the pattern of population. Two small burgh districts were dissolved, while Aberdeen and Dundee now had two members each, Edinburgh four and Glasgow seven. Among the county seats also the representation of industrial areas was increased, with two MPs apiece for Fife and Renfrewshire and six for Lanarkshire. The most significant result of the changes was the virtual disappearance from the Commons of the influential body of Whigs representing rural Scotland whose return the efforts of the landed class had always been able to secure. The House elected in 1880 was the last in which country gentlemen sat in large numbers.

All this had a decisive effect inside the Scottish Liberal party, where the Whigs had been fighting a tenacious rearguard action. The SLA was run by an executive on which they were over-represented. They bore down on radical opinion by banning discussion of disputed matters at its meetings. Their attitude hardened after the 1884 Act—only by entrenching themselves in the SLA could they hope to hold on. But the association also had a council drawn from local parties. Here radicals dominated, but against obstruction from the executive they still could not impose their ideas on the party or win the support of the leadership in London. Their frustration grew with the approach of the 1885 election, which they hoped to fight on a full-blooded radical programme. The result was the formation of the NLFS. The more impatient radicals decided that only by acting independently of the party hierarchy could they successfully mount pressure for their policies, especially on the Church of Scotland.

Gladstone had never imagined things were so far gone as to produce this perilous rift. While unwilling to take sides, he could not endorse the radical programme in detail and balked particularly at immediate disestablishment. In effect this meant favouring the SLA, though the NLFS was not deterred. The Liberals' coming schism was prefigured at the 1885 election when radicals ran their own men against some of the leading Whigs. But the latter, led by Robert Finlay and Sir George Harrison, an Edinburgh MP, were better organised and able to fight off the attacks without letting in the Conservatives. There were twenty-seven double Liberal candidatures, but such was the party's strength that only one seat was lost on a split vote.

With Gladstone still opposing its basic plank, the NLFS was now stalemated. The SLA had proved its loyalty but could not rally the dissidents. All was overthrown once more when Gladstone resolved to go for Irish Home Rule early in 1886. The shocked SLA dithered over the question, while the NLFS gave him immediate support. This almost reversed the previous attitudes of the two towards their leader, but the resulting puzzles solved themselves. Offended in their deepest constitutional attachments, the SLA Whigs left the party in droves. The distinction of Liberals and Unionists marked out by the 1886 poll was not, however, quite the same as that between Whigs and radicals. A remnant of the Liberal Right stayed loyal to Gladstone. With all else collapsing, Rosebery took the chance of at least reconciling the party organisations. The rump of the SLA and the almost intact NLFS were united in a new Gladstonian SLA. Outnumbered there, the Whigs were soon overridden. At the end of the long battle the radicals were left in possession of the field.

This should not be facilely construed as the victory of one class over another, as the final triumph of the Scottish bourgeois revolution. Unionism had strong middle-class roots and some of the aristocracy continued to support Gladstone. In Scotland class conflicts were hopelessly entangled with all others. The workers, for example, had in class consciousness not advanced by 1880 much beyond their fathers in the 1820s.[15] Their pride was in the individualist traditions of artisan and craftsman. Their organisations were impermanent. Loud in demands for specific reforms, they had no long-term aim for society as a whole. Their attention was confined to their own trade or burgh rather than given to the interests of workers as a class.

This lack of class feeling was exploited by the Conservatives in their not unsuccessful appeals to the proletariat in the 1870s. They promised paternalistic social reform with protectionism as the remedy for unemployment. But the development was brought to a halt by the Midlothian campaigns, which inspired religious adulation of Gladstone in Scottish workers. In any case the Conservative advance never went so far in Scotland as in England. The Scots remained overwhelmingly loyal to the Liberal party and especially to the radical wing. Its programme—the destruction of privilege, the limitation of government power, the extension of civil liberty and the improvement of popular education—represented public opinion in Scotland much more faithfully. The consonance of political aims obscured, however, an underlying economic issue. The Scots radicals were rigorously purist in their *laissez-faire* principles and unsympathetic to demands for higher wages, shorter hours and unemployment relief. Some even raged against the Factory Acts and the very institution of trade unions. This reflected their relative lack of contact with the working class.

One product was the independent political line which some trade unionists tried to follow. The Midlothian campaigns put a stop to that too, but did not remove the underlying causes of dissension. After fifty years of rapid development in Scotland with only rare intermissions, there had followed in the 1870s a long depression. It culminated in 1878 in 'the greatest disaster that had ever befallen the commercial community of Great Britain',[16] the collapse of the City of Glasgow Bank with huge debts which reduced pillars of Western society to beggary and crippled enterprise for years. The classical doctrines of *laissez-faire* and free trade no longer appeared worthy of the veneration accorded them and the general repute of Liberal orthodoxy suffered. Some workers' leaders began to advocate active interference with market forces to protect the interests of their class. Keir Hardie made his debut in Scottish public affairs as a miners' union official in the disputes of 1879–81, when he agitated for the restriction of output as an alternative to wage cuts if recession produced a fall in profits. It was not yet realised, but this manipulation of the market logically committed him, and those who were starting to think like him, against everything that Liberal economics stood for.

Soon afterwards Scots radicals received new inspiration from the American proto-socialist, Henry George, who argued that the use of land should be regulated by the community for the good of all and that exploitation by idle landlords should be outlawed. His speaking tour of Scotland in 1882 prompted the formation of two bodies advocating his views, the Scottish Land Restoration League in the West and the Scottish Land and Labour League in the East. The latter affiliated in 1884 to the London-based Social Democratic Federation, the first Marxist political organisation in Britain. Though concerned with the problems of industrial or agricultural workers, the members of these land leagues were usually middle-class intellectuals.[17]

For a native and more proletarian initiative the country had to wait on the Liberal split in 1886. This established radical control over the Gladstonian wing, but it was still averse to identifying itself too closely with the workers and reluctant to accept the political and legislative commitments they might impose. These were not very extreme. In fact, apart from specific demands such as an eight-hour day in the mines, the main desire was for the Liberals to select working-class candidates. Though the reform of 1884 extended the vote to a much larger number of workers it did not, contrary to expectations, alter the exclusively bourgeois nature of the Scottish parliamentary party. The internal structure developed by the Liberals since 1868 actually hindered changes here by placing control of the constituencies more firmly in the hands of activists, who were mainly drawn from the middle class. Keir Hardie was among the workers' leaders whom this angered. By 1888 his vexation had gone so far that he put himself forward on a labour platform at a by-election in Mid-Lanarkshire. He did poorly, polling only 617 votes. These discouraging experiences convinced him of the need for a proper working-class political organisation. Soon afterwards he founded the Scottish Labour Party. It was a small, weak body dependent on support from the miners' unions and various extreme radical groups. Keir Hardie shortly left to seek his fortune in the South, and the party dissolved itself after a few years. Its programme was not distinctively socialist and, even if it had been, political consciousness among voters had not yet advanced to the point where they could easily have distinguished between its aims and those of radical Liberals.

The land, rather than industrial problems, remained the Scottish political issue which produced most clearly a division on class lines.[18] Land ownership was heavily concentrated in Scotland, and the law of entail could still preserve this state of affairs through generations. Political reform had not by the 1870s eliminated the land as a source of power. For the great noblemen, huge estates and huge influence went together. There was much antagonism between the rural classes. The land laws were Scotland's last bastion of feudalism and the tenant suffered many disabilities. He had no security of tenure, and was on occasion evicted if he voted against the laird's wishes. By the law of hypothec his crops and stock could be seized in lieu of rent arrears. The game laws afforded him little protection against aristocratic sportsmen.

The Whigs' resolve to defend this position also started to shift them into opposition to Gladstone. His Land Act for Ireland in 1881 ended there the strictly contractual relations of landlord and tenant. That set a precedent which radicals might well have wanted to see extended to Scotland. The big Highland landowners were especially worried because of the likenesses between their territories and the West of Ireland. The tensions grew acute for Argyll, the Whigs' elder statesman. He had agreed only with misgivings to serve in Gladstone's Cabinet and was dismayed enough by its Irish policy to resign. He gathered round him a small band of other Whig magnates—Minto, Sutherland, Zetland and Elcho—who were thereafter consistent critics of Gladstonian Liberalism. Argyll, unusually for a nobleman also an intellectual, set out in his own writings to defend property rights and produce a detailed refutation of Henry George's theses. Apart from general moral and political considerations, he argued that the Highland problem was essentially one of over-population. The resulting congestion and poverty could be relieved only by concerted action on large estates, like his own.

Reformers asked why the land laws alone should remain sacred when the tenants' communal sentiment and customary, if unwritten, rights were so often ignored. Their answer lay in fundamental structural change. The aim, necessarily a long-term one, was to break up the large estates and create a sturdy class of smallholders. A little progress had been made. Disraeli, with his Entail Act of 1875, did away with more of the ancient restrictions, and he later modified the game laws. Honouring pledges given in Midlothian, Gladstone got rid of hypothec and granted tenants some security of tenure and compensation for improvements.

Radicalism was strong in the Scottish, unlike in the English, counties because of the tenants' robustly progressive views. The 1880 election inflamed them with resentment towards the landlords, kindled by the battle in Midlothian between Gladstone and Buccleuch. It won more lasting expression in the land leagues formed in response to Henry George's visit, which were soon in contact with the like-minded in the Highlands and in Ireland. The magnates' influence was anyway waning, and before long only Argyll, Bute and Sutherland were left as pocket counties for them. After the Whigs' defection from Liberalism, radicals had no qualms in turning on the lairds in general as parasitic obstacles to progress.

The case was first a moral one: the land was justly the heritage of the people and, once given back, would restore rights long abused. But practical proposals had also to be made. The redistribution, even nationalisation, called for by the most extreme could at best be only a distant goal. Meanwhile, something might be done through taxation. The reformers held land to be the ultimate source of all riches, and predicted a yield from a levy on its value so huge as to allow the abolition of every other tax. That was why they called themselves the Single Tax Movement (the notion survives in British Liberal thinking, and the name in some foreign countries). If released, the wealth locked up in land could be used to deal with a range of social problems.

Business would flourish, its confidence sustained in freedom from any threat of crippling burdens imposed by the state. It would be better able to satisfy workers' wage claims. Government would have more to spend. And the whole of society would benefit when landlords, to meet their obligations, were forced to put their property to its most profitable use.

Because the development of the cities and towns might then be improved, the Single Tax Movement became more of an urban than a rural one. Glasgow was its hotbed. There the land league even fought the General Election of 1885, though all its candidates failed badly. Yet by 1892 a majority of the corporation was pledged to some degree of land reform. Along with seven others, it petitioned Parliament for the right to take land values as the basis of local taxation. While the reformers hoped to make their movement as mighty as the Anti-Corn Law League had been, they never united all classes behind them. One success came with the introduction of death duties in 1894. But, at least over most of the country, there was no land legislation proper till after the turn of the century.

Quick action was required in the Highlands, however.[19] The clearances were past, but their results still bitterly felt. The 1880s saw the latest in a line of violent outbreaks by crofters that had long been going on. Their legal position remained insecure, with no defence against rent rises, eviction and loss of land to sporting estates. A depression in agriculture and successive poor harvests were immediate causes of their distress. The landlords continued to collect rent as before. In cases of default, eviction was ordered. It was also resisted, for local agents of the law were too weak to enforce it. Eventually in one instance on Skye a contingent of fifty police had to be brought from Glasgow, and in April 1882 they fought the 'Battle of the Braes' against a mob defending a number of men from arrest. In 1883 a gunboat and marines were sent to the island to ensure the capture of more offenders. In 1884 and 1885 the disturbances grew worse. All over the Hebrides thousands refused to pay their rents, and some of the big sheep farms were taken over by force. On Skye, the centre of the trouble, order could only be restored by stationing a garrison of 300 on the island.

Though spectacular, these events might have had little effect without the concern they aroused beyond the Highlands. The region now possessed able spokesmen among its many emigrants. Gaeldom was decadent, but would not die quietly. Exiles had formed societies on both sides of the border to revive their native culture. Through these, links were formed with Irish nationalists. Interest in land reform was shared by Lowland radicals. All agreed that Scotland needed an equivalent of the Irish Land Act. The sentiment alarmed the Government. Superficially, the Highland troubles recalled those in rural Ireland, though lacking the racial and religious overtones which brought the latter to such a pitch of savagery. Still, the Ministry was persuaded that crofters' affairs merited serious treatment, and in 1883 it set up an inquiry under Lord Napier of Ettrick.

To advise the witnesses he called, and to organise further protest, a Highland Land Law Reform Association was established in London. This galvanised the situation. Through local branches it recruited many crofter members. Its morale was boosted by the Napier report, which recommended concessions to its views, and by Gladstone's subsequent pledge to legislate. The 1884 Reform Act opened up a more exciting prospect. Crofters now had the vote, and with it the ability to end the landlords' monopoly of Highland representation in the Commons.

The association chose five parliamentary candidates. All had Highland connections, but were really Lowland intellectuals. Four were elected in 1885—for Argyll, Caithness, Inverness-shire and Ross and Cromarty—and once at Westminster they were joined by an independent from the Wick Burghs. The Crofters' party, as it was now known, has been described as the first populist movement in Britain, even as Labour's precursor. Yet it was not socialist and brought not one actual crofter to prominence. Its rise is best explained by the results in the Highlands of the 1884 Reform Act. Liberalism there had been a landlord preserve, and nowhere else in Scotland was it left so divorced from the new mass rural electorate. With no Liberal tradition among the illiterate Gaels, the reformers had little incentive to associate with the ruling party and much to gain by rejecting it. Apart from labels, however, the contests were similar to other double candidatures of Whig and radical in 1885.

But the victories impressed Gladstone and he legislated at once. His Bill gave security of tenure and set up a Crofters Commission to fix rents. The Crofters' party opposed him, with Irish support, because he failed to meet all its demands. This did not appear to harm it, for at the 1886 election it maintained its strength. The Bill's passage put it in a dilemma, though, by weakening the case for its continued separate existence. The reforms eventually ended the violence which had brought it into being. In addition, the Crofters' party had reciprocated Irish support by endorsing Home Rule, which alienated one of its own MPs and identified the rest with the Gladstonians. Soon it looked to be no more than an adjunct of the newly radicalised Liberals, and internal squabbles weakened its own cohesion.

The crofter movement scored a notable success in establishing the foundations of the Highlands' modern administrative system. But it allayed neither the Highlanders' sullen disaffection on the one hand, nor the landlords' frequent contempt for them on the other. Without closer co-operation among its classes the region continued to decline. And despite the novel populist character of the Crofters' party, its philosophy and policies were not distinctive enough to give it a future outside the broad mainstream of Gladstonian Liberalism which by 1892 had absorbed it. Thus it shared the impermanence and factiousness of most other movements among the lower orders in the nineteenth century.

Too much political importance can be attributed to the crofters' movement. Its main achievement was to add particular urgency to the land question in Scotland. Round this more general focus of discontent there gathered groups of men for the moment obscure and of disparate interests, but significant in that they contemplated setting up an independent opposition to the left of the Liberal party. This stood in contrast to the situation in England, where industrial conditions gave the impetus to a similar movement.

The attraction of the land question for the Scots was that it could *par excellence* be presented as the people's struggle against archaic privilege. It allowed the land reformers to forge close links with other radical groups, including even the liberationists. Henry George was important in building a bridge between Scottish agrarian reform and socialist theory. When his ideas were applied to urban problems too, a further connection was laid down between the land issue and the distress of the proletariat. Many of the coalfields were owned by noblemen who extracted large royalties from them, so that the land could also be seen as a relevant economic question by a miners' leader like Keir Hardie. Beyond that, it established common ground with the Irish nationalists: the advanced radicals among the latter had strong links with a wider Labour movement in Britain. The Irish encouraged Gaelic revivalism, which in turn fostered contact with the crofters and the romantic school of Scots Home Rulers. The motley collection which joined in the Scottish Labour Party in 1888 contained representatives of all these tendencies. The only thing they really had in common was the land question. In this itself, however, there was already a fundamental divergence in social and economic doctrine between them and the Liberals. The logical position for *laissez-faire* Liberalism was to defend the landlords' free disposal of their property. The Scottish dissidents, by insisting on the recognition of tenants' rights, were demanding collectivist control of individual actions. This theoretical stance gave them a basis for the development of mutual interest in their originally very diverse ideas. Here lay the importance of their formally coming together in the Scottish Labour Party. From the agrarian reform movement there arose an identifiable leftist opposition in Scotland, weak at first, but with a growing coherence that enabled it to survive a long stagnation and eventually to emerge in strength.

As change in Scottish society accelerated, its governmental structures were exposed as inadequate. They had changed little since 1832. The main innovation in England, the civil service reform of 1870, was not enforced in Scotland, where administrative posts were still filled by patronage rather than on merit. The deficiencies, aided by the tumults of the time, intensified the pressure for more autonomy. The MPs were active here, but for a determined initiative the country had to wait on Rosebery. He regarded it as vital that the Scottish Secretaryship of State, abolished in 1746, should be resurrected, and had set his own appointment to it as his first political goal. He was already an intimate of Gladstone's through his sponsorship of the Midlothian campaign. That, and his abilities, gave him the leading place among Scots Liberals. He was thus offended when offered no post in the 1880 Cabinet. But events came to his aid. William Harcourt, the radical Home Secretary, soon tired of his Lord Advocate, John McLaren, a son of Duncan. This hapless and none too able man had held office since the election but twice failed to get into Parliament. To expedite Scottish business, Harcourt put the Camperdown proposals into effect and recommended the appointment of Rosebery as an Under-secretary in his department.

Though displeased with a subordinate job, the Earl agreed to serve and set eagerly about his duties.[20] He used his personal status to keep Gladstone abreast of Scottish affairs and to try and persuade him of their importance. But he was given no time for his legislation and suspected the Prime Minister of going back on a promise to promote him to the Cabinet. He also had problems with the Lord Advocate, when McLaren was eased out and replaced with the more competent John Blair Balfour. By the end of 1882 Rosebery was threatening to resign. He wrote to Gladstone that his standing was

> derogatory to the national position and injurious to the national interests . . . I serve a country which is the backbone of our party, but which is never recognised.

Matters drifted till the Earl, getting no satisfaction, finally did step down in May 1883. Though Gladstone was anxious to employ his talents, it was not before 1885 that Rosebery was at last called to the upper ranks of the Ministry as Lord Privy Seal, and then he found his colleagues exclusively pre-occupied with Ireland and foreign affairs. He too became immersed in them and never did fulfil his ambition of ruling Scotland from the Cabinet.

With his resignation popular sentiment became the main force behind devolution. Great indignation was provoked when the Lords rejected a Bill of Gladstone's to place all local Scottish agencies of government under a central board presided over by a senior Minister. In response public opinion declared his plans too timid and moved in favour of a fully-fledged Scottish Secretaryship on the lines advocated by Rosebery. In 1884, at a National Convention in Edinburgh, vigorous support was given to the idea by leading figures among both the Liberals and the Conservatives. Since Scotland was all but unanimous, Gladstone acceded to the demands. Soon afterwards he introduced a Bill to set up the Scottish Office. After delays it was passed with all-party agreement by Salisbury's Ministry in 1885.[21]

There had been some Whitehall bickering about the department's functions. Finally it assumed a wide range of Home Office powers and also, against much opposition, control of education. But the legal system, with all residual matters, remained under the Home Secretary and the Lord Advocate. The first Scottish Secretary was a Conservative, the Duke of Richmond and Gordon, who had no taste for the office and did not try to develop it. His Liberal successor, Sir George Trevelyan, took a step forward by sponsoring the Crofters Bill even though it lay outside a strict interpretation of his statutory powers. More expansion came under A J Balfour who held office in the winter of 1886–7. The Highlands were still disturbed and he was annoyed to find that the Home Office retained control of law and order in Scotland, while he was merely expected to supply police and keep local government running. He persuaded the Cabinet that the distinction was absurd and in 1887 a new Act gave him the extra powers he wanted. He also won disposal of Scottish patronage from the Home Secretary.

But the pattern of Scottish Office authority was still unsatisfactory. One drawback was that the department's headquarters were at Dover House in London, with only a small representative office in Edinburgh. The early Secretaries had almost a ceremonial role. They kept out of the major Scottish controversies, and once these had died down in the 1890s spent much time merely travelling the country reassuring people that Westminster had not forgotten them. They assumed no large political responsibilities, but devoted themselves to maintaining contact with local worthies, promoting petty legislation and distributing patronage.

In keeping with this role the early Secretaries were usually peers. That meant the Lord Advocates continued to take charge of Scottish legislation in the Commons. Though the latter were often more able than the former, the MPs still felt they could not effectively scrutinise Government activities in Scotland. This was especially true in the case of the administrative boards, whose control of most day-to-day business was undiminished. The Secretary answered for them in Parliament but did not in practice direct their work. Relations between him and the Lord Advocate were sometimes difficult too— a number of disputes arose over the responsibility for judicial appointments. The problems encouraged demands for all matters with a distinctive Scottish aspect to be brought under the Secretary.

But the degree of decentralisation now established was the most the Conservatives would tolerate once they had been placed in power in 1886. Scottish Home Rule won, however, a measure of support across a wide spectrum of the country's opinion. Popular nationalism was growing but had not so far produced a demand for legislative devolution, for Scots believed their aspirations could be satisfied at Westminster, given more sympathy and flexibility there. Since Gladstone's declaration in Midlothian the subject had been more fully explored. The Irish controversy seemed to open up the real possibility of a Parliament in Edinburgh of some kind. Just before the 1886 election, the Scottish Home Rule Association was founded. Its leaders included the crofters' MP, Dr G B Clark, the socialist Cunninghame Graham and the Celtic revivalist Prof John Stuart Blackie. The SHRA's official aim was 'Home Rule all round', if anything with Scotland's coming before Ireland's because the Scots had lost their independence first.[22]

In the specific context of 1886 this placed the SHRA in opposition to Gladstone. He wanted an immediate and extensive arrangement for Ireland alone, which in many respects would have granted her virtual independence. But most Scots favouring devolution believed it should be given simultaneously and in equal measure to all the countries of the British Isles— and Gladstone had promised as much in Midlothian. They saw Home Rule as a step towards greater democracy within a United Kingdom still firmly united.[23]

Yet the party affiliations of the SHRA were not at all clear. It inclined at first to the Liberal Unionists, among whom the idea of Home Rule all round had taken firmest root. Ready to hand they had a scheme of limited devolution applicable to both Scotland and Ireland worked out in 1885 by Joseph Chamberlain, the most prominent of Gladstone's deserters. There was, however, great enthusiasm for Home Rule on the Left and inevitably the SHRA formed close links in this quarter—Keir Hardie was one of the vice-presidents while Dr Clark promoted several unsuccessful Home Rule Bills in the 1886 Parliament. But the SHRA also had an incentive to work with the Gladstonians, the strongest opposition to a Conservative Government which had set its face against any moves which might curtail the imperial Parliament's power.

Everybody saw it as a step forward, therefore, when in 1889 Gladstone changed his mind about Ireland. Previously he had intended to exclude her MPs from Westminster when she got Home Rule, but now he agreed that she should continue to have some representation there. This seemed to open the way for a general scheme of devolution covering each nation of the United Kingdom, thus bringing him much more closely into line with opinion among Scots. Many were confident of getting Home Rule all round when a Liberal Ministry returned in 1892. The Scottish Secretary, Sir George Trevelyan, exerted himself to gain approval from the Cabinet for a new Bill. But there was no consensus on the question, even among its Scots members, and Gladstone's energy was anyway being squandered in the final agonies of his struggle over Ireland. Rosebery, by now opposed to devolution for Scotland, became Prime Minister in 1894 and tried to appease the discontents by establishing in the Commons a Scottish grand committee. Its duty was to take the committee stage of government or non-controversial Bills. All the Scots MPs sat on it, but they might be diluted by up to fifteen others if they did not themselves reflect the party composition of the whole House. This, for the first time since 1707, gave them a chance to deliberate formally among themselves without having to contend against the majority of Englishmen in the Commons chamber. But for the moment the cause of Scottish Home Rule got no further.

The controversy aroused by any of the great Scottish questions might have been capable in the long or short run of disrupting the Liberals' national coalition. Scotland's society and politics had many distinctive features, but it is a measure of her integration with the United Kingdom that the break, when it came, was the result of a purely imperial issue. Though bearing a resemblance to some other divisions, the split corresponded exactly to none of them. It was *sui generis*, and not indigenous to Scottish politics at all. This explains why the event was so complex, and why it is so difficult to characterise in terms of previous Scottish political history.[24]

Before 1886 Scots cared little about Home Rule for Ireland, though after centuries of close and often antagonistic contact they had strong feelings on the Irish. Anti-papist sentiment in Scotland was powerful, as was sympathy for the embattled Protestant minority across the water. There was hatred in all classes for Irish immigrants. Scots workers were infuriated when they allowed themselves to be used as strike-breakers, keeping down wages and crippling trade unions. The higher orders deplored the squalid social habits to which they saw them irretrievably given up. The Irish, in the face of such bitter hostility, were unassimilated, maintaining their own identity and institutions.[25]

So Scottish attitudes did not provide receptive ground for their complaints. Despite the revival of local nationalism, attachment to the United Kingdom and its constitution was genuinely strong in Scotland. And Scots had never been troubled in these feelings by their political leaders. Thus when in

December 1885 the word got out that Gladstone wanted to do something on Irish Home Rule, it came as something of a shock. It came as an even greater shock when the extent of his plans was revealed in the Bill put before Parliament in the following April. These went much further than his remarks during the Midlothian campaign would have suggested. For many, politics now became a painful struggle between their personal admiration of and loyalty towards Gladstone and their conviction of the profound rightness and goodness of the British constitution. Bitter battles broke out everywhere among the Liberals of Scotland. Within three months their party had split into a Gladstonian and a Unionist wing.

In retrospect the great schism of 1886 was broadly between Left and Right. But it did not look that way at the time. It is true that many of the Whiggish MPs and most of the peers—men like Robert Finlay, George Goschen, the Duke of Argyll and the Duke of Fife—did indeed turn Unionist. Yet Rosebery, who had almost become the archetypal Whig, of noble blood, moderate opinion and imperialist sentiment, stayed with Gladstone. There were anomalies on the radical side too. In England the most advanced of all, Joseph Chamberlain, broke with his leader, though followed by few outside his Birmingham fief. In Scotland a wider defection took place, headed by the Secretary, Sir George Trevelyan, and by the doyen of radicalism, the retired Duncan McLaren. Of twenty-three Scots who voted against the second reading of the Government of Ireland Bill—defeat of which led directly to the 1886 election—twelve were radicals.

Class analysis in Scotland at large also reveals complexities. Most workers remained loyal to their hero Gladstone. But the Protestant proletariat of the West, which had suffered most from Irish immigration, swung to the Unionists and much of it stayed stolidly with them for decades afterwards. On different grounds Gladstone was deserted by numerous business and professional people, to whom his new Irish policy was the culmination of years of creeping subversion. A great blow to him was the defection of the two leading newspapers, the *Glasgow Herald* and the *Scotsman*. He had been idolised in the Scottish Press, but now had no organ of authority to speak for him. All these forces were strong in the cities and towns, so that Unionism became primarily an urban movement. The instinctive conservatism of the small burghs and counties expressed itself this time in a fidelity to the mainstream of Liberalism.

Religious allegiances further complicated the matter. Catholics of Irish descent naturally supported Gladstone, though many were not voters. In reaction the Unionist secession was strongly Protestant. It was joined by numerous members of the Church of Scotland above all because they feared the growing influence of liberationists in the Liberal party. The Free Church declared for Gladstone, but was accused of doing so only to get in return his assent to disestablishment. Yet the liberationist movement split too and there was a strong minority current of Unionism among dissenters.

The confusion meant that one could discern between Unionists and non-Unionists no clear-cut difference on general principles: rather, a delicate gradation of views about the future relationship of the three kingdoms. The most violent Scottish objections were directed not at Home Rule as such, but at Gladstone's subordinate proposal that Irish MPs should be excluded from Westminster. If this was to set a precedent for Scotland, it meant the country would be shut out from consideration of those imperial affairs in which, commercially and emotionally, she had invested a great deal. Gladstone himself had little sympathy for these fears. So obsessed was he now with his mission of pacifying Ireland that he became openly irritated with Scottish claims for equal treatment, because he knew it could only be given at the cost of toning down his Irish plans. His opponents found these both premature and pusillanimous. They saw him offering self-government to Ireland before Scotland and perhaps offering more of it than Scotland would ever get. This would clearly break his previous promises. Moreover, they believed, he was doing it under the threat of Fenian violence. The reservations were in no way inconsistent with support for Scottish devolution in principle which was shared with the Gladstonians by many who felt forced to declare for Unionism. They took their stand against the specific terms of Gladstone's Irish Bill, without prejudice to their ultimate aims for Scotland and the United Kingdom.

The simple political labels of the 1886 election thus concealed a vast array of nice distinction.[26] Neither Liberal faction sought a permanent split. Liberals of all persuasions made much of Scottish Home Rule during the campaign, with Unionists asserting any scheme would have to satisfy hopes on both sides of the North Channel and Gladstonians claiming a measure for Ireland was but the first step to one for Scotland. These similar lines of argument threatened the integrity of Gladstone's party. They may explain why so many sitting Unionists were able to retain their constituents' confidence. The commitment to devolution also helped the Unionists in their insistence that they were quite different from the Conservatives. The anti-Gladstonian parties eventually concluded an electoral pact, but closer identification would in many places have been a distinct liability to the Liberal defectors.

Considering his rout elsewhere, Gladstone's performance in Scotland was a remarkable success.[27] Of the seventy-two constituencies, forty-three returned Gladstonians (including four Crofters), while Unionists won seventeen (including one Crofter) and Conservatives twelve. In 1885 there had been fifty-seven Liberals, ten Conservatives and five Crofters. The Gladstonians' share of the vote also held up quite well at 54 per cent, compared with 62 per cent for Liberals and Crofters combined in 1885. The Unionists took 33 per cent and so were greatly under-represented in Parliament. But evidently a large part of their support came from Conservatives. These had fought fifty-nine seats in 1885, but now intervened only where they had a chance of winning. A mere sixteen candidates were fielded and all else was left to the Unionists. That difference of 8 per cent in the Liberal vote gives the measure of the defection, small but significant. Scotland still mistrusted Conservatism. But the new body of Liberal floating voters discontented with their leadership was enough to make many seats marginal. The main Liberal party could no longer rely on an impregnable stronghold in Scotland.

Both sides were able to draw some satisfaction from the results. The Gladstonians scored a psychological victory by defeating the two leading Unionists, Trevelyan and Goschen. But they lost ground heavily in the West. Among its thirty seats the Liberal share dropped from twenty-one to twelve, with the Conservatives taking ten and the Unionists eight. Except for the two university constituencies which they picked up uncontested, the Conservatives' strength was confined to this region. Outside it they fought, unsuccessfully, only West Lothian and the Aberdeenshire seats. By contrast the Unionists' forty-three candidacies, while concentrated in urban or industrial areas, were scattered round the country and half their wins came in the East and North. Sitting Unionists had the best chance and thirteen out of twenty-two got back; of the twenty-one new candidates only four were elected. Incidentally, the result helped to reverse the previous geographic distribution of the Liberal factions in Scotland's parliamentary representation. In the counties the 1884 Reform Act granted the vote to many tenants, as well as to such depressed groups as miners and crofters. These constituencies thus became radical rather than, as before, Whig strongholds. And a good number of the formerly radical burghs followed the Unionists in moving steadily rightwards thereafter.

Despite the reservations 1886 must count as a turning-point in modern Scottish history. For the Liberal party the split in Scotland proved far more complex and damaging than anywhere else in the United Kingdom. Most alarming of all was the fact that particular, homogeneous social groups now permanently lost faith in it. This was the big innovation. The Scots opposition grew from a tiny, landed coterie to a true political party containing some of the leading citizens, grounded on a popular base in the West and espousing a patriotic, Protestant ideology. The official Liberal party also developed in consequence, becoming more united, radical and proletarian. Scotland started to change from a one-party state, where politics were conducted by individuals and cliques, to a country with a modern, formally pluralistic political system of organised group interests.

But the change was more than formal. Scottish politics till 1886 had an ethical basis. In voting Liberal, Scots voted for a view of man as a free, independent being—and for not much more. The party had been hopeless at devising Scottish policies, however well it responded to moral appeals. But ethical politics had severe limitations. Chalmers forgot that moral enlightenment can be proposed as the answer to anything, but is of little help with urgent problems and difficult options. Gladstone never learned that government by public debate leads most often to messy stalemate. The ethical approach had allowed defects to develop in Scottish society for which morality alone provided no relief, and for which the Liberals were blamed. The way was opening for ethical consensus to be replaced by secular party struggle, and for the reduction of the Liberals to merely one faction among several.

But was the great rift inevitable in 1886? In a Scottish context the Liberal split on Ireland was after all fortuitous. And though it proved permanent, it was also untidy. In fact Liberal ideology retained its force throughout society till 1914, little corrupted by class conflict. In philosophical terms there was still more to unite than to keep apart the two Liberal factions, especially in the period immediately after 1886. Nevertheless political divisions did now correspond more closely to underlying social divisions. The class politics of the future had been germinated in Scotland, even if it took thirty years before class differences were to a significant extent defined and articulated in political terms.

For the moment the most striking distinction was regional. Glasgow forsook Gladstone in 1886 to a remarkable extent.[28] It was Unionist because imperialist; it was imperialist because its prosperity was bound up with Empire. But the change had started outside party politics. Glasgow now had relatively little in common with the rest of Scotland. It had moved far ahead of a country otherwise of gracious, old-fashioned cities, small burghs and thinly peopled uplands, the seedbeds of traditional Liberalism. Its connections with America and Europe were closer than those with London, or even with Edinburgh. It had cast off parochialism and liked to think big. That was reflected in the philosophy of the corporation, a pioneer of municipal reform, active in building up public utilities and services. It was also notoriously authoritarian. It cared little for private property interests in pursuit of its ends, and on the populace it enforced its sanitary and temperance regulations with rigour and zeal. A critic called it 'the oppressor of the West', using Parliament merely as a 'means of registering its decrees'.[29] A new political spirit was being born in Glasgow: collectivist, interventionist and in the end alien to the libertarian radicalism of most Scots.

But other citizens seemed glad of it—one noted in awe that 'our municipality is a microcosm of our state . . . our imitation of imperial housekeeping is very faithful.'[30] In some ways Glasgow actually organised itself better than the state. City government rested on two principles: strict economy in finance and the welfare of the people. A council composed of businessmen saw to the first, but the second they were strangely reluctant to entrust to the mechanics of capitalism. They had first placed investment at the service of the public good rather than of private profit as early as 1854, when they had solved the problem of water supply by a scheme to tap Loch Katrine. They strove systematically during the next decade to raise the standard of the population's health. With the Glasgow Improvement Act (1866) they acquired powers to clear slums and soon started to build their own housing. In 1869 they took over the city's gas companies and in 1892 began to generate electricity. From 1894 they operated the tramways and in 1901 set up a telephone network. Nor did they stop at material wants: they also provided high and low culture, in public concerts and the excellent art gallery, or at the People's Palace. Their enterprise and efficiency, which made profits while keeping prices to the consumer lower than elsewhere, were a source of pride to the whole city.

The inspiration was part-foreign and part-native. The experiment had started in imitation of Birmingham's under Chamberlain, though Glasgow's went further and did better. The principles also had a startling similarity, however, to those of Scotland's defunct ecclesiastical constitution, long vainly upheld by the Free Church—of which it was perhaps no accident that two outstanding Lord Provosts of the period, Sir Samuel Chisholm and Sir Daniel Macaulay Stevenson, were members. It accorded to the state only the duty of providing the werewithal to the institutions catering for the people's welfare, which otherwise acted in the freedom they chose for themselves. Glasgow corporation had a visionary ambition to create an ideal industrial society, where the energy of capitalism and the morals of the citizens would be brought into harmony through strict regulation. That gave social control to the bourgeoisie, but also offered much to the workers. If, as a result of the city's rapid development, their housing and health were still poor—though improving—they were more mobile and could mix more freely with other classes than elsewhere. They were certainly kept tranquil at a time when labour was rising as a political force in England. It is true that religious and associated motives anyway attached many to Unionism till the First World War. But the corporation's policies reinforced their assent to a system in which clashes of capital and labour were deliberately defused. Though different parties were represented on the town council, they acted in a non-partisan manner and removed divisive issues from politics.

In the main Glasgow still regarded itself as a Liberal city, though Unionist too. This Unionism was a reconstructed form of ethical Liberalism, in which the fierce, anarchic pursuit of personal rights was transmuted into a co-operation for the general welfare that might equally ensure them: out of it today's system of Scottish government was to grow. Unionism thus defined need not have divorced itself from Liberalism without the catalyst of the Irish question. That forced Scots Liberals to look beyond their individualism and to formulate the concept of a British—even an imperial—community. Many decided that the most important task was to build and maintain it, an aim with which they thought Home Rule for Ireland incompatible. But they had only given such an answer when Gladstone asked their assent to one specific reform of the imperial structure—to their mind the most extreme among a range of options. In other ways the new spirit and the old Liberal values were still mutually consistent.

That Unionism still felt itself Liberal was evidenced by its representatives' conduct in the 1886 Parliament. It was unclear who would form the Government, for while the Tories held the most seats nobody had a majority. As Prime Minister the Unionists wanted Hartington, leader of the Whig secession, rather than Salisbury, the Conservative candidate. When the latter won, they declined to coalesce with his party, agreeing only to support him informally from the Opposition benches. At this stage there was in Liberalism no clear dividing line between a Unionist Right and a Gladstonian Left. People whose sentiments were hardly to be distinguished from Unionism stayed with the main party, forming a wing notable mainly for its imperialism, while the Unionist ranks contained a good number of radicals. In 1886 the commitment to basic Liberal principles was still powerful and general enough in Scotland for most to hope that the two factions could be quickly re-united. It was assumed this would become possible as soon as Gladstone had been taught a lesson and defeated in Parliament and at the polls. Perhaps it was only prevented by his obstinate refusal to retire. But, though sitting side by side at Westminster, Gladstonians and Unionists spent as much time in mutual recrimination as in scrutinising the Government, with each group proclaiming itself the guardian of Liberal tradition and damning the other as its betrayer. A conference called in 1887 to arrange a reconciliation failed completely.

Salisbury himself was pitifully weak in Scotland. He had only twelve MPs out of seventy-two and yet remained in office for six years. No-one had ruled the country for so long from such a narrow base. Once Balfour was transferred from the Scottish Office in 1887, the Prime Minister had to resort for a replacement to an obscure and mild-mannered peer, Lord Lothian, who was not admitted to the Cabinet. So the Unionists on whom the Government had to rely were in a position to extract some of the legislation they would have introduced themselves. In Scotland they had a range of their own anti-Conservative policies on education and welfare, the land, local government and Home Rule.[31]

In these circumstances it was not surprising that Lothian presented himself as a non-partisan Secretary. His policies bore all the same a striking resemblance to the Liberal Unionists'. In the Highlands he set out to foster development rather than just encourage emigration. For the country as a whole he set up county councils, brought in free school education a year ahead of its introduction in England and further reformed the universities. He was helped by Goschen, his colleague at the Treasury, who answered the old grievance over lack of public spending in Scotland by devising a formula which guaranteed her an allocation for each of the Scottish Office's responsibilities equal to eleven-eightieths of the sums disbursed for the corresponding purpose in England and Wales. The Unionists naturally did not get all they wanted. In particular the Government had set its face against any dilution of imperial unity, so there was no prospect of further devolution.[32]

The Scots Unionists were superior to the Conservatives in leadership and organisation, and had their satisfactions. Their position was all the same tricky. Their party held the balance of power at Westminster, but what would happen to it if either the Gladstonians or the Tories won an absolute majority? Its *raison d'etre* was commitment to existing links with Ireland, a nebulous basis for a permanent appeal to Scots voters. It was clearly necessary to work out something more convincing. Joseph Chamberlain, once the hero of radicals, came north in 1887 and 1889 to campaign on the land and education in the hope of persuading people that Unionists were better democrats than anyone else. The effort was vain, for most of his sometime admirers were now firmly wedded to Gladstone. The drift was rather in the opposite direction to that which Chamberlain intended. A new intolerance had entered political life after 1886—Unionists and Conservatives resorted too easily to personal abuse of the Liberal leadership, to sneering at the Irish and to the mouthing of imperialist slogans. This was often repugnant to the radicals who had at first defected. Lured by Gladstone's new, progressive policies and driven by their reluctance to persist in tacit league with Conservatism, many of them—Trevelyan the most prominent—returned to their old allegiance. At the same time, Unionists who had retained membership of Liberal organisations were being steadily expelled.

Given all this, it was perhaps inevitable that Unionists and Conservatives should have begun co-operating in more regular fashion. Joint associations appeared and the first combined parliamentary candidacy was arranged as early as 1889. But in this coming together it was really the old Conservative party that was killed off, with its reliance on the landed interest, its emotional resistance to reform and its attachment to detested privileges. In Scotland the Right was increasingly dominated by its progressive, urban and especially by its Glaswegian wing. In alliance with Whigs and with Protestant workers, it was by no means identical in aims and outlook to English Tories. There was no formal control from London over the Scottish Unionist party, so that it was free to act according to its own lights. It was not especially closely associated with the upper class and retained a commitment to such old Liberal ideals as land reform and free trade. As a result, it escaped the fate of English Unionism, soon subordinated to and absorbed by the Conservatives. In its essentials, it was to survive for a very long time.

In Scotland, on the contrary, a Unionism still rather Liberal absorbed Conservatism. This may be illustrated by the personal odyssey of Lord Balfour of Burleigh, appointed Scottish Secretary when Salisbury returned to power in 1895.[33] He had started in politics as a Conservative. A strong campaigner for the Kirk in the 1880s, he maintained an enduring concern with religious matters, above all with Church reunion. No other Conservative was so engrossed in specifically Scottish questions or so intimately involved in the nation's life. The effect on him was remarkable. In the Highlands his policy was if anything more radical than the Liberals', encouraging small-holders, assisting emigrants and, through a new Land Court, subjecting crofters' disputes to a judicial instead of a merely administrative process. By the turn of the century he was for some more general scheme of land reform. All this brought in the North striking electoral dividends. Then, in 1903, he resigned from the Cabinet over its wish to abandon free trade. He led a sympathetic inquiry into Clydeside workers' grievances in the First World War and afterwards took close interest in all aspects of commercial and industrial policy. He was certainly no remote aristocrat isolated from the country's real problems, on the usual Conservative pattern. By espousing active social reform in combination with imperial unity and strong government, he had in effect moved to a Liberal Unionist position.

The Unionists were in this period far better than their separated brethren at securing Liberal measures for Scotland. But they remained a sectional party without the appeal to all classes and regions that united Liberalism had enjoyed. Vigorous enough in their areas of electoral strength, they won little support elsewhere, for they themselves showed no anxiety to build up a popular coalition outside the West. In time their distinctive features faded. They went in 1895 for the first time to sit with the Conservatives on the Government benches at Westminster. Though they had once been devolutionaries, they now also acquiesced in the immediate abolition of the Scottish grand committee.

Even then they had much in common with at least a section of the Liberals opposite. For the battle in Scotland was being primarily waged not between the still untidily divided party organisations, but between two interpretations of the ethical tradition, the purist and the reconstructed. Unionism stood for the second, but so did the new talents and forces stirring within Gladstonian Liberalism. To its ranks there was now introduced a different type of Scottish MP. The outstanding younger members were Anglo-Scots, such as Robert Haldane and Ronald Munro-Ferguson, or English carpet-baggers like H H Asquith and Augustine Birrell. Their horizons were not bounded by the line of the Cheviots, they were at home with the ruling circles in London and a number of them were to achieve great distinction. They found a leader in Rosebery. His latest pet cause was Efficiency, a somewhat nebulous doctrine. But it acknowledged that Britain had many problems which could not be solved by radical libertarianism and *laissez-faire* economics. Instead, the Earl said, the Government should set its own social goals and legislate positively to achieve them. This he linked with the need to equip the country for its imperial vocation. His disciples were themselves a socially exclusive group, stressing the superiority and moral necessity of leadership, especially in pursuit of progressive policies, by an elite. For all their abilities, they remained a minority in the Scottish party. Nor did they make much appeal to the nation at large. The analysis by these Liberal imperialists of the future of Scotland, Britain and the Empire was more profound than any by the Unionists or Conservatives. But the latter parties always had the more imperialist image and reaped a greater electoral benefit when voters were in chauvinist mood.

The difference between the imperialist and the orthodox radical stream of Gladstonian Liberalism may be illustrated by their views on Scottish Home Rule.[34] Rosebery turned against it after 1886, but those about him offered a glowing vision of Scotland in a reformed imperial structure. The case was expounded by his cosmopolitan crony, Lord Reay, a former colonial governer and junior Minister in his Government, during the rectorial address he gave at St Andrews:

> If we had a Scottish Parliament sitting in Edinburgh, I have no doubt that the organisation of the universities would be the first number on the legislative programme . . . This is not a question of local importance. It concerns the greatness of the Empire. Development of more brain-power in Scotland means increased national efficiency and less danger from democratic ignorance.[35]

More generally, it was contended that Home Rule all round would give her justice and self-respect, while freeing the imperial Parliament from legislative triviality and leaving it the scope for a mission of economic and social reconstruction. That was anathema to radicals. They wanted Home Rule because they were for local autonomy on principle—as an end, not a means. They abhorred the idea of Westminster arrogating to itself these supreme powers.

But imperialists could fairly accuse them of not thinking through the arguments they had long advanced on the question. It was largely on account of radical pressure that the Scottish Office had been set up. Opposition to it came from those who feared for their own position, in the administrative boards and Parliament House: because of that, Whigs in general were unfavourable. They objected that the subordination of all Scottish government to a central department would, as Moncreiff once put it, have 'a tendency to denationalise the conduct of Scottish business'—though in view of what they had done since 1832 the point was rather hypocritical. But it was a real point. The Lord Advocate's job was a quirkish survival, yet it did keep Scottish affairs in Scottish hands, not much interfered with, if often obstructed, by London. Now that a Scottish Office had been created in Whitehall, there was a danger that it would follow other departments in its methods and impose English norms on the country. Radicals insisted that this made Home Rule a necessity. Imperialists agreed, but added that a rationalised system of government in the United Kingdom alone might still make of Scotland a mere province. Their answer was complete renewal within an imperial framework, as the basis of an eventual federation which by its nature could not be so anglocentric.

The imperialist ideal, if developed in practice, might have prevented Scotland's utter subjection to central government amid her economic collapse after the First World War. The radical model would in any case have been inadequate. This important debate about Scotland's identity and role was, however, never carried through to a conclusion. Under a Conservative Ministry nothing was attainable anyway. And even within the Liberal party the radicals came under no pressure to rethink their position, for the Unionist defection had left them dominant there, and overwhelmingly so in Scotland. That freed them of the constraints at which they had bridled ever since 1832. They no longer had to fight the Whigs or compromise their ideals in the interests of Liberal unity. Their reforming, democratic, internationalist and pacifist enthusiasms could now be given full rein, and they pressed their demands over the whole field of public policy. Under their control the SLA voted for disestablishment and land reform in 1887 and for Scottish Home Rule in 1888. By 1892 it was taking an even more radical stance than Gladstone in his Newcastle Programme, advocating an eight-hour day for miners, abolition of the House of Lords, more land for crofters and women's suffrage. For the first time the Scots Liberals were formulating coherent policies. Their reward came in the General Election of that year. Their party was returned to power and in Scotland it advanced from forty-three to fifty seats. This was, however, the only break in the twenty years of Conservative ascendancy established by the Liberal schism in Britain as a whole.

It was not the sole reason why the burst of energy among the Scots Liberals produced so few results. The English party hierarchs, as before, heeded only their own countrymen and ignored policy proposals from Scotland. Their increased dependence on her votes since 1886 had done little to change their attitudes. Gladstone's pursuit of Irish Home Rule had been in one way an attempt, only partially successful because revolutionary in its novelty, to impose the executive's will on a resistant party and country. This was an

augury of the centralised politics of the future, and in fact it did impose
more central control over the remainder of Liberalism. That cancelled out
the greater numerical importance of the Scots for, with their own national
interests and organisation, they were even more of an anomaly in the new
dispensation. They never learned how to persuade the leadership in London
to accord them their due weight.

Their inspiration was still the Liberalism of old, unreconstructed, grounded
in ethical imperatives and insensitive to social and economic change. It made
them indifferent to the problems of power. Their tactics remained the same
as in McLaren's day—they hated compromise, believing that if the Scots
demanded something loud and long enough and reinforced their case with
moral arguments, then this was reason enough for it to be done. The consequences were seen in their lack of achievement during this decade. Soon it
was evident that the great motor forces which had sustained them were spent.
Always dwelling in the shadow of the English Liberals, the Scots became
demoralised and apathetic.

That was reflected in the persistent mediocrity of their radical representatives. The only exceptions were Charles Cameron, now the doyen of Glasgow members, and Henry Campbell-Bannerman, who had been pursuing a
solid if unexciting career in various minor departments of state. The rest were
men of no great ambition or ability but rather, like their predecessors in mid-
century, well-meaning, respectable provincials. Office rarely came their way.
Rosebery, elevated in 1894 as Liberal leader, had long lost interest in forcing
the nation's claims on southern politicians, and there was nobody to replace
him. The one source of renewal within practical reach, the adoption of
working-class candidates, was neglected. The party was punished for its poor
performance when it had to go to the country again in 1895. It was left with
just thirty-nine seats against thirty-three for its adversaries, the narrowest
margin since 1831.

The frustrated Liberals could not even unite against the Conservative
Ministry which followed. It pursued a policy of imperial expansion which the
radicals furiously opposed out of moral horror at such oppression of helpless
foreign peoples. The imperialists, however, could not in all conscience disapprove. They believed in a British mission to the world and criticised the
Government rather for its failure to bring in at home the social and economic
reforms which they thought the essential basis for success. But the men and
the ideas were quite out of touch with the individualist values and organic view
of society held by the rest of the party, especially in its Scottish stronghold.

Never liking to be thwarted, Rosebery found in 1896 a pretext to resign
the leadership. In Britain as a whole his party with its radical programme
had just been electorally thrashed. He was convinced that it would be saved
by nothing less than a complete re-orientation on the lines he advocated. He
disdained politicking in any case and felt he now needed a philosophic distance
to develop his ideas. The dissension had spread down to the Liberal grassroots, and his departure only made it worse. Harcourt assumed the leadership
in the Commons, but by the end of 1898 he too felt his position impossible
and resigned. Great hopes were reposed in Campbell-Bannerman, who took

over. Though by nature a conciliator, his prospects of quiet progress in re-uniting his colleagues were ruined by the outbreak of the Boer War in 1899. Radical outrage at this attack on the sturdy, God-fearing republics of South Africa was boundless, while an impassioned Rosebery endorsed it with fervour. Once more the Liberal party appeared in danger of dissolution.

The war proved very disruptive in Scottish politics, unlike in England, where it was widely supported. In Scotland a radical, pacifist tradition scarcely diminished in strength confronted a school of imperialists highly esteemed and of exceptional ability, so that public opinion was more equally divided. Unionists naturally backed the Government; it was the Liberals who suffered most from the conflicts, not least because Rosebery had left behind in key positions men of his own who did not always reflect opinion among the rank and file. In the Commons, the Scottish whip, Ronald Munro-Ferguson, was a fervent disciple, but the dozen or so imperialist MPs around him were out-numbered by pro-Boers. His friend Thomas Gibson Carmichael was chairman of the SLA, though that could not disguise the presence of a radical majority within it. The most desperate desire of the hapless Campbell-Bannerman was to avert another schism, so he dared not show favour to either side. He attempted instead the impossible task of maintaining a critical but neutral attitude to the war. His reward was to be attacked from every quarter for weakness and vacillation. A series of embarrassing Commons divisions on various military issues demonstrated his lack of authority. He persisted in abstention but could not carry the party with him—at one time or another a majority of Scots Liberals repudiated his line, either by combining with the Government or else by voting against its South African policy.

When the Ministry suddenly called an election in 1900, the Liberals were in the utmost confusion. Though they held reasonably firm in England, in Scotland they lost the majority they had enjoyed since 1831, returning only thirty-four of the seventy-two members. Against one gain they suffered eight losses, four of them by pro-Boers. So it seemed clear that the issue of the war gave the decisive final push in toppling their long ascendancy.

The election showed conclusively how much more precarious their hold on Scotland had become since 1886. In particular many of the industrial districts were now very marginal. On this occasion the West was a disaster area, as signified by the fall of the Liberals' last two seats in Glasgow. Unionists also took most of the Highland constituencies which the crofters' movement had apparently secured to the Gladstonians, whose reforms were, however, now being outdone by Balfour of Burleigh's work. The residual Liberal coalition evidently contained elements that could not be relied on. Even small dis-ruptions were more serious than they could ever have been in former years: according to Campbell-Bannerman, the balance had been tipped by the defection, on a relatively minor education issue, of the previously loyal Catholics. Still, one must not underestimate the strength of a party which for most purposes could still count on them, on the urban working class in general, and especially on the Gladstonian East. It was several times proved in the period up to 1914 that the opposing Unionist coalition, based on the imperialistic West, the bourgeoisie and on anti-Catholic workers, was not constant or coherent enough to secure a majority. But the circumstances of 1900 were exceptional, with the Government calling an election to rally the country in the midst of war and the Opposition divided on the question of what patriotism might excuse. Thus the Scots Liberals' great century ended on a baffled and disappointed note.

Chapter 5

'Its Platforms Were Pulpits'

Scotland's story in the twentieth century is one of national decline. In 1900 she was among the world's richest industrial countries. Her native traditions remained strong despite the forces shaping the structure of her society in ever close conformity to England's. While her affairs weighed little in imperial politics, her material success was evidently enhanced and secured by the Union and she was happy to trust in the many leaders of Britain who were Scots or had Scottish connections. But even before the First World War there were disturbing signs of a change in fortune. In the years after the peace they manifested themselves in the cruellest fashion. Prolonged economic depression dissipated Scotland's wealth and sapped her social cohesion. The national consensus on which Liberalism had nourished itself was undermined by so many forces at once that it crumbled beyond all hope of reconstruction. It was replaced by the barren polarity of a simplistic, moralising socialism and an unimaginative conservatism. Between them the historic Liberal party collapsed. It had presided naturally and integrally over the prosperous and self-confident Scotland of the nineteenth century. The two disappeared together.

Amid the consternation of 1900, however, few Scots Liberals spared a thought for the distant future.[1] The immediate and pressing task was to resolve the conflict between the imperialists and the rest. The struggle posed a peculiarly Scottish dilemma, which did not strike the more disparate and adaptable English party with equal force. Domestically, Liberal imperialism was a response to Britain's growing social and economic difficulties. English Liberals were already starting to accept that these demanded a more active role of government and from now on, in espousing the so-called new Liberalism, they in fact moved closer to Rosebery's position.[2] But the Scots, holding fast to the old Liberalism, drew back from this novelty and left others to build on the collectivist spirit of the twentieth century.

It may be that Rosebery's flatulent idealism and disruptive tactics hindered a peaceful transition in Scotland. He was no longer interested in serving his party and seeing it back in power unless he could use it to impose his own views. But now that he had stepped down from the leadership he needed some means of maintaining his influence. He reverted to the strategy he had tried in the 1880s, of establishing control over a territorial interest in the same way as Chamberlain had once done in Birmingham. Scotland was the place he chose to transform into his personal fiefdom, as the base for his renewed ideological advance.[3]

He was optimistic about his position there, for he remained popular among the Scots. Modern judgements of him are equivocal, but at the time he struck people as a glamorous and exciting figure. Though still a comparatively young man, he had been at the summit of British politics for fifteen years and his beliefs seemed imaginative and futuristic. He had gathered round him the most brilliant of the rising generation in Scottish politics. Through them he still held, if somewhat loosely, the leading-strings of local Liberalism. The imperialist city of Glasgow, with its bureaucratic and paternalist but reforming corporation, was already showing that his principles of Efficiency could be successfully applied. He was weaker in the East, but that region had elected several of his friends to Parliament and from his seat at Dalmeny he could exert an influence in the Lothians. Though the Earl himself opposed Home Rule, his followers were fond of holding before the Scots the promise of a special role for their country within his dirigiste imperial framework. They were scathing about the older school of Scottish Liberalism and the latent conservatism of its unsullied libertarian ideals. These points struck home. The SLA had continued to decline and was neither original nor inspiring in the years after 1900. The Liberals' defeat at the General Election was taken as clear proof of its debility. Moreover, Rosebery's greatest enemies within the party had been palpably trounced. Of the fifteen Scots pro-Boers in the previous Parliament, only nine survived. One had retired and four had lost to Unionists, while in a double Liberal candidature in Caithness the radical Dr Clark had been turned out by the imperialist Cecil Harmsworth.

But Rosebery's optimism hid from him some underlying weaknesses in his position. The great majority of the Scots Liberal party was still Gladstonian in outlook and simply not open to his persuasions. For all the forward-looking nature of the doctrines of Efficiency, real commitment to them was confined to an intellectual coterie. They struck no chord with the nation's presbyterian spirit and aroused little interest in the mass of voters.

Most of the Earl's true constituency in Scotland, those who had been converted or were convertible to imperialist collectivism, was captured by the Unionists in 1900. While he offered a more constructive, less hysterical alternative to the jingoism of the Right, it was perhaps, as one radical said, only 'Chamberlain wine with a Rosebery label'.[4] The Earl was prepared to make the major concession of dropping his party's pledge to Irish Home Rule in order to win back those who had defected in 1886. But, though the Unionists did still maintain a political organisation in Scotland separate from the Conservatives', the anti-Gladstonian alliance was now of long standing and not to be broken easily.

That was a problem which troubled Rosebery little, as little as the accusations of rank treachery heard from his fellow Liberals. His manoeuvres never got much beyond the planning stage, however, for he had a great dislike of politicking. He sought a transformation of attitudes, which he thought best achieved through the diffusion of his moral influence rather than by his direct political engagement. He left the more sordid work to lieutenants, himself withdrawing into long silences punctuated by the odd enigmatic and abstract statement of his position. Beneath the public image was an unfathomable character quite capable with its contradictions and evasions of destroying what meagre chance the imperialists had of capturing Scottish Liberalism. But since he had chosen Scotland as his battleground, the struggle between the two factions there assumed a special importance.

Both set energetically to work as soon as the 1900 election was over. In London, Rosebery's friends had already formed a Liberal Imperialist Council. At home, Munro-Ferguson felt obliged to resign as Scottish whip and effective head of the electoral organisation after the defeat. But he was then willing to place his services fully at the Earl's disposal and carry out the tasks of propaganda and co-ordination for him.

One of Rosebery's mistakes was to consistently underestimate Campbell-Bannerman. Clearly the leader had been gravely weakened by the result of the election. But in Munro-Ferguson's place he was able to appoint his confidant, the radical John Sinclair. With Sir Robert Reid, a popular MP and lawyer, and the former whip Edward Marjoribanks, now Lord Tweed-mouth, they set out to tighten their grip on the party. They encouraged the activities of a new Liberal ginger group, the Young Scots Society. Originally formed to protect public meetings from disruption—for pro-Boer campaigners often got a riotously hostile reception in the West— it went on to agitate for the whole range of radical policies. An important point in Campbell-Bannerman's favour was that he managed to keep the SLA faithful. It passed a resolution in 1901 giving 'strenuous and unreserved support' to the leader against the imperialists. He felt able to claim: 'Everything I hear in Scotland is satisfactory . . . we have captured the local associations.'[5] He was altogether much cannier than the Earl gave him credit for. Britain's victories earlier in the Boer War soon turned sour; its end was long drawn-out and bloody. Sensing the turn of the tide, Campbell-Bannerman restored party consensus not by condemning the war itself, which would have been too much for the imperialists, but the 'methods of barbarism' used in a vain attempt to finish it.[6]

Having demonstrated the strength of his position, he set out to conciliate Rosebery if he could. The tetchy Earl proved no easy man to bring to a compromise, simply refusing to recognise the claims of party loyalty. This so exasperated Campbell-Bannerman that in February 1902 he demanded a firm statement on whether Rosebery still counted himself a Liberal. The reply was couched in the usual ambiguous terms, but did employ the phrase 'definite separation'.[7] The degree of definition was all the same still far from clear, for shortly afterwards Rosebery, aided by Asquith and Haldane, launched from Glasgow a Liberal League dedicated to spreading the gospel of Efficiency within the party.

The Liberal imperialists were meanwhile themselves becoming unsettled, for Rosebery's deviousness puzzled them as well as Campbell-Bannerman.

Even as the league was being formed Munro-Ferguson wrote of his worry about 'a split between Rosebery and the rest of us—a finale which one always feels to be within the bounds of possibility but which we must try to avoid.'[8] The league's Scottish organisers were unable to make much headway. In July 1902 Munro-Ferguson noted ruefully than in the South it was doing 'much better than in Scotland'.[9] For the imperialists, engaged in the quiet, cunning work of winning converts and easing supporters into key positions in the constituencies, Rosebery's recent statements had been a great embarrassment. Each group tried to shift the blame for disruption on to the other, so that the Earl's equivocating over his allegiance was a gift to the radicals. They really had only to bide their time while he alienated the rank and file. Gibson Carmichael told Rosebery in August 1902 that Tweedmouth was urging the SLA to 'show no hostility to the league but rather to let the hostility come from us.' The danger, he added, was that if an open battle broke out, 'whichever party begins it will turn popular sympathy to the other.' It was a strange revelation of his true loyalties in a man who at that point was still actually chairman of the SLA. The next year he felt obliged to resign.[10]

Before long the imperialist campaign was generally faltering. In March 1903 Munro-Ferguson wrote in vexation; 'It may be that belonging to the league will so hamper us through his (Rosebery's) treating it as a personal appanage that we shall have to get quit of it.'[11] The straggling band managed to hold together, but little more. Rosebery was supported by the upper class, even by much of the Press. Elsewhere he found few adherents. Propaganda apart, the imperialists devoted most effort to getting candidates of their persuasion nominated for Parliament. They succeeded in only three con- stituencies—Glasgow College, Midlothian and West Renfrewshire—which they did not already hold. The struggle ended in a resounding victory for Campbell-Bannerman. The Scottish party steadily re-asserted its old- fashioned radicalism against the bloodless intellectuals round Rosebery. Except for Haldane in the field of education, the champions of Efficiency in fact made little contribution to the reformist debates of the time. It was Campbell-Bannerman who proved the more efficient by holding the Liberals together and enabling them to return to undisputed power.

The last resistance to him came as he was forming his Government in 1905. The two outstanding imperialist MPs in Scotland, Asquith and Haldane, had with the English member Sir Edward Grey formed the so-called Relugas compact, named after a fishing lodge on the Findhorn where it was concluded. They resolved to refuse office under Campbell-Bannerman unless he agreed to go to the Lords. This would have left their faction pre-eminent in the Commons. The manoeuvre was too clever by half. Fortified by the King's commission, the leader could not be bullied. The compact dissolved as soon as he started offering round the Cabinet posts.

With his chief allies reconciled to the new Prime Minister, Rosebery's influence rapidly waned. His demise as a public figure of the first rank was marked by an extraordinary speech in June 1908. He chose Glasgow, if you please, to defend the dukes as a 'poor but honest class' and called that year's Budget 'the end of all, the negation of faith, of family, of prosperity, of monarchy, of Empire'.[12] These inanities, exposing him as an increasingly reactionary Whig, killed off the wilting Liberal League and destroyed his popular following in the West, the only region where it remained substantial.

The Liberals had been helped to power by a rapid deterioration in the position of the Scots Unionists.[13] Despite their solid support for the Government during the Boer War, these had not been able to escape dissensions over imperial issues either. Even now the image of the party, still filled with Whiggish gentry and hard-headed businessmen, was stamped with the impress of the Liberal defection of 1886. It was also persistently reluctant to be absorbed by its partner—the first negotiations for a formal merger of the Scottish Conservatives and Unionists were started after 1900, but the response was unenthusiastic and no progress was made. Above all, the Scots Unionist MPs refused to be taken in by the besotted imperialism of some of their colleagues in the House. This was shown by their conduct when in 1903 the irrepressible Joseph Chamberlain, who had once helped to wreck the Liberal party, rent the Government from top to bottom by his campaign for the abandonment of free trade in favour of imperial preference. A J Balfour, the Prime Minister, now faced internal problems not dissimilar to those which had afflicted Campbell-Bannerman during the war. Chamberlain was opposed by a determined group of Unionist Free Traders, while Balfour tried unsuccessfully to maintain a compromise position between them.

Scotland, an exporting country, was a centre of the resistance to Chamberlain's plans, which would have subverted one of the most fundamental and long-standing Liberal principles. But the resistance was joined by many Unionists too. Seven MPs from the West staunchly defended free trade with their votes and were warmly supported by commercial and other interests in Glasgow. From the Lords they were encouraged by Balfour of Burleigh, the Scottish Secretary, a member of the Cabinet group which felt forced by the Prime Minister's temporising to resign at the end of 1903. These were great blows to the Scots Unionists' morale, not to mention their popularity.

After his predecessors had evaded legislating on disestablishment of the Kirk, it was also the hapless A J Balfour that was forced into action, at least on a side-issue. The main battle had exhausted itself, but it remained for the survivors to divide the spoils. A small section of the Free Church, already rejoicing in the nickname of Wee Frees, had stood aloof from the merger in 1900 with the United Presbyterians. It now presented a claim to all its parent body's endowments, arguing that the seceders of 1900 were the true successors to those of 1843, since they clung to the principle of Establishment. This, they asserted, was essential to the constitution of a Free Church, yet the new United Free Church had abandoned it. After long litigation they got the House of Lords to agree, with the absurd result that half the property of the largest dissenting body was to be devolved on a tiny sect. Scotland was so outraged that the Government felt obliged to step in. It passed a Scottish Churches Act reversing the judgement and recognising that a Free Church could alter its constitution at will. This affair nevertheless also damaged the Ministry. Scots felt that the House of Lords had caused all the trouble and turned further against the Unionists as the defenders of its prerogatives.

The Government had been steadily forfeiting support in any case. After November 1902 it lost every single by-election in Scotland. Through these gains the Liberals achieved parity in the country's representation by late in 1903. A further win at the Ayr Burghs in January 1904 gave them back their majority. At the time of the General Election they held forty of the seventy-two seats.

The Unionists also had trouble in finding men of calibre to run the administration. After Balfour of Burleigh's resignation there was no obvious replacement. Andrew Graham Murray was promoted from Lord Advocate, but had a 'foolish habit of not answering letters.'[14] When he went on to the Bench in 1905 the Government had to turn for the Secretary to an obscure retired colonial governor, the Marquess of Linlithgow, an embarrassing contrast to the galaxy of talent among the Scots Liberals. By the end of the year the Ministry was crumbling and A J Balfour limply handed over power to the Opposition.

Campbell-Bannerman went straight to the polls in January 1906.[15] The result was a crushing victory for his party, which took fifty-eight seats and 56 per cent of the votes. The Unionists, with 38 per cent, survived in only twelve constituencies. They suffered a spectacular reverse in Glasgow, where they had made a clean sweep in 1900. Now it was represented by four Liberals, a Labourite and two Unionist Free Traders, so that A J Balfour's policies were well and truly repudiated. Socialists entered ten contests and made their first gains. In Dundee Alex Wilkie took one seat with Liberal support. The performance of George Barnes, who won Glasgow Blackfriars, was the more commendable because he, in common with the remaining Labour candidates in Scotland, had no electoral pact with the Liberals as those in England did.

It is interesting to compare the Liberals' situation in 1906 with that after similar overwhelming victories in the nineteenth century. In the old days a scattered and ineffective opposition had persisted only in rural pockets under the corrupt influence of landlords. Unlike them, the Unionists had never been alien to the national ethos. Their basic electoral position was correspondingly different. A modern political party is tested not in triumph but in defeat, and the real test is whether it can survive in some loyal heartland which may form the foundation for renewed advance. Six of the remaining Unionist seats were in the imperialist West—representing a core irretrievably alienated from the simplistic radicalism prevalent elsewhere—while a further four were decidedly middle-class in character. Unionism thus retained a coherence and resilience which Conservatism had never shown.

At the other end of the spectrum Scottish Labour was in this period of meagre importance and remained weak till 1914. But it is noteworthy that where candidates were put up—though all in selected, favourable areas—they did reasonably well. The Liberal landslide did not, then, entirely obliterate the new patterns emerging in Scottish politics. Opposition survived not through isolated personal influence but because of divergences in regional, religious and class interests that were genuinely appreciated, if only by small minorities.

What the triumph did appear to do was settle the argument between imperialists and radicals in Scotland. The Unionists were reduced to a tiny rump, while within the Liberal party Rosebery's disciples submitted to Campbell-Bannerman. The radicals had indeed gained the upper hand, but their position was not so good as it seemed. Imperialist, even collectivist sentiment had been spreading among English Liberals, and at Westminster the Scots were starting to look like some old-fashioned, fundamentalist sect. They were also failing to rise to positions from which they might determine the future course of Liberalism. The imperialists were by contrast advancing rapidly. Asquith succeeded as Prime Minister within three years. A cautious elitist, he gradually neutralised the Scots radicals and deprived them of influence. They soon found themselves once more ignored as provincials whose allegiance could be taken for granted. Their victory in 1906 did not fulfil its promise.

But for the moment they at last felt they had their hands on the instruments of power. Their local dominance was undisputed. More important, they could for the first time count on co-operation from the central government, where Scotland was strongly represented through the presence of nine MPs or peers in the Cabinet, under Campbell-Bannerman as Prime Minister and with Sinclair as Scottish Secretary. Another radical, Thomas Shaw, was appointed Lord Advocate and at home party affairs were ably controlled by the bluff and wily Master of Elibank as Scottish Whip. This Government is rightly renowned for its achievements in social and constitutional reform. Scottish interest in them was great, but they belong essentially to British history in general. The Scots Liberals were not so outstandingly innovative. True to their nineteenth-century principles, upheld stolidly against Rosebery, they regarded with suspicion ideas for an active welfare policy or for economic intervention. For no good reason, they did not attempt either to bring the lower classes into Parliament.

Their programme was in fact based on the unfinished business of the previous century. Though no longer troubled by internal conflicts, the SLA was not turning out a very creative body, and there was none of the policy-making fertility of the early 1890s. Thus the interest of Campbell-Bannerman in Scottish affairs, at a time when he was content to leave English matters to some colleagues, was a wasted asset. The unfinished business consisted in three major items—all else had either been settled by 1895 or had faded from public attention since.

Land reform was the one from which the greatest social benefit was expected.[16] Most Scots supported it. The Prime Minister and his Scottish Secretary were strongly for it. Sinclair declared that 'one need stood first: what Scotland wanted most was land for the Scots.' Every Liberal favoured it and had made it one of the big issues on the hustings. So had both the Labour MPs. Even some Unionists were sympathetic. They themselves had devised a policy for development of the Highlands and were ready for further action there, if with reservations about a similar programme in the Lowlands. Their old Scottish Secretary, Balfour of Burleigh himself, had come out in 1901 for a scheme of moderate land reform.

Liberal policy had two aims. One was to encourage smallholdings, a radical ideal for nearly a century. They were thought likely to erode landlord power, create a free peasantry and offer a better life to those in the cities who could not endure overcrowding and the risk of unemployment. The second aim was the taxation of land values, which had been part of the reform package since the 1880s. The purpose of this was to place the social burden firmly on those who were regarded as owning the ultimate source of wealth. It was also hoped that the central government's capacity for raising taxes would be greatly expanded, to the point where a surplus would be created that could be offset by reductions elsewhere or by expenditure on public works and welfare. Finally, radicals believed taxation would encourage economic development by forcing landlords to bring their property into profitable use in order to pay it. Land reform was thus seen as the answer to all sorts of problems, urban and social as well as agricultural.

Sinclair's plans were very radical indeed. His Small Landholders (Scotland) Bill really sought to extend the Crofters Acts to the whole country. It provided for the creation of new smallholdings, the enlargement of uneconomic ones, for security of tenure, fair rents and compensation for improvements. Despite wide public support for the Bill in Scotland, furious opposition came from the Unionists and from Rosebery; it also went too far for Haldane and some other Liberal Leaguers. Still, it passed the Commons with huge majorities in 1907, only to be thrown out by the Lords. The same thing happened the next year. Now suddenly, Sinclair's efforts were halted. Campbell-Bannerman died in July 1908 and was succeeded by the more circumspect Asquith, who promptly dropped the measure. Sinclair would not give up, but it took him three years to bring in a new Bill. This became law in 1912 and was known as the Pentland Act after the title he had meanwhile assumed. It was not as successful as he hoped. Up to 1914 only 500 new holdings were created and less than 300 existing ones enlarged. Even a longer period of operation proved that the demand for smallholdings had been overestimated and in 1933 the policy was quietly abandoned.

Sinclair had more luck, though no more ultimate effect, with his ideas for land taxation. The essential basis was a general scheme of valuation. In 1907 Sinclair brought in a Bill to establish this. It was also twice wrecked by the Lords. But because of its popularity the provisions were incorporated in Lloyd George's controversial Budget of 1909 and came into effect in 1911. Progress in their complex execution was slow, however. Finally it was over-taken by the war and the Unionists exacted the sacrifice of Scottish land valuation in the jobbery which accompanied the formation of the 1916 coalition. It was never re-introduced.

The resurgent land reform movement quickly lost its force, though faint echoes of it persist still, especially in the Highlands. There a Land League contested two seats in the 1918 election and the next year a Settlement Act provided for some redistribution of land in the region. But otherwise the results of this long agitation were curiously nugatory, both in the political benefit they brought the Liberals and in their impact on Scottish society. The party failed to recognise that the biggest problems were now irrevocably urban and could not be tackled on the assumption of a common interest between city and countryside.

The second issue was temperance reform.[17] A majority of Scots MPs had supported it for years without attempting to legislate. Of late conditions had become more propitious, for relentless propaganda had altered the climate of opinion. Once, temperance cranks had been derided, but now their views were almost the conventional wisdom. Since 1901 the country had possessed its own Scottish Prohibition Party, led by an excitable, evangelical Dundonian, Edwin Scrymgeour, who called for the manufacture and sale of alcohol to be banned everywhere in Scotland. The Liberal and Labour parties were all but unanimous in favour of some milder reform, while the Unionists had a temperance faction too. That left only the Conservatives, on this account often ridiculed as the Beerage, offering serious resistance.

It was still a surprise that the vague Liberal commitment turned into the 1913 Temperance Act, a Scottish measure not imitated elsewhere, mainly because it failed in its objects. It allowed local electorates to vote their areas dry, upon which all public houses there were to be shut without compensation. The polls could not be held till 1920, when only fourteen parishes, fifteen small burghs and twelve wards of burghs, including four in Glasgow, took the local option. This meagre success destroyed the point of the exercise. There was no use in a prohibition so limited in its coverage, which people wanting a drink could circumvent simply by crossing into a wet area. Consumption of alcohol had anyway fallen below the spectacular levels of the nineteenth century, and now social redemption was sought rather through economic measures. The movement's one later success was the defeat of Churchill by Scrymgeour in Dundee at the 1922 election. But it owed more to his socialist leanings than to the city's desire to go dry. He introduced a Bill for national prohibition with some support from the Scots Labour MPs, but it was laughed out of the Commons. Over the years the local bans were gradually repealed, till only a handful of places were without public houses. The country stuck to its hard-drinking habits and in 1976 a Licensing Act finally abolished local option. Its liberal reforms seemed to do more to cut down abuse than temperance had.

The third issue was Scottish Home Rule, on which again the Liberals had returned to office with only vague ideas, most favouring Home Rule all round.[18] Clearly it could only be taken up in conjunction with a measure for Ireland. It was thus a matter of great delicacy, and no fit subject for hasty legislation. Campbell-Bannerman thought it could be linked with the abolition of the House of Lords. He would have liked unicameral legislatures for the four nations of the United Kingdom, subject in imperial matters to a further single elected chamber for the whole. Wariness about disturbing the settled state of Ireland, as well as the certain opposition of the Lords, meant, however, that such large schemes were postponed. Some immediate progress could be made by restoring the Scottish grand committee. It started work again in 1907, this time surviving permanently.

In any case the system established in 1885 seemed to be working reasonably well: the record of reform in the twenty years since had been infinitely better than in the corresponding period before. But there were still difficulties. The lack of sympathy and time for Scottish issues in a predominantly English

Parliament was illustrated once more by the struggles over Sinclair's Land Bills. While the systems of tenure on each side of the border were quite different, the Lords made so bold as to reject any principle in his legislation not found in the English Bill going through at the same time. So the Small-holders Act for England passed quickly, but Sinclair's was delayed for three years. Complaints grew about the position of the Scottish Secretary too. He, head of the country's administration, appeared in practice to have little say on most government policies there. Not being a Secretary of State, he was in fact formally inferior to his colleagues. His essential role was as a co-ordin-ator, smoothing relations between Scotland and Westminster in matters aris-ing mainly from the legislation of other Ministers. His daily round was in the minutiae of government, dealing with complaints and injustices and guiding through Parliament minor amending measures or Scottish clauses tacked on to English Bills. The unsatisfactory split persisted between the regular Scottish Office powers and the duties of the administrative boards, while the Lord Advocate retained his independence: in 1906 the old dispute over the appoint-ment of judges recurred between Sinclair and the law officers.

Such problems gave Scottish Home Rule a continuing allure. The sentiment was shared with Liberals by the nascent Labour movement. It even engaged some young Unionists, such as Philip Kerr, destined for an eminent and varied career as Marquess of Lothian, though their leaders were now firmly opposed. The Government also needed convincing. Till 1912 the Scots MPs, who had set up a committee under Munro-Ferguson to promote the idea, made little headway here. But then, with plans afoot for Ireland and the Lords no longer capable of obstruction, they managed to extract an under-taking from Asquith. Thomas McKinnon Wood, just appointed Scottish Secretary in succession to Sinclair, lent support to a series of private member's Bills. But a new obstacle arose in the form of reservations by English MPs. Their doubts centred on the problems that would be created if, as seemed likely, there was now to be a gradual move towards a general scheme of devolution for all four constituent nations of the United Kingdom. England's size would unbalance the structure; in any case it appeared superfluous to establish a Parliament for her in addition to the imperial one. Churchill was asked by the Cabinet to report. His answer was regional devolution within England. But this was too elaborate and gained no support. Without enthusi-asm the Government allowed itself to be persuaded by the Scots MPs that Home Rule for Scotland and Ireland should proceed more or less in step. When Asquith rose in the Commons to introduce his Government of Ireland Bill in 1912 he told members that it was but the start of a comprehensive devolution policy. The Scottish Bill of 1913 provided for a Parliament of 140 legislating broadly for the existing responsibilities of the Scottish Office; in addition there would be a Scottish Privy Council and a Lord High Com-missioner to represent the Crown in Edinburgh. It passed second reading in the Commons in August 1914 but then had to be abandoned—somewhat to the Government's relief.

Talk of administrative reform was similarly inconclusive.[19] The system of specialist, autonomous boards, general in Britain during the previous century, survived now only in Scotland. In fact new ones were still being set up, compounding the problem of how to build an efficient central administration for the country. The whole subject was submitted to a Royal Commission in 1914. It advised that the boards' semi-independence should be ended and that they should be placed under the direct authority of the Scottish Secretary as normal departments of the civil service. But again nothing could be done till after the war.

The unfinished business which the radicals took up in 1906 was thus sadly incomplete. Land reform was carried yet did not have the expected effects—the decline of rural Scotland continued and urban problems were untouched. Till the last moment, and then it was too late, Home Rule proved far too complex an affair. But unlike in the rest of the United Kingdom the years were politically tranquil for Scotland, reminiscent of the long, peaceful stretches of the nineteenth century rather than of the turbulence which preceded and was immediately to follow.

The radicals slipped easily into the attitude that their old programme was adequate to the country's outstanding problems. Their own decadence was already evident. It accelerated after Asquith became Liberal leader. Unlike his predecessor, he was eager to restrain what he saw as their wilder schemes. All the more prominent soon fell from favour or otherwise disappeared. Asquith greatly disliked Sinclair, whom he described as having 'the brain of a rabbit and the temper of a pig.'[20] The Secretary did not survive the controversy over his Land Bills, for which his fervour won him too many enemies in the Government. Asquith, having made him a peer, coolly asked for his resignation in 1912 on the grounds that the holder of his post ought to be in the Commons. The same year Shaw went on to the Bench, Tweedmouth died insane and financial embarrassment obliged the Master of Elibank to leave public life. Even the most humane and progressive of the imperialists, Haldane, in the end fell victim to bigotry in the establishment: in 1915 he was unjustly hounded from office as a pro-German.

Scottish politics sank back into mediocrity. The new spirit of complacent moderation suited Asquith well, however. It was reflected in the Scottish Secretaries whom he chose. McKinnon Wood (1912–16) was an untalented conservative with an aversion to social legislation. His successor, Harold Tennant, owed his promotion to his brother-in-law, who happened to be Prime Minister, and was cast in the same Whiggish mould. The fall of the radicals was a great loss to Scotland. It cannot have been mere coincidence that their ascendancy covered one of the few periods, from 1880 to 1910, when—despite the lack of many permanent achievements—parliamentary democracy worked really quite well there, when Scottish leaders were lively and creative and Scottish issues excited wide interest. The contrast with the periods of apathy and dullness before and afterwards is eloquent.

Not that such failings greatly affected the Scots' loyalty to their governing party. John Buchan used these terms to describe it in 1911:

Its dogmas were so completely taken for granted that their presentation partook less of argument than of tribal incantation. Mr Gladstone had given it an aura

of earnest morality so that its platforms were also pulpits and its harangues had
the weight of sermons. Its members seemed to assume that their opponents
must be lacking either in morals or in mind. The Tories were the 'stupid' party:
Liberals alone understood and sympathised with the poor; a working man who
was not a Liberal was inaccessible to reason, or morally corrupt, or intimidated
by laird or employer. I remember a lady summing up the attitude thus: 'Tories
may think they are better born, but Liberals know they are born better'.[21]

The obverse of such moral certainty was smug complacency. New forces
appeared elsewhere in Britain, often with great violence, but from Scotland
they looked too remote to require a political response. One can trace here
the consequence of the traditionalist victory among the Liberals after 1900.
In England the social situation demanded fresh thinking from all parties, and
increasingly it moved in collectivist directions. In Scotland the strains were
less visible, but the Liberals would have done well to be more sensitive and
observant. When tensions emerged, the party paid dear for clinging to an
outworn ideology.

For the moment the opposition in Scotland was ill-placed to exploit this
weakness. The Unionists' position had not improved at all. In the January
1910 election they won eleven seats on less than 40 per cent of the poll. In
December there was a small rise in their percentage of votes but no net gain
of seats.[22] It did not go unnoticed how feeble Scottish Unionism had become
compared with English Toryism, which revived greatly in 1910. The old Scots
Conservatives were often regarded as an anglicised party, and there was a
danger that this stigma would be attached to their successors. It was decided
therefore to give them for the first time a leadership of their own. The form
was one long employed by the Liberals—a Scottish whip at Westminster with
responsibility also for constituency organisation in Scotland. Sir George
Younger, MP for the Ayr Burghs, took up the post in 1911.

At the same time negotiations started again for a formal merger of the
Unionists and Conservatives, a matter which had been pursued desultorily
for some years. Though the two parties were practically identical by now, the
talks were surprisingly protracted. They took seven months longer than the
corresponding English ones, being finally concluded in December 1912. The
results were also different. In the South it was the Conservatives who dominated with the Unionists as a decayed appendage. But in Scotland, Conservative was a label with a regrettable past and, so far as could be told, an
unpromising future. The Scottish Right continued to draw its main strength
from those groups which had deserted the Liberals in 1886. Thus it was
appropriate for the combined party to assume the name of Unionist. The
importance of repudiating the Conservative tradition was appreciated by
Austen Chamberlain, who took some interest in Scottish party organisation
and who later wrote: 'Our only chance of winning Scotland is to change the
issue on which Scotsmen vote. As long as it is the land, the landlords and the
rest of the radical programme we shall be beaten.'[23]

Unionists were not, however, prepared to countenance reform in other
spheres of Scottish political life. Their small band of MPs vehemently opposed

Home Rule, with Sir Henry Craik, a university member, in the forefront. He issued dire warnings to the country against seeking devolution by mere analogy with Ireland. He claimed that Scotland would degenerate into a provincial backwater, that she was too heterogeneous to sustain a stable political structure of her own and that in the end she would be taken over by the Clydeside proletariat. At least some of this was blind prejudice, reinforced by the fact that Scottish Home Rule was so widely favoured on the Left and above all by disdain for Irish aspirations. In the great crisis which developed over Ireland before the First World War there were many Scots who felt an emotional sympathy with Unionist support for Ulster. The temper of the nation was still firmly Protestant. And though the Churches this time held themselves aloof on the question, that temper was stiffened by the militant Orangemen in Glasgow and elsewhere often closely linked with the Unionist party. But the tensions which racked other areas and institutions of the United Kingdom with such disturbing force did not greatly trouble Scotland. The extremists of Orange and Green certainly made their views known. But Ireland was not now an issue which the weakened Unionists could use to win over large new blocs of voters.

Another tide of social discontent, the movement for women's suffrage, also left the country relatively unmoved.[24] In Scotland it had very worthy antecedents. Duncan McLaren's wife, Priscilla Bright, had formed a suffrage society in the capital as long ago as 1867. Chrystal Mcmillan, who in 1892 became the first of her sex to matriculate at Edinburgh University, was one of the most active in the cause about the turn of the century. As an intellectual, respectable, professional woman, she was typical of the Scottish school of feminism. There were Scots among the militants in the South, but at home the suffragettes came from the middle-class establishment and were prepared to work within it. They had no taste for vulgar antics designed to embarrass their own Liberal Government. In general Scottish society remained a conservative one where women were expected to know their place.

Systematic efforts began in 1906 with the formation of a Scottish Federation of Women's Suffrage Societies under Dr Elsie Inglis. At first it pursued its aims strictly through peaceful propaganda and the lobbying of MPs. Their response was never encouraging but only after repeated rebuffs did the Scottish movement turn to more unsavoury tactics. Churchill's and Asquith's public meetings were frequently interrupted and the latter was once assaulted by a mob of women near Bannockburn. But when real violence occurred it was usually imported from outside. Militancy was not to the taste of the native suffragettes. Their character was revealed by the outbreak of war, at which they immediately relapsed into good works. The suffrage societies used their funds to finance hospital units on the Eastern Front, where Dr Inglis directed matters in person. She led a heroic existence and died a moving death.

The United Kingdom's third social upheaval of these years, the rise of the Labour movement, likewise touched Scotland little.[25] Till 1914 she was distinguished by the feebleness of both her trade unions and her socialist parties. The forces militating against them were as strong after 1900 as before—the ascendancy of Scots radicalism, and the failure to break down either the religious allegiances which kept many Protestant workers Unionist or the firm paternalist authority of the bourgeoisie in the West, Scotland's natural arena for labour activity. The movement was also divided within itself. Many on the Scottish Left saw themselves simply as very radical Liberals, and had no interest in an independent political party. But there were others, more doctrinaire, aiming at a clean break with Liberalism.

These men were not downcast by their lack of progress. In a parallel but different process to that in England, they resolved to set up in co-operation with the unions a proper Labour party. Thus the Scottish Workers' Representation Committee was born in 1900. The organisers got the support of the Scottish Trades Union Congress (founded in 1897), which on its industrial side was, however, a small, weak body. It received a more militant impulse from the adhesion of often socialist-dominated trades councils, which were excluded from the TUC. Inside the SWRC large concessions were made to the views of moderate union leaders. But overall it was not they but the committed socialists who ran it. This contrasted with the position in England, where the unions were the guiding spirits of the Labour Representation Committee, formed a few weeks after its Scottish counterpart. There were corresponding divergences of policy between the two. While the LRC was ready to co-operate with existing parties, the SWRC was not. This suited the anti-collectivist Scots Liberals, till in 1903 their English colleagues concluded an electoral pact with the LRC.[26]

The Scots were now torn between loyalty to party policy and hostility to the militant little band of socialists they faced at home. There were, however, seats where a Labour man had been adopted early and where as yet no Liberal was selected. In these few cases the Scottish party swallowed its pride and offered a pact. But the overtures were rebuffed. The SLA then voted to oppose all socialist candidates, though eventually the one in Dundee was excepted. Labour's resulting failure in 1906 to match in Scotland the scale of its success in the South convinced the Liberals that they had nothing to gain by accommodation, and their antipathy continued.[27]

Few shared Campbell-Bannerman's fears that Labour would become a drain on the party's progressive wing or his belief that co-operation was therefore desirable. Scots Liberals saw that they had scored a great triumph and that they owed the socialists nothing for it. In the new Parliament they denounced Labour with an unremitting vehemence which in English politics was rivalled only by the Conservatives. This fervour did not represent a lapse into reaction for the party's radicalism was unimpaired, if by now slightly antiquated. There was something of a modernising impulse to extend it into social welfare, but a total commitment would have smacked too much of Roseberian Efficiency. Still, when Churchill was elected for Dundee in 1908, Scottish Liberalism gained an advocate in this field far in advance of anyone in the Labour party. On Campbell-Bannerman's death the same year, he was succeeded in the Stirling Burghs by Arthur Ponsonby, who yielded to none in his calls for state action to correct inequality. By 1913 he was reckoned the leader of a like-minded 'gang', though it consisted of only five Scots MPs.

The socialists made some attempt to improve their position. The SWRC was merged with the more effective LRC in 1909. Labour won West Fife, its third parliamentary seat, in the General Election of December 1910, though otherwise its performance at the polls that year was dismal: Liberal strength still hemmed it in on every side. This weakness left room for unconventional political action. In the pre-war period young agitators such as James Maxton and John Maclean first made a name for themselves. Syndicalism, a subversive movement which had won support in Europe and North America, came to Scotland too and found adherents among miners and engineering workers. Under the slogans of industrial democracy and the general strike it fomented labour disputes and even violence.

But the Liberal leadership was careful not to antagonise the working class. During the great railway strike of 1911, for example, the soldiers sent into several English cities to maintain order sometimes clashed bloodily with workers. Pentland, however, steadfastly refused to call troops to Glasgow. The Scots Liberals could be comforted by the fact that a conservative frame of mind ruled their own proletariat. The trade unions had little time for socialist militancy and were mainly concerned to uphold craftsmen's privileges and restrictive practices.

Here, as for the whole country, the decisive turning point was the First World War. Scotland had been virtually immune to the general social disturbances in Britain before 1914. She was characterised by stability, tranquillity, almost universal Liberalism. Afterwards came unrest, dissolution and the rise of bitter class politics. But this is a contrast too sharply drawn. One can see a dreadful irony about the position of the Scots radicals at this point—since attaining power eight years before they had only proved their inadequacy to deal with the needs of a new century. The one thing lacking was for the country to realise and articulate the need for political renewal. War gave the impetus to this.

It was not wholly the radicals' fault that their reforms had proceeded sluggishly and achieved little. But this failing was painfully exposed by the bewildering acceleration of change in wartime. Economic conditions were transformed.[28] Even before 1914 Scotland's position was becoming less favourable, though she remained one of Britain's great centres of heavy industry. For the war effort her economy was, however, grossly over-expanded and suffered with special harshness when peace produced a slump. Then it became oppressively obvious that she was far too dependent on heavy industry, because new demand was concentrated in consumer goods. She was defeated by foreign competition in her traditional products and built up little capacity in the alternatives. War brought other traumatic disruptions of this conservative society. Rural workers and women were hauled into unfamiliar industrial jobs. Under official goading both management and labour had to adopt unpopular new working methods. Prices rose rapidly. So did rents, exerting pressure on an already difficult housing market. This showed up how for many years social conditions had been improving much more slowly than in England. Liberal welfare measures had been far too modest to remedy the appalling distress caused by poverty and bad housing.

There was of course social advance, especially in the emancipation of women through their war work. But the setbacks outweighed the gains and after 1918 the country was crippled by the twin evils of high unemployment and heavy emigration. More and more Scots demanded a complete new set of social and economic initiatives with the intervention of central government as the only agency powerful enough to carry them through. Their Liberal party, which had never pretended to any long-term aims for society, was ill-placed to respond.

Its gradualist, idealistic, libertarian philosophy of reform was discredited all the more by the fact that Liberal Ministers promptly abandoned it with the outbreak of hostilities—thereafter, indeed, they acted in precisely the opposite spirit. The nation's leaders now had only one aim: the efficient prosecution of the struggle against Germany. Sectional interests had to be overriden and cajoled, even coerced, if they resisted. A people which placed individualist values above all found itself, with the active connivance of its own political establishment, subject to the levelling, bureaucratic apparatus of a modern state engaged in total war. The workers, whom this struck most forcibly, had no effective channel of opposition—despite the Liberals' reforming interests they still showed a stubborn reluctance to bring working men into the Commons, as had happened on a considerable scale in England. Only when the whole proletariat was at last enfranchised in 1918 did its mass discontent find legitimate political expression. Liberals could then make no convincing claim to represent the radical libertarianism which might have prevented the ferment being directed into socialist channels.

A final illustration of how the war changed Scotland was the dissipation of her pacifism. It had been a potent radical rallying cry since the 1850s. In Midlothian, Gladstone spoke for almost the whole nation when he damned aggression on foreign peoples as an affront to God and man. By the Boer war feelings had changed. It appalled many Scots. But others, of all classes and especially in the West, were swept away by strident nationalism. In 1914 the old sentiment still survived, but the balance against it had tilted further.

Pacifism remained stronger in Scotland than elsewhere in Britain. This was especially true of the Labour movement, where war was opposed by Keir Hardie and Ramsay MacDonald. The Liberals too had a peace faction led by Ponsonby. But peace candidates standing in one or two by-elections fared poorly. In general, pacifists spent the war years in disgrace, overwhelmed by the jingoism which seized the country in 1914. In fact Scotland proved one of the best recruiting grounds and stoically took very heavy casualties in the fighting. For the vast majority, then, pacifism was dead as a guiding political principle. That was a severe blow to the coherence of the radical corpus of ideals.

But the outbreak of war produced a rapid deterioration in relations between governors and governed in Scotland, arousing there stronger opposition to authority than anywhere else in Great Britain.[29] The Ministry intervened promptly to control key sectors of industry, with the fervent support of a ruling class in the West long accustomed to collectivist public policy. It now started with relish to lay the foundations of a corporate state. Scottish capitalists, previously content to mind their own business, moved into national politics in force. The production effort in Scotland was organised by the Glasgow industrialist, William Weir. He gave his own war profits to charity, but was ruthless and uncompromising in his insistence that employers' interests should be paramount for the duration. To him this meant ideally a wage freeze, an end to restrictive practices and the direction of labour, on the argument that the state must assume the disciplinary function in industry because the unions had made skilled men uncontrollable. Glasgow paternalism was thus extended with a vengeance.

Its proponents became powerful in London too. Weir reached the Cabinet as Air Minister in 1918. Meanwhile three Clyde shipping magnates—Andrew Weir, later Lord Inverforth, Sir John, later Lord, Maclay, and James Mackay, Lord Inchcape—had all been making vital contributions to the war effort in various official capacities. The Edinburgh family of Geddes more or less took over servicing the armed forces, with Auckland in charge of conscription and his brother Eric directing transport, while their sister Mona Chalmers-Watson was first controller of the Women's Auxiliary Army Corps.

Opposition was fostered by the obscure socialist agitators who had worked away unavailingly before 1914, but who were now aided by a unique constellation of forces which made Clydeside especially a crucible of political change. Here they rapidly extended their influence and taught many workers to regard their Liberal leaders as enemies.[30]

The Scottish economy had difficulty in moving quickly to a war footing and 1915 saw recurrent unofficial strikes on the Clyde, met with repression by the inflexible McKinnon Wood. The unions, playing a conciliatory role, lost the confidence of their members. In such inauspicious circumstances the Government launched a campaign to raise war production. It was embodied in the Munitions Act—at that time munitions denoted every kind of military supply from boots to bombs, so that the law's application to industry was very wide. One of the innovations enforced was dilution, the use of unskilled labour in shops so far closed to it. Skilled men, a majority of the Glasgow workforce, had no objection to this as part of the war effort so long as they could be sure that demarcations would be restored in peacetime: their call was thus for workers' control of dilution. The Act also banned strikes in munitions companies, and a number of men were imprisoned as the disputes continued. That brought the Clyde Workers' Committee to prominence. It had been formed by a group of shop stewards, three of them destined to be MPs—David Kirkwood and John Muir for Labour and William Gallacher as a Communist. They set out to organise the agitation through a chain of unofficial shop committees in direct contact with the workers, filling a communications gap which the bureaucratic union structure disregarded.

But the CWC had ambitions beyond the merely industrial. A statement of aims issued in January 1916 was really Scotland's first important socialist manifesto. It promised to 'organise the workers on a class basis and to maintain the class struggle until the overthrow of the wages system, the freedom of the workers and the establishment of industrial democracy have been obtained.' But that sentiment did not yet correspond to the aspirations of the rank and file, whose grievances were over conditions in their factories rather than the organisation of society.[31]

Still, the troubles were intensifying. Late in 1915 there was a successful rent strike. Lloyd George was howled down when he came to Glasgow at Christmas trying to win the workers for dilution. As a result, *Forward*, the leading socialist newspaper in Scotland, was suppressed. Resentment grew further when conscription was introduced in January 1916. Serious efforts by the Government to take the situation in hand were now urgent. An official committee was set up to arbitrate in disputes over dilution, giving the men in practice much of what they hoped from workers' control of it. Their good intentions established, the authorities next moved against the militants. Three were imprisoned and ten others deported from Clydeside. The CWC then virtually ceased to function. Its importance lay not in its own limited activities, but in the way these were developed and diffused (see chapter 7 below).

The effects of the labour troubles on Scotland were profound. The working class learned the value of solidarity, which replaced the individualistic traditions whose defence had been the object of the strikers in 1915, if not of the CWC. This prepared the ground for the shift among Scots workers away from Liberal values. It gave the unions an attraction they had never enjoyed, and through it the Labour movement began, despite its divisions, to flourish. It sharpened the resentment caused by the Government's misreading of the protests as subversive, even revolutionary, rather than mainly industrial. Repression alienated people with genuine grievances and raised the standing of the militants. These were now able to define the terms of political debate among workers, to whom the vocabulary of class struggle became familiar. In a country used to disputing in the language of Burns or the Bible, it was a fatal blow to the old national ethos and the political allegiance which it underpinned.

Capital and labour had both espoused new philosophies grounded in collectivism. Yet they were brought into a sharp antagonism which persists in Scotland even today. Capital's aims in the new era were in no sense socialist. It sought a continuance of the state support and regulation of wartime, especially in cartels, to maintain traditional industries during the long recession which followed, with the workers kept firmly in order. They, threatened with unemployment, were equally conservative; at the same time, their new strength made them unwilling to co-operate with the capitalists. For the first time in its history, Glasgow resisted change instead of innovating and diversifying to meet it. That was the start of an inexorable economic decline.

There had meanwhile been far-reaching developments at the summit of politics. Asquith's formation of an all-party coalition in 1915 failed to still the discontent with his conduct of the war. At the end of 1916 Lloyd George staged a coup which ejected him from the premiership. That completed the rout of the Scottish Liberal elite. Only one transferred his allegiance to the new Prime Minister. This was the Lord Advocate, Robert Munro, now promoted to Scottish Secretary—the first time that in filling the office the Liberals had had recourse to Parliament House. A majority of Scots Liberal MPs, together with the SLA, remained loyal to Asquith when he went into opposition, partly because the Ministry was dominated by Tories and partly because of Lloyd George's very un-Scottish brand of Liberalism. The split was formalised by a vote of censure against the Government in May 1918. On the division twenty-two Scots Liberals stood by their old leader while seventeen supported Lloyd George. In the Liberal party as a whole it is generally reckoned that about 100 were for Asquith and 150 for the Prime Minister.

Within six months the war was over and a fresh General Election followed at once. It was held under a reformed franchise which extended the vote to all adult males and to most women. That created a working-class majority in many constituencies. A redistribution of seats shifted the political weight of the country into the Clyde Valley, which had turned most decisively against the existing order. The startling new tendencies of which all this gave evidence in Scotland were, however, obscured by the confusion of the time. People were asked not to vote for party but to confirm the coalition in office. As a guide for voters, an endorsement, nicknamed the coupon, was issued to candidates prepared to back the Government. It was agreed that the Liberal wing of the coalition should be given a certain number of seats and a share of these was allocated to Scotland—necessarily, it was reckoned, if she were not to be lost to the Opposition. But Sir George Younger, the Unionist whip, was put in charge of the coupon's detailed distribution. There were some odd manoeuvrings. In one case the sitting Coalition Liberal MP was refused it in favour of a new Unionist candidate. Yet, perversely, it was granted elsewhere to the uncommitted or even to adherents of Asquith. In the event, though, nearly all Unionists in Scotland got the coupon while most Liberals did not. In a country both Liberal and loyal it made for much perplexity.[32]

But the election produced three indisputable results. First, there was the triumph of the coalition, which took 52 per cent of the votes and fifty-seven seats out of seventy-four. Inside it, the Scots Lloyd George Liberals were in a minority to the Unionists, who secured 31 per cent and twenty-nine seats. Secondly, there was the rise of Labour to be a major party in Scotland. Its vote climbed from insignificance in 1910 to 29 per cent, though the vagaries of the electoral system gave it only eight MPs. Thirdly, there was the rejection of the pre-war Liberal establishment, as represented by Asquith, the existing Scottish parliamentary party and the SLA. Asquith himself failed to hold East Fife, and anti-coalition Liberals won only eight seats.

Even taken as a whole, the Liberals suffered a great reverse. Their share of the poll sank from 54 per cent in 1910 to 37 per cent, about three-fifths of it being secured by coalition candidates. With only thirty-seven seats in all— the worst performance since 1900—the party had been dealt a heavy blow, but not yet a mortal one. It still accounted for exactly half the country's parliamentary representation, and thus remained her biggest political force. The results also certainly understated the true level of Liberal strength. Both the Asquith and Lloyd George factions regarded themselves as members of the one, temporarily divided body. And because of the erratic distribution of the coupon, many Liberals wanting to support the coalition had no choice but to vote Unionist.

But there were real points of Liberal weakness. Lloyd George's main strength lay outside the West, where he left the Unionists to spearhead the Government's attack. This caused the virtual disappearance of Clydeside Liberalism, a somewhat fugitive phenomenon ever since 1886. In fifteen western seats the party was unable to put up a candidate of any kidney or else came a poor third to the Unionists and Labour. From now on these two were the only real contenders for power in this key to political dominance of the country. More generally, the Liberals could no longer claim to be the unique and exclusive agents of Scotland's political will. The people's experience of unity and struggle during the war made party distinctions look unimportant. Lloyd George skilfully exploited this feeling and promised a golden age of welfare to reward the nation for its exertions. Most Scots happily subscribed to that. If the traditional-minded still looked to Asquith, he could offer no distinctive Liberal vision, only the pursuit of an old feud.

Yet within weeks the Government was faced with what it saw as a major crisis in Scotland. All bourgeois Europe was shaken by the events in Russia. In early 1919 there were people prepared to entertain the notion that Glasgow was to be the centre of a British Revolution. A subversive-looking Scottish Workers' Committee, descendant of the CWC, was flourishing. The Bolsheviks had appointed the local agitator, John Maclean, as their consul in Britain. Some romantic members of the Glasgow trades council wanted to turn it into a soviet. But behind the posturing, the strength of the Clydeside socialists still lay in their skill at organising industrial disputes. With the end of war production, workers grew anxious about their jobs and saw shorter hours as a way of fending off unemployment. In the campaign to cut the working week there was some rivalry between the regular unions, under the trades council president, Emanuel Shinwell, and the old CWC group under Gallacher. But they all united on the demand for a 40-hour week, and in support of it workers in Glasgow and Edinburgh went on strike from 27 January, 1919.

The Scottish Secretary became highly excited over all this. When by the second day of the strike 70,000 men were out, Munro had already got Cabinet consent to a hard line. The chance for a show of strength came on 31 January as a large crowd gathered on legitimate business in George Square, Glasgow. The police tried roughly to keep it under control and a riot broke out, with workers advancing under the red flag into uninhibited fights with the forces of order. The Cabinet was sitting in London and, the minute records, 'the Secretary for Scotland said that in his opinion it was more clear than ever that it was a misnomer to call the situation in Glasgow a strike—it was a Bolshevist rising.'[33] That day 12,000 troops were sent in and tanks rolled through the city's streets. The strike leaders, who had no interest in violence, were horrified. Gallacher, Shinwell and Kirkwood were nonetheless arrested. From then the strike began to collapse and by 11 February it was all over. Ministers had once more imputed political motives to essentially industrial demonstrations. They furthered the political expression of class differences which started in wartime, and opened wider the cleavage between the workers and the political establishment. Remaining links were severed: the last went with the resignation from the Cabinet in 1920 of George Barnes, MP for the Gorbals and only survivor of the coalition Labourites. The Government continued to fear labour more than anything else.

For about the deeper problems of the economy little could be done. Once war production had ended and a burst of investment to repair the losses was over, every major industry faced severe recession in 1921 and 1922. The Scottish capitalists, many of whom had stayed on in official posts, responded in two ways. One was to continue the co-operation of government and business, now with the aim of rationalising and deliberately sustaining economic activity. Weir was to the fore in creating cartels or corporations to run, among other sectors, electricity, shipping and railways. There was also a strong desire to return to the pre-war practice of strict economy in finance. Inverforth and Sir Auckland Geddes helped to disengage the state from its many contracts with industry. Under Sir Robert Horne, MP for Hillhead, who rose rapidly to become Chancellor of the Exchequer, a concerted effort at retrenchment was made. He entrusted it to Sir Eric Geddes, who chaired a committee trying to reduce expenditure to 1914 levels. The result was the infamous 'Geddes axe' which imposed painful cuts but failed in its basic purpose.

Amid all this the pre-war Liberal programme for Scotland was nearly lost from view. The one item outstanding was Home Rule. It was now taken up again, though in desultory fashion. A Speaker's Conference considered it in 1920 and once more recommended a Scottish Parliament. But in the post-war crisis people saw the problems as economic rather than constitutional. The discussion aroused little public interest and the Ministry ignored the findings. Greater administrative devolution began to replace Home Rule as a practical goal. A flurry of activity from the Scottish Office was, however, hindered by its creaking, old-fashioned structure. As a step in re-organisation, a Health department was set up inside it under a junior Minister. The first, John Pratt, MP for Cathcart, at last repaired the omission of the 1845 Poor Law and, in the face of widespread hardship, gave relief to the able-bodied unemployed.

The modern system of public sector housing was also now inaugurated. A Royal Commission, appointed by McKinnon Wood but reporting only in 1917, revealed that large numbers of Scots lived in appalling circumstances. Its conclusion was revolutionary: 'the state must at once take steps to make good the housing shortage and improve housing conditions, and this can only be done by or through the machinery of the public authorities.' That was accepted. Soon the Local Government Board acquired powers to enforce minimum standards. The Housing Act (1919) brought in subsidies for construction from central government to the local councils.[34]

Munro's greatest work was the Education Act (1918) which, among other things, at last granted state finance to Catholic schools. It was most important for Scotland's social evolution, in being the biggest single step towards peaceful assimilation of the Irish minority. Since 1872 Catholics had run separate schools. They were then taxed twice, through the rates for the national system, and through voluntary contributions for their own. Their poverty starved such schools of resources. Munro described them thus:

> generally speaking, inferior as regards building and equipment, their teachers . . . zealous but poorly paid, their provision of secondary schools . . . totally inadequate and the educational outlook of the mass of their children . . . unduly narrowing.[35]

Ownership of them was now transferred to the education authorities, which were empowered to build new Catholic schools; to all, however, only teachers acceptable to the church might be appointed. The Act was a sort of concordat, making compatible the aims of Catholic education and good education through a denominational system financed by the state. Catholics could henceforth rise in life without losing their identity. Soon the despised Irish proletariat was producing a middle class, especially in the teaching, legal and medical professions. The community as a whole acquired a stake in society.

Any support thus won for the Government was, however, dissipated by Lloyd George's policy in Ireland. One of his party's mainstays in Scotland in the period of instability since 1886 had been the Catholic vote.[36] It usually clung to Liberalism as the guarantor of eventual Irish Home Rule; the spread of socialism in the working class was also thus checked. Sinn Fein's victory in Ireland at the 1918 election broke the link. Even worse, Liberal Ministers now attempted there a savage coercion. In turning to Labour, Catholics could both reject that and assert their proletarian identity. Nor did this put Protestant workers off, for to the party's good fortune it had avoided any particular religious association.

The Asquithians failed to exploit similarly their opposition status. At first the most devout wish of the divided Scots Liberals was a reunion, and the Master of Elibank tried without success to reconcile Asquith and Lloyd George in 1918. After that the two groups drifted further apart. Asquith's faction in Parliament, led in his absence by Donald Maclean, MP for South Midlothian and Peebles, took an aggressive attitude towards the Ministry. It persuaded five members who had got the coupon in 1918 to cross the floor. And it seemed to make a big breakthrough in 1920 when at the dramatic Paisley by-election Asquith returned to the Commons.[37] But he had little new inspiration to offer. His Paisley speeches were full of the compromises of a tired political creed needing above all to appease Unionists for the sake of their anti-Labour votes. If Asquith relied on a broad centre-right coalition at local level, he helped to wreck a similar re-alignment at national level. His victory appeared to open up a new future for independent Liberalism. It destroyed Lloyd George's hopes of reuniting the two party factions under his own leadership and led quickly to the expulsion of his followers from the Scottish Liberal Federation (as the old SLA had been known since 1918). Personal rivalry thus obscured the fact that all three non-Labour parties were coming to rely on variations of the same constituency—an alliance of county voters and the urban middle class. By struggling to build up their individual coalitions of voters within these sections, they only created artificial squabbles which ruined the possibility of unity among themselves.

It was again Labour that benefited. More workers were won over to it as a result of the economic crisis. It possessed by far the most active local associations and in Glasgow an electoral machine of high efficiency was built by Patrick Dollan. Many of the wartime agitators had gone into regular politics, a few in the Communist party but most in the Independent Labour Party. This also attracted the support of middle-class intellectuals. By 1923 Labour was able to win such a prestigious convert as Haldane, who with numerous others of progressive views now saw little future for the old parties. He himself judged the growth of Labour to be the best way of restoring social cohesion—a notion with an obvious appeal to other Scots Liberals. In 1918 Scotland's parliamentary Labour party had been dominated by pedestrian trade unionists, typified by its leader William Adamson, the miner MP for West Fife. Developments since had transformed the movement into the country's liveliest political force.

As the time for a General Election approached the outlook was most unclear. The coalition was losing the allegiance of the English Conservatives, but not of the Scots Unionists. They and the local Lloyd George Liberals had grown attached to one another. In Scottish terms, after all, their alliance merely undid the work of 1886, and the more easily for the departure from the parent Liberalism of its most radical elements. Sir William Younger, now chairman of the Conservatives, said in 1919 that he 'personally entertained the hope that the present coalition would form the foundation for a permanently fused party.'

Thus when in October 1922 the majority of the parliamentary Conservative party decided at the Carlton Club, London, to end the arrangement with Lloyd George, it was joined by just seven Scots Unionists, while eighteen voted to carry on.[38] The decision ran counter to the advice of the man who was to be the next Tory Prime Minister, Andrew Bonar Law, MP for Glasgow Central. He feared that the construction of a bourgeois bloc would strengthen Labour by making it the sole alternative, and Younger had come round to supporting him. But the Scots were not deterred. They avoided a repudiation of Lloyd George and told Bonar Law they would only follow him if he left alone their alliance with the National Liberals, as their partners now called themselves. Thus Unionists still supported a Liberal candidate in twenty-seven seats, and Liberals a Unionist in eighteen. So in most Scottish constituencies there persisted something like the co-operation produced by the coupon in 1918, and the coalition was in effect maintained.

Relations between the two Liberal factions in the run-up to the election were ambiguous. In strength there was little to choose between them. Asquith had a numerical majority of Liberals on his side, but the local associations which had opted for Lloyd George in 1918 were well supplied with funds from him. After the Paisley by-election the quarrels grew fiercer. The president of the SLF was deposed for his coalitionist sympathies. He then defected to build up National Liberal organisations, which by the election were widespread. As the polls approached it seemed unwise, however, to split the party beyond all hope of reconciliation. In the end the Asquithians fielded forty-eight candidates to the National Liberals' thirty-three, but they fought each other in only eighteen seats.

In England the 1922 General Election was a Conservative triumph. But in Scotland there was a big swing to the Left. The two coalition partners of the previous Parliament retained only twenty-seven seats, while Labour took over as the largest single party with twenty-nine. The ILP could claim eighteen of these. The Asquithians, with sixteen seats, overhauled the National Liberals, who held only twelve. Unionist representation was almost halved to fifteen seats. The Communists made their first gain at Motherwell and in Dundee Edwin Scrymgeour, the radical Prohibition candidate, spectacularly succeeded in unseating Churchill, a National Liberal. Labour's share of the poll rose three per cent on a much larger turnout. The Unionist vote fell from 30 per cent to 25 per cent. Asquithians secured 21 per cent against the National Liberals' 18 per cent. With a combined vote of 39 per cent, an actual increase of 2 per cent on 1918, the Liberals were still Scotland's biggest political movement.

There was a clear pattern to the results. It showed massive Labour gains in industrial Scotland. This was at its most remarkable in Glasgow where Labour's share of the fifteen seats rose from two to ten. The trend brought a corresponding disaster for the National Liberals who now held just two urban seats, among which, except on Clydeside, they had previously been quite strong. With Churchill gone, their only MP of real ability was Archibald Sinclair, newly elected for Caithness and Sutherland. The Liberals lost Donald Maclean, while Asquith held Paisley against a fierce Labour challenge by 300 votes. In general his party gained from the Right but yielded ground to Labour. As for the Unionists, the outcome emphasised their urban middle-class side: only three of their remaining seats were rural. The result in Scotland was altogether strikingly different from that in the rest of Britain. Asquith spoke of a 'sullen anti-bourgeois feeling which is sweeping like a tidal wave over the whole West of Scotland.'[39] Certainly the events of the last four years had united the workers more solidly with Labour, and it was now able to reap a fuller benefit from the enfranchisement of 1918. It was also helped by the collapse of the coalition at the national level and the consequent removal of a patriotic counterweight to class feeling.

For Scotland the election result in the United Kingdom as a whole was unsatisfactory. Only a small section of her opinion favoured the diehard Tory pattern imposed on government by Bonar Law. It was exemplified by the large quota of obscure peers in his Cabinet. They included Viscount Novar, otherwise Ronald Munro-Ferguson in his final incarnation as a Unionist Scottish Secretary. The Ministry was so weak in Scotland that it had to suspend the grand committee: even the extra fifteen English MPs could not produce a majority there.

The most spectacular event of the new Parliament was the arrival of the Clydeside ILP contingent, including several leaders of the wartime agitations. Seeing themselves as harbingers of social revolution, they were bent on shocking the complacent Commons with a sustained display of rowdiness. A notorious incident occurred in June 1923 when Maxton, irate over cuts in Scottish health spending, called those who would vote for them murderers. In the ensuing uproar several Clydesiders were expelled from the chamber. But from a mere faction these efforts had few results. Its main achievement was to swing the choice of a new Labour leader in favour of Ramsay Mac-Donald, an action afterwards rued. Still, it made up in pugnacity what it lacked in consequence, and this satisfied its constituency. The Clydesiders were anyway elected not only for their socialism but also, perhaps rather, for their moral fervour. They were the heirs of the Scottish school of fighting radicalism.

In other ways the body of Scots MPs returned in 1922 was remarkably reminiscent of its Victorian predecessors. The county interest was represented in the National Liberals, the Unionists were bourgeois in the strict sense of the term, while the Asquith Liberals were a much reduced microcosm of the old party. All the components of traditional Liberalism lived on, but divided into three parties rather than united in one. They were in fact complementary. Left to themselves, their logical course would have been to merge in a broad anti-socialist coalition. Even Younger had returned to the view that 'if the parties in the North have any sense they will make a mutual arrangement with regard to seats at the next General Election.'[40] But the patterns of metropolitan politics now excluded any such ingenuity. Instead, the dividing lines were redrawn on an earlier pattern. Baldwin, succeeding Bonar Law in 1923, reconciled the coalitionist Unionists. When he suddenly espoused protectionism and went to the country on it, the two Liberal factions were reunited against him.

The election followed in the winter of 1923. Bonar Law's economic policy of retrenchment had worked to the disadvantage of a Scotland gripped by recession. This favoured Labour, which made further important gains in the central belt. It took thirty-four seats and 36 per cent of the vote. The Liberals got only 28 per cent, a loss of 11 per cent. Their last Glasgow MP fell and the remaining ones were concentrated in the northern counties, Edinburgh being the one city where considerable strength persisted. The Unionists, with 31 per cent of the poll, were unlucky to win only sixteen seats.

Ramsay MacDonald now took office with a minority Labour Government. It was, as soon became clear, intimidated by its lack of a majority and by the novel, awesome responsibilities of power. It was so inexperienced that Haldane had to be drafted in as Lord Chancellor, while in Scotland the independent (in reality Unionist) Hugh Macmillan became Lord Advocate. In disregard of the eager army of Left-wingers available, the Scottish Secretaryship went to safe, dull William Adamson. The sole Clydesider given Cabinet office was John Wheatley as Minister of Health. He produced this Government's one important reforming measure, a Housing Act. It replaced that of 1919, which had come to grief through its open-ended subsidies to local authorities. Wheatley found the means of reconciling the need for public economy with the demands of a concerted effort at tackling the shortage of homes. Suspended building programmes could resume, and the covering of Scottish townscapes with council schemes could proceed.

The next election came only nine months later in the autumn of 1924. It was another sweeping victory for the Conservatives in England. In Scotland the Unionists won thirty-eight seats. That gave them their first majority, though a narrow one, since 1900. It was partly achieved through twelve gains from Labour which, however, held reasonably firm with twenty-six seats in industrial areas. The most notable result of the swing to the Unionists was the decimation of the Liberals outside the Highlands. The whole business was a disaster for Scotland's old ruling party. Having supported Labour in office, it was ill-placed to attack the outgoing Ministry in the campaign. The anti-socialist voter turned rather to the Unionists. Asquith, the leader, fell at Paisley and only nine of his followers survived. The votes were distributed in true two-party fashion, with Labour and the Unionists each winning about 41 per cent and the Liberals far behind on a mere 17 per cent.

Sir John Gilmour, MP for Pollok, now took over the Scottish Office. He introduced the first major reforms in the country's government since 1907, though interest in these matters was waning. The Liberals' support for devolution was neutralised by their collapse, while feelings in the Labour party grew ambivalent. In 1918 it had stood strongly for Home Rule. But many of its MPs now saw the Scottish people's material condition as best ameliorable through economic centralism. Still, it was from the Labour side that the post-war Home Rule Bills came. One was introduced in 1924, but Ramsay MacDonald's Ministry declined to sponsor it. A second in 1927 was talked out, an incident which aroused great indignation and led indirectly to the foundation of the National Party. The Unionists still disliked devolution, and the benefits of the measures which Gilmour brought foward were disputed.

In 1926 he finally won the full status of Secretary of State. From this eminence he set out on what he intended as a definitive reform of his department. He and it did not at this stage actually devise and execute policy. That was done by the administrative boards, in which alone statutory powers were vested. Their members were not civil servants, but appointed from outside either for their expertise or as guardians of the public interest. The MPs' usual assumption that the Secretary was responsible for the boards was thus in the strict sense wrong—his duties stopped at liaising among them or seeing that they did not step out of line with the Government's general intentions. So there were good grounds for the complaints about lack of political control. In 1928 Gilmour made two main changes. He replaced a large part of the nominated staff by regular civil servants with the normal Whitehall recruitment and career structure. Then he amalgamated and regrouped a number of the boards so that their work could be better co-ordinated. But in making these improvements he also did away with much of the loose system of administration which, for all its faults, had allowed the Scots to conduct their business without excessive reference to Whitehall norms. In its new, centralised shape, the Scottish Office was becoming a government department like any other. So in one way, Gilmour's work represented a step away from autonomy. As if to prove it, he undertook in 1929, with little consultation, a sweeping reform of local government which diminished the powers of many burghs and was seen as an attack on civic pride.

Internal quarrels meanwhile pre-occupied the Opposition. The ILP, long Scotland's largest socialist group, deplored the caution of the Labour leadership. A mighty row broke out over the General Strike in 1926. Under the direction of the STUC it won all but total support from unionised workers. There was a hard core of militancy among Scots miners, where Communist influence was strong. Violence marked the dispute in Glasgow and Edinburgh as well as in the coalfields. But the Government did not stand passively by: the Lord Advocate, William Watson, headed a Scottish Emergency Organisation which supervised transport and the distribution of food and fuel. To all this there was no decisive reaction from the Labour leaders, while their allies in the unions were throughout anxious to compromise. The ILP thought the whole performance shameful and was bitter in its recrimination when the strike collapsed. The split between the radical Clydeside socialists and Ramsay MacDonald thus widened. Temperaments on either side did not help. Maxton had taken over as chairman of the ILP in 1926, but he was a romantic, magniloquent agitator rather than a serious politician. On the other hand, Ramsay MacDonald grew ever more complacent and unenterprising.

There were even sections of the other parties now more progressive than he and his closest colleagues. Among Liberals traditional radicalism was a spent and irrelevant force, and their Left had embraced collectivist principles. They had fought the two previous elections on a new social and economic programme devised by John Maynard Keynes. It came too late, for the party was in full process of disintegration. The Asquithian old guard looked thoroughly effete. Haldane, once one of its pillars, had already deserted to Labour. He was followed in 1927 by William Wedgwood Benn, MP for Leith and leader of the advanced Liberals in the Commons. The Scottish Right-wingers, under Sir Godfrey Collins, MP for Greenock, stayed in the party, but they had little liking for the new policies and objected to Lloyd George's leftist line on such matters as the General Strike. Amid these disputes Scottish Liberalism wasted away. In 1925 the SLF complained of 'a lack of interest in about two-thirds of the constituencies in Scotland.'

The Unionists, according to their new MP for East Aberdeenshire, Robert Boothby, were 'a small band without many personalities or traditions, or indeed much hope.'[41] For years their benches had been filled with stern old-fashioned capitalists and farmers, among whom, however, the latest arrivals had re-introduced a radical strain. There was even a Glasgow working man, William Templeton, MP for Banff, but notably a group of younger members—Boothby himself, Walter Elliot, MP for Kelvingrove, and John Buchan in his university seat. They drew their inspiration from Noel Skelton, MP for Perth and East Perthshire, reputed inventor of the phrase 'property-owning democracy' which summed up the ideal of this more enlightened conservatism.[42]

For the moment it made little impression. In fact Labour was restoring its electoral position, and through three by-election victories had by the summer of 1929 robbed the Unionists of their Scottish majority. The General Election later that year gave the Left once more the upper hand in Scotland, with thirty-six seats for Labour, plus one independent Labour and Scrymgeour in

Dundee. Labour took 42 per cent of the poll. The Unionists' share fell to 36 per cent and they retained no more than twenty-two seats. The depleted Liberals put much effort into the election and had some success, including five gains from the Unionists. But their total of seats was still only fourteen and, with just over 18 per cent of the vote, they had not decisively reversed the trend towards a two-party system.

Had matters taken their natural course, Scotland would doubtless have settled down to such a system earlier than she did. But soon she was overtaken by the great political and economic crisis of 1931, in which all these post-war developments were stifled by the electoral weight of the National Government. The year of 1930 is thus a convenient date at which to break off the history of the last triumph and ultimate destruction of Scotland's old Liberal party.[43] It is important not to confound this with the parallel but essentially different process in England. The difference lies in the starting point: for whereas in 1914 the English Liberals were merely a single element in a two-party system, the Scots ruled over something akin to a one-party state. There was more to this than simple success at the polls. The essential factor was the social and ethical integration of party and people which, though weakened by the beginning of this century, was founded on a tradition which stretched far back into the last.

As for England, one group of historians there takes the view that the Liberal collapse was the largely accidental outcome of the squabbles between Asquith and Lloyd George. Another maintains that it was the result of long-term social and economic changes, and in particular of the way these were allowed to manifest themselves through the extension of the franchise in 1918. There then appeared on the Left of British politics a new electoral force composed of people who had really long ago withdrawn their allegiance from the Liberal establishment. And they appeared in such numbers that they simply displaced the Liberals as the main party of the Left. With that Liberalism's natural role in a two-party system was played out.

Neither thesis is irrelevant to Scotland, but reservations must be made. The Scottish historian has to stress the extraordinary survival of a Liberalism itself unchanging—or at best slowly and reluctantly changing—which could yet preside over a nation transformed beyond recognition from the time when it first put the Liberals in power. That was permitted by the Scots' blind loyalty to their social myths which, however, also gave the party a woefully limited view of what was going on in the country. It looked, after the unpleasant interlude of war, for a restoration of the old order and for the resumption of Scotland's tranquil progress. Used to weathering tempestuous crises, it might have been forgiven for thinking that of 1918 just another, which time and skilful accommodation could again overcome.

Attempts at re-orientation were not lacking. Asquith's Paisley speeches, though insipid, acknowledged the need, and Haldane's conversion to Labour was perhaps a bolder version of the same tendency. Some Glasgow Unionists, the most creative—if separated—element of the former Liberal coalition, strode on with resolution to a collectivist future. But most Scots Liberals regarded the advance in state power during wartime as an unfortunate and temporary, if unavoidable, deviation from the true social path. They had rejected fresh ideas after 1900 and still hesitated to open the party to them, even to the limited extent that they were now represented by Lloyd George. Orthodox Liberals thus had little to say when an endless economic crisis confirmed for many of their countrymen the need of more active government.

And so long as they were split, Liberals could not move quickly or decisively in any direction, neither towards Unionist paternalism nor towards compromise with the brash appeal of socialism. Yet till 1923 they remained the largest party in terms of votes and still yearned for popular unity: hence the constant hankering after coalition with someone or other. On a more profound level than tactics, however, the time had passed when the Liberals could present themselves as the party of the Scottish people without qualification. In the mid nineteenth century the Liberal national consensus was the fairly passive expression of a society where there was little disagreement on fundamental aims and not much call for policy. But now the country's values had been deeply eroded. Opposition to Liberalism was based not on the vagaries of aristocratic influence or sectarian resentment, but on organised group interests reinforced by ideology.

In the intervening decades a more secular society had continued to develop, industrialisation had proceeded and social problems had grown worse: Scotland was altogether more divided, more sectional than before. It had become increasingly difficult for any one party to understand and cater for such marked divergences of outlook as those between East and West, Highlands and Lowlands, Protestants and Catholics, city and countryside, radicals and collectivists, labour and capital. As politics grew more complex, moral enlightenment and individual self-reliance could no longer be cited as the automatic answer to every question—especially after the war when, on the contrary, the individual seemed quite helpless before new economic forces hardly comprehended. Liberal myths were suddenly seen as void of political meaning. This gave the ruling party's rivals scope to elaborate an appeal on some other basis.

The distinctive feature of politics after 1918 was the polarisation along class lines, one which soon pushed all the rest into the background. But its inevitability should not be over-stressed. The elements of class division in Scottish politics can be traced back to 1886. By 1914 there were two opposition parties with constituencies perceptibly based on class. Perhaps it was that which constricted them. Liberals still drew mass support from all classes. In any case there is no evidence, of an electoral or any other kind, that Scots workers were not—unlike much of the English proletariat—overwhelmingly prepared before the war to entrust their interests to the old Liberal party.

Thus one must look to the tensions of wartime for the decisive break. Then the state made demands for large and rapid changes in Scotland's ways of life and thought, enforced if necessary by mildly oppressive means. Especially on Clydeside, centre of her population and industry, they produced a strong antipathy of rulers and ruled. This was exploited by a socialist minority which implanted a class interpretation of it firmly in the popular mind. The social variety of pre-war Liberalism then became a weakness. So, as the economic crisis continued to defy solution, did its indifference to policy. Moreover, attempts to formulate new policies for the new conditions were now likely to be tested on class criteria and might lose as many votes as they gained. When in 1922 Labour was able to consolidate the support it had won during war and recession, a return to the classless, non-doctrinaire, Liberal national consensus was excluded.

After ninety years of almost continuous dominance in Scotland, the Liberal party dissolved in a welter of centrifugal forces. With the advent of class politics the bourgeoisie had good reason to think it was safer supporting the Unionists than the ostensibly classless Liberals. If there was a brief chance to forge a new, broad alliance, it was lost when the English Tories seceded from the coalition and eventually carried the reluctant Scots Unionists with them. Some Right-wing voters stayed with the Liberals for a while, but as the English party disintegrated even more completely than its Scottish counterpart they concluded that their interests could indeed be better served by Unionism. Socialists had been largely content to go along with Liberalism before the war, but they now had their own vehicle for power which attracted the support of both workers and advanced radicals. The Irish settlement loosed the bond between Catholics and Liberals. With the prospects for Home Rule within the conventional party system dimming, Nationalists formed a political organisation of their own.

Scottish Liberalism had always contained many varied and conflicting elements. They had, however, had a common allegiance in their ethical view of the world, and this had allowed Scotland to retain an identifiable political personality. People and politicians alike found Liberal ethics impossible of application to the immense social and economic problems of the post-war period. Reduced to a tiny faction at Westminster, the Liberals could offer no hope of fulfilling anyone's moral imperatives or political aspirations.

The results were disastrous. In 1832 Scotland had lost the decrepit survivals of her ancient constitution; in 1843 she lost the central pillar of her native social structure; from 1886 she was visibly torn between a self-satisfied parochialism and new ambitions in the wider world; now, amid the upheavals of the greatest crisis she had ever faced, her political personality dissolved. With the Liberals apparently in their last agonies, with the Unionists' independent vitality smothered by their London masters' stodgy conservatism, and with centralising tendencies, as we shall see below, gaining ground in the Labour party, Scottish politics moved rapidly towards conformity with the pattern in England. Thus by 1930 Scotland had forsaken her own political tradition and had collapsed into a depressed and subordinate province.

Chapter 6

'All This Will Belong To The People'

Keir Hardie thought the Scots natural socialists, for they were and still are a more egalitarian people than their southern neighbours. The reasons are to be sought not only in their centuries of poverty but also in their presbyterian religion, in the aspirations towards universal education which it implanted and in its teaching that the merely political was a subordinate part of the moral order. To Keir Hardie there would have been no great difference between a Christian and a socialist commonwealth.

All this long gave Scotland's socialism a special character. Like her Liberalism it was often more idealistic than its English counterpart and often more intellectual. Robert Owen, whose activities north of the border allow British socialism to claim in him a spiritual ancestor, remarked: 'Even the Scotch peasantry and working classes possess the habit of making observations and reasoning thereon with great acuteness.' Yet these qualities produced not a generous but a narrow-minded tradition with a Calvinistic urge towards doctrinal purity.

Frustration also contributed, for Scotland had no state structure through which principle could easily be turned into practice. Faced with that insurmountable obstacle, her socialists confined themselves largely to local interests and ignored the problem of how to take and hold power. Political compromise did not appeal to them and realities could not constrain them to it. In the national crisis during and after the First World War, a wave of popular, radical indignation raised them from nothing to become in less than a decade their country's most dynamic force. This miraculous transformation was far from the experience of their English comrades, who owed their rewards to patient groundwork. The Scots placed their faith instead in emotion, rhetoric and daring. That could not stop their being swamped by the construction of an efficient mass Labour party covering the whole of Britain and inevitably led from England. A distinctive Scottish socialism then died. [1]

For a century after the Union, Scotland was on the whole a peaceful and well-ordered country, where rumblings of popular discontent were local and short-lived. This changed as the industrial revolution destroyed the old social system sustained by traditional institutions, principally by the Church. The working class was exposed to forces it could not understand or resist. Against them the ruling hierarchy, even at its most benevolent, offered scant protection. The even tenor of Scottish life was now more often disturbed by irruptions of the mindless, violent mob. But such revolt was easily dealt with. It had no programme apart from a general desire to overthrow oppressors. It was in essence an inchoate reaction to dire social and economic conditions, only lightly touched by ideas derived from the French Revolution. But it did give an impetus to more thorough efforts, notably in the start of trade unions. Banned under the Combination Acts till 1824, they had already sprung into existence in various embryonic forms: in the burgh guilds formed to protect craftsmen's privileges; in the attempts to join together by downtrodden workers flocking into the towns to man new industries; and in the friendly societies which, while primarily offering insurance against sickness and incapacity, also opened the way to other forms of co-operative action. These groups were, however, always small, local and limited in outlook.[2]

A theoretical inspiration largely ignored, though close at hand, lay in Owen's colony at New Lanark, one of the most remarkable of early socialist experiments.[3] If the idea of model villages was not new in Scotland, his notion of combining it with social reform was. His charges were subjected to a paternalist regime with no democratic tendency whatever. But they were sobered up, well fed, properly clothed, educated and taught to work industriously at their machines. Underlying all this was Owen's conviction that men were moulded entirely by their circumstances—if these were put right, men would become good. But he was also interested in trade unionism and advocated the formation of general unions, that is to say, federations of workers in many places or trades.

Yet Owen's theories failed to find an audience in the Scots working class. In his time and afterwards its agitation remained comparatively violent and thus repugnant to the bourgeois reformers on whom hopes for progress in Scotland really rested. The more radical of them, however, were attracted by the moral and social aspects of Owen's teachings. They strove to order spontaneous proletarian activity according to his systematic ideas. The most prominent of his disciples was Alexander Campbell, a journalist who played an energetic role in various radical causes over four decades.[4] At this stage he devoted himself to the encouragement of general unions. The first of them, the Glasgow and West of Scotland Association for the Protection of Labour, was set up in 1831, but soon disintegrated. Undeterred, Campbell and his circle continued their efforts and had much to do with the upsurge of labour activity in the 1830s. It ended with the defeat of the cotton spinners' strike of 1837. It could not be revived amid the subsequent repression and economic hard times. Besides, trade unions had in Scotland powerful—and to the people of the time often more relevant—rivals in religious dissent and Chartism, both at heart pacific. Thus militancy failed in these years as a vehicle for the general advancement of workers.

But those three movements, which issued in the Disruption, the triumph of 'moral force' and the collapse of the earliest unions, produced in the period round 1840 a turning point in the history of the Scots working class. They meant severally the death of the old social order, the discrediting of violence and a commitment to peaceful methods; together they meant a clamant need for new ways of defending workers' interests. The memory of proletarian effort independent of any bourgeois inspiration was a spur to the search for them.

While these lessons were being absorbed, Scotland entered the second stage of her industrial revolution. It was marked by the growth of heavy industries such a steel and shipbuilding. There trade unions began to take root as prosperity revived. The greatest success in organisation was achieved by the miners, whose leader, Alexander MacDonald, set up an at least nominally all-Scottish union in 1852. Equally important were renewed attempts at co-operation among different groups of workers, in the trades councils formed in Edinburgh and Glasgow during the 1850s.[5]

This was, however, a moderate phase of trade unionism, and for good reason. It was struggling to flourish in a society still intensely individualistic. Most agreed that a man's success was due to his personal moral qualities. Thus it was possible to see in temperance or universal education means of progress for the working class quite as potent as labour organisation. Industrial issues were often commingled with others. At Airdrie in 1854, for example, the miners went on strike 'till all the Roman Catholics should be expelled' from their jobs. With so little sense of solidarity in the proletariat, the pursuit by unions of long-term strategy was impossible. Each would contain only a fraction of those engaged in a trade. Workers in a different one or even in the same trade in another town rarely supported strikers. These weaknesses meant that labour leaders, especially MacDonald, normally advised their men to avoid disputes: he told a Commons committee that workers 'should endeavour to meet their employers as far as they can.' He accepted the tenets of capitalism, and saw winning friends in Parliament as the best way of getting legislation in his members' interests.[6]

The climax of this phase of labour activity was the formation of a United Trades Confederation of Scotland, a general union, in 1872. But it soon collapsed. That was above all the result of the severe recession which now set in and lasted a decade. In the face of it, moderate ideas were found wanting. With many workers having their wages cut, unions could do little to help. MacDonald simply recommended them to accept their fate. Even he soon learned that moral suasion availed nothing against economic instability. By the end of the 1870s he was advocating the 'wee darg' to deal with the worst effects of depressed trade, a scheme which would have required employers and unions to co-operate in restricting the miners production; work could then be shared or else lower output would keep up the price of coal, allowing profits and wages to be maintained. But the fierce competition among the Scottish coalmasters made this unthinkable. MacDonald's liberal capitalism had turned into a plan of controls and labour immobility which could never have worked in Victorian Scotland.[7]

MacDonald did not especially want to be tied to the Liberals, because they accepted only the workers' constitutional and not their social or industrial aspirations—though he himself became a Liberal MP for an English seat in 1874. For Scotland his career provided no answer to the question of how, if at all, the unions were to participate in politics. In this respect they were still immature, not knowing with whom to work or in what way. That was why they could turn to Elcho, a reactionary who scarcely counted as an ally, but who happened to share with them opponents on a single issue of labour law. In general their position seemed to counsel political neutrality. Participation in public debates might not only make them enemies without but could also be divisive within. A reluctance to risk schism was one of the lessons learned from the Chartists, who had ruined themselves largely through factionalism. Thus, several times before 1868 the Edinburgh trades council refused to join in the agitation over the franchise. There were, however, signs of growing confidence in the years after the second Reform Act. Both the Edinburgh and Glasgow trades councils then started contesting local elections, if un-successfully.

The individualist attitudes all through society made not the labour leaders but the Liberal party the hope of the workers. The price of their winning a place in its ascendancy was respectability and co-operation with their rulers. The artisans enfranchised in 1868 were part of the living tradition of ethical Liberalism: thrifty, often teetotal, members of a kirk, deferring to authority outside the home as they were deferred to inside it. There was no great ideological difference between them and their political leaders, the bourgeois radicals, who were hostile to labour organisation. Unions could not persuade many that class interests were more important than the victory of Liberalism, especially when the horrible alternative was Conservatism. In any case the emergence of a strong opposition on the Left was for the moment made impossible by Gladstone's triumphs in Scotland, which attached the workers more firmly to the Liberal party than at any time since 1832.

In the 1880s the most pregnant innovation was the arrival of socialism in Scotland, though only as a minor intellectual movement, a cranky foreign importation.[8] It came from England as a result of efforts by her leading Marxist, H M Hyndman, to extend support for his Social Democratic Fed-eration. In 1884 he brought into existence its first branch north of the border by securing the affiliation of the Scottish Land and Labour League, the middle-class group of agrarian reformers in Edinburgh. One of them attested that the federation was 'neither indigenous to Scotland nor proletarian in composition.'[9] In any case it split almost at once over objections to Hynd-man's autocratic leadership. Most of the Edinburgh branch departed with his main opponent, the artist William Morris, into a new Socialist League. It was romantic, anarchic, idealistic to the point of unreality. An attempt was made to re-unite the two in a Scottish Socialist Federation in 1888. This soon died in its turn and of its parts the league died with it. But the Social Democratic Federation lived on.

Meanwhile the unions had been recovering, though on nothing like the scale of the so-called New Unionism in England.[10] The textiles, building and heavy industries all achieved a fair degree of organisation. The most active and militant group remained the miners. They were remarkable also for their political involvements in various radical pressure groups. They had a parliamentary spokesman in Cunninghame Graham, MP for North-west Lanarkshire 1886–92.[11] Alexander MacDonald had died in 1881, but even before then was beginning to lose influence. The rising star of the Scottish miners was Keir Hardie. Born illegitimate in industrial Lanarkshire, he typified in his younger years the attitudes of the Scots working class. He did not distinguish politics from morality: self-help and temperance were his programme, Burns and the Covenanters his heroes. Naturally he was a Liberal.[12]

His first venture into public affairs came as a miners' agent in Ayrshire. There he won notoriety, and soon lost his job, for leading the 'Tattie Strike' of 1879. Supporting himself precariously from journalism, he continued his work and by 1886 had made enough progress to set up a union covering the whole county. After extending his efforts to Lanarkshire, he felt able within a few months to make another attempt at forming a national union, the Scottish Miners' Federation. But its existence was more hope than reality: it indicated an intention to organise rather than actual organisation.

It met with a vehemently hostile reaction from the employers. Yet the miners were heartened, and in February 1887 the Lanarkshire men struck for an eight-hour day and for the setting of national wage rates (the purpose of which was to stop an individual company cutting pay when its pits did badly). At Blantyre riots following the masters' introduction of blacklegs were so severe that troops had to be brought from Glasgow to restore order. Soon the miners were forced into complete surrender. In consequence the federation collapsed by the middle of the year. Another effort at building up union organisation was in ruins. Keir Hardie, a proud, even vain man, was furious at the employers' contempt for the workers and depressed that these had got no help from outside. The main reason, he felt, was the unions' subservience to official Liberalism, manifested in the way the TUC handled its political relations. When he attended congress that autumn he launched a blistering attack on the committee responsible and especially on its secretary, Henry Broadhurst, as the mainstays of an alliance in which the Liberals were inevitably the stronger partners.

It seemed to Keir Hardie that only labour representation in Parliament would rectify matters. The 1884 Reform Act provided even stronger arguments for that. In England the Liberals were actually starting to do something about it, through sponsoring trade unionist candidates in selected constituencies—Alexander MacDonald had found his seat by this means. But it was not happening in Scotland, and could not while her ruling class wished otherwise. The age of monolithic parties had not yet dawned. The Liberals had not so much as a central election fund, and the constituency associations retained absolute autonomy. They were usually controlled by local notables likely to take a dim view of such people as miners coming forward as candidates, for it could still be assumed that the Liberals would be able to hold the allegiance of the working class without making further concessions to it. The very attempt to press a different view from the centre spelled danger, for the party was under the strain of trying to keep together a great number of divergent forces released by successive Reform Acts. Gladstone managed it for a time, but he could not push the party decisively in any new direction: when he tried the Unionist schism resulted. That showed no-one could impose unpalatable policies on the constituencies.

Despite these obstacles to his progress, it is difficult to imagine that at this stage Keir Hardie's loyalty to Liberalism was seriously shaken. He knew almost nothing of Marx and would have regarded the handful of Scottish socialists as to a man too theoretical. What were their doctrines to him but a demand for greater state intervention in the economy which could be incorporated into Liberalism if it willed? Of course he was a union activist and remained so—but because it was the element in radical agitation at which he was best and through which he could aim for reciprocal support. Of course he also felt disappointed at the failure to promote working-class candidates— but because it was to him a failure to promote the brotherhood of man which he and the official Liberals alike proclaimed. One must conclude that for the moment he wanted labour representation not as the basis for a new party but as a means, to be used in association with pressure from the unions, of working towards his objects within Liberalism.

That is confirmed by Keir Hardie's immediately offering himself as Liberal candidate when in 1888 the sitting MP for Mid-Lanarkshire resigned. Predictably he was not well received by the constituency association. Despairing of persuasion, he afterwards withdrew his application. Yet he was still determined to go ahead and stand on his own account in the hope of teaching the official Liberals a lesson. He could find only a motley collection of support— the local miners, the Glasgow trades council, odd groups of radicals and land reformers—and got a discouraging result.

The effort seemed at the time to be of no great significance. It was after all usual to argue out every problem within the Liberal party, and a candidate did not automatically divorce himself from it by failing to receive a proper constituency endorsement. In view of what had happened in the 1885 and 1886 General Elections a double Liberal candidature at a by-election could be regarded as nothing out of the ordinary. Indeed the Liberal disarray meanwhile had encouraged minority interests to try and secure a place for themselves in Parliament. Hardie stood on a largely Liberal platform and insisted that a vote for him was a vote for Gladstone.

But the Mid-Lanarkshire by-election was important in retrospect, because it at once led Keir Hardie to found the Scottish Labour Party.[13] Preliminary moves were made within weeks of the defeat and the inaugural meeting was held in August 1888. Hardie took on the job of secretary, while Cunninghame Graham was elected president and Dr G B Clark, the crofters' MP, one of the vice-presidents. The number of bodies willing to affiliate was satisfactory: they straddled the Left from trades councils to Liberal groups such as the land reformers' associations in Edinburgh and Glasgow. But the real significance of the SLP lay in its being the first party in British history to aim specifically at promoting the workers' interests. With that a seed had been planted: as the politicisation of the labour movement proceeded it grew steadily away from Liberalism.[14]

The immediate intentions were less ambitious. In one sense the SLP may have been no more than an expression of Keir Hardie's hurt pride.[15] He, a well-known miners' leader, Home Ruler and local man, had been done down through the nomination of a London lawyer by a narrow-minded and snobbish constituency association. At the very least his experience showed that the Left was too disorganised. But what sort of party had he now founded? The main plank in its platform was labour representation, which it united with the usual radical programme and with ideas for advanced social legislation such as the eight-hour day. Its closeness to the normal run of radicals also explains the Scottish orientation. Home Rule within the framework of the United Kingdom was one of their main demands. It was therefore natural that a labour group, being by definition radical, should give itself a Scottish label. Most of all, perhaps, it was educational in intent, seeking to spread its opinions rather than to gain power. In that it was typical of many groups given life by the high ideals of Liberal democracy. True, its stated aims also included nationalisation of land, railways, banks and mineral rights. But it hesitated to use the word socialist of itself. It was not founded on economic analysis, still less on a materialistic view of the world. It was not a proletarian party, but a populist coalition. Yet even if only one or two of its leaders were closely linked with organised labour, its roots did lie in trade unionism. And it did intend to appeal to the whole working class.[16]

The ambiguities were reflected in the SLP's practical action. Like any political organisation, it sought to found branches and propagandise, though often the more it tried to expand the more it fell apart, suffering many disputes and resignations. It never quite decided whether it preferred to put up its own candidates in seats where the big parties were not prepared to champion labour interests, or to form electoral pacts in return for concessions to its view. Neither course was followed consistently. On the one hand, when the SLP stood independently in by-elections it failed miserably. On the other, it could not come to terms with the Liberals, from whom it hoped for the more fruitful co-operation. Cunninghame Graham was entrusted with the business of pacts. The nearest he came to success was in talks with Marjoribanks, the Scottish Liberal whip, in 1890. Their proposed agreement would have given SLP candidates Liberal backing in three winnable seats at the next General Election. But an attempt to get Graham himself officially adopted at Greenock foundered on the opposition of the local Liberals, and the whole idea was dropped. The SLP fought five seats on its own account at the 1892 election, in all of which it did very badly.

Gladstone had taken careful note of the latest schismatic tendencies among radicals and was now revising the Liberal programme to keep them in the fold. Keir Hardie had nothing much extra to offer than a demand for working-class candidates. But even the proletariat was not greatly excited about that, so in Scotland the Liberal local associations could still not be coerced into helping. Perhaps the only permanent result of this failure was the embitterment of the Scottish Left. That made impossible the reconciliation which took place in England a decade later in the form of Lib-Lab pacts.[17]

These experiences brought a decisive shift in Keir Hardie's views. The

Liberals' refusal to espouse labour representation seriously meant to him that they were declining to enter into the spirit of a new broad alliance, to become a people's party as electoral reform had promised. He turned to the trade unions instead. From now on his main purpose was to persuade the TUC to come out in favour of a parliamentary labour party. In future the workers were to rely on their organised strength in winning their way to Westminster, and no more on the condescension of Liberalism.

Given the weakness of Scottish unions, there was no point in carrying on with the SLP. Keir Hardie accepted nomination for a London seat, and won it in 1892. Henceforth he was much more important in England than in Scotland, which he left without being elected to any more exalted body than Auchinleck parish council. Meanwhile he had succeeded at the 1892 TUC, which took place in Glasgow, in persuading the delegates of the need for a labour representation fund. He also got agreement to the summoning of a national conference of the political and industrial sides of the movement. It took place in Bradford in 1893 and set up the Independent Labour Party. The SLP affiliated to it and was dissolved the next year.

Though Scotland now had no native Left-wing party, the ILP was an improvement on its precursor. It established a centralised structure without the rag-taggle of affiliates which had weakened the SLP. Moreover, its status as an all-British group attracted wider support, and in Scotland notably from people who gave it a more socialist character. But this was not a decisive influence. If the ILP was to flourish it had to find friends of other persuasions, especially moderates in the unions on which it was meant to rely for money and organisation. It was an improvement, too, on the socialist societies of the previous decade, those coteries of bourgeois intellectuals who had learned more of the workers from Marxist texts than from experience. Of course the ILP found room for intellectuals; indeed it had great cultural pretensions. But in Scotland, where possession of a university degree was not restricted to a narrow elite, that meant it could call on a pool of educated men themselves working-class, at least by origin or sympathy. Through them it had access to the proletariat and some appreciation of its needs. It was innocent of any real connection with Marxism, repudiating the idea of class war, preaching a high-minded, rather sentimental socialism, often shot through with Christianity. Certainly it had little time for scholastic disputation or for fomenting industrial trouble, preferring to concentrate on practical good works, mainly in municipal government. It built up a fair strength in Scotland, with about forty branches soon after its foundation, most of then round Glasgow. These, based on the former SLP and exploiting local issues, enjoyed a relative independence of the national leadership.

Since the ILP was not greatly interested in success at the hustings, it had little. At its first test in the 1895 election all seven Scottish candidates were heavily defeated, while for good measure Hardie lost his London seat. Emphasis on the middle way emasculated it as a political force. It wanted to follow a parliamentary rather than a revolutionary path. But it was too idealistic to take easily to the opportunism needed in building a mass party, and neglected chances to woo the workers. In any case they remained indifferent, believing the issues promoted by radical Liberals the most important, and content for these to be otherwise socially conservative. And the ILP disagreed, after all, only on the second point. It did not think of displacing them. On the contrary, it identified with their achievements and would have settled for their becoming a bit more radical.

Moderation meant that it could not even unite all the forces on the Left.[18] The Social Democratic Federation survived into the 1890s, but in an altered form which excluded merger with the ILP. Once a circle of bourgeois intellectuals—as the main body of Hyndman's friends in England still was—it had been taken over in Scotland by militant proletarians advocating revolutionary Marxism. Their leader was James Connolly, born of Irish immigrants in the Edinburgh slums. He disliked Keir Hardie for his doctrinal slackness.[19]

Others were less fastidious. This period of dissolution in old political patterns laid workers open to blandishments from all sides, even from the Right. In the West the Irish question had polarised religious and political feeling, with Catholics usually voting Liberal and many Protestants firmly committed to Unionism. There seemed to be a chance, better than at any time since Disraeli, of making conservative principles attractive to the masses. The idea found a highly intelligent advocate in the Glasgow campaigning journalist, Michael Maltman Barry. This rather mysterious figure managed to combine close friendship with Marx and chairmanship of the English section of the First International with a devotion to imperialism and repeated Conservative candidacies.[20]

The course was pursued most eagerly by a roguish Englishman of Scots descent, H H Champion.[21] He was active in the Labour Electoral Association, which since 1886 had been sponsoring independent working-class candidates, though all in Liberal seats. He was thus suspected of being financed by Tory gold. Champion helped Keir Hardie in Mid-Lanarkshire, but then built up contacts in Aberdeen, where he stood for Parliament himself in 1892. He courted the trades council with ideas for progressive social and industrial legislation coupled with protective tariffs. In 1894 he got it, and even the local ILP and Social Democratic Federation, to recommend a Unionist rather than a Liberal vote at the impending election. For several years Aberdeen followed an eccentric course as the Scottish bridgehead of Tory socialism.

The most fruitful development came not in politics but in the unions. Progress was still slow, and by 1892 no more than a quarter of the workers on Clydeside had joined them. But new ones were formed in heavy industry and some old ones became more ambitious. The Scottish Miners Federation, revived in 1894 under Robert Smillie, then led a four-month strike of 70,000 men. It was surprisingly socialistic and, unlike its English counterpart, refused to work with the Liberals. The usual channel for more radical tendencies was the trades councils, now found in most big towns. They were the liveliest working-class groups in Scotland, often in competition with the ILP and often more successful. With Champion's aid, Aberdeen and Falkirk had already tried their hand at politics in an initiative which set up a Scottish Trades Councils' Labour Party in 1891. Led by Chisholm Robertson, a miners' agent who had fallen out with Keir Hardie, it was meant largely as a counter-stroke to the SLP. But it had no resources to do more than endorse certain sympathetic candidates, and eventually joined up with the ILP as well.

This independent spirit was soon to bring, however, another important innovation. The militancy of the trades councils, which was not confined to Scotland, alarmed the cautious TUC. It therefore decided in 1895 to exclude them from membership. The Scots were so incensed that two years later they broke away to form their own Scottish Trade Union Congress, which allowed the councils to affiliate. With 40,000 members at the outset, the STUC was strong enough to maintain its separate existence. All the same, unions in Scotland were generally smaller, weaker and poorer than those in England, with parochial attitudes that did nothing to foster a sense of proletarian solidarity.

'The Scottish nature does not lend itself to combination,' Beatrice Webb bleakly noted after a visit to Glasgow in 1897.[22] Keir Hardie's quest for a union of the political and industrial sides of the labour movement had indeed thus far met with scant success. In Scotland, on the contrary, there had been further fragmentation. So long as large schemes were impracticable, co-operation could only be practised on a lower plain. But it was in the development of ideas for municipal socialism that leftist thinking first made a more general impact among Scots, though it did little more than call for the experiments of the entirely capitalist corporation of Glasgow to be pushed further. On that platform a combined Left-wing attack was mounted in the local elections of 1894, when in Edinburgh and Glasgow the ILP, the unions and the co-operative societies formulated a common programme, allocated the candidacies among themselves and bore expenses jointly. By the end of the decade the alliance was yielding its first fruits, with its representatives holding ten of the seventy-five seats on Glasgow town council.

After these encouraging omens, Keir Hardie was authorised to approach the STUC with a view to extending the arrangements to the national level. The prospects for this seemed to have improved, for while the Left remained weaker in Scotland than in England, its greater militancy made it more eager for unity. Perhaps only politics could provide a release for energies unsatisfied by the limited opportunity for labour agitation. In any case proposals for the nationalisation of land, mines, railways and industrial capital were approved by the STUC in 1897. The following year Keir Hardie publicly suggested that it should link up with the ILP. In response the unions undertook to support the existing socialist parties, something to which the English TUC had not so far proved amenable. After he had personally outlined his ideas to the 1899 STUC, it passed at the prompting of the socialist delegates a resolution in favour of united working-class action at the next General Election. A further conference of the two sides, together with the Social Democratic Federation and a few co-operative societies, was summoned to Glasgow in January 1900. This established the Scottish Workers' Representation Committee.[23]

The SWRC was the first example in Britain of a Labour party on modern lines. But it proved a false start in the task of mobilising the workers to strive together over the whole range of public affairs. Scotland simply did not possess the resources and scope for such a venture. Though there was still enough national sentiment about to impel the Scots to act alone and in advance of the English comrades, it was no counterweight to the growing political and economic power of London—the SWRC was always over-shadowed by the Labour Representation Committee formed there a few weeks later. It had to contend with the dislike and aggrandising intentions of the LRC leaders, especially of Ramsay MacDonald. A battle ensued about whether they ought to be allowed to recruit support in Scotland. In practice this could not be stopped because so many of them were Scots.

Nor was the militancy which might have been a basis for continued inde-pendence fully reflected in the SWRC's programme. That was kept mild for fear of alienating the non-socialists. The 1900 conference rejected a motion from the Social Democratic Federation calling for wholesale nationalisation, and the list of objects adopted still stressed most of all the need for labour representation. Such caution failed to place the committee on a sound footing in terms of membership and finance: the opening subscription from the STUC was £5 and from the ILP two guineas. The SWRC had constantly to struggle to make ends meet and before long was reduced in effect to being the political wing of the miners' federation, its only source of regular funds.

It could not resolve either the Scottish Left's usual dilemma over how to work with others.[24] A pact like that into which the LRC entered with the Liberal party had little point while the latter's constituency associations in Scotland spurned joint candidacies. Obstacles also existed to the merger of the two Labour committees. The main one was that the miners in England would not support theirs—they were still staunch allies of the Liberals and wanted nothing to do with a Labour party.[25] Nevertheless the LRC was much better integrated into the English political system than was the SWRC into the Scottish. Aided by the pact, the LRC was soon doing quite well at the polls. The SWRC neither sought nor was offered official Liberal collaboration, and only languished.

Its electoral record was poor all through the nine years of its existence. At the 1900 election it presented just one candidate. By-elections were obviously more promising, and the best chance came in Northeast Lanarkshire in 1901, when the chairman, Robert Smillie, was chosen to stand. Being against the Boer War and for Irish Home Rule, he got much initial support from radicals. There was talk of adopting him as the official Liberal candidate, but as usual the local association would have nothing to do with a worker. Smillie went ahead by himself and lost heavily. The SWRC also fought the 1906 election independently. It contested five mining constituencies, coming last in all of them. Though outside the coalfields organised labour was weak, the LRC insisted on standing in four seats. It won two, one each in Glasgow and Dundee, neither of which can have been owed to the backing of the miners. That only exposed the electoral feebleness of the SWRC.[26]

In 1908 the LRC asserted its right to accept affiliation from Scottish unions. The next year the miners, having repeatedly rejected the move in the past, did affiliate. The SWRC was promptly disbanded. But that meant there was for a time no effective machinery for running Labour candidates in Scotland. Hence their pitiable performance in the 1910 elections.[27] The problem could only be solved by establishing some special organisation for the country once again. A Scottish Advisory Council of the Labour Party was set up in 1913.

These frustrations had made the Scottish Left more militant. Having nothing to lose, it set itself further apart from the Liberals. The ILP attracted an active younger generation acquainted with Marxism. One was James Maxton, chairman of the Scottish region in 1912. Another was Thomas Johnston—founder of *Forward*, the ILP newspaper—whose books, *Our Scots Noble Families* and *History of the Working Classes in Scotland*, began to sweep away the kailyard myths and effect a re-interpretation of Scottish history. A third, John Wheatley, was remarkable in being both a Catholic and a socialist at a time when his church would have no truck with materialism. In 1906 he founded a Catholic Socialist Society which in 1908 affiliated to the ILP—the first significant contact between Labour and Irish workers in the West. As these men rose within the ILP they made it a more socialist party, though they could not yet build bridges to the mass of the industrial working class.[28]

There, given the distance of the ILP and the weakness of the unions, opportunities opened for militant agitators. Direct action in industry was for the next two decades almost wholly unorthodox and extremist, divorced from the broad, moderate alliance sought by Keir Hardie. One instigator of it was the Social Democratic Federation, renamed Social Democratic Party in 1908. It had soon disaffiliated from the SWRC, staying independent till after the First World War. A few hundred Scottish members were concentrated on the Clyde and in the Fife coalfield but united in their own regional organisation. They had little in common with Hyndman, wanting to work for, rather than talk about, the revolution. Their greatest asset was John Maclean, teacher, writer, orator, founder of the Scottish Labour College and a hero of the country's Left ever since. In 1911 they associated with other groups to form a British Socialist Party, which became the nucleus of the Communist party after the war.[29]

James Connolly, having sojourned in Ireland and America, came home in 1902 imbued with yet more radical ideas. He forced a split in the federation and led off its Left wing (though without Maclean) into a Socialist Labour Party. Its entirely Scottish membership was reflected in Calvinistic insistence on purity of belief, not only in Marxism but in the doctrines, new to Scotland, of syndicalism or industrial unionism. They aimed to solve two problems: the fragmentation of unions and the tendency of their leaders, damned as the 'labour lieutenants of capitalism', to come to terms with employers. The answer offered was the formation of one union for each industry, to end craft prejudices and unify the rank and file, who were also to be trained in militancy which union officials could not ignore. Come the revolution, provoked by class war and carried to victory through rigid obedience to the party hierarchy, these industrial unions would be the foundation not just of economic but of political life, for they would then also become organs of representation and replace parliaments; government would be a sort of confederation of them. Such notions, if far-fetched, had relevance on the Clyde, where large-scale industry co-existed with many overlapping, competing unions. The party did manage to foment industrial conflict and win some influence in the region, staging its biggest effort in a major strike at Singer's factory, Clydebank, in 1911. During the war, its ideas were the starting point for the activities of the militant shop stewards.

But all this agitation has to be placed in perspective.[30] Scottish unions did not care for confrontation because they were bound to suffer great handicaps in any contest with the extremely hostile employers. The workforce was hard to organise, not least in the West. There it consisted at one end of shiftless and despised, often Irish, labourers, living in slum tenements, godless and violent, squandering their meagre wages on drink. They were an affront to the Scottish values which the labour movement also shared, so it left them in their degradation. At the other end the labour aristocrats, the skilled craftsmen, sometimes even scorned to join unions. Harry McShane, a member of the British Socialist Party, wrote: 'It wasn't easy to rouse up the engineers; they were very respectable with their blue suits and bowler hats and used to come to mass meetings with their umbrellas.'[31] Scotland had no strong national unions but only local ones, often impermanent, loosely joined in fragile federations. Trades councils remained more effective, but with the result that strikes tended to cover a number of occupational groups in one district rather than to develop into disputes involving all the workers in a given trade. Besides, industrial harmony generally prevailed. In a reversal of the roles today, Glasgow looked down on London as a hotbed of unrest.

Glasgow actually had more Marxist education than any other city in Britain, but still the socialists could win no wide political following. Scots persisted in thinking socialism inimical to their individualist outlook, not respectable enough and irreligious. Not even many trade unionists were persuaded by Keir Hardie's schemes for a common front. In England strong unions overshadowed the socialists, but were ready to provide money and organisation in plenty; this had the advantage that in some industrial areas there was already a broad-based working-class party bringing together many shades of opinion. In Scotland weak unions left Labour prey to the small numbers and schismatic zealotry of her socialists, condemning the movement to factionalism and frustration. It looked and was a minor political sect offering no competition to the Liberals. Though Scottish Labour's resources were inadequate, an independent spirit meant it could not reconcile itself to throwing in its lot entirely with the English. Yet so far experience had proved that the choice between local and London-dominated direction was no more than a choice between incapacity and vacuum.

After 1914 the position of Scottish socialism was transformed.[32] The First World War aroused unease in the country's radical, pacifist conscience. The Left in Scotland, unlike in England, did not in the majority abandon its internationalist principles. The Scots leaders in London, Keir Hardie and Ramsay MacDonald, refused to endorse the war, the latter resigning leadership of the parliamentary Labour party when it decided to support the Government. The response of the local activists was yet more resolute. They damned the conflict outright as a capitalist affair and declared they would fight only in defence of socialism. This was an attitude shared alike by the relatively moderate ILP, by a number of union leaders and by the extremist groups.

Nevertheless there were differences in approach. The unions were anxious to avoid domestic collision and would not, out of fear of antagonising the Government, back the Clydeside strikes of 1915. The ILP's position was similar. Thus the main thrust of anti-war agitation came from the militants. They saw in it a more hopeful means of undermining the capitalist system, something their previous efforts had done nothing noticeable to achieve. But while workers' industrial grievances could be exploited, it proved difficult to imbue them with a political impulse.

The motives and aims of the Clyde Workers' Committee were mixed. Some of its leaders, William Gallacher the most prominent, were members of the extremist parties. Others, such as David Kirkwood, were simply shop stewards trying to do the best by the men they represented. They were induced to co-operate as the authorities forced the pace in putting the economy on a war footing. When the CWC was formed it genuinely filled a gap between insensitive official policy and workers' protests against it which could find no other outlet. If the Government had been quicker to deal with the problems, the militants would probably not have been able to bring matters to a head at the end of 1915. But once the authorities had properly appraised the seriousness of the threat to industrial peace, they did move fast, as they had to for the sake of the war effort. The conflicts were certainly not intractable, and the Government largely succeeded in defusing them by the compromise offered over dilution early in 1916.

That compromise mixed concession with repression: agreement to let the unions control details of dilution was balanced by the arrest and deportation of the more prominent agitators. These terms were accepted by the rank and file. A dangerous affair promptly fizzled out and the risk of industrial turning into political unrest was averted. There had always been a contradiction in the militants trying to use as the basis for a mass movement the protests of the most privileged, conservative craftsmen at the threat to their restrictive practices. These could hardly be presented as a cause for concern to other workers, whom they were designed to penalise. Even if it had been possible, there was no means of mobilising such concern, since general unions, for both skilled and unskilled, did not exist in Scotland.

The contradiction split the labour leaders on the Clyde. Extremists rejected the deal with the Government and censured the CWC for being too practical. Deprived of real wrongs to exploit, they could only fall back on vague and in the circumstances laughable demands for the nationalisation of all industries and a general strike to enforce it if they were denied. Others went still further. John Maclean, revealing himself not as a uniquely brilliant revolutionary but as an absurd fanatic, called on workers to have nothing to do with war production at all. He expected this to bring a display of international proletarian solidarity that would halt the fighting and destroy capitalism. But no such thing had followed similar appeals in 1914, and more likely it would just have put the men involved out of a job. To workers needing to make a living, it appeared merely that the most militant activists had ceased to care about negotiating better conditions.

Those who had accepted the compromise began to develop more trust towards the Government. They appreciated the value of having forced it to recognise the informal workshop organisation; legitimacy was lent to workers' indignation and benefits accrued. This helped restore the standing of the unions and the Glasgow trades council. The latter, led by Emanuel Shinwell, now avoided confrontation because it saw in the new arrangements a potential for improving the workforce's lot. Thus Scotland remained relatively quiet for a while.

The first phase of agitation had arisen from the rude shock dealt by war to an industrial structure ill-equipped to meet its demands. The second sprang out of the universal weariness brought on by the endless fighting. It reinforced the unrest over wages and prices, poor housing and rapacious landlords found commonly in Britain, but often in more acute form in the West of Scotland. There, meanwhile, membership of the unions had expanded greatly and new ones were being formed for the unskilled workforce which had not been organised. Most were still local and highly responsive to members' grievances, and when necessary they could support each other through the Glasgow trades council. In time came a fresh upsurge of labour trouble, with militants again the catalyst. The deportees were freed in the summer of 1917 and soon the CWC was functioning again with Gallacher as its chairman. Their ideas had also spread. The shop committee system had been found of great utility in pressing workers' interests, and disputes were fomented in trades other than the skilled engineers whom the CWC had led in 1915. Its network, which had never quite vanished, now expanded: a shop stewards' committee was formed in Edinburgh on the pattern of Glasgow's and more followed elsewhere, till it was possible to set up a Scottish Workers' Committee, lasting till 1923, through which action might be co-ordinated and broadened.[33]

Two outside forces helped to win more general support during this renascence. One was the increasing desperation of the struggle in Europe, demanding a search for ever more men to offer to what Lloyd George called the 'military Moloch'. In January 1918 Sir Auckland Geddes, director general of National Service and himself a Scot by birth, was sent to persuade the Glasgow shop stewards of the need to extend conscription to the so far exempt skilled workers. He only succeeded in undoing the relatively good relations built up by the authorities in the past two years. The Government now seemed intent on resuming the previously defeated campaign against craft privilege. Instead of agreeing with Geddes, the stewards passed an anti-war resolution. For the first time there was an explicit link between industrial discontent and pacifist agitation.

The second was the impact of the Russian Revolution during this last dreadful winter of the war, when politicians began to despair of restoring peace or of calling forth much more sacrifice from their peoples. To socialists it was proof that the proletariat could actually seize power instead of just revolting now and again. There was quite wide sympathy for the Bolsheviks in industrial Scotland, and some gun-running to them. May Day 1918 saw many workers expressing at least verbal support for revolution in a huge demonstration in Glasgow which has been called 'the peak of Marxism in Scotland'. The militants, especially Maclean, hoped to reproduce the Neva's victories on the Clyde. Now it looked as if they might be winning a mass following. Though that proved in the end deceptive, the industrial front remained disturbed till the great confrontation early in 1919, with the climax of the 40-hours strike and the George Square riot.

They marked, however, the defeat of the revolutionaries' hopes. Their agitation could not be sustained through the surge of joyous relief that greeted the armistice. Conditions turned against them in politics, by reason of the return of the Coalition with a huge majority in the 1918 election, and in economics, as the problems of recession replaced those of wartime shortage. The masses, threatened with unemployment, grew apathetic and hostile to strikes. The shop stewards' network was forced to yield to the regular trade unions. These were no longer inhibited in negotiations for fear of the Government, but they could do little to ease the painful transition to new circumstances.[33]

The extremists, who still expected a world revolution to follow inevitably upon the events in Russia, did not adapt quickly enough. Instead they busied themselves with the formation of a Communist party, even then disagreeing on its shape. Maclean advocated a purely Scottish one, with the argument that Clydeside was nearer to the necessary upheaval than any other part of Britain. But Gallacher, who had just visited Moscow and fallen under Lenin's spell, returned with orders to found a British party and seek its affiliation to Labour. Gallacher's forceful personality and Lenin's authority propelled the idea through against strong opposition. Maclean refused to join and tried vainly to set up his own party, socialist and nationalist at once, on the model of Sinn Fein. Thereafter he faded into obscurity, and died in 1923.

Meanwhile, in 1920, the Communist party had been formed out of the British Socialist Party, the Socialist Labour Party, the Left wing of the ILP and a number of shop stewards. Though its attempts to affiliate to Labour were rebuffed, individual Communists were free to infiltrate. For some time it had a modicum of success, enjoying relative strength in Scotland because the founding groups were better organised and bigger than in England. It was a force to be reckoned with on Clydeside and in the Fife coalfield, where in 1929 it established the first Communist trade union, the United Mineworkers of Scotland. Two party members have been returned for Scottish seats: Walton Newbold, who slipped in for Motherwell in 1922, if only through Labour's confusion over his credentials, and William Gallacher, who sat for West Fife 1935–50. Even so, the Communists remained a tiny minority. As Labour centralised itself, they proved too much at odds with the rest in ideology and were all expelled in 1925. After that they were a nuisance rather than a serious threat.

The extreme Left was anyway losing influence. It was not that during or indeed after the war that Scots workers were easily cowed. Only in 1919 did they start to shy away from industrial action, which thus far had brought real benefits. But it might only cost jobs when demand for labour was falling. The proletariat was not necessarily reconciled to the powers-that-be, but its freedom of action narrowed. Prudence, however, did not nullify the previous leftward shift in its sentiment spurred by the extremists. The result came nowhere near revolution, but brought far more militancy than before 1914. At the same time, labour had forced the authorities to recognise it as a legitimate interest group. For unions the effects in power and membership were soon evident. Craftsmen learned that pride and privilege were not enough to protect them from economic misfortune, while the unskilled had discovered the value of getting organised. The working class accustomed itself to industrial conflict and was ready to follow tougher leaders. In politics, too, there were consequences. Different loyalties were staking their claims just as workers were shaking off their historic Liberal allegiance and being fully enfranchised for the first time. So now thousands of old and new electors were prepared to do what they had never done before and vote Labour, which in Scotland meant above all voting for the ILP.

As the extreme forces on the Left overreached and spent themselves, it was to the ILP that leadership passed.[34] Though at odds with the establishment, it had never given way to revolutionary fantasies, even when they seemed to be mesmerising the masses. Its inhibitions during the war sprang from its paucity of industrial experience and from an appreciation of the dangers in its pacifism, easily misinterpreted as seditious. Public opinion was at first overwhelmingly in favour of fighting Germany, and the Government was ready to pounce on dissent. After August 1914 the ILP could not rely either on the new Labour leaders in London, who wanted to avoid too close an association with anti-war agitators.

But the industrial unrest was not necessarily unpatriotic, as the authorities chose to think. It arose rather from workers' resentment at what they felt to be exploitation of their patriotism. The ILP seized on this, concentrating its fire on the social and economic aspects of wartime dislocation: prices and rents, the evils of profiteering, the welfare of soldiers' families. So while keeping out of the troubles in industry, it was able to extend its influence among the proletariat. Its Scottish membership tripled between 1914 and 1918 and it gained wide sympathy in a Glasgow working class thoroughly fed up with the Government.

Thus the ILP seemed to have proved itself the best fitted of the Leftist groups for the challenges of peacetime. A number of the industrial militants were attracted to it as a way into regular politics, which were in any case scorned by the minor socialist sects. Glasgow became the centre of a new, popular and decidedly socialist ILP. Its candidates accounted for nineteen, including ten previously active in the CWC, of the forty-six Labourites who stood in Scotland at the 1918 General Election. England then responded to the coalition's jingoism, but Scotland voted heavily socialist for the first time. Working-class Scots had shown much less support for Labour before the war than the English. Yet the war itself strengthened the Left rather than the Right instead of—as in England—the reverse. The patriotic hullabaloo obscured the underlying trend: in the number of seats won the coalition triumphed in Scotland as everywhere else, with Labour taking only eight seats. All the same it gained one-third of Scottish votes, ten times the proportion at the previous election.[35]

Enough grievance had been generated in the working class to give it the coherence and continuity of outlook lacking in the nineteenth century. Peace had solved some economic problems but created worse ones, notably unemployment, which never in the following two decades ran at less than fourteen per cent on the Clyde. Socialism could easily take root among frightened, frustrated workers, especially among the skilled whose privileges had been eroded and to whom the dole was an insult. Important, too, was the conversion of Catholics to Labour, to which they have ever since been remarkably loyal. This was partly the result of the 1916 Easter Rising in Dublin. It destroyed their allegiance to Liberalism and demonstrated, in the person of James Connolly, the possibility of being both a socialist and an Irish nationalist. But it was also due to their improved economic position. Their rigid exclusion by Protestants from the crafts and from union office could no longer be sustained. Some Catholics—such as Wheatley, the dominant figure in the Glasgow ILP, and Patrick Dollan, his electoral organiser—were now numbered among the foremost Labour politicians.

Altogether the developments of these years had allowed the socialists to break through from being isolated sectaries to become leaders of a mass movement. Old divisions dissolved within the Scottish working class, which grew more independent and united. Being identifiably Scottish and working-class, the ILP made itself the symbol of that evolution. It loved to evoke the spirit of Bannockburn, of Wallace and Bruce, in its appeals to the people. It remained committed to Home Rule, to which the rest of Labour was indifferent and in time hostile. Above all it formulated its policies out of the experience of an economically stricken Scotland and devoted itself to finding remedies for her.

Though the Liberals still had residual claims to represent the common man and for years afterwards continued to hold industrial seats, they offered no inspiration to compare with Labour's. Among them the idealism and fervour of the radical tradition were dead. That inheritance now passed to the ILP. Sometimes it was carried over personally by men like William Graham, elected for Edinburgh Central in 1918, who was to all intents and purposes a plain, old-fashioned Border radical. Where Keir Hardie, Thomas Johnston and their like made a difference was by re-interpreting the tradition to link it with the rise of the working class. Scottish socialism was given a history and Scottish history made to seem socialist.

The feat in the West was the most remarkable. It brought not just labour representation, the essential accomplishment in England, but a socialist proletarian party unique in Britain. Its backbone was a group of men harder, more combative, more intellectual than the English Labour leaders, who were mainly trade unionists, often dullards and not always socialists. This difference in personalities seems to have been decisive in producing on Clydeside what Keir Hardie had thought impossible: a breakthrough which did not rely on the unions. Since they remained politically diffident, there must have been at work a class feeling independent of them. Its inspiration may have come from men with the force and vision to win influence out of all proportion to their numbers or to the real proletarian support for their ultimate aims. But that does not necessarily detract from the achievement.

Yet what now happened in Britain as a whole had a greater effect on the future of Scottish socialism.[36] In England, Labour broke its links with the Liberals. It adopted a new constitution in 1918, socialist in philosophy but granting the crucial weight in its counsels to the unions—a historic compromise between the two forces brought together by Keir Hardie. Till then Labour, despite a powerful presence on the national scene, had not progressed in organisation beyond the LRC's loose confederation of affiliated groups. It was one of these—the ILP, a union, the Fabians—that a supporter had to join; he could not be a member of the Labour party as such. The constitution gave it an existence of its own. Now any citizen could join it directly through the network of constituency parties, separate from the affiliates, set up to represent it at the local level.

While that was being built the structure remained decentralised. But Labour's ambitions to rival the old parties meant it could not continue thus. Scotland's importance was hence diminished. So far she had been the only area outisde London with a proper organisation. An advisory council for the country had been established in 1913 to deal more effectively with electioneering. It at once sought greater independence and in 1917 put forward proposals to this end, all rejected by the party bosses in the South apart from the right to a Scottish election manifesto. The council was fitted into a general regional structure set up in 1921. As the organisational gaps were filled, central control became increasingly tight, leaving less and less initiative in the hands of local activists.

Integration was hampered, though, by the different character of Labour in Scotland. There it consisted in little more than the ILP, with which no other affiliate could compete. It had never been close to the unions and grew uncomfortable in a unified structure dominated by them. The spread of constituency parties was perceived as a threat, even if in Scotland they did not develop fast—within five years nearly every seat had one, but many long remained nominal, being nothing but glorified trades councils. More discouraging was the very fact that Labour as a whole now possessed a socialist constitution. The ILP lost its sense of purpose in being an intellectual vanguard and found no new one. Carping at official policy often seemed the only way to maintain its identity. Willy-nilly it became a bolthole for disaffected socialists, who further soured its relations with the main party.[37]

But for now these trends were concealed, especially by the ILP's triumph in the General Election of 1922. It swept Glasgow and sent to Westminster eighteen of Scotland's twenty-nine Labour MPs, including Wheatley, Maxton, Shinwell, Johnston and Kirkwood. The wonder of it moved them and their following to an almost religious fervour. Before the victors left Glasgow they held a service of dedication at which their splendid speeches on the promise of socialism were interspersed with the congregation's singing of Covenanters' hymns. Hundreds came to give the MPs an emotional send-off at St Enoch Station. Kirkwood looked exultantly around and proclaimed: 'When we come back all this will belong to the people!'[38]

In retrospect some took a more sober view. Shinwell wrote that as early as 1922

> the Scottish contingent was, in fact, composed of a typical cross-section of an industrial country representing, not so much the political attitudes of the electors, but their disillusion with the policies of Westminster, especially as regards housing and unemployment.[39]

Yet this is too casual a dismissal from the pragmatic point of view of one who later changed his mind. For a few years after this election they stood at a pinnacle of popularity. With Gladstone they share the distinction of having been the only politicians in modern Scotland to have provided a focus for mass commitment. Like him they aroused hostility, but even among opponents won respect. In the West they inspired a sort of tribal proletarian enthusiasm.

The Clydesiders felt they represented the real needs of the time against the old guard, including that of the Labour party. Yet while calling for a revolution through social and industrial legislation, they remained naive and narrow-minded. The poverty of Scotland was their burning concern, but their response to it was rarely more than emotional. Having served their apprenticeships on town councils or as union organisers on the Clyde, they showed no vision wider than the local one—the only serious policies they had were on essentially municipal questions such as housing. One reason for their failure to break through and win the respect and confidence of the whole Labour movement was their inability to sublimate their passions and address themselves to problems beyond their parish pumps. They did not seem to expect power, contenting themselves with a parliamentary platform on which to air their constituents' grievances.

Still, the ILP had an immediate effect in swinging the Labour leadership election held at the start of the 1922 Parliament in favour of Ramsay Mac-Donald, then regarded as candidate of the Left.[40] This induced the false impression that he would feel himself in its debt and join with it in committing Labour to a precise and immediate programme of socialism. On the contrary, he was trying to give the party an aura of respectability. Within a few months his relations with the Clydesiders had cooled drastically, as their truculence and deliberate rowdiness in the Commons aroused his deep displeasure.

Nevertheless Wheatley, their unofficial leader, was invited to join the Cabinet when Labour took office in 1924.[41] This did not placate his friends, few others of whom found preferment. They distinguished themselves in these precarious months of Labour power by absolute refusal to admit that practical politics might be allowed to modify ideology. They denounced the Prime Minister's compromises with the Liberals—and even more his social life among the aristocracy—for they expected a Labour Ministry to bring an advance towards socialism, not uneasy tinkering with capitalism. Except for Wheatley's Housing Act, their own interests were ignored: their Home Rule

Bill failed. By the end Wheatley himself was disillusioned enough to conclude that Labour had abandoned its ideals. Since the Clydesiders had exerted little obvious influence on the Government, they were quite relieved when it fell. Opposition would permit them to resume a fighting stance.

In the next Parliament, elected at the end of 1924, the Clydesiders resolved to bring Labour back to what they saw as its true path.[42] Wheatley's answer to the dissipation of doctrine lay in restoring the role of the ILP as an internal powerhouse of socialist ideas. Now retired to the back-benches, he worked out, mainly in pamphlets, an alternative economic strategy of higher public spending, nationalisation, trade controls and a minimum wage. His plans were brought together in an ILP document, 'Socialism in Our Time', published in 1926. He also sought ways of countering the increasingly firm central direction of the party by giving more power to its conference. But conference itself rejected them. These were the Clydesiders' first serious intellectual efforts since they had entered the Commons. They came too late to divert a party now set on a gradualist path.

Another possible way forward was for the ILP to exploit more ruthlessly its residual strengths. Having attracted those angered by the Labour leadership's compromises, it was in the country often a party of committed Left-wing activists. These were first mobilised to get rid of obstructions to new, militant methods. The main target was the ILP chairman, Clifford Allen, in truth a radical but also a London intellectual and friend of Ramsay MacDonald's. That was enough to condemn him. Quarrels were picked and Allen was induced to resign in 1925. The wild, impulsive Maxton was elected in his stead. Steps were then taken to control ILP in Parliament, where it had almost ceased to function as a separate entity. But it still held occasional, poorly attended meetings, which were thus all the more easily packed with Clydesiders. At one, an executive for the parliamentary ILP was set up consisting of Maxton and two other Glasgow MPs. They now claimed the right to give orders to all their colleagues. The manouvre had three objects: to legitimise a Leftist ideology as ILP policy; to permit the use of party discipline on those who might otherwise not accept it; and to strengthen ILP influence in Labour as a whole.

Thus Maxton sought to prepare the ILP for his messianic conception of its future. He wanted it to be not just a socialist think-tank but the spearhead of a neo-Marxist, eventually revolutionary mass movement. He did not worry about damaging Labour in the process, for to him the advancement of the working class was more vital than the fate of any mere party. He was fierce in support of the General Strike, attributing its failure only to the lack of solidarity on the Left, and afterwards violently denounced Labour's and the unions' timidity. He consorted with Communists too, notably with Arthur Cook, a miners' leader, with whom in 1928 he issued a manifesto, 'To the Workers of Britain', calling on them to halt the drift towards compromise with capitalism. This alienated many ILP members, outraged the Labour hierarchy and stiffened its resolve to resist him.

His strategy was misconceived. In the movement and in the country there was little interest in purist socialism.[43] Disruption in its name seemed folly when Labour had progressed so far through moderation and won the workers more power than ever before. It already valued unity as such, and Maxton's fury made it the less amenable to dictation from the Clydesiders. This was true of the ILP as well—the bulk of it was in effect merged with the general run of the Labour party, to which it gave its first allegiance. Graham, who was by any standards a moderate, saw nothing inconsistent in belonging to the ILP too. In Scotland generally the changes set in motion by the 1918 constitution were bringing socialists with different aims from Maxton's to the fore and a growing number of union members into her parliamentary representation. Led by William Adamson, they were anxious to direct industrial, indeed all other disputes into safe, institutional channels. The Scottish Council of the ILP itself took a dim view of Maxton's antics. Now a loyalist faction formed. Shinwell and Johnston had been led through the realities of ministerial office away from their Left-wing attachments. The exigencies of running the party machine did the same for Dollan, who in Glasgow was actually stronger than Maxton. Still they could not outwit him, failing in an effort to depose him from the chairmanship in 1929. Under these pressures there was no chance of Maxton rallying the whole ILP to his ideals, support for which was more or less confined to the small band of humdrum Glasgow Backbenchers round him and Wheatley.

They moved rapidly towards a clean break with Ramsay MacDonald when he returned to office in 1929. Their behaviour in the Commons was rude and unpredictable. They hampered, even endangered a Government anyway in a minority and forced to be circumspect by the need for Liberal support. Some hope remained that Wheatley might act as anchor to his wayward, impetuous leader. But he was not re-admitted to the Cabinet and died in 1930. Maxton, with little to lose and nothing to restrain him, was free to transform the quarrels into a power struggle against the Labour leadership. There could be little doubt of the outcome.

The position of the 140 MPs, nearly half Labour's total, who held on to at least nominal ILP membership was uneasy.[44] With their parliamentary executive determined to impose on them an extreme Left-wing policy to which few could subscribe, a clash of loyalties seemed inevitable. It came when the executive ordered a vote against a Government Bill on unemployment insurance, because it did not fulfil the Labour conference's injunction to keep the number on the dole down. According to the rules, this decision was binding on all MPs still attached to the ILP, and those defying it would automatically expel themselves from its parliamentary party. Only nineteen conformed. The move thus achieved nothing but the gratuitous reduction of the ILP in the Commons to a mere rump. In retaliation the parliamentary Labour party passed a standing order allowing MPs to abstain on a matter of conscience while forbidding them ever to vote against one of its formal resolutions. This the nineteen continued to ignore—indeed they set out yet more defiantly to harass and embarrass the Ministry. Even the crisis over the formation of the National Government failed to repair the breach. In the 1931 election the ILP ranged itself with Labour in campaigning against the cuts in unemployment benefit, the issue which had caused the rupture between

Ramsay MacDonald and his former comrades. But to all intents and purposes it stood as a separate party. Maxton and three others were returned.

The rout of the Left prompted feelings that the two sides ought to come together again. Tentative moves for a reconciliation were made. But Maxton's behaviour had caused much bitterness in the Labour ranks, where many believed the ILP no longer worthy of a place among them. George Lansbury, the new leader, insisted that any rapprochement would have to come on his terms, which included full acceptance of the standing orders. Maxton would not give way. Meanwhile the ILP loyalists, backed by *Forward*, were loudly pointing out that the party could hardly remain affiliated to Labour while striking out on a line which contradicted its policies. Inevitably, therefore, the question of disaffiliation arose.[45]

A special conference was called to consider it in July 1932. Maxton had reached the conclusion that no other course was possible. In the absence of an obvious compromise, three-fifths of the delegates voted to quit. Thus ended an alliance which had lasted since the foundation of the Labour party and was largely responsible for setting it on its feet. Nevertheless the main body of the ILP parted without remorse. On the contrary, such emotional force had built up behind the secession that, in a mood of suicidal wildness, the conference proceeded to sever every link with Labour. Dual membership of the ILP and other parties was forbidden, so that nobody could fudge the choice. But that ensured the disintegration rather than the independence of the ILP. It plainly miscalculated the reaction among the rank and file, many of whom had spent years in the service of the movement. It also meant losing the ILP's share of the political levy from the unions, cutting its one tangible link with them and promising it a bleak financial future. Most members could not accept all this. The Scots were especially unhappy and defected in droves. They formed a Scottish Socialist Party under Dollan which remained affiliated and later merged itself with the constituency parties (thus giving Labour the proper local organisation almost everywhere which it had so far lacked). The other leading loyalists, Shinwell and Johnston, also stayed in the Labour fold, while even Kirkwood, one of Maxton's close associates, returned to it within a few months. Scots membership of the ILP dropped catastrophically from 16,000 in 1932 to only 4,000 in 1935.

The ILP thus condemned itself to become merely a socialist splinter group and was soon competing, even in its Western stronghold, from an unfavourable position for the working-class vote. If the figure it now cut was distinctive enough, its contribution to politics was yet not great. The flow of economic ideas died with Wheatley, and policy consisted in little more than an interest in housing and furious hostility to the Labour leadership. Yet Maxton and his circle remained confident. They truly believed that capitalism was collapsing and that only the ILP was qualified to formulate policies for the dawn of a new era. Labour was dismissed as too timid to represent the workers, as a party whose gradualist philosophy had utterly failed. Thus, it was asserted, disaffiliation was the finest thing the ILP had ever done: when economic depression had brought popular discontents to boiling point, its new freedom of action would enable it to lead a proletarian crusade on principles little short of revolutionary. In token of that, the ILP formed in 1932 a United Front with the Communists. It was remarkable, though, only for its disunity, and Maxton withdrew from it two years later.

There was little substance in all this posturing, but it did allow the ILP to keep up its morale and to exercise an influence disproportionate to its size. It gained some ground in the local authorities and formed an alliance with Labour to control Glasgow in the mid 1930s. But Parliament was its true arena. It never had more than three or four MPs—though that sufficed to make it larger than the orthodox Scottish Labour contingent for a time after 1931—but it could maintain the semblance of a real party. It was recognised by the Speaker of the Commons as fully independent, and Maxton enjoyed all the rights and privileges of a party leader. Loved at Westminster for his waywardness and passionate eloquence, he became one of the best known politicians of the decade. Given the depleted numbers of the Opposition and the dullness of the Labour remnant, he could play an unusually prominent role. The ILP survived because of his mastery of Parliament rather than of any great rapport with the proletariat, except in the East End of Glasgow.

But there was no sign as the years passed that the ILP could expand this narrow base. It stayed resolutely pacifist, so that an attempt at reconciliation with Labour in 1938 foundered on the latter's support for re-armament. The ILP also opposed the Second World War, though only at the cost of a further split. While performing a useful opposition function which might have been neglected in the wartime Parliament, dominated by a grand coalition, it really had no future when peace came. Maxton died in 1946. His successor in his seat at Bridgeton and his two ILP colleagues in the Commons, faced with the choice of fading into obscurity or taking part in the socialist reconstruction, rejoined Labour the next year. Thus the ILP's role on the national political stage came to an end, though it fought elections for another two decades and maintained some local branches for three.

What had been achieved after all? For Britain as a whole, the ILP helped to keep alive the aspirations of idealistic socialism, and thus the current of critical thought in a Labour movement not remarkable for its spirit of intellectual adventure. Wheatley's programme had provided an alternative to conventional economic thinking, one which still has a following today. All the same, it could establish no equation between the return of a Labour Government and the introduction of socialism. For the movement, organisation remained more important than doctrine, and organisation was bound to win when the two came into conflict. Voters agreed with this order of priorities. Most who stayed loyal to the Left in the 1930s saw not the Clydesiders but the Labour orthodox as their hope. They could not accept that the ILP was fighting the party establishment on their behalf.

Yet the ILP had long defied the trend in an era of centralisation by preserving its character as a peculiarly Scottish political force. In Scotland the concept of a Labour movement went deeper than the dominant English one of mere working-class representation. For the ILP, socialism was a crusade—its evangelical politics aimed at the transformation of the whole man, and could comprehend everything from economic and social policies through education and culture to the healthy outdoor life and amateur theatricals. This was a Scottish inheritance. But the ILP failed to develop it into an adequate and relevant political programme for Scotland, still less for the United Kingdom.

It might have been done with Home Rule, to which the ILP remained faithful. Its commitment descended through Keir Hardie from Liberal populism, which abhorred overbearing government. But the methods advocated of getting action for Scotland, now the most depressed part of Britain, stood in contradiction to that. When help arrived in the mid 1930s, it was given—to applause from the Clydesiders—through laying the foundations of the modern system of central economic planning. Once it was accepted that the essential initiatives must come from Westminster, the idea of devolution, not to mention of an ILP confined to Scotland, appeared increasingly redundant.

Such sentiment was all but killed by the inevitable subjection of Scottish Labour to the party bosses in London. The STUC abandoned its support for Home Rule in 1931, though it managed to avoid merger with the TUC. By the next year, when another devolution debate was held in the Commons, many Labour MPs were clearly coming to regard it as a bourgeois interest. Partly through admiration of the Soviet example, Labour was adopting centralism as an integral element of modern social and economic theories. In Scotland it was embraced with a vengeance. Labour turned into the most unionist and rigidly disciplined of all the parties. In Parliament adherence to the official line became obligatory, while at home nonconformity was shunned as tending towards schism. Thus democracy itself often fell victim to a remote leadership desiring from the rank and file no more than service in a professional electoral apparatus. Intellectuals and other free spirits sought satisfaction in splinter groups, leaving Labour to the machine politicians, the dullards and authoritarians. This trend was especially marked in the West and continued long after the war.

For many years Scottish socialism remained ossified in the postures of the 1930s. The mouthing of class slogans was preferred to any serious attempt at the promised social regeneration, of which there is little sign even fifty years on. As the almost exclusive repository of the working-class vote, Labour had the chance of exploiting the radical tradition bequeathed to it, but squandered the legacy.

Chapter 7

'Undue Scottish Susceptibilities'

By 1930 the foundations on which the Scots' modern polity had been laid, prosperity for the nation and power for the Liberal party, seemed broken beyond repair. Some reacted by fleeing into outright Nationalism. But, with its practical objects confused and in any case clearly unattainable, it could offer them few hopes. Most therefore accommodated themselves to the new dispensation and were reconciled to unionism as the best way forward. On every hand, Home Rule was being forgotten.

The unionist experiment took two forms. One was to find means of working more closely with the apparatus of central government. It was a natural consequence of the collectivist spirit which for fifty years had increasingly informed politics, first in the West and then elsewhere. That spirit took no notice of the traditional Scottish institutions with their merely moral rather than material outlook. Those of most importance in the past, the Church, the law and the universities, anyway mattered much less. The main presbyterian sects had come together again in 1929, but religion had long been demoted from a political force to an interest group. Scots law was being overtaken by an ever greater volume of uniform legislation for the whole United Kingdom. The universities stagnated, admitting fewer students, losing their scientific pre-eminence, yielding to the forces of anglicisation. Henceforth the institutions with the strongest influence in public affairs were those of recent date, products of the growing scale of government and industry. The capitalists were active, if as yet in an unorganised fashion, trying to arrest economic decay. The STUC was surmounting, largely by assimilation to the British trade union movement, the problems of promoting labour's claims through its feeble and disunited member bodies. The Scottish Office had so far principally been a supervisor of local authorities and administrative agencies, without playing a wider part in the political guidance of the country. Soon it was equipped to do so.

The second half of the experiment lay in the acceptance of a leading role for the Unionist party which continued, except during Attlee's Ministries, for nearly thirty years. It satisfied the hopes entertained by many Scots of moderate opinion. Liberals might not have expected to be quite so subordinate as they turned out inside the desired grand coalition. But that was what they had been advocating and, having got it in 1931, they were broadly content. The idea anyway had its origins in the generous traditions of nineteenth-century Liberalism. The new men brought now in such numbers into Scotland's parliamentary representation resembled their Victorian forebears in forming a broad bottom, moderate, dull, content to underwrite London's policies. The famous carpet-baggers were gone, though there was still a leavening of waspish radicals. Even so, Scots MPs no longer served a territorial interest with its own causes. The enfeebled presbyterian tradition was only carried forward, in the work of such as A D Lindsay, John Reith, John Grierson and John Boyd Orr, outside politics.[1]

The National Government's triumph in Scotland was staggering—much greater than, for example, in Wales, where the roots of the Labour movement seemed to have struck no deeper. While on the surface a genuine coalition, with a Labour Premier and Liberal Ministers, it was in truth a facade for the Unionists' dominance. They, well organised by Sir Robert Horne and Sir John Gilmour, would surely have swept the country on their own, for they anyway took fifty seats. Liberals or National Liberals, generally as yet unseparated and not opposed by Unionists, had sixteen. The sitting MP at Kilmarnock held it for National Labour. This gave in all sixty-seven for the Government. To the opposition it left only seven members, of whom three were official and four unofficial Labour—these soon to join together as the ILP parliamentary party. What had hurt the socialists most was Liberal hostility, which allowed them to win only where they enjoyed a real majority. The political pattern for the 1930s was thus set. It was assumed that class-based voting had ended, yielding to a huge Unionist majority round which lesser groups, some of which it was to absorb, struggled for existence.

The Scotland over which the National Government presided was deeply stricken. Dependent on heavy, exporting industries, she was terribly vulnerable to world depression.[2] That weakness was recognised after the First World War, but little had been done to cure it. Perhaps only the position of farmers, now strongly Unionist, was eased—certainly the protectionism adopted after 1931 helped them most. But in the cities unemployment had been higher than in England since 1923. Between 1929 and 1932 the Scottish rate more than doubled to 28 per cent. In some black spots, such as Greenock and Motherwell, it reached three-quarters of the insured workforce. In the same period national income declined in money terms by 22 per cent, compared with 15 per cent in the United Kingdom as a whole, so that Scotland was left with a smaller share of fewer resources. During the next three years, her proportion of industrial output sank by one-fifth, the fall concentrated in shipbuilding, mining and engineering.

What was to be done? On the Left, Wheatley had devised the programme for a siege economy, though its case was not argued by his successors with any understanding. In the Labour party, economic thinking was still conventional, except in its insistence that at all costs welfare benefits should be maintained. The National Government thought tariffs the key, though they proved self-defeating when other countries introduced them too. Keynesian ideas of state intervention often appealed to younger politicians of all parties—to Mosley, Elliot and Johnston, for example—but for the moment won only limited acceptance.

Scotland was in any case labouring under extra burdens dating from the war. Though the danger of any real social upheaval had always been remote, she had won herself enough of a bad reputation to deter investors, but not enough to bring decisive government action on her problems. A little, but not much, unrest continued, organised mainly in the National Unemployed Workers' Movement, of which the leading figure in Scotland was Harry McShane. Demonstrations in Glasgow and elsewhere against the cuts in unemployment benefit in 1931 sometimes degenerated into violence. Hunger marches followed from Edinburgh and Glasgow in 1933 and from Glasgow again in 1934. Such activity was carried on, ineffectually, all through the decade.[3]

Even so, Labour proved resilient, and was in the end to upset the assumption that there could be no alternative to Unionism. The performance was all the more remarkable because it had lost its strongest native component, the ILP. That and the rout of 1931 ended Scotland's primacy in the party established by its pioneers. Of those still alive, Ramsay MacDonald and Maxton had departed, leaving the older generation at home to be led only by the obtuse Adamson. If it had not been for his early death in 1932, an important role might have been played by William Graham, a talented economist who had been President of the Board of Trade since 1929 and became deputy leader in 1931. It was largely his legacy that Scottish Labour remained a gradualist force, eventually able to appeal to broad masses again, rather than isolated in extremism. Orthodox in his finance and moralising in his socialism, he did live long enough to deter an outward stampede of moderates into support for the National Government. He helped to persuade them that the fault lay not with Ramsay MacDonald's policies but with the man himself, and they stayed loyal.

Labour itself soon joined in the unionist experiment, in the sense that Scotland's interests were in future bound to count much less to it. The victory of the machine in the struggle with the ILP ended disciplinary problems, but also alienated many able men. Labour was left weak at the local level, where it was now led mainly by manual workers. Power gravitated instead to the ever more authoritarian and centralist national Labour party. It speedily gave up any serious commitment to Home Rule. Other anomalies were cleared away, as when in 1938 consent was secured from the STUC to the separation of the trades councils and constituency parties. The structure, consolidated under a Scottish Council of the Labour party, was then identical to that in the regions of England and fully integrated with the central apparatus. This was, however, also a lifeline for the Scots, bewildered at their crushing defeat and dispirited by their own dissensions. Though Labour's prospects in the country at large looked grim, it was yet not broken and did recover.[4]

It had a second lifeline in the trade unions, from which the ILP had so wilfully estranged itself. Thus far the STUC had assumed no major political role, for the interests of its members were parochial. But, step by step with the influence and prestige of the wider union movement, its own were rising—which was one reason why it too acquired an ever more centralist outlook. The general secretary, William Elger, had in 1923 guided through a new constitution which ensured its survival by averting conflict with the English TUC. He struck a bargain which allowed affiliation to the STUC by the Scottish membership of British unions—already accounting for a majority of the 500,000 workers now organised—on the same terms as the membership of Scottish unions. Hence it could fairly claim to represent the whole movement in Scotland. It was moderate and easily able to ward off the Left. Secessions among miners and dockers only confirmed it in its anti-Communism.

Above all Labour had retained in 1931 a bedrock of support, one-third of the electorate indeed, in the industrial working class. That was consolidated by the threat of unemployment and by the party's main economic demand of the moment, the safeguarding of welfare benefits. It was otherwise preoccupied, as before, with municipal matters, especially the expansion of subsidised council housing and the maintenance of separate schooling for Catholics, now among the most trusty components of its vote. Those policies brought it early success in recapturing the burghs, of which it ruled nineteen by 1935. The jewel in this somewhat alloyed crown was Glasgow, controlled by Labour and the ILP in coalition from 1933 and by Labour alone from 1938, with Dollan as Lord Provost. The tradition of active city government was still strong, and the corporation did what it could to ease economic conditions with fair wage clauses in municipal contracts and direct labour departments.

All this showed Labour recovering from its trauma through the humdrum but necessary tasks imposed by centralism: building a presence in the local authorities, patching up the party's machine and co-operating with its British organs. The old utopian fervour with its nationalist overtones was little regretted. As Thomas Johnston said: 'What purport would there be in getting a Scots Parliament in Edinburgh if it has to administer an emigration system, a glorified Poor Law and a graveyard?'[5]

Labour was thus also equipped to withstand competition from its socialist rivals. The Communist party had in Scotland one of its few areas of strength, but it aroused more fear than its size or activity justified. Its bid now for the leadership of the far Left was ruined by its opportunism, which even in these favourable conditions repelled potential recruits. As things stood, it was at Moscow's behest against co-operation with fellow-travellers, thus isolating itself save in pockets of Clydeside and in Fife. In that county it had a base in its own union, the United Mineworkers of Scotland, and returned a number of councillors. Such efforts, though small, bore fruit in William Gallacher's victory over Adamson in West Fife at the General Election of 1935. Meanwhile, again at the Kremlin's dictation, the Communists had changed their line, seeking a common front of all progressive groups against Fascism. They looked for causes to share with other socialists and even with Liberals, including Home Rule. The omens were all the same bad. In 1933 the ILP had responded to similar approaches, in joint policy committees and the like. But Communists were rarely willing to take any but their own interests into account and Maxton, who had come to distrust them, withdrew from the arrangement. That left them again in an isolation which could not be broken.[6]

Other options for the ILP were limited after its disaffiliation from Labour. It chose, as recounted above, the full independence which brought its rapid decline.[7] Yet the fact that it had in the 1931 Parliament more Scots MPs than the official Labour party filled it with delusions. While its pugnacity won it much admiration from workers, Maxton's hope that it could escape at the local level the consequences of its break with the wider national movement proved vain. It lost most of its existing supporters and gained few new ones, since activists preferred to join the Communist or the Labour party. An effort was made by the latter to entice its membership back when Dollan, Shinwell and Kirkwood set up to take its place in the parent body an affiliate equally dedicated to education and propaganda, the Scottish Socialist Party. As the ILP withered, the task became redundant. In the 1935 election it regained one seat, but desertions continued. Complacent in its unrealistic policies, it was not forced like Labour into a thorough re-appraisal of aims and methods. The price was paid in a loss of touch with the proletariat, except in Glasgow. Socialism in one city was hardly possible, however.

National Labour offered no serious alternative either. Of the home-based Scots in the previous Government, only the Lord Advocate, Craigie Aitchison, MP for Kilmarnock, and the Solicitor General, John Watson, went over to it. Otherwise it had hardly any presence at all. But two exalted candidates, Ramsay MacDonald and his son, Malcolm (both defeated in their English constituencies in 1935) won it by-elections in Scotland afterwards. The former Prime Minister was, though, an embarrassment. Such a distinguished figure was useful to the Government in promoting national unity, and it wanted him in Parliament again. Yet he could not now be trusted to win any industrial seat, and no Unionist MP was willing to resign in his favour. A chance came with the death of Noel Skelton, sitting of late for the Scottish Universities— except that Ramsay MacDonald had always opposed, indeed had tried to abolish, their separate representation. The political associations of this mainly Unionist constituency were shocked at his eagerness to use it as a springboard back into the Commons. The efforts of the official machine eventually foisted him on them all the same. He was returned, as was his son for Ross and Cromarty in 1936.[8]

The Liberals had meanwhile been reduced to a bunch of squabbling factions united only by a name and its memories. Most had reckoned their co-operation with the Labour Government unprofitable. They were thus naturally drawn in the other direction. In fact they became dependent on Unionist charity, and were not always grateful either. In the first National Government there sat three Scots Liberals, with Sir Archibald Sinclair as Secretary of State. They did not stay long. Among its first measures was the introduction of imperial preference, offensive to their doctrine of free trade. In September 1932 they resigned, but stayed for the moment in the coalition. That nevertheless marked the opening of the split between them, the independents, and the National Liberal faction which consented to take their vacant places in the Ministry.[9] It widened when they went over into Opposition the next year. Liberalism was breaking up in the struggle between Left and Right, though its adherents still regarded themselves as members of the one party. They were driven into wasting their energies on battles for control of its organisation.

Sinclair, who held the SLF for the independents, had to leave room for reunion in Parliament, yet try to make sure of their dominance in the constituencies. Thus, while avoiding a breach with the National Liberals, he was constantly manoeuvring to ease friends into key positions. Each of his many setbacks had to be meekly accepted, since he was reluctant for the two wings to be seen fighting each other. But at times he could still take the offensive. He was behind the conference resolution of 1933 which called on the whole party to repudiate the coalition, though many Scots defied it. Other attempts to recapture ground had an air of desperation. Sinclair even turned to the embryonic Nationalist movement. The project of merger foundered, not least on the fact that some leading Scots Liberals were now against Home Rule.[10]

The National Liberals struck back just before the country went to the polls again in the summer of 1935. Conspiring with the irrepressible Lloyd George and helped by his mysterious funds, they took control of the SLF by winning over its chairman. He felt the need for finance more important than what he regarded as minor quarrels with the Unionists. In a painfully moderate statement, he went on record in favour of 'genuine (if to some extent qualified) co-operation with the National Government, especially at the coming General Election.'[11] This ploy still only enabled Liberals to contest ten county and six burgh seats. The independents, with no organisation to speak of, were all but wiped out, Sinclair alone being left on the Front bench. He was then chosen leader of a party staring extinction in the face. Even at by-elections it was humiliated. Sinclair wrote in 1937: 'While at the centre the federation is doing what it can, most of the associations throughout the country are simply dead.'[12] Despite his efforts, the rift with the National Liberals had been formalised after he overthrew the conspirators in the SLF in a counter-coup at the end of 1935. They then set up their own electoral machine. Sinclair was glad that they could therefore be saddled with the blame for the trouble. And while they declined to merge with the Unionist party till after the war, they always fought with its support and could not escape the accusation of being Tory stooges. Yet they usually bested the independents—not least because they had attracted most of the Liberal talent, including the incumbent Secretary of State, Sir Godfrey Collins, as well as two of his successors, Ernest Brown and the Earl of Rosebery.

Other parties on the fringe similarly failed to make headway against the overwhelming weight of Unionism. Two Nationalist ones existed. The larger, the National Party of Scotland, founded in 1927, was under John Mac-Cormick close to Labour in its social and economic ideas. The second, the Scottish Party, was formed by dissident Unionists in 1932. Neither was very clear in its strategy. To aim at independence seemed mere fantasy, and in practice they just provided a refuge for old Home Rulers. Nor were their efforts attended with much fortune, even after they merged in 1934 into a Scottish National Party consciously moderate in outlook. Its vote at General Elections was not to rise above 30,000 till 1964, its only consolations coming in the municipalities or in rectorial contests at the universities (but see chapter 9 below). Attempts to find a middle way brought greater confusion, as in the bungled attempts to unite Nationalists and Liberals, which did little for either.[13]

Fascism was a negligible force in Scotland. There had been some imitation of the Italians during the 1920s by a group of Scottish Loyalists, said to be 2,000 strong, under the Earl of Glasgow. When Sir Oswald Mosley broke with Labour in 1931, he took with him two Scots MPs, one of them Dr Robert Forgan, of West Renfrewshire, who became deputy leader of the British Union of Fascists. Mosley's New Party fought five seats in Scotland at the subsequent election, four in or near Glasgow together with Galloway, but was routed in all.[14] Perhaps the most extreme of the Scots members then returned was Archibald Maule Ramsay in South Midlothian and Peebles, whose views took on a gloss of pan-European anti-Bolshevism not so different from Nazism in its more philosophical moments. He was interned in 1940.

The most notable native movement on the further Right was Protestant. Prejudice against the Catholic minority intensified during the depression, though the flow of new arrivals from Ireland slowed to a trickle. The Kirk showed much rancour on the subject, enunciating 'the elementary right of a nation to control and select its immigrants'. Unionism was, however, no longer willing to exploit such feeling openly by providing a respectable vehicle for the Orange Lodge. In response there arose two groups, the Scottish Protestant League in Glasgow and Protestant Action in Edinburgh, virulently anti-Catholic and anti-socialist, which won several seats on their respective town councils when left a clear run by the Unionists.[15]

But the ruling party itself was not viciously conservative, as the popular mythology grown up since tends to depict it. There were within it advanced elements which saw themselves as defenders of liberty on a programme just as radical as its rivals', yet more realistic. They could justly claim that Unionism had proved itself socially progressive—it had, after all, been the main channel through which the Scottish capitalist class had risen from merely local standing to national leadership, a privilege usually reserved by the old Liberal party to aristocrats. Nor were they complacent towards the distress of the proletariat, even if unable to find quick or easy remedies. What they now sought was a coherent version of liberal values relevant to a mass urban society which had lost unquestioning faith in individualism and free enterprise. It would aim neither at the pure ideal of efficiency, as espoused by the wartime tycoons on the Clyde, nor at the socialist destruction of private ownership. It was, at least in embryo, corporatist. It accepted that large concentrations of economic power had come to stay, in the shape of both organised capital and organised labour. Indeed it believed that the state ought to encourage them as agents of efficient production and full employment, while setting the conditions by which they should be held in balance. The practical result might be managerial paternalism, but it could reasonably be presented as a type of industrial democracy fulfilling the demands of the age.

It took a decade and more for these ideas to be worked out. Skelton had been the first to put them forward, and in the 1920s he was already gathering round him a growing body of disciples.[16] They included not only native Scots, but also rising stars among the English MPs such as Anthony Eden and Harold Macmillan. At first they were, almost by definition, rebels. Yet a number of them won their first ministerial posts in 1931, rising thence to positions from which they could decisively influence the future course of the British Right. As things turned out, they had in Scotland their first opportunities to practise what they preached. Forming there a national party which drew support from all regions and classes, they could hope to build a new consensus in between discredited Liberalism and suspect socialism.

Along with Skelton, the most distinguished of them was John Buchan, with his idealistic imperialism, his romantic dreams of lads o' pairts making good in the establishment, his friendship for the Clydesiders and his agonising over expenditure cuts after 1931.[17] More brilliant but more eccentric was Robert Boothby, driven by the poverty of the Aberdeenshire he represented into a hostility to international finance almost as fierce as a socialist's. He later wrote that 'the system of "laissez-faire" capitalism which enshrined the principle of enlightened self-interest is not only dead but in a state of putrefaction', arguing that free trade, the gold standard and foreign competition exerted on the farmer a grip which had to be broken. It was an intriguing evolution of agrarian radicalism. By the end of the Second World War, Boothby was an advocate of the welfare state and of forceful government intervention in the economy, even of limited nationalisation.[18] Most flamboyant of all was the Duchess of Atholl, elected in 1923 for Kinross and West Perthshire as the first Scottish woman MP. A tigerish anti-fascist, and deprived of the whip for her opposition to Neville Chamberlain, she resigned in 1938 to fight a by-election against the Munich agreement. She was supported by the Popular Front—which united such diverse elements as the Communists, the Young Liberals and Boothby—losing only narrowly to the official candidate.[19]

Overshadowing all these in both political vision and practical expertise was the outstanding figure among the progressive Unionists of the time, Walter Elliot. His book of 1927, Toryism and the Twentieth Century—granted the accolade of an introduction by Stanley Baldwin—was the earliest attempt to set out in extended and lucid form the theories which he and his friend had been discussing. The programme it proposed was indeed essentially corporatist, though not coercive on the contemporary European model. He believed instead that the task of politics was to erect a framework within which corporatist bonds could emerge, in an entirely voluntary way, between capitalists and workers. That was how they could together meet the unpredictable and uncontrollable forces always ruling the real world, with a better chance of success than the rigidities of socialism would ever offer. More significant still, Elliot—having already done sterling work as a junior Minister at the Scottish Office—was soon to be Secretary of State.

By then there had been a response at home in Scotland. While labour's calls for action were loudest, capital was not dormant either. We have noted above the role taken by Scottish capitalists, especially those brought up on Glasgow's collectivism, in the state's reorganisation and sustenance of industry after 1918. Despite the drastic change in their fortunes, they were as self-confident as ever. Their work went on. Weir was president of the National Employers' Federation, and the wartime generation which he had led found its successors: Sir Steven Bilsland, an inventive banker with a wide range of industrial interests, Sir John Colville, a steel magnate who became Secretary of State, and Sir Andrew Duncan in shipping, coal, steel and electricity.

The most energetic was Sir James Lithgow, scion of a famous Clyde dynasty.[20] He was chosen president of the Shipbuilding Employers' Federation at an early age in 1920, then followed a well-trodden route through various public industrial bodies. His most controversial project was the National Shipbuilders Security Ltd, founded in 1930. This private corporation sought to cure the ills of a crippled sector through rescue operations and planned contraction. It bought up loss-making firms and then, as the unhappy term had it, sterilised them. Thus construction capacity was cut and more business left for the remaining yards. Though he got help from the Labour Ministry and the Bank of England, Lithgow provided much of the finance from his own pocket. Even so, his altruistic motives were misconstrued by the workers. He had always been regarded by them as a hard taskmaster and now seemed to be mounting a savage attack on their livelihoods. Because the company was owned by shipbuilders, not by the Government, its activities were taken as an especially shocking example of heartless capitalism. Lithgow became the symbol of everything to be feared and hated in rationalisation. But the alternative might have been more instability, more sudden closures and more unemployment. His was a bitter, arduous and thankless task which only bore fruit when rearmament started.

His public spirit was seen in a better light in his promotion of the Scottish National Development Council, set up in 1931 to bring labour and capital together in the first of many similar efforts at co-operation. He went on to devise plans for saving the engineering and steel industries, again subsidising companies himself if he felt their survival essential to a recovery. In 1933 he was made, with Weir and Sir Arthur Balfour, a member of the official working party on rearmament, advising on where demand would arise in wartime and how to meet it. From 1935 he was active in the Scottish Economic Committee, which sought the aid of interested parties in surveying national resources and ways of mobilising them. Little progress could be made, however, with his suggestion of a corporation to finance new ventures funded by the Scottish banks. In general there was as yet a lack of experience in planning and of instruments for putting it into effect. It was also often vitiated in practice by the class hostility between employers and unions.

Lithgow rejected compulsory projects devised by politicians and civil servants, holding that intervention ought to be voluntary. This was an old-fashioned Scottish view. But the ruin of the economy had persuaded other capitalists that the state itself should help to restore the conditions for their traditional vigorous enterprise. This attitude was a product of their rise during recent decades in the apparatus of a stronger state, and a logical development of Glasgow Unionism. So far it had reacted to recession through cartels and rigorous retrenchment. These were still in vogue, but were supplemented by further ideas. One was provision of finance from the Exchequer at least in dealing with the worst effects of the most intractable problems—naturally nobody yet thought to make it the motor of the economy. Many also felt that government ought to be nearer, not to direct industry itself, but to be more accessible and responsive to those who would.

Between the formation of the National Government and Johnston's appointment to the Scottish Office in 1941, there were five Secretaries of State. Three were Liberals, they being reckoned to have a certain lien on the post in view of the need for a harmonious coalition. The other two could be counted among the liberal Unionists. Scotland thus had, by contemporary standards, a progressive regime throughout.[21]

Sinclair's term might have been fruitful had it been longer and come at a time more propitious to Scottish measures. When he resigned in 1932 he was succeeded by Collins, head of the publishing house, leader of the National Liberal rump and remarkable for holding the working-class constituency of Greenock through nine elections.[22] He concurred, in the teeth of opposition from some of his Scots colleagues, with the need for public economy, especially in his Housing Act (1933), which phased out subsidies. But under him began the reforms which were to transfigure the modern government of Scotland.

The main innovation during his own tenure of office was regional aid, brought in under the Special Areas Act (1934).[23] It applied to the whole of Britain, but Collins got Scotland a commissioner of her own to administer it. In the districts designated—West Lothian, Fife and Clydeside, though without Glasgow—he had a brief to help existing industries and stimulate new ones. Initially this meant programmes of public works, on which nearly £5 million was spent, much of it in the establishment of trading estates. Steps were also taken to maintain health and welfare services where local authorities were in financial straits. The commissioner's annual reports showed a slow improvement. In 1935 he was gloomy: his measures had assisted a selection of existing companies and some incomers, but he concluded that the schemes offering the best prospects were tardy in their impact and did not immediately yield large numbers of jobs. The next report spoke of an all-round increase in activity in both old, heavy industries and new, light ones. But again, there remained pockets of high unemployment with a surplus of workers unsuitable to the changed demand for labour.

It would have been impossible for the Unionists to hold at the 1935 election all the ground previously won.[24] But the country's confidence in them was confirmed when they came back with thirty-seven of the National Government's forty-six MPs. Only three independent Liberals survived, while the ILP restored its strength to four and one Communist was returned. Labour made good progress in central Scotland and, to general astonishment, took the Western Isles, for a total of twenty seats. Thus it restored itself as the main opposition to Unionism. This election finally established the modern system of two parties. Each was now entrenched in areas of homogeneous social composition, Labour in the industrial ones, Unionists in the suburbs and counties. The latter remained all the same much the larger party in the popular vote, with just a shade under 50 per cent. While Labour, with 37 per cent, added four points to its previous share of the poll, it won fewer seats than at the time of its first breakthrough in 1922.

So, with the anti-Unionist forces still feeble and divided, the revival was only limited. The secretary of the Labour party, Arthur Woodburn, was in his report on the election studiously unimpressed with the gains. They had not, he wrote, shaken the prestige of the Government. There persisted a general lack of confidence in Labour, above all in its economic policies and particularly in nationalisation. Its pacifism, too, had been a handicap in a campaign fought to an unusual extent on foreign policy; its faith in the League of Nations seemed misplaced amid growing fears of war. In Scotland, moreover, it faced socialist, not just conservative critics: 'People would not have believed our enemies—they did believe our own people,' Woodburn commented.[25] The major improvement was in personnel. As Adamson's career had come to an end with his ignominious defeat at the hands of Gallacher, Johnston was appointed Scottish spokesman in the Commons. He moved towards the centre, supporting the measures of administrative reform brought in by the Unionists. Labour won two by-elections in this Parliament, but could almost certainly not have restored its majority had a General Election been held in 1940.

After Collins' sudden death in 1936, his designs were pursued with great vigour by Elliot.[26] Among the most attractive personalities to have occupied the Scottish Office, he was a man of broad and humane interests who certainly had the potential to become great. His zeal for ordered reform sprang from a high intellect which, however, also made him sceptical, so that he could appear disordered in his thinking, wordy and reluctant to commit himself. Despite many misgivings, he was among those Cabinet Ministers who accepted the Munich agreement, with a fatal effect on his own subsequent career. He was sacked by Churchill in 1940 and never held office again.

He wanted the Unionists to be a progressive party, ready if necessary with state intervention, able to hold the centre ground occupied by former Liberal or Labour voters. In the economic field he identified two problems. One was housing. He raised the number of homes built to a record level, and in 1937 founded the Scottish Special Housing Association to answer neglected needs such as those of incoming workers not on the long waiting lists. The other was to create jobs rather than just stave off unemployment. In 1938 he set up the first industrial estate outside Glasgow, and had the powers in the special areas extended so that incentives might be offered to small firms. The commissioner's report that year noted a widespread revival, largely due to re-armament, which had cut the number on the dole by one-third since 1934. But it granted that intractable problems persisted, notably in mining.

Elliot's great work came in the re-organisation and transfer to Scotland of the Scottish Office. It was more than administrative reform. It had immense symbolic value, making Edinburgh once again a seat of government, truly a capital rather than just the headquarters of the Kirk and judiciary. It was, with Home Rule now excluded on all sides, a real attempt to raise the standing of a department which so far had had relatively trivial duties. This was stuck in the mould of 1885 in its conceptions of the state. The then limited role of government had meanwhile been vastly expanded, but all new powers had gone to United Kingdom Ministries. In the fifty years of its existence, the Scottish Office had fully solved only one big political problem, that dealt with in the Education Act (1918).

Gilmour's reforms of the department in 1927 had been attacked as anglicising, as subjecting it too much to Whitehall norms. The criticism struck home. There was genuine worry about the direction of events, and Unionists such as Horne and Buchan were foremost in calling a halt. In response, some staff had already been transferred from London to Edinburgh. Under Collins, discussions started about a wider overhaul. Elliot took the decisive step in 1936 by appointing Gilmour head of another inquiry, which reported the next year.[27]

It found the definitive answer to one major problem which had dogged Scottish government for a century, that of the status and operation of the administrative boards. They had conducted most day-to-day business, but were not really devolved bodies, rather the products of convenience as London sought to draw on expert knowledge for the technical tasks of ruling a distant country with its own laws. In his first attempt Gilmour had tried to balance the demands of tradition and efficient government. It produced untidy results, however. Some boards were amalgamated and recast as departments, but others survived. Some now required civil service standards of entry, but others continued to employ patronage, occasionally of laymen. Most answered to the Secretary of State, but the Scottish Education Department was formally a committee of the Privy Council, and their location was still divided between Edinburgh and London. In all, Gilmour's effort to strengthen his and his successors' responsibility for them had not worked. If it was real, then their independence was illusory. In fact the chain of command remained obscure, and the overriding need was to lay down a clear one.

It was done by application of a simple rule. Previous statutes had vested powers in the boards or departments, giving the Secretary of State a vague supervisory role. Now the powers were to be vested in him. The organs of the administration, including the surviving boards, would be refashioned into four departments (Agriculture, Education, Health, Home) all of equal status, all part of one Scottish Office with a permanent Under-secretary in charge of the whole, transferred to Edinburgh and there subject directly to the Secretary of State, leaving only a parliamentary and liaison staff in London.

The headlong anglicisation started by the first set of Gilmour reforms was thus slowed, if not in the long run halted. All the same a certain independence at St Andrew's House was assured for the future. It could adopt distinctive working methods, for the suggestion of letting at least the administrative grade of civil servants stay behind in Whitehall had been rejected. It might assume fresh functions piecemeal. It could even turn itself into a Home Rule administration overnight. More important, the Secretary of State was now able to regulate as he liked its internal organisation and policy-making procedures. Before, its constituent parts had followed their own ideas, subject to his sanction. Henceforth he could through them enforce his personal preferences, providing the driving force instead of just oiling the machine. Gilmour alluded to that wider political role in these terms:

> The duties of the other great offices of state are in general defined functionally. The duties of the Secretary of State are, on the other hand, defined on a geographical basis . . . He is popularly regarded as 'Scotland's Minister' and our evidence shows that there is an increasing tendency to appeal to him on all matters which have a Scottish aspect, even if on a strict view they are outside the province of his duties as statutorily defined . . . there is a wide and undefined area in which he is expected to be the mouthpiece of Scottish opinion in the Cabinet and elsewhere.[28]

That was the first official recognition of his function of promoting Scotland's interests generally. In time it was to become his most important function.

Thus a firmer, more coherent approach to public questions became not just feasible but almost inevitable. In a system centred on one man, Scottish interest groups could work out with him and the department a national line on particular issues and, so long as it was compatible with general policies pursued in London, have it promoted there and translated into law. It was also frequently possible to get the general policies modified in Scotland's favour. While that encouraged consensus among the interest groups, it also subordinated them to the executive branch of government, thus established as the prime mover in Scottish affairs. This was the central achievement of the unionist experiment, the essential antidote to its programme of integration.

In 1938 Elliot moved on. The necessary legislation was completed by his successor, Colville, under whom the Scottish Office took up residence the next year on Calton Hill in Edinburgh.[29] He was typical of the Clydeside capitalists in their governing role. He had little interest in social problems, though the special areas report of 1939 pointed to them as a principal reason for the lack of further progress: standards of health and housing below those elsewhere reinforced the poor morale of workers and deterred useful immigrants. His own outlook was protectionist, which equipped him to promote Scotland's interests keenly as the state took on the mammoth burden of re-armament. She at last followed the rest of Britain with a decisive fall in unemployment. The same pattern continued under Brown, the ebullient English MP for Leith and Secretary of State 1940–1. The function of the Scottish Office, accorded a second Under-secretary, was now simply to carry out the duties imposed by war.[30]

So it might have continued had it not been for the arrival there of the legendary Johnston.[31] He professed reluctance to be elevated—and never took the salary—for he had been intending to leave politics. But he stayed for four years, during which, as he declared in his memoirs, 'we . . . got Scotland's wishes and opinions respected and listened to as they had not been respected or listened to since the Union.'[32] He has generally been taken at his own valuation. The best modern Scottish historian wrote: 'When every allowance is made for the unusual latitude he enjoyed, Tom Johnston emerges as easily the greatest of the Secretaries of State for Scotland.'[33] Later re-appraisals have not altered that judgement, though it is being accepted that he was no betrayed pioneer, nor even much of an advocate, of Home Rule. This does not mean his achievement was fatally flawed; it must be viewed in its context. Johnston largely shared the centralist outlook of his own party, with which the strengthening of the Scottish Office was not incompatible. But, without our hindsight, he could not have foreseen Labour's victory in 1945 or the consolidation after an interval of its rule in Scotland. A sensible contemporary observer might have assumed her Right-wing majority to be invincible and Unionist government as likely to continue indefinitely. So it was essential to give his party and its philosophy a secure place inside the consensus established by Unionism, which was not at all averse to progressive ideas. Thus Labour could come in from the wilderness to take a full part in the unionist experiment.

Johnston, though a university man of bourgeois stock, had started his career an *enfant terrible*, editing *Forward*, abusing the aristocracy. He entered Parliament for West Stirlingshire as part of the ILP contingent in 1922, but soon drew apart from the Clydesiders. He had too clear and orderly a mind, was too disinterested and modest, to follow in their anarchistic wrecking. By 1929 he was Under-secretary at the Scottish Office and by 1931 in the Cabinet as Lord Privy Seal in charge of relief schemes. He learned to love admin-istration and to abhor distractions from it. He now argued that the quest for jobs should be 'lifted entirely out of the arena of partisan political strife'. Government by consensus was his theme after he became Labour's chief Scottish spokesman in 1935. He agreed with liberal Unionists on the need for administrative devolution rather than Home Rule. He concurred when that conclusion was reached by Gilmour, dissenting only in a desire for better democratic control through meetings of the Scottish grand committee in Edinburgh. On the outbreak of war, he was appointed commissioner for civil defence in Scotland with powers also over food and fuel supplies, transport, direction of labour, evacuation and information. With the Lord Advocate he worked out plans to take full control if Britain were invaded and London fell. Rosebery was his deputy and ally against bureaucratic inertia. The task was performed with a vigour that marked Johnston out as a superlative administrator and made him a natural choice for Secretary of State after Labour had joined the Government.

Thanks to Lithgow's committee Scotland was this time better prepared for war. It brought a prompt and vast expansion of central government at the expense of local agencies. For example, every measure of regional aid introduced in the 1930s, and anyway viewed with suspicion in Whitehall, was suspended. Now firms were simply told from London where to set up and what to make. All available manpower was directed to war industries, some-times sited in England, or forced to remain in other essential ones: those factories deemed non-essential were denied labour and raw materials, if not turned over to storage or closed down. With one in seven of all war projects allocated to Scotland, she got more of the extra productive capacity which Lithgow and others had fought for. But most was in the old, heavy industries and little in those supplying armaments and other modern goods.[34]

She was at least more easily organised than England. Military installations were built in the central belt and round the Highland seaboard, but the forces' presence was not so overwhelming as in southern England and the disruption—with just 65,000 evacuees—not so great. Only in the bombing of Clydebank in March 1941 was any major destruction wrought. It did not depress morale in the West where, for instance, more ships were built the next year than ever before. On the contrary, it helped to get this faintly recalcitrant region really working on the war effort. For its sake, government was so far as possible being consciously run for the people's benefit, and the scandal of the depressed areas could no longer be afforded. Higher output and investment eventually mopped up nearly all the unemployment. Vigorous encouragement of agriculture and controlled distribution of its produce actually improved the nutrition of the working classes.

Government became truly national in 1940 when Labour entered the coalition. Politics went into abeyance. A pact ensured that by-elections were not contested among the main parties, though on occasion the ILP, Nationalists or independents intervened. Resistance to war came only from these and, at first, from Communists. A few dissidents were imprisoned. Pacifism, till recently the official line of the Labour party, remained relatively strong within it, however. In November 1939 a negotiated peace was called for by twenty of its MPs, seven from Scotland. She was the strongest base for opposition to its support for war.[35] More generally, Whitehall still harboured some doubts of her belligerency. One survey noted:

> It is not that Clydeside workers are against the war or for peace. They want to win it as much as anyone, though there is a considerable Maxtonish minority. It is rather that Clydeside workers are also having a war of their own, that they cannot forget the numerous battles of the past 30 years and cannot overcome the bitter memory of industrial insecurity in the past ten years and their distrust of the motives of managers and employers.[36]

In 1942 another report found the sentiment that 'we would be as well off under Hitler'[37] disturbingly prevalent in the Scots coalfields; they also saw most of the prosecutions under the order in council which banned strikes. The Germans even thought it worthwhile to start broadcasts from a Radio Caledonia. This was a meagre catalogue of mutiny. But it allowed Johnston to beguile Reith, and no doubt others, with talk of a 'sort of Sinn Fein movement', a notion he exploited shamelessly.[38]

It had indeed helped him, when pressed to take office in 1941, to extract the concessions which gave him more independence than any of his predecessors. Churchill saw through his wiles and distrusted them. But, probably wrongly, he thought a price necessary for a tranquil Scotland and was willing to pay. Johnston's exaggerated attention to the feeble, feckless Nationalists did prevent their becoming anything else. Of much greater consequence was the strengthening of his own hand as Secretary of State.

The system he instituted has been called 'informal Home Rule'.[39] Its informal nature was not the least of its pecularities. A constant purpose of devolution has after all been to bring government nearer the Scottish people. But the suspension of politics had deprived them, as the British people generally, of serious influence on their rulers. Johnston did nothing to restore it. The centrepiece of his innovations was the raising of himself into a position of quasi-premier, heading a Council of State composed of the ex-Secretaries for Scotland. These were five: in order of seniority Munro (now Lord Alness), Sinclair, Elliot, Colville and Brown. They first met in September 1941, monthly till the end of 1942 and sporadically for the duration. They did not stop at merely vetting Scottish measures, but launched thirty-two inquiries into possible reforms that might be combined into a programme of their own. Elliot was keen on long-term plans for education and housing, while Colville stressed the threat to the industrial future in non-essential firms being penalised in favour of war producers bound to close down at the end of hostilities. Action on all this was approved by the Council of State with unanimity. That was the condition Churchill had set for the Government's support. Then, however, the proposals could go through Parliament without a division. Thus opposition was disarmed, and residual opportunities for democratic scrutiny by-passed. Even so, the council lost its initiative because it had no executive powers. It could contribute little to plans for reconstruction once they were past the first stage of identifying and investigating problems.

An impetus might have been preserved by Johnston's scheme to have the Scottish grand committee summoned from time to time to Edinburgh. This proved worthless. It was not even the committee, only an informal convention—attended by just twenty-seven MPs, of whom fifteen were Labour—that he was able to bring to the capital in October 1941. Nothing resulted, so he fell back on meetings at Westminster.

Johnston expected more of his 'industrial Parliament', properly the Scottish Council on Industry.[40] Representing the major economic interests, it got to work in February 1942. Its ideas and energy were meant to solve the problems with which lesser bodies had grappled for a decade and fit the Scottish Office as the nation's planning authority. Its best efforts came in the allocation of war industries—by 1945 it had brought in 700 projects with 90,000 jobs. Johnston egged it into standing up to Whitehall, which lacked contacts in Scotland and disliked her lobbying. In practice there was a good deal of co-operation, especially with Duncan, between 1940 and 1945 alternately President of the Board of Trade and Minister of Supply. Thus the council became Britain's most effective pressure group. Success warranted permanence: it was merged in 1946 with the Scottish National Development Council to become the Scottish Council (Development and Industry), which survives today under the same cumbrous name.

Johnston publicised and popularised this work with vigour, appealing to the national spirit of solidarity to get things done. His biggest single initiative was to set up in 1943 the North of Scotland Hydro-Electric Board, providing cheap energy and fostering development in that neglected Highland region covering one-third of the country. The proposal met with much opposition, but the Council of State, not least the Unionist members, stood firm on it. Johnston took immense pride in this Scottish exercise in public ownership, the first corporation of its kind to be run from outside London. He assumed its chairmanship after the war and stood guard over it when it was threatened with absorption into the nationalised electricity industry. Other projects were not on such a scale but were widely accounted useful. With an industrial division inside the Home department, the Scottish Office began to equip itself as a planning Ministry. The machinery was extended downwards in partnership with committees of local authorities in East and West. Progress was made in agriculture, not only in the boost to output in the Lowlands, but also in remote areas through aid for hill-farming; in addition the Scottish Office won joint responsibility for the Forestry Commission. An emergency hospital scheme, precursor of the National Health Service, provided some free treatment for civilians in the central belt. Unlike in England, housebuilding was continued through the war in Scotland, where the first rent tribunals were also set up.

Most of these social and economic innovations survived Johnston's retiral from the Scottish Office in 1945. The constitutional frills did not, even with a Labour Government soon in power. It evidently saw no place for them under its own centralist regime of radical reform, and Johnston did not stay in Parliament to try and change its mind. For despite his hopes to the contrary, politics could hardly be forever conducted in the form of public inquiries by-passing the normal democratic procedures in the cause of a Scottish consensus. And since that was bound to comprise elements about which the parties disagreed in London, they could not, once their habitual strife resumed, be expected to stand together on it in Scotland.

The Unionists suffered most from its end. On it they had, with their majorities in the parliamentary representation and in the Council of State, exercised great influence. Care had been taken to bring the capitalists into the war effort, Weir, for example, occupying the splendid post of director general of explosives. The Council on Industry, in particular, had assured them a powerful voice in Johnston's arrangements. And in his quest for consensus he had always stopped short of offending Unionist sensibilities. In fact he quite forgot his antecedents in a doubtless necessary deference to the establishment. His appointments were all of figures from it—unlike those of Elliot, who had preferred outsiders. Johnston thus entered that tradition of Scottish government which liked decisions taken by enlightened men behind closed doors, the tradition of the Whigs rather than of the fighting radicals whom he had emulated in his youth. But the Unionists gave more in return. They appreciated that war required positive cultivation of popular solidarity. Thus they accepted an extension of state power and an active welfare policy to unite the nation. They did so all the more easily because Johnston's work was viewed kindly, almost encouraged, by a Churchill with too many memories of Scotland in the First World War. He wanted her quiet and co-operative and Johnston made her so. But in the process the balance of power within the system of government set up in 1938 was tipped from the Unionists to Labour.

Labour was brought right into a hierarchy which had long shunned it and even by 1939 still only felt able to deal with it at arm's length. Now it was helped to build a power structure matching the Unionist one so far dominant at every level of government and industry. The base was secured by the local authorities. Numbers of them had been learning to hold the support of their client electorates through housing policy, with its low rents, large deficits and gross inefficiency. Some councils had able leadership, such as Glasgow under Dollan, but they too could be riddled with corruption; others were in an appalling state. Yet after 1945 their spending was increased, and with it their power, by Labour's expansion of local services. Then Johnston raised the STUC's status and gave it a part in economic decisions. Elger was assigned as honest broker to incoming firms, in return for which pay and conditions were fixed by the unions. Since 1940 these had been officially encouraged and drawn into close consultation on war production. Soon after the peace the STUC had 900,000 members, nearly half the workforce. The whole edifice was crowned by the Labour Ministers at St Andrew's House—and they were there for ten years almost continuously from 1941. They formed a provincial outpost of the set of collectivist-minded politicians which rose inside the British establishment during the war. But those in Scotland were not visionaries, still less militants. They were machine men, content with a stable power structure. That built, they considered the needs of their time answered. Their socialist ardour cooled, and they became at most conservatively pragmatic in going further. They assumed that all basic problems had now been, or would soon be, finally solved: Labour had found its formula for Scottish government for the next 30 years.

It was in essence a highly centralised system. But Johnston's decisive leadership had persuaded many that it was also devolutionary. At the least, he had shown people that the recent reforms might be valuable in their own right, rather than a consolation prize for lack of Home Rule. If at heart no unionist, he like every other serious politician had probably long given up hope of a Parliament in Edinburgh. The whiff of disloyalty about the Nationalists did not help in a country raised to new heights of British patriotism by the war effort. But then it was actually safe to grant more scope to Scotland—reforms could be Scottish without threatening the Union, as well as collectivist without seeming socialist. Channelled through St Andrew's House, they were a reasonable alternative to Home Rule.

Johnston demonstrated not what devolution could do, but a strong state. He taught the Scots not to be afraid of it, for special consideration could be given them within it. They were duly impressed, and his claim to represent their best interests was acknowledged on every hand. But there was also a price to be paid. His innovations hardly released the energies of the people, who now had little control over their much more powerful governing caste. The result was not in practice greater autonomy: Scottish government became instead a process of constant adjustment by the political and administrative hierarchy to entrenched pressure groups. Any could be brought into it, and those judged unacceptable could be excluded and neutralised. That was what happened to the Nationalists, who were in effect to be quelled by Johnston's reforms. The simple expedient of making the bureaucracy more efficient quite cut the ground from under their complaints and rebutted their most important argument for Home Rule.

The glaring omission from all this was any serious attempt to tackle the basic weaknesses of the economy. The need was to restore the competitive position of the heavy industries, or else to find substitutes which could compete. War actually increased dependence on them. Dispersal from the South and diversification at home were too limited to redress Scotland's lack of capacity in the new industries which were to ensure prosperity in other parts of Britain. For example, she acquired little in the way of high technology, of which armaments production was a major source: even in the midst of war she had less factory space devoted to that than to storage. Equally, when mass manufacture of consumer goods was allowed again, companies supplying them mostly went elsewhere. Johnston never applied his energy to correcting these shortcomings; perhaps he simply failed to see that they were there. In consequence there was much misdirection of effort as the state took over the key role in the economy performed by the Scottish capitalists during and after the First World War. The irremediable decline of their own industries served meanwhile to make them more conservative. Under the imposition of central control the spring of native enterprise all but dried up.

At the end of the war in Europe the National Government dissolved. The subsequent caretaker Ministry replaced Johnston by Rosebery, who had served as regional commissioner since 1941. He was the first peer to be appointed Secretary of State and the last Liberal to occupy the Scottish Office. Described as arrogant and insensitive by his civil servants—for he was a foe of bureaucracy—he was regarded as jovial and cavalier by the rest of the country. He always insisted that, as a National Liberal, he had not betrayed the ideals of his father, who would have followed the same path. Many other Liberals agreed.[41]

Contrary to expectations, Scotland swung rather less dramatically to the Left than the rest of Britain in the General Election of 1945.[42] Labour, with 48 per cent of the poll, had a small plurality over the Unionists' and allies' 45 per cent. It gained fifteen seats in the central belt for a total of thirty-seven, while three ILP members hung on in Glasgow, the Communist held West Fife and Boyd Orr was elected as an independent for the universities. Against those forty-two on the Left were thirty-two MPs on the Right: twenty-five Unionists proper, five National Liberals and two others. For the first time not a single independent Liberal was returned, though candidates failed narrowly in five constituencies, Sinclair by only seventy votes. The enmity between him and Brown, leader of the National faction, had ruined attempts at reconciliation. The independents set themselves up again as an autonomous self-financing party in 1946, but by then most of their old followers were also supporting Unionism. That apart, Scotland fell into the same pattern of voting as the rest of Britain.

The Unionists did not feel themselves crushed—on the contrary, they saw

Scotland as an anti-socialist stronghold. Weaknesses went unremarked. The main one was the decline of the Scottish capitalist class, from the self-made local businessmen to the dynasties of the Clyde. The former survived in municipal politics to which, however, the Unionist organisation did not deign to extend itself. The latter retired, prematurely but decisively, from public life in general. They believed in a strong state but found a socialist one intolerable. In Parliament, the only figure of substance to fight the losing battle against nationalisation was Duncan, and he as MP for the City of London. Bilsland alone leavened the weight of Labour opinion in the Scottish Council.

In the Unionist party itself, leadership was being taken over by landowners and lawyers. After Elliot's defeat in 1945, the chief spokesman in the Commons was the advocate MP for Hillhead, James Reid. A skilled debater, he often embarrassed the mediocre Labour Ministers, but went on to the Bench in 1948. Elliot, meanwhile returned at a by-election, did not try to replace him. Still, he did coin the phrase that 'for Scotland, nationalisation means denationalisation' which gave point to the campaign against remote bureaucracy. By the end of the Parliament the Government was on the run. The Unionist party's structure was now strengthened. In 1950 Churchill ended the whips' control of it which had lasted since 1911, setting up a chairman's office in Edinburgh under James Stuart, MP for Moray and Nairn—who had, though, also been his chief whip. Regular associations were formed in the constituencies to supersede the old informal caucuses.

Labour, coming at last to unfettered power in London, was there equally confident of itself and its values—but not so much in Scotland.[43] Its atrophied local organisation under cliquish and sometimes corrupt councillors did not revive even with the victory of 1945. It still suffered from the departure of its freer spirits in the previous decade. Scotland's socialism had been, like her Liberalism, individualistic and devoted to moral principle. Centralist discipline ran counter to that. At home a Right-wing leadership was entrenched and the Left weaker than in England. The ILP, too, became moribund once Maxton had died and the other MPs had rejoined Labour. Idealists were driven into agitation in splinter groups. The party itself concentrated on the workaday tasks of rebuilding the cities with vast schemes of council housing and ensuring that union practices were enforced in industry, being otherwise the merely passive protector of its clients' interests. The essentials could be dealt with by local authorities. In 1945 Labour won thirty-seven of them and usually continued to control the big ones, except Edinburgh. Their representatives were also the most active in the Scottish Council, in which an exasperated business community scarcely took part. But wider aspirations were treated with cynical disregard.

Home Rule, expected as part of the reconstruction, figured in the Scottish, if not in the British manifesto. It could rightly be concluded that the reference was a sop. Typical of the latest attitudes on the Left were George Buchanan's. MP for the Gorbals since 1922, Under-secretary for Scotland 1945–7, then in the Cabinet as Minister for Pensions and finally first head of the National Assistance Board, he had once contended that the Scots' poverty justified

Home Rule. Now their equal benefits were his clinching argument for rigorous unionism.

Their influence in London anyway fell. The Labour MPs were such a sorry lot that Attlee had problems even with his appointments to St Andrew's House. Only one Scot sat in the Cabinet, the Secretary of State himself, unless Shinwell, of late an English member, should be included. So there was no resistance to the tightening of central control by that new collectivist elite in Westminster and Whitehall. To it, as to the generation of 1918, peace opened up the prospect of utopia. To these younger men it actually seemed this time, by reason of their greater powers, more attainable. They pursued it with a sense of their own moral rectitude which often degenerated into insensitive arrogance. They were anyway too easily seduced by empty, pretentious gestures of action and by the notion that bureaucracy could be radical.

Impatient of special interests, Attlee wanted sweeping, thus uniform measures of social equality. It was readily enforced in prices, wages and terms of employment, soon similar all over Britain. But then Scotland could no longer attract industries from outside through low pay. Priority was given by planning to the existing heavy ones, though that only aided her till they declined again. Meanwhile, some promising new companies closed down and the southward drift resumed. Official regulation at the same time made venture capital scarce and hampered investment, generally stifling native enterprise. So enfeebled was it that moves against centralism had themselves to come from the centre. The Distribution of Industry Act (1945) cajoled firms into leaving the South of England for certain beneficiary areas, including much of Scotland. There its operation was supervised by committees on which St Andrew's House was represented. This did not disguise the reality of a control from London which rapidly extended the powers of Ministries based there, as all the new ones were.

The system had high ideals, but its techniques were not well developed. It thought little of cost or consultation, so that large sums could be lavished on people, such as the Scots, who remained unsatisfied. They were certainly better off than before the war, not least because they found it easier to get a job—though unemployment still running at twice the national average encouraged emigration and union militancy. Objections on any wider grounds injured Labour's *amour-propre*. Suspicion about the alternative of Home Rule turned into an antipathy, even a contempt, which is nevertheless rather hard to explain. After all, socialists still cherished such autonomous Scottish institutions as served their purposes. And the Nationalists in their post-war upsurge (see chapter 9 below) believed themselves heirs of Johnston, too, in seeking to solve all problems by consensus. It says little for their political nous that they failed to understand how impossible this was amid fresh party strife, and little for their understanding of what Johnston had been about. Hence the naive manoeuvrings of MacCormick, canvassing now Liberal, now Unionist support, trying single-handed to undo the ruling parties' discipline. His National Covenant, adventurous enough to unsettle, too cloudy in its aims to succeed, only antagonised them. He won a hearing from institutions obscurely perceiving the centralist threat. But the Government correctly assessed the agitation as an emotional protest rather than a demand for specific changes. Its main result was to create extreme Labour hostility to devolution.

In any case the new Cabinet would not countenance the independence for the Secretary of State once enjoyed by Johnston. His influence was not entirely lost, however. Both his successors had been at St Andrew's House with him, Joseph Westwood as Under-secretary, Arthur Woodburn as his parliamentary private secretary. But like all later incumbents they were unionists by personal conviction. Thus they acquiesced in a new order which gave them limited responsibility for the biggest post-war problems, so that the Scottish Office declined again as a centre of power. To them there was still a net gain in the fact that it remained more influential than before, if only as an agent of Whitehall.

Westwood, the ex-miner MP for the Stirling Burghs, was voluble and sincere but plainly unfit for the Cabinet.[44] He entered it not on merit but because someone or other had to fill his post. Willing to speak there only on Scottish questions and carrying no weight, he was brusquely dismissed by Attlee after barely two years. Though he gained some new responsibilities— notably over the National Health Service, and town and country planning— they were mere shadows of the corresponding English ones. Westwood's own economic initiatives were minor: the creation of the Scottish Council, the designation of New Towns and the drawing-up of particular plans for cities and regions.

His successor Woodburn, MP for Clackmannan and East Stirlingshire, was more impressive—a party man certainly, having been for years Labour's Scottish secretary, but better than a party hack.[45] Yet while warm, generous and avuncular, he lacked the political skills which would have enabled him to win support in Cabinet and assert himself in Whitehall. He could do little to shake the Government's indifference to Scotland. Concessions to her in the great spate of nationalisation were extracted only in the form of tame advisory boards supposed to safeguard her interests. He tried to revive the more lively debates of wartime in a Scottish Economic Conference, a gathering in Edinburgh of the usual pressure groups. But it turned out to be a talking shop superfluous to the similar bodies recently established, and was wound up in 1950. Woodburn's energies were turned to greatest effect in housing. His policy was abetted by his Left-wing Lord Advocate, John Wheatley, nephew of the ILP leader, who seemed to object to private construction on principle and did what he could to obstruct the granting of licences for it.

Woodburn had once been in favour of Home Rule but now, stung by Nationalist attacks, became a fierce opponent. Still, it would have been imprudent of the Government to repudiate its promises openly. Instead, hopes were unobtrusively damped. Thus, a select committee recommended in 1947 that no change should be introduced in the arrangements for Scottish legislation lest it be made to look inferior. Yet the Home Rule agitation would not die down and the Government had extremely heavy commitments. It was therefore persuaded to take a second look. In 1948 Woodburn issued a White Paper which, while curtly rejecting even an inquiry into devolution, proposed a reform of the procedure for Scottish Bills in the Commons.[46]

The grand committee, consisting of the seventy-one MPs with ten to fifteen others, had since 1907 taken the committee stage, that of detailed discussion and amendment. Now it was to take also the second reading, the debate on general principle. Then only the largely formal first reading, report stage and third reading would come before the whole House. Since usually the Scots members alone would be interested in the legislation, this was an apparent rather than a substantive change. Woodburn all the same applied stringent safeguards. It would be for the Speaker to certify which Bills were Scottish and which might be referred to the committee. The objections of ten MPs might prevent it, and even afterwards the objections of six would still require a second reading on the floor of the House. Because most Bills were non-contentious and went through without debate, no more than a quarter of them were referred in the following decade. But those the Scots members were free to vote on and amend as they liked—the Government normally accepted their decisions without demur. There followed a minor but useful improvement in the flow of Scottish business. In addition, the grand committee was given the job of debating the estimates for Scotland on six days a year. The experiment as a whole was successful enough to be amplified in 1957.[47]

Woodburn was briefly succeeded in 1950–1 by Hector MacNeil, MP for Greenock, a former journalist with a precocious political reputation earned at the Foreign Office, where he had been a junior Minister since 1945.[48] Now he was given his first Cabinet post, and would surely have gone further but for his untimely death in 1955. On the Right of the party, he did not share the parochial concerns marking the limits of his Scots colleagues' horizons. He was a thoroughly professional politician, ready to speak in Cabinet on many subjects, respected for his skill at constructive solutions. As Secretary of State, he was entrusted with the specifically political task of quelling the Nationalist agitation, which he himself hated for its narrow-mindedness. He received the leaders of the Covenant but made no concessions of substance to them. He dealt dexterously with the Stone of Scone incident. Otherwise, he was anxious to get Scottish industry moving again: to some of his fellow-socialists he seemed too ready to work with the capitalist foe. But he had no time to devise a coherent policy.

In the General Election of 1950 Labour found little new to say and was really asking for a vote of confidence in its achievement to date. Scots again declined to ape the more volatile English, and the swing to the Right was smaller than in the South. A redistribution and a few changes in marginal seats largely balanced out, allowing Labour to hold a small lead. With seventy-one members to choose after the abolition of the university seats, Scotland returned thirty-seven socialists against thirty-two Unionists and allies. The great surprise was the Liberals' capture of two seats, despite a generally disastrous performance. The Nationalist vote was negligible. Attlee's tired Government was given too small a majority in the Commons to last for long, and soon was at the hustings once more. In 1951 the Tories took office again in London, while in Scotland the Unionists won three seats to gain parity with Labour at thirty-five, the Liberals retaining only Jo Grimond in Orkney and Shetland. The system of two parties was now firmly established, votes for all others being very small.[49]

Elliot was a natural choice for the post of Scottish Secretary and would surely have filled it with distinction. But he was still remembered as a man of Munich by Churchill, who passed him over in favour of his crony, James Stuart. Having the Prime Minister's ear, and in Cabinet certain of sympathy from 'hidden Scots' such as Harold Macmillan and Sir David Maxwell Fyfe, this languid, laconic aristocrat, partly royal in ancestry, was influential enough to get special consideration whenever he wanted it. But he did not often want it.

The Unionists were elected on promises to dismantle socialist controls and loosen the grip on Scotland of a distant bureaucracy, though that had to be reconciled with their acceptance of the welfare state.[50] The Scottish Office might have returned to the more independent position it had enjoyed under Johnston, or at least become again, as in the 1930s, a focus for Scottish opinion rather than merely the local agent of central planners. Stuart made a start by strengthening the team at St Andrew's House with a third Under-secretary and a Minister of State. The latter was to reside mainly in Scotland and look after business, such as the attraction of industry and some aspects of local government, which could not be easily handled from London. But Stuart was too willing to delegate his work to junior Ministers. His department settled into routine administration of minutiae. It was happiest when generating no controversy in Whitehall or Westminster, for it was still nervous about asserting itself there. It preferred to leave the lobbying to unofficial bodies such as the Scottish Council, and itself conformed to general policy unless there were specific reasons for not doing so.

The country had anyway grown weary of law-making. That entirely suited a Secretary of State who disliked too much legislation or interference and who, for all the modesty of his talents, was hardly stretched by a lacklustre Labour Opposition under Thomas Fraser, MP for Hamilton. Stuart seldom exploited his scope for independent action, though he won some extra powers—in 1954 over roads and in 1956 over electricity. Nor did he summon up the energy to break the socialist hold where it was being consolidated. In fact he maintained a remarkable continuity with Labour policies, notably on public sector housing. An Act of 1953 doubled subsidies for it, and greatly increased the number of completions by the next year. This was well-meant, but scarcely the best thing for the future of the Unionist party.

Discounting Labour's challenge, Stuart also felt able to ignore the Nationalist one. In his view, it had only grown because people disliked those socialist controls which his Government was curbing. He seemed much less worried by it than his chief, who was exhibiting his habitual nervousness about the temper of the Scots. Churchill urged the first Minister of State, Lord Home, to 'go up to Scotland and see if you can get rid of this embryonic Scottish nationalist thing.'[51] Home manfully did so, while Stuart satisfied himself with asking the contentious questions over again. A committee was appointed under Lord Catto to inquire into Scotland's financial relations within the Union. It proposed a separate return of her revenue and expenditure which, when published, showed her providing 10 per cent of the former and getting 12 per cent of the latter. An inquiry under the Earl of Balfour reviewed her government, though not the issue of Home Rule. Its report of 1954 was elaborately diplomatic, ascribing any ill feeling to 'needless English thoughtlessness' but also to 'undue Scottish susceptibilities'. It dismissed the myth that Scotland was exploited, but accepted that the status of her administration should be enhanced. It acknowledged the loss of autonomy through centralism, but rejected every remedy put forward at the time— meetings of the grand committee in Edinburgh, a Highland development authority and industrial powers for the Secretary of State, all to come in the end. Amid the solemn platitudes, two principles were set down which have since been universally accepted. One was that British Ministers should own the Scots' standing as a nation and consult fully on matters touching them. The other was that the role of the Secretary of State as 'Scotland's Minister' should be recognised and in no way limited.[52]

But this was on the whole an era of good feeling. Labour, anyway preoccupied with internal disputes, had few grounds for bitter complaint against the paternalistic, gently progressive Unionists, and did not press them hard. They were rewarded in the General Election of 1955, when for the second time—or the first in normal circumstances—they achieved an absolute majority in every sense, winning thirty-six seats on just over 50 per cent of the poll. Labour retained thirty-four seats on 47 per cent. Grimond held his too, but the national vote for all minor parties was tiny.

Stuart took the chance of retiring when Macmillan became Prime Minister in 1958. The Unionists were at this stage doing better than the Conservative party in England and their subsequent rapid decline could not yet be foreseen. But it had been a period of lost opportunities for them. They had not decisively secured their position, either by capitalising on their anti-centralist stance or by reviving Scottish industrial enterprise. On both fronts a little more effort was made by Stuart's successor, the pleasant but unassertive John Maclay, MP for West Renfrewshire and last chairman of the National Liberals. The decision to bring him back into the Government, from which he had been hounded by a dissatisfied Churchill some years before, was strategic: it was intended to hold what remained of the old Liberal vote. But it was still not enough.

Maclay's most notable work in the period before the General Election of 1959 lay in further reform of the legislative process. The grand committee had become too unwieldy for its many tasks, so that measures were still being rushed through with inadequate discussion. Yet MPs complained that the time they had to spend there restricted the attention they could give to wider political affairs. The committee stage of Bills was therefore handed over to a smaller Scottish Standing Committee. It was to contain at least thirty Scots and up to twenty others to reflect the party balance in the whole House, but its composition might vary according to the issue on the agenda. The grand committee would continue taking second readings and estimates, acquiring also the yet grander function of debating, on two days in each session, any general matter of interest to Scotland. Broadly, all this meant that henceforth exclusively Scottish business would be looked after exclusively by Scottish MPs. They became more of a legislature, with the result that still more work was loaded on to them. So this was not a final answer to problems of congestion at Westminster.

The prosperity which made the Unionists popular also hid persistent economic weaknesses. A boom during the Korean War was followed by a recession in which Scotland again fared badly. Stagnation had continued underneath, but the signs had not been read. Now the heavy industries were about to enter another, this time irreversible decline. That was not appreciated even as the crisis deepened in the winter of 1958 and the number out of work, having doubled in a year, reached 100,000 for the first time since the war. A corresponding shift in politics also took the Unionists by surprise, though pointers were there in by-elections: they lost their majority when Kelvingrove fell to Labour on Elliot's death in 1958. Dissension in the ranks was heard, with a Highland MP resigning the whip in protest at neglect of his region. The Government, boasting that the people had never had it so good, called an election in 1959. While in England the Conservatives made large gains, in Scotland the trend was opposite. Labour won three seats from the Unionists, and thus the lead which it has enjoyed ever since.

What had gone wrong with the Unionist part of the experiment? One unperceived problem lay perhaps in the fact that it represented, if somewhat tenuously, a last echo of the old Liberal tradition, on which the Scots had turned their backs. Elliot might have remedied that, but he never tried to set himself at the party's head and was anyway spurned by Churchill. Instead it got the languid inactivity of Stuart. Nobody better illustrated how Unionism was cutting itself off from its roots, notably in choosing its MPs from the anglicised upper class. It began to lose the centre ground which it had held for thirty years. That was occupied partly by former Liberals, now dying away—their offspring would soon start to flirt again with a Liberalism that had only just escaped extinction before moving over in their thousands to the SNP. Unionists had also attracted a large working-class vote, founded on the Protestant patriotism which had been part of their ideology from the outset. That too was being dissipated—with the wild Clydesiders gone, the Labour party's solid work in the local authorities and the STUC was giving it a firm hold on the whole proletariat. Unionism was to find itself ever more strictly confined to the counties and the bourgeois districts of the big cities. Then, with little ideology left of its own, it was practically identical to English Toryism. The forces which since 1886 had sustained its specifically Scottish character were spent.

The unionist part of the experiment was not for the moment called into question. But henceforth it was to be conducted under Labour leadership. As it had evolved, it was actually rather better suited to being run by socialists than by Unionists: the latter favoured at least some degree of economic self-reliance. For the moment, Scots did not seem to mind that the post-war system had further provincialised their country. They were to demand and get a phase of yet more intense state intervention before breaking away into a Nationalist reaction. It was not now expected that any initiatives or ideas should come from Scotland, nor was her public life quickened by any higher instinct than the extraction of as much money as possible from Westminster. This was indeed the opposite pole to the old ideology of ethical Liberalism.

But the victory of the new provincialism was not quite complete. Above all, it had so far failed in its basic rationale, the restoration of the economy. With that the issue of central controls was intimately related. Since the end of the war they had never faded from political debate. For while they had not proved satisfactory, nor had the Unionists' lifting of them. The argument was circular: no prosperity without controls, no respect for national aspirations with them. This produced an inherent instability, most obviously expressed in deviant voting behaviour. From 1959, Scotland started to move to a more independent and important position in British politics, notably by becoming more indispensable to the Labour party. It was bound in turn to become more responsive to her wishes. Elements of it continued to call for devolution against its generally hostile line. Given its dislike of internal discussion, there seemed little hope of an early or easy change. But while the sentiment lived, Labour, as the new guiding force in Scottish politics, would surely have to face the question of Home Rule again one day.

Chapter 8

'An Intensity of National Feeling'

The rise of the Scottish National Party, the attempt at devolution and the prospect, as it once might have seemed, of rapid progress towards independence, produced an assumption, not least among historians, that nationalism was a central thread, perhaps the most important single one, in the story of Scotland's last two centuries.[1] This was misleading. For while her sense of identity persisted with surprising strength, it was for nearly all that time quite overshadowed by British nationalism, the necessary consequence of a successful Union. The Union had its faults, of course, many to be blamed on the facile assumption by the English that it implied uniformity. Yet in this was one advantage: that, ignorant of the reality, they seldom interfered—when anglicisation took place, it was on the initiative of the Scots themselves. The deeper sin was indifference. It made Parliament extraordinarily reluctant to grant major reforms in Scotland, even when widely supported by her own people and of no possible detriment to England. Generally concessions were extracted only after all scope for evasion was exhausted. But the Scots, and in particular their nearly always solidly unionist establishment, can equally be blamed for lack of energy in their own institutions and political life. It was they who often declined to follow their stand through to its logical conclusion at the cost of damage to other ambitions and loyalties.

In such half-hearted forms, Scottish nationalism nevertheless endured. The old sentiment survived the events of 1707, though as little more than innocuous nostalgia. It was sustained by the advent through popular government of the radicals, with their devotion to individualism and local interests. It was transformed and deepened when the great prize of the Union, the prosperity of Scotland, slipped away. Even then it long appeared too eccentric to gain wide support. Nationalism's moment came during the crisis of the British state in the 1960s and 1970s, when indifference was aggravated by centralisation and failure compounded by immobility.

The Union was at first deeply unpopular. But the Scots, apart from those in the tribal Highlands, were not so remote in language and culture from their southern neighbours as to make co-operation in one state impossible. Moreover, the Glorious Revolution of 1688 had marked the end of attempts in Britain to emulate the unifying absolutism which at the time was the main vehicle of progress in the rest of Europe. The diverse social forces previously subjected to England's monarchy were preserved distinct and robust—in this, she lost less of the varied medieval heritage than any continental country. So to England the Union presented no novel problems. When Scotland entered it, bringing her own laws and institutions with her, they could be easily accommodated. And in the end it was a relatively painless transaction. Blatant breaches of the 1707 Treaty did take place, such as the Patronage Act of 1712 and the abolition of heritable jurisdictions after the 1745 rebellion. But they were rare. The Scots during the eighteenth century were actually much more fortunate than other small peoples drawn into the orbit of larger neighbours. Effectively they could pick and choose for themselves which elements of their nationhood to retain and which to discard, so that nationality was taken out of politcs.[2]

In fact for nearly three centuries after 1560 the development of Scottish society formed a continuum. There was no sudden break at the Union and no need for the Scots to adopt a defensive nationalist stand against their loss of statehood. Their Parliament had never been the same revered wellspring and focus of national life as England's. It had been merely one among a range of institutions—the nobility, the burghs, the law, the education system, above all the Kirk—through which Scotland's national character manifested itself. All these others were maintained by the Treaty of Union.

In the eighteenth century Scotland was pervaded by a rational, universalist spirit.[3] Her culture attained a European significance. Her best sons thought and wrought for a public bound by no frontier, mental or political. They always wondered that their obscure little land should take the lead in elaborating great principles for the guidance of mankind. Much of this intellectual activity was inspired by the drive towards the material development of their country. The fact that Scots could now turn their energies to this end, undisturbed by faction and feud, was counted the greatest blessing of the Union. So the men of the Enlightenment were unionists. But they left a legacy to the nationalist issues of the future in their belief that Scotland was to be improved by the application of rational axioms and the example of superior models—by the latter they meant England.

Yet their attitude was not unambiguous. On the one hand they felt some contempt for Scotland's barbarities. It might express itself in embarrassment at their provincialisms of manner and speech or, in a sublimated form, in their building on to their capital a New Town which in its grace and nobility was consciously intended to match the best in Europe. On the other hand, they could not shake off an affection for Scotland's eccentricities: they loved the intimacy of her life and the human individuality it produced. Certainly the intellectual universalism did not prevent in the literary sphere a counter-reaction. In the works of Ramsay, Fergusson, Burns and Scott the previous rapid decline of Scots language and literature was halted and temporarily reversed. The leading circles in Edinburgh were often patronising about it, but nearly always approved. There was a constant underlying nostalgia for the old ways and even for the political independence which had preserved them. But the nationalism that survived was above all cultural in spirit, requiring no dissolution of the Union. For in that cultural universe diffusing its glow from Edinburgh to St Petersburg, from Stockholm to Naples, no shame attached to being provincial—even London and Paris were in their way only provincial centres of the same Enlightenment. Only when the universe dissolved into self-conscious and often aggressive nation-states did the problem of provinciality present itself.

These conflicting emotions are seen most clearly at work in Sir Walter Scott. He was painfully aware that historic Scotland was dying: in his poems and novels he both celebrated and mourned her, acknowledging that the price of maturity was the loss of her most typical features. In his public life he insisted on the need to treat a nation's history with reverence, stressing that reform, however inevitable, should always respect the past and avoid imposing uniformity for its own sake. In the true realisation of this ideal, Scotland would have to remain in many ways special and different; but he feared and suspected she would not. This led him into a Toryism often extreme, yet also endearing: he wept at the thought of reorganising the Court of Session, sniped entertainingly at interference with the Scottish economy and blustered ineffectually at parliamentary reform.

It did soon become clear that the astonishing development of Scotland in the later eighteenth and early nineteenth centuries was causing a steady assimilation of her underlying social and economic structure to England's. This in turn demanded an assimilation of the superstructure: those ancient customs and institutions, political, legal, religious and educational, which were the tangible evidence that Scotland had once been an independent nation. It was less possible to be confident that she would stay herself. On the contrary, as the old ways were outmoded, it seemed evident that further progress would have to be at their expense.

There was a range of political reactions. The Tories were the most nationalist party of those days. They justified retaining Scotland's distinctive institutions by claiming these had been unalterably established through the free choice of her last Parliament in the Treaty of the Union. There was, of course, another side to their stand; underneath one could perceive easily enough a cynical expediency ready to seize on any means of keeping power. Even after the battle against reform had been lost, there persisted a minor school of Conservative romantics inspired by Scott with the same deep historical consciousness of their country as was found in contemporary national movements elsewhere. But in practice it meant little more than defending the residual privileges of the aristocracy. That ensured the extinction of this group as a political force.

Against it the Whigs linked reform with anglicisation. To them Scotland's heritage amounted to little more than archaic uncouthness, with even its virtues preserved at the cost of extreme political backwardness. This had to be corrected by the imposition of political principles and methods drawn from England, the paragon of a free civil society. But the Whigs showed all the same a sneaking affection for that heritage. Henry Cockburn, as a member of the Government which carried reform, helped it to pursue a resolute anglicising policy. Yet he viewed the effects of the same trend outside politics with dismay and regret. He called the early decades of the nineteenth century 'the last purely Scotch age' and his writings evinced a passion for recording its picturesque details before they passed into oblivion.

The common nationalist ground which the two ruling elites could thus find in Scottish culture was undermined by its rapid descent into philistinism. Locked into the backward-looking forms extracted by the popular mind from Burns and Scott, it was no more than depressingly provincial under the influence of lesser imaginations and talents, drawing sustenance from regiments and tartans, from a tawdry-heroic view of history, from ben-and-glen paintings and from kailyard literature. The contrast with the Enlightenment is staggering to the modern mind, though the Scots were not perturbed. Still, the lack of much culture to be proud of deprived cultural nationalism of political force. Since it was the one well-developed form of nationalism, the only obvious alternative was stoical acceptance of the tide of history and the only obvious substitute was to grouse about the trivialities of anglicisation. The real motor of national feeling was the pride the Scots felt in the rapid development of their country and its contribution to the Union. They were energetic, intelligent, educated and self-confident, made money easily and ruled the Empire. They had invented new sciences, revealing to the world the secrets of political economy and pioneering the study of man as a social animal. They succeeded above all through loyalty to Scottish values, scorning the subservience which seemed the main ingredient of any Englishman's success. All this actually gave them a strong sense of superiority over their southern neighbours. But they were level-headed enough to recognise in the Union its precondition.

The national spirit seemed vindicated, but was in reality vitiated, by the struggles of the 1830s and 1840s. In politics the new order was an unsatisfactory compromise, based on a constitution at once more representative in the legislative and less workable in the executive branch. A political nation was created but could not coalesce into a coherent Scottish interest. A society undergoing profound changes had to adapt, and popular government translated the necessity more easily into pressure for reforms. But the expectations raised were dashed. The pressure was itself confused in its objects: at the same time nationalist, as pressure for more attention to Scottish issues, and unionist, as pressure for the benefits of the Union to be shared equally by Scotland.

The net effect, however, was to extend the power of the English secular state. That was an unspoken issue behind the Disruption, for the evangelicals' social thinking and activity were in one sense concerned to limit such power. The argument set out in the Claim of Right rejected the purely English doctrine of the absolute sovereignty of Parliament. In Scottish constitutional theory the relationship between the state and the Church was a federal one, according the latter a sovereignty of its own. Unfortunately for Scotland, the dispute came at a time when that doctrine was hardening, and the Kirk was its first major victim. Still, here again there was no nationalist reaction. The inevitable resentments were turned inwards, into conflict within Scottish society, rather than outwards against Westminster.

The Scots were all the same proud of having defied the attempt to control religion by the state, and having shown by their sacrifices the bounds of its authority. The practical benefits of this stern moral resolution were less clear. For amid the upheavals the continuum in Scottish life dating from the Reformation was broken. The institutions guarding semi-independence were destroyed, divided or otherwise debilitated. In particular the Church, the one institution which had always taken on the labour of dealing with social questions, ceased to play an active role, and the cement of Scotland's social structure for the last 300 years was dissolved. Efforts to find substitutes were long, wearisome and not always successful. If legislation came, it had to follow English precedents for lack of native ones. But this was a procrustean work, and the simple Whig answer of anglicisation turned out unsatisfactory.

A different answer came from the radicals. They, in the vanguard of ethical Liberalism, were the most typically Scottish of all the factions. They too had their literary antecedents, in Burns' poetry and his implicit social philosophy. But respect for the past did not figure in their sentiment. They saw history as the often dismal narrative of man's struggle to raise himself above barbarity and injustice. They preferred to look to the future, where his infinite progress could be assured by acceptance of their own ideals.

They were often nationalist too, though far from prejudiced in favour of anything and everything Scottish. On the contrary, unity of the British peoples, the comradeship-in-arms of Scots and English radicals in tearing down privilege, was a primary aim. Measured against it, residual differences between the two nations seemed unimportant. The main one, in the Scots' own estimation, was their greater boldness and consistency—or, as it appears to us, their narrowness and fanaticism, unhappy products of their religious roots. But with their help, Scotland retained a political personality different from England's. Her religiously inspired Liberalism determined her politics till the next century.

Even when defending specifically Scottish interests the radicals were concerned with abstract principle rather than with national self-assertion. They highly valued strong local institutions, which Whig policies had gravely weakened. That was not necessarily a cause of regret to most Scots, who saw the old system as discredited and worthless, no longer an expression of their nationhood but the means by which a corrupt ruling class defended its privileges against the just demands of the people. Soon radicals were calling for the reversal of the process where it eroded local autonomy, though not where it extended civil liberty—they had after all supported the anglicising Reform Act so far as it went. If local institutions did not preserve privilege, as they had done before 1832, then Scots radicals were for them; if they did, they were against them. So there was in their outlook no anti-English antagonism or belief that Scotland deserved a unique status. They stressed rather that overbearing central government, ignorant and even destructive of local individuality, was an offence to the absolute rights and dignity of man.

And radicals took this view whether the community in question was, as in the 1850s, Scotland or, as in the 1870s, Armenia or Afghanistan.

That was at any rate the rationale of the first identifiably nationalist agitation of modern times, which gave rise to the National Association for the Vindication of Scottish Rights in 1853.[4] It also drew strength from the Tory romantics, indeed was directly the result of some vigorous campaigning by two eccentrically conservative brothers, James and John Grant. Through a steady stream of letters to the Press and numerous pamphlets they drew attention to the many complaints, major and minor, which had come to light since 1832. Their protests were skilfully contrived to appeal to as wide a section of the public as possible, and in preparing to launch the association they managed to drum up 3,000 subscriptions. Help came from the burgh councils, from professional bodies, from noblemen such as Eglinton, Hamilton and Montrose, from the radical leader Duncan McLaren and from Charles Cowan, the Edinburgh MP. To inspirit the campaign a statement of grievances was issued. It listed thirty-one points, among them forgotten breaches of the Treaty of Union, the under-representation of Scotland in Parliament, the low levels of public expenditure there, the difficulties attending her legislation, the weak position of the Lord Advocate, administrative centralisation and a great number of lesser matters from the recognition of Scottish medical degrees to the display in Scotland of English heraldic emblems and flags. It is remarkable how long-lived some of these issues have been.

By the end of 1853 the groundwork was complete. The association's inaugural meeting, held in Edinburgh in November, attracted an audience of 2,000, while a similar demonstration in Glasgow the next month brought in 5,000. The motions they adopted called for various constitutional reforms, notably the resurrection of the post of Scottish Secretary of State. In general they agreed that anglicisation was a clumsy way of effecting reform—a perfect Union would give the Scots enough self-respect and power to do things in their own way, so that her social and economic advance could proceed to the satisfaction of everybody.

But otherwise these gatherings were unsuccessful. They exposed the differing political outlooks of the disparate membership. It proved impossible to persuade high Tories and rabid radicals to subordinate their partisan interests in the wider cause of their country. Their resentment could not be directed at England as such because a Scots radical had, as a radical, more in common with a like-minded Englishman than he had, as a Scot, with a Scottish Conservative; and the same was true for every other element in the association. The corresponding movements in Europe overcame similar obstacles to unity. The Scots' failure to achieve it excludes them from the ranks of classical nationalism. In any case they all had an overwhelming attachment to a Union which guaranteed their material well-being; they sought no change in its basic structure, but rather fuller equality for Scotland within it.

The reaction of the country at large to the association was indifferent or hostile. The Whig establishment condemned the exercise as atavistic nonsense. The MPs were not pleased to have their own failings shown up: among them,

Cowan remained the only one prepared to lend his support. The Scottish electorate was too prosperous and complacent to take much notice; it was in any case enjoying one of its phases of imperial patriotism under the stimulus of the Crimean War. It did not yet connect the laggardly treatment of the country's problems with a need to reform her political system. A further difficulty for the association was that particularism within Britain risked being linked with the mounting disorder in Ireland. The *Times* ran a haughty leader remarking that the English were above nationalism and that 'the more Scotland has striven to be a nation, the more she has sunk to be a province'. Faced with all this, the enthusiasm of the National Association faltered and by 1856 it had disappeared.

But the causes of its protests did not disappear. In fact it set off and laid down the pattern for a steady, if hardly intense, agitation over the next thirty years. A singular aspect of it was that only a few radical politicians and intellectuals took part, while the rest of the bourgeoisie—in Europe the backbone of the national movements—was content to channel its patriotic interests into history and literature. The agitation was sustained by idealist conviction rather than by the people's will. The Scots MPs now started demanding redress of the grievances to which the National Association had drawn attention. They got the Camperdown inquiry in 1869, and thereafter took every chance to voice their discontents and mull over the various possible correctives. London politicians were slow to respond, Gladstone being among the most obtuse. But he was obtuse on a great number of popular demands: nationalism could not expect any priority, and the radicals themselves gave it none.

In many ways it was difficult to distinguish from their fairly innocuous interest in strengthening local institutions. With that the Scots' aspirations could be fitted in even after being spiced by the romantic ideas of Rosebery. He too, when being practical, was at bottom concerned with making such institutions more efficient. Once Gladstone had been induced to respond to Scottish pressure, it was with the Bill of 1883 for a central Local Government Board in Scotland, overseeing the burghs and the various administrative agencies. The same purpose lay behind a scheme which Joseph Chamberlain produced for both Scotland and Ireland in 1885, and on which Rosebery co-operated closely. As late as 1887 Lord Hartington, the Unionist leader, wrote to Chamberlain: 'It would not be very difficult to devise several schemes for the extension of local self-government in Scotland which might be tried without much risk, because the demand in Scotland, such as it is, is on the part of a vast majority really limited to local self-government'—the contrast being drawn here was with the aims of the Irish which, as the Unionists appreciated, were in the end directed towards national self-determination. The crowning achievement of the radical campaign was the Scottish Office: till recently that too was above all the co-ordinator of tasks delegated to local government.

It is important to make clear the emphasis of the campaign because of the frequent assumption that it was a forefather in direct line of the twentieth-century nationalist movement. The agitation up to 1886 was nationalist only in a very limited sense. The Scottish people, while doubtless approving of these efforts, saw no decisive conflict between their national sentiment and their continued membership of the United Kingdom. Above all they did not demand a Scottish legislature, believing their essential interests could still be represented by Westminster. The British body politic remained integral: if the Scots were unhappy that their aspirations could not always be fulfilled within it, their reaction was no different to that of any other given group of citizens. To the reformers Scotland happened to be a convenient local unit with customs and institutions of its own; her standing or lack of it as a nation was a secondary matter. They called for political equity through decentralised administration, not for a distinctively Scottish form of government—only the latter would have made their claims nationalist in the modern sense.

We have, however, to explain why in 1886 or soon after the demands went much further than local government reform. The aim was now Home Rule under a Scottish Parliament, and it aroused increasing interest in a so far quiescent public opinion. The origin of this change is to be sought largely in the fact that during the 1870s and 1880s the discontent spread outwards from the ruling circles. One product of bourgeois emancipation had been the tremendous upsurge of voluntary activity and organisations. Fiercely independent in outlook though they were, they usually had as their object some legislative change. They grew ever more restive at the difficulty of obtaining such at Westminster, even when they had considerable support among MPs. On a more material level, business interests and town councils objected to the high cost of getting private Bills through. It was thus in the end the Convention of Royal Burghs that called a great public meeting in Edinburgh in 1884, where both Liberals and Conservatives united on resolutions which persuaded Gladstone to abandon his own limited plans in favour of a proper Scottish Secretaryship. By then there was extensive popular commitment to reform—this was the vital factor that ensured success in the campaign for a Scottish Office against the reluctance of Westminster and Whitehall.

But legislative devolution was still a novel idea. Not till 1877, in an important debate on Scotland in the House of Commons, was it for the first time warned, by the Liberal MP Sir George Campbell, that Home Rule might be the only solution to her ills. Rosebery felt moved to point out to the Lords in 1881 that Home Rule was starting to be openly discussed among his compatriots. The turning point on this question came, as for so much else, in the year of 1886. Gladstone's espousal of Irish Home Rule suddenly made nationalism a live issue in British politics. Among the Scots, however, the main result was to stir the radicals' concern for consistency and equity—if Ireland was to have a Parliament, then Scotland should get one too. The Irish measure was anyway never popular and for electoral reasons it had to be toned down in tandem with some wider and less revolutionary plan. That, rather than a subterranean popular aspiration, raised the question of Home Rule all round, and the Scottish Gladstonians endorsed a plan for their country in 1888. In this politically respectable form it proved to have great appeal. It stayed part of the Liberals' programme and as such won the voters' repeated approval. But for many years the main agitation came, as the old one had done, from the parliamentary representation and a few radical groups outside it, rather than from the people.

The first expression of this new current was the formation of the Scottish Home Rule Association in the summer of 1886. By seeking through some sort of federal system a basic re-organisation of the Union it went further than the National Association of 1853, and was thus more properly an ancestor of twentieth-century nationalism. Nominally it transcended party, by attracting Unionists, crofters' and labour leaders, as well as orthodox Liberals. But, though at first severe on Gladstone's policies and viewed with suspicion by his MPs, it soon felt able to make common cause with them. From the 1890s to the First World War nationalism could be easily contained with Liberalism and there was no need for separate political activity by the SHRA.

In that period Scottish Home Rule was brought before the Commons thirteen times, and on the last eight was approved in principle. From the start—the motion put forward by the radical Dr G B Clark in 1889—the majority of Scots MPs supported it. Similar moves followed till in 1894 a resolution was passed by the House as a whole. Yet the growing agitation inside the Liberal party coincided with a loss of interest among its leaders. The Government returned in 1892 was divided. Gladstone had always been hesitant about Scottish Home Rule and Rosebery had turned against it, though other Ministers were sympathetic. But in reality the Cabinet, while acknowledging the defects in Scottish government and the desire of most MPs for reform, wanted above all to dispose of the matter with as little delay and trouble as possible. In the end it went no further than to set up the Scottish grand committee. The Liberals concluded then that for the moment they had done enough. For the lack of further action they had plausible excuses—till 1905 the long interval of Unionist government and then the impossibility of getting controversial legislation through the Lords.

It is surprising, perhaps, since these exertions were only ever spasmodic and ultimately fruitless, that no independent nationalist movement appeared. But this was a time when the state had encroached little on the life of the citizen, who did not believe himself oppressed by a distant Government—the radicals intended to keep things that way. In these years about the turn of the century, moreover, Scotland's devotion to imperial ideals was at its most ardent. From the beginning she had been sending out into the Empire her administrators, soldiers, businessmen and missionaries. Her pride in their achievements was profound. Scots could not regard the concerns of their own small country as significant when faced with this field of enterprise. Nor, if they took advantage of it, did they have to sacrifice their Scottishness. It offered scope for all the virtues of a masculine, Protestant Christianity which they thought of as peculiarly theirs. Here nationalistic feeling may actually have led away from a desire for national self-determination, except in the context of some much more grandiose and unlikely scheme of imperial federation. It was nevertheless in that context that most Liberal imperialists, ignoring the views of their leader Rosebery, continued to support Home Rule.

Home Rule was one point on which imperialists and radicals could unite, but it was the latter's victory in the Liberal party after 1900 and its triumph at the General Election of 1906 which brought the issue to life once again. A group of backbenchers, led by the imperialist Ronald Munro-Ferguson, formed a committee to promote it in 1910. That prompted the party managers to establish their own official group to control and co-ordinate the efforts of others—they certainly did not intend to let native enthusiasm get out of hand. In Parliament another series of motions and measures culminated in the Ministry's backing the Government of Scotland Bill in 1913, which would have created a legislature to deal with all purely Scottish matters. It was expected to be passed in the autumn of 1914.

This was the radicals' best but also their last chance to fulfil their hopes before their final decline. They were still failing to satisfy their highest ambitions. Though they had a Scottish Office, the Secretaries had turned out on the whole ineffectual. Though they had a majority in Scotland's representation at Westminster, they were always swamped by the English and were now starting to be driven out by the Liberal Right. Bad luck and judgement had robbed their measures of the intended effects. A Parliament in Edinburgh might have afforded them scope for a more thoroughgoing programme and secured their position. In any case the Bill, having been read a second time, lapsed on the outbreak of the First World War.

Even then the nation showed no deep resentment or regret. The Bill was carried along on the coat-tails of the Irish one, and it was perhaps only Westminster's wish to stress that the reform was meant to benefit the whole United Kingdom, rather than just to appease Ireland, that produced a Scottish measure at all. Public opinion remained above all committed to Liberalism and was broadly content with the existing administrative devolution. A legislature on top seemed a dispensable luxury if it was going to cause problems for the Government. Only some of the Liberal elite gave it a higher priority, partly as an idealistic consummation of the old radical programme, partly, perhaps, because they sensed that power was slipping away from them, to new impulses stirring within Scotland and to centralising forces without. But they were hardly likely to rebel against the Liberal leadership on this issue alone, and their opportunity passed.

The war brought for nationalism, too, a new departure. With its aftermath, it all but completed the political assimilation to England: the Scots, having lost their independence in the eighteenth century, and their central native institutions in the nineteenth, now lost the ethical Liberalism which had since kept them distinct. The collapse of the Liberal coalition diminished Scotland's influence at Westminster, dispersing it among squabbling factions incapable of devising the kind of programme based on common Scottish interests which the radicals had once had.

Other events helped to banish the prospect of further devolution. The argument from parity for all the countries of the United Kingdom fell with the secession of the southern Irish. Having had its most intractable national problem solved, Westminster could regard Home Rule all round as superfluous. The remaining arguments also diminished in force. The proto-nationalists of the previous century had wanted equal treatment for Scotland where through historical accident or oversight she was unfairly dealt with. Their grievances—maladministration, under-representation, fiscal injustice and so on—were being redressed, and now have been. The Scottish Office rationalised government, slow population growth gave Scotland over-representation and eventually a large flow of assistance brought public spending per head well above the British average. So it was increasingly hard to see what Scottishness meant in any politically relevant sense. Besides, economic catastrophe apparently condemned Scotland to being a bankrupt client of England. The answer to the distress seemed to lie not in nationalism, but in centralisation. Even if a Parliament had been secured in 1914, its powers would have been inadequate to the enormous problems of post-war reconstruction. Instead, the Scots felt there was little choice but to accept growing central control of their national life.

Yet the fact that Scotland now seemed incurably depressed, perhaps even doomed, proved in the long run fruitful for nationalism. As the moderate sentiment in the political parties turned out ineffectual, various unconventional groups took up the cause: militant socialists, Gaelic revivalists, the leaders of the Scottish literary renascence. They were not bothered about administrative efficiency or constitutional tinkering—their concern was with the soul of the nation and with independence as the one way of restoring it. But political opinion was again growing more unionist and support even for Home Rule was disappearing. So the whole work had to be started afresh, on a different base and with different methods from those which had almost brought a Scottish Parliament in 1914.

The most radical solution came from Clydeside's Marxist firebrand, John Maclean. He had hailed the Easter Rising of 1916 in Dublin as the first blow against English capitalism and imperialism, and the post-war unrest in Scotland as harbinger of a great crisis destined to bring a similar repudiation of the Union, with the establishment through revolution of a Scottish socialist republic. But his unyielding fanaticism isolated him and he had no lasting influence after his death in 1923. Foremost among the Celtic romantics was a whimsical aristocrat, Stuart or Ruaraidh Erskine of Mar, who organised a Scottish National League which helped two land reformers to stand in the Highlands in the 1918 election. His purpose was the revival of Gaelic as the prelude to national awakening, though this made a limited appeal to most Scots. In fact Gaeldom never played much of a role in the subsequent growth of nationalism.[5] A more important cultural phenomenon was the Scottish National Movement, as the young literary lions of the 1920s—Hugh MacDiarmid, Neil Gunn, Eric Linklater and Lewis Spence—grandiosely described themselves. It was certainly a wonderful flowering of a tradition all but dead. Yet the step from that to consistent and effective political activity was a long one, and these writers had difficulty in winning acceptance even in the later nationalist parties.

The largest and most politically active group was the SHRA which, after dying quietly in 1912, had been refounded in 1917 by Roland Muirhead, a wealthy businessman, and Thomas Johnston, the socialist. It took a moderate line and advocated Home Rule all round, placing great hopes in the fact that both the Liberals and Labour kept it in their programmes. This did not advance the cause either, though they continued to command a majority of Scottish votes till 1931. But at Westminster their MPs formed only a minority within their respective parties and there was no guarantee of their combining on Scottish issues—their overriding loyalty was to their leaders in London rather than to Scotland. Anyway the Liberals were soon to be rendered ineffective as a vehicle for devolution by their collapse. And Labour's relative strength in Scotland meant its stand on the question could not be unequivocal. On the one hand, its construction of a permanent power base would be easier in a Scottish legislature than if it waited for the conversion of Tory England. On the other hand Home Rule seemed bound, after the example of Ulster, to bring some reduction in Scottish representation at Westminster, which would not be to Labour's advantage there; the same was true for the Liberals.[6] And besides, by the later 1920s both parties were advocating collectivist, centralising policies basically contradictory to the principle of devolution. Neither bothered to revise its plans in the light of them, assuredly a sign that their interest was no longer keen.[7]

But it took some time for this to become evident. At first they co-operated quite closely with the SHRA. In 1922 and 1923 conferences of a wide range of organisations were held to work out a united policy on Home Rule. The result was the 1924 Bill which Ramsay MacDonald's Government declined to sponsor. Undeterred, devolutionists later in the year summoned to Glasgow a further conference to which they gave the grandiloquent title of Scottish National Convention. This set up a committee to work out firm legislative proposals. A thoroughgoing plan was produced which in effect would have given Scotland full dominion status. It was embodied in the Bill talked out of the Commons in 1927, amid wild and angry scenes. With all the effort gone for nothing, there seemed to be no way forward except through some more radical initiative.

Muirhead's solution was to start fighting elections on a straight Home Rule platform. But he won only a minority of the SHRA to this view and for success it was vital to enlist the support of other nationalist groups. Because of their disparate policies, this proved difficult. Then a young lawyer, John MacCormick, arrived on the scene. A former member of the ILP, he too had become convinced that Home Rule could not be pursued in disorganised fashion from within the existing parties. After setting up a Nationalist Association at Glasgow University he began lobbying energetically for a united movement. He achieved that at a conference in Glasgow in May 1928 when the National Party of Scotland was formed.[8] It was initially intended just as an experiment in co-operation with the limited aim of getting the veteran socialist and nationalist, Cunninghame Graham, elected rector of the city's university. He failed narrowly, but his sponsors were impressed enough with their support to establish a more permanent structure at a further meeting in Stirling. There Graham was chosen president, Muirhead chairman, Spence vice-chairman and MacCormick secretary. Only the last had any political talent and the rest relied heavily on him. His interest lay not in doctrinal purity but in gathering together as broad a movement as possible in favour of any form of effective Home Rule. He presented Nationalism as safe, reasonable and non-exclusive. At the same time he was intolerant of extremists.

The party next tried its hand at serious political business, though with no success. Spence stood at a by-election but polled poorly. At the 1929 General Election, MacCormick and Muirhead were candidates and got just 3,000 votes between them. Yet they were re-assured by the fact that both the Liberal and Labour parties had been prompted to affirm their Home Rule commitments. Membership of the National Party grew and it saved its deposit for the first time at a by-election in November 1930. It scored a propaganda victory when its nominee, Compton Mackenzie, was chosen rector of Glasgow University in 1931. Still, in that year's General Election the party's five candidates won only 20,000 votes.

MacCormick was all the same encouraged in his view that a broad, non-doctrinaire Home Rule movement could be built up—he suggested the idea of a National Covenant as early as 1930. The National Party had a well-defined policy stance, leftist on social and economic issues and for full independence under the Crown. But MacCormick was prepared to jettison all detailed undertakings if he could win outsiders to the principle of Home Rule. One further nationalist body had been formed meanwhile, an amalgam of Unionists and Liberals under the Duke of Montrose and other worthies, calling itself the Scottish Party. It was against full separation from England and if anything rather reactionary in its general outlook. But MacCormick was impressed by its personnel and determined to effect a merger. The idea outraged many in his own camp, especially the radical literary men. Others were uneasy about diluting the commitment to independence and sinking the National Party in some wider movement of less definite aims. At the cost of a major disruption MacCormick got his way. Many of the dissidents resigned and others, such as MacDiarmid, were expelled—action which gained Nationalism a persistent reputation of being anti-intellectual. After an experiment in electoral co-operation, the two older groups combined in 1934 as the Scottish National Party.

It was, however, a quite different animal from the SNP of today. MacCormick pushed his latitudinarian policies so far as to risk making it completely amorphous. He put up no bar to simultaneous membership of other parties. He was still willing to let in cranks and romantics provided they were not associated with his personal enemies. In fact he was prepared to admit people almost without regard to their opinions so long as they said they were for Home Rule. Having just welcomed the Unionist Duke of Montrose to his ranks, MacCormick adhered in 1935 to Sir Stafford Cripps' anti-Fascist Popular Front, an organisation of near-Communist sympathies. Montrose himself became alarmed at the number of extremists entering the SNP and deserted to the Liberals in 1936. MacCormick's efforts to broaden the party's base could not save it from a poor performance in the 1935 election. It fielded eight candidates and got 29,000 votes. But it saved only three deposits and lost ground in most of the seats it had previously contested.

MacCormick's aim now was a new National Convention on the 1924 model, which he planned to hold at the end of 1939. His patient preparation was not rewarded, for the SNP continued to decline. A major problem was how to make headway against the electoral strength of the National Government. Baldwin, the Prime Minister, was an enemy of Home Rule, though he moved to allay Scottish discontents with further administrative devolution. Another difficulty was that Labour had re-emerged as a credible opposition. It did not now appear, as it might have in the period after the 1931 crisis when all parties except the Unionists seemed to be disintegrating, that a vote for the SNP was as useful as any other. In addition, some socialist MPs were working to hold the Labour leadership to its increasingly shaky commitment on Home Rule. Thomas Johnston formed in 1936 a London Scots Self-Government Committee, which requested and received assurances from Attlee. There was also the perennial problem of SNP relations with the Liberal party—the two had always been close and had complicated each other's electoral difficulties. People tended to drift indiscriminately back and forth between them, making difficult a clear Nationalist appeal to voters. The SNP itself was taking the form of a small middle-class pressure group rather than of a true political party—it had after all been chosen to throw out the most active and prominent Nationalists. Yet despite MacCormick's ruthless purge in 1933, it still had unrealistically extreme and idealist elements. Its 1937 conference, for example, approved a resolution calling on Scots to refuse service in the British army on the grounds that this would breach a provision of the Act of Union.

But when war broke out in 1939 many Nationalists happily joined up. MacCormick encouraged this and for himself suspended his Convention plans till the fighting should be finished. The war at least brought to an end the crippling stagnation of Scotland's economy. The problem of depression was, however, replaced by the new one of detailed, centralised economic planning by a London-controlled bureaucracy, creating fresh Nationalist complaints. The SNP thus ignored the gentleman's agreement among the major parties to avoid electoral confrontations while the hostilities lasted. At a by-election in Argyll in 1940 it achieved its most impressive poll ever, taking more than one-third of the vote. To many Nationalists, though, its political strategy seemed timid and ill-equipped to match the opportunities which the general party truce presented.

In fact all was far from well inside the party. Those who wanted an undiluted commitment to full independence were again becoming active under the quixotic young poet and academic, Douglas Young. An upholder of the 1937 resolution on conscription, he was in dispute with MacCormick on the SNP's whole attitude to the war. Matters came to a head in a furious row at the 1942 conference. The decisive point was the election to the party chairmanship which, amid much tension and acrimony, Young narrowly won against MacCormick's nominee. MacCormick immediately resigned his post of secretary and quit the SNP altogether, setting up with his own supporters a new nationalist body, the Scottish Convention. But this traumatic split only made explicit conflicts which had been latent for a decade. MacCormick felt it much more important to demonstrate the truth of his conviction that there was broad public support for greater devolution, in however mild a form, than to create a cadre which could focus, intensify and extend popular commitment to separatism. He had shown to his own satisfaction that a nationalist movement of the latter kind could not make much electoral headway. The overriding need, he concluded, was to build a national consensus on Home Rule which Westminster would not be able to ignore, under an organisation which should therefore be neutral as among the existing parties (though he himself fought the 1945 election as a Liberal and actually flirted with the Unionists afterwards). While appreciating that the consensus would probably stop short of independence, he saw it as the easiest means of effecting practical improvements in the government of Scotland. Now he was certain the SNP had isolated itself in extremism.

It must have been galling that the party still prospered without him. In a by-election at Kirkcaldy in 1944 Young secured 42 per cent of the vote. Even more spectacularly, Robert McIntyre won the SNP's first parliamentary seat at the Motherwell by-election in April 1945, though he lost it again at the General Election six weeks later. This brief interlude of success for the truncated SNP was not, however, the result of any sudden conversion of Scots opinion. The long and tiresome suspension of political activity in wartime encouraged protest voting and the SNP benefited as one of the few organisations prepared to fight official candidates. These votes returned to the normal allegiances at the 1945 General Election. Then it was demonstrated that the SNP had hardly advanced since the last one. In the eight seats contested it got only 30,000 votes, just 1,000 more than in 1935.

Yet again war had wrought great changes in Scottish politics. The economic and social administration of the United Kingdom was firmly centralised in 1940 and the machinery strengthened after 1945: the influence and intentions of the state now impinged directly on most areas of people's lives. But Scotland, through the establishment of St Andrew's House and Thomas Johnston's work as Secretary of State, had a greater degree of administrative devolution than ever before. The Scots' traditional reliance on local agencies for the structuring of their society was no longer adequate: they had to formulate on many major issues a national interest and win Government favour for it. At the Scottish Office, however, the impetus was in the opposite direction. It did not see itself as anything other than a Whitehall department which happened to be sitting on Calton Hill, nor did it interpret the discretion won for it by Johnston as a licence to step out of line with policies laid down for England. On the contrary, when given extra responsibilities it tried to step into line. So while the Scottish pressure groups, and public opinion generally, tended more and more towards particularism, their demands were often met by a wooden refusal in the civil service to depart from Westminster precepts.

A similar stance was soon taken by Labour, now eagerly transforming itself into a credible party of government. Though its 1945 manifesto had repeated the old promises on Home Rule, it quickly turned against them to adopt the most extreme centralist position of all. Since the Unionists continued in their hostility, Nationalism had to reckon with the fact that parties endorsed by 90 per cent of voters had set their face against any significant further devolution. MacCormick nevertheless pressed forward with the long-delayed plans for a representative gathering to rally support for his cause. The so-called National Assembly, which met in 1947 and 1948, produced detailed plans for a Scottish Parliament with powers over all the main domestic policies, including economic ones. The Government replied that it did not accept the views of a self-appointed assembly as reflecting the aspirations of Scotland. An indignant MacCormick set out to prove that contention wrong. His instrument was the National Covenant.

This document declared that regardless of party political considerations it was necessary for the good government of Scotland to establish an effective system of Home Rule under the Crown and within the framework of the United Kingdom. Voters were invited to subscribe to it, and two-thirds of them did so. Though an impressive achievement in itself, the Covenant showed nothing more than wide assent to its aims. It did not prove that people were prepared to throw up their other interests and allegiances to secure them. Here MacCormick's non-partisan approach was a weakness. Instead of inspiring London politicians to act out of disinterested respect for public opinion, he only caused them to calculate that they would neither gain nor lose whether they responded or not. They therefore ignored the issue. Scottish lobbying was met with the riposte that no-one would move till Nationalists fought and won elections on their own platform. This meant MacCormick's attempt to find a short cut through the electoral barrier had failed. His policy of the last twenty years was played out.

The rump of the SNP had been eclipsed by these efforts. But now, under the leadership of McIntyre, it was more united and had acquired a detailed political programme with a new constitution issued in 1949. Democratic and populist in spirit, this aimed to restrict the power both of the socialist state and of capitalist big business. Still, general aspects of policy were not important in unifying the party and were little stressed in its appeals to the electorate. Independence for Scotland became in effect its sole rallying cry. That exposed the SNP to charges of being simplistic, but also ensured that it would not lay itself open to the compromises which had in the end defeated MacCormick. For the moment single-minded resolution held out little prospect of success. With few resources of men or money, the SNP was hardly able to participate at all in the General Elections of 1950 and 1951. The establishment scorned it, the issues it raised were stifled by discipline inside the big parties and its advance was blocked by the insurmountable obstacle of the electoral system. Nationalism was reduced to pointless gestures of frustration like stealing the Stone of Scone. The whole movement had visibly degenerated and even in Scotland was regarded as ridiculous and irrelevant to the country's real problems. Thus it limped miserably through the next decade.

The very spirit of the age was against the Nationalists. The 1950s were a time of stability in British politics when all minority movements, even the most moderate, got short shrift from the electorate.[9] As a philosophy, nationalism was widely held responsible for the agonies through which Europe had just passed. Idealists looked rather to the subduing of strife among peoples by co-operation in supranational units such as the Commonwealth or the EEC. Scottish Nationalism's revival in the 1960s thus owed little to the naive faith in higher visions of political morality which had guided it under MacCormick. Its starting point was plainly self-interested, based on the failure of the London Government to respond to the sudden deterioration in the Scottish economy after 1955. This brought home the fact that it had been performing poorly since the First World War. For the whole of that period, most Scots had seen their salvation in economic centralism, in giving Westminster more and more power to re-allocate the resources that would raise them from backwardness and poverty. Now this view seemed to have been misconceived.

Thus came Scotland's first deviation from the national political pattern which she had closely followed since the 1930s. Contrary to the trend, she swung against the Conservatives in the 1959 election. The SNP, however, polled just 0.8 per cent of the Scottish total, representing 20,000 votes—about the same as in 1931. For the moment Scottish discontent expressed itself through the Labour party and then through the Liberals. But in time there was also some encouragement for the Nationalists. At a by-election in Bridgeton in 1961 they saved their deposit comfortably; at another in West Lothian the next year they beat both Unionists and Liberals, taking second place to Labour. This stimulated the SNP into a liveliness it had not known since the end of the war. At last there was a big influx of young, active supporters: finances improved, a national organiser was appointed and a central office set up.[10]

The approach to the 1964 election saw a lull. But the SNP then fought fifteen seats, three times as many as in 1959, by dint of which it also tripled its vote to about 65,000. The performance in 1966 was still better. Nationalist candidates secured 130,000 votes, 5 per cent of the total, and came second in three constituencies. This still modest achievement gave little indication of the events to follow during the new Parliament. Immediately after the election Labour was forced to bring in deflationary measures which plunged it within months from unprecedented success at the polls to the depths of unpopularity. In March 1967 at the by-election in Pollok, a seat held by Labour, its position was so eroded by a high SNP vote that the Conservatives won. In November 1967 came the greatest sensation of all when Mrs Winifred Ewing swept everything before her to take Hamilton, one of the safest Labour constituencies in Scotland. There were soon also big gains on the local councils.

So far the SNP had been written off as a small pressure-group of eccentrics and enthusiasts. Now, having overcome its tendencies towards crankiness and schism, it was starting to look a formidable force with a mass following. The fact that so many were not being adequately catered for by the existing parties came as a great shock because in Scotland, unlike in England, voting habits were setting yet more rigidly into a class mould in the decade after 1959. That stopped the Conservatives benefiting, as they did in the South, from Labour's misfortunes. The Scots Tories were in a sorry state: their interest in economic and industrial problems was sluggish, and they perversely insisted on choosing their parliamentary candidates from the anglicised upper class. As a result Scotland was reverting to her old anti-Conservative tradition. The Liberals, in any case without appreciable support or organisation in urban Scotland, had this time been discredited by a poor performance in 1966. The SNP would have had to be supremely incompetent not to capitalise on these trends, even if it had not turned professional. Scotland was unique in the United Kingdom in having a fourth party with a reasonable record and prospect of success, which could thus be used by the governed as a radical alternative to teach their governors a lesson.

Yet it might have been difficult to interpret the Nationalist upsurge of the 1960s as anything other than protest voting. Its main function lay in articulating, without much coherence, a host of disregarded grievances; a secure socio-economic base in the electorate and a consistent line in public policy were still lacking. But beneath the stagnant surface of Scottish society there was all the while a stirring of forces which could not be accommodated in political institutions that had taken on their essential form long ago and refused to change. That was bound to produce an impulse for renewal at some point.

The 1960s saw the breakdown in much of the central belt of the old pattern of close-knit, poverty-stricken communities, utterly reliable in their allegiance to an authoritarian Labour movement. Workers were still conscious of living in a deprived country, but were also richer, more socially mobile and more independent than before. They were not so prepared to act as voting fodder—ironically, that resulted largely from the improvement wrought in their lives by socialist policies. For the Conservatives the problem was to become still more acute. The prejudice against them among industrial workers was great and growing, and even in their rural strongholds the SNP was soon to make wide gains among people who for fifty years had refused to go over to Labour. Meanwhile many among the bourgeoisie were beginning to despair of fulfilling their aspirations through such an antiquated party.

The hold of class ideology on these voters had loosened. They gave little thought to the theoretical merits of capitalism or socialism, demanding progress by the most convenient means to hand, just as the SNP did. It benefited from its very incoherence as a political party, from its refusal to define itself as belonging to Left or Right. This allowed it to present at least a facade of constant unity, but also to seize on single issues as they came along. Thus it could draw on all sorts of local or individual protesters who might otherwise never have emerged from pressure groups. Because Scotland was a nation, their protests came out as nationalism. Attracted, too, were those sunk in apathetic alienation from the existing system—most of the activists had never engaged in political work before. If people did not feel at ease in the peculiarly constricting class structure of the other parties in Scotland, then national allegiance was a natural alternative.

So the Nationalists had the chance to exploit the failings of an establishment which on both sides of the political divide was dull and conservative, while giving the geniune discontent with it a Scottish interpretation. The post-war weakness of the United Kingdom was now striking forcefully home. Since Scotland was worse off than England, the gap between present reality and past glory or future expectations proved all the more painful. And the problems seemed to be compounded rather than solved by more centralised government—many Scots remained firmly convinced, despite ever rising aid to them, that economic policy was run for the good of South-east England. The big parties moved to appease Nationalist opinion, but only with the classic delaying tactics: a committee of inquiry under Sir Alec Douglas-Home was set up by the Conservatives and a Royal Commission under Lord Crowther (later under Lord Kilbrandon) by the Labour Government.

This half-hearted approach seemed justified when at the end of the decade the SNP went into decline and gave way to internal squabbles. With no well-defined popular base, it depended above all on maintaining its electoral impetus. Yet it failed to emulate its previous achievements in the remaining by-elections of the 1966 Parliament and soon forfeited most of its seats on the local authorities, where it was not served by the low calibre of its councillors. The General Election of 1970 turned out a tougher proposition than these lesser contests, in which the Nationalists' limited resources could be concentrated. They did double their vote to about 300,000 or 11 per cent of the total, and gained the Western Isles. But Hamilton was lost, no progress was made in urban areas and by common consent the SNP acquitted itself badly. Returning to the serious business of electing a Government for the United Kingdom, voters had with little hesitation taken up again the old allegiances. Opinion polls showed consistently that a willingness to vote SNP was much more widespread than a desire for independence—converts to full-blooded Nationalism, ready to give it their primary loyalty, were relatively few. Even so, its temporary successes had at least established it as the natural vehicle for the expression of Scottish discontent in future. Thus it survived the defeat of its offensive in the 1960s.[11]

British economic failure soon came once more to the aid of the SNP. Labour's deflation in its last months of office, and the Conservatives' in their first, produced a deep recession. Meanwhile the extent of the oil resources under the North Sea became apparent. The contrast of present misfortune with the potential for regeneration if only Scotland could get her presumed share of the revenues sharpened the discontents. The issue was seized on with the glee by the Nationalists, whose energetic campaign on it made a wider appeal than anything they had ever done. It seemed to show that, far from being inevitably reliant on the generosity of the English, the Scots were now held back by their neighbours; for the first time independence looked an attractive possibility rather than a romantic pipe-dream.[12] More generally the SNP was, despite the debacle of 1970, still in good heart. A fresh leadership under William Wolfe, chosen chairman the year before, had not been discredited. A series of encouraging by-elections culminated in the capture of Govan from Labour late in 1973. This coincided with the publication of the Kilbrandon report, the fruit of four years' exertions which had been all but ignored by the Scottish public. It proposed extensive devolution with an Assembly controlling most important domestic affairs.

The impetus given the Nationalists by these events could soon be exploited at the General Election suddenly called in February 1974. Then they won 630,000 votes, 22 per cent of the total, and seven seats—a sensation which almost at once shocked the new Labour Ministry into a commitment to devolution. The sight of other parties falling over themselves to concede its case set the SNP up for further spectacular progress when another election followed in October. This time it took 840,000 votes or 30 per cent of those cast, though returning only four more MPs. But its eleven seats understated its threat to the old order—it came second, often a close second, in most Labour ones.

A turning point in the life of the nation seemed at hand. With all parties favouring some form of devolution, its passage into law looked a certainty. In anticipation, lively debates burst out in every area of Scottish politics, which blossomed in a display of idealism and energy of which few had thought them capable.[13] Labour's response initially appeared to have the opposite of the intended effect by making Scotland more rather than less Nationalist. With the fall of the first devolution Bill in February 1977, the Government might well have been forced to go to the country. That could have been decisive for the SNP, then forging ahead of all other parties in the opinion polls. But Labour was saved by its pact with the Liberals, and the crisis passed. To general surprise, Nationalism steadily declined thereafter. Failure in the referendum and the General Election of 1979 only confirmed the trend.

These had been a few, brief years during which the SNP might have transformed itself into the national movement it longed to be, but failed. It did not strike roots deep enough. Even in 1974 and afterwards the main reason for its success still lay in its own electoral momentum. Few Scots accepted its claim that they were so different from their Southern neighbours as to make separatism a necessity, or that central government was to be equated with oppressive English government, especially with Labour in power. Thus they did not repudiate the dual nationality which, in the absence of full assimilation, had made a successful Union. To be sure, the Scottish aspect of it became more attractive amid the crises of the 1970s. But if loyalty to Britain was shaken, it never broke. The Nationalists' opponents could therefore establish a distinction in the public mind—in Scotland, if not always in England—between independence and a lesser degree of constitutional reform. An improved Union was what most Scots in the past had wanted and most in the present still did. By espousing it, if only in the dubious form of the Scotland Act, a Labour party at heart unionist was able to seize the mantle of leadership of national sentiment from the SNP, which did not have the political skill or experience to win it back.

In fact it had little altered the spread of opinion shown consistently by survey. A strict unionist balanced a strict Nationalist minority—though the latter, of course, formed part of the huge majority favouring some change. Within it were electors who might opt temporarily for the SNP, believing that the best way forward was to vote for the extreme in the hope of a settlement coming to rest somewhere in the middle. Others took little thought of the constitution—the SNP might appeal to them as an instrument of protest, but progress towards independence would require several electoral tests in which they would be unreliable. Perhaps the one description covering them all came in the Kilbrandon report:

> The greatest significance of the Scottish Nationalist movement lies not in its advocacy of separatism but in the means which it has provided for the people of Scotland to register their feelings of national identity and political importance. Nationalist voters, and the obvious sympathy they have attracted from a good many others who would not themselves be prepared by their votes to endorse a separatist policy, have drawn attention to an intensity of national feeling in Scotland which people outside that country were not generally aware of.[15]

It certainly reflected discontent with the way she was being run, but it was in the end no national movement bent on self-government.

The support the SNP had got was patchy and shallow. It did not decisively break down the class allegiances which had long determined party preferences. Some dissolution in them began among Scots as among others at the time, but the vote thus released was more volatile than that yet attached to the big parties. And despite appearances, Scotland was in important respects not so deeply affected by the change as other parts of Britain. Especially in the West, which the Nationalists had to take for ultimate success, class differences were still felt to be a reality—class loyalties and class politics remained extremely strong. The SNP's breakthrough took place mainly in faraway rural seats, For all its exertions, it never persuaded the workers to identify fully with it. And finding that progress towards its goal would not be quick, but on the contrary long and arduous, it was more depressed by setbacks than the senior parties with their experience of vicissitude.

If unable to rely on class, the Nationalists might have turned to the other great force in modern Scottish politics, the institutions. Of the older ones, the Church showed much sympathy to devolution, but the law was wary and the universities bitterly hostile, while the SNP's excursions into local government did more harm than good. Of the newer ones, business was vehemently opposed, the unions tied to Labour and the Scottish Office discreetly ready for any outcome. Real commitment was everywhere lacking. The SNP was unlikely to inspire any, since its populism made it rather indifferent to institutions, even scornful of their compromises with unionism. Yet while expecting the Scottish people to break their grip, it did not seem to want to change things greatly. The picture of an independent Scotland it painted was of one where matters would carry on much as before, except that North Sea oil would provide more bounty to share out. That allowed the old interests to respond in kind: in particular, Labour's devolution scheme was blatantly designed to protect its own power structure. In pork-barrel politics, the Nationalists could not compete with the existing apparatus. It was thus the more difficult to wean Scots away from their traditional allegiances.

Failing to consolidate its position, the SNP was vulnerable to internal strains. With the prospect of success for Labour's legislation, it could not decide whether to accept devolution or reject it for falling short of independence. Some Nationalists argued with conviction that they had only reached their present eminence by sticking to their principles. To others, the refusal of all compromise seemed unreasonable when most Scots would clearly settle for Home Rule: pursuing a hard line too stubbornly might make explicit the lack of wide support for separation. The SNP could not therefore afford to alienate doubters while it was still far from the majority of seats it claimed as a mandate for dissolving the Union. The outcome was merely hesitation and a mishandled choice. The Nationalist MPs played only a small part in the parliamentary debates on the Scotland Bill, where the running was made by Scots of other parties, mainly opponents, even by Englishmen. Equally the SNP was unable to join with unanimous enthusiasm in the referendum campaign. The initiative was thus lost at crucial points.

The advance had all the same been a great achievement, won without any formidable leaders or wealth of ideas in the face of the whole English establishment, and much of the Scottish one. In the process Nationalism had transformed itself from a mere pressure group into a member of a four-party system on a par with others. After breaking the mould of politics, however, it found itself faced with demands for which it was unprepared. It could no longer be content with purity, but had to cope with difficult choices, compromises and setbacks. At the first assay, it did not cope well.

The sentiments it awakened were anyway not automatically translated into a vote for the SNP. At bottom there was still no strong will to fundamental reform in a people long mollified by patronage for lack of real influence over its rulers, and canny enough to avoid risking false moves. Even less had there been, as in 1832, 1886 and 1922, any decisive breakthrough by a rising movement seizing the leadership of forces unleashed amid social and constitutional change. This time they mainly issued in periodic surges of protest voting—if, indeed, they did not bring a long-term shift to Labour which could only be taken as an affirmation of the United Kingdom. Having once already proved inept at playing a waiting game, Nationalism could spend itself before any renewed British failure gives it a fresh chance.

Yet in the course of the century it had unmistakably risen. It had necessarily in passing loosened the Union's links somewhat, though not definitively even amid the enthusiasms of the 1970s. The formula for satisfying a national sentiment in this uneasy, intermediate state proved elusive: conflicts about nationhood do not, after all, readily admit of intermediate remedies. As things stand, it would take an uncommon astuteness to reconcile Scotland's peculiarly finicky aspirations with the interests of all others involved—and her politics have never been astute. So far, Nationalism offers no guarantee that she can come to a better resolution of her problems than at any time since 1707.

Chapter 9

'How Deep Is The Separation'

The crisis in the Union of which the modern Nationalist movement was the catalyst must also be ascribed to wider causes. Often disregarded in the analysis is the sudden decay after 1959 of a major ideology, the Unionist, which among other things had fostered and harnessed the British patriotism of all classes, including many workers. Socialism, the only real competitor left, was allowed to consolidate itself and secure an unrivalled dominance. Scotland thus broke with her recent conformity to the general pattern of politics in the United Kingdom and recurred to her own of former days, likened above to a one-party state. True, Labour never emulated the absolute majorities habitually won by the old Liberal party, and twice even by the Unionists. But it established a decisive lead in votes and, more important, an unshakeable hold over at least forty seats capable of surviving large swings against it in the rest of Britain. Through that alone it set the agenda for Scottish politics, and to some extent all other parties imitated its programme. Strangely, though, the confrontation grew harsher, for they also thereby fed its self-confidence and aggression towards Governments unable to match its own degree of popular support.

This, too, contributed to making the Scots feel more different. Yet it would be wrong to suppose that their polity had restored to it the pronounced national character, ultimately owed to religion, that it had shown before 1914. Sermonising rhetoric was still heard, but it articulated no distinct moral outlook. The secular socialist creed sought in practice little more than a centralised welfare state, contenting itself at home with the humdrum round of power-broking and patronage in the local authorities and trade unions. Many of those disliking it or excluded from its rewards were soon to fall for the more exciting allure of Nationalism. Labour, in playing the people's party, had in its turn to attempt some coming to terms with that persistent sentiment. Here, however, was a contradiction which the history of the period proved it unable to resolve.

If the trend in British politics was towards consensus, in Scotland it was already past its prime. Originating there under Elliot and Johnston, it saw its heyday in the 1950s, that decade of easy-going Unionist government in the face of an acquiescent, not to say ineffective opposition. It was replaced, in a system of politics becoming rather void of content, by a straight fight over the raw material of power, for votes, offices and spoils. The struggle was perhaps on that account all the more bitter, though the pantomime of confrontation obscured a good deal of actual consensus on policy. Under the Unionists, representation at the centre for Scottish interests left little to be desired. They were not only promoted by the Secretary of State, but could be sure of a sympathetic hearing from several of his senior colleagues, including the Prime Minister, Harold Macmillan, who himself took care to cultivate contacts in, for example, the STUC. The net of influence was also spread through the versatile MPs. They moved easily to posts other than Scottish ones and were, despite a nominal distinction, better integrated with their own side than Scots Labour members were with theirs.

The general cast of mind, long inherent in Unionism, was collectivist. But it was too uncritical in welcoming the latest extensions of the Scottish corporate state, which hammered more nails in its coffin. In the end they buried any remaining ideology of the party's own, because in collectivism it could always be outbid by Labour. The electoral benefits were certainly meagre. Unionism had after all from the start reflected more than anything the values of its largest group of supporters, the very Scottish bourgeoisie, which on the whole disliked the inefficient squandering of taxpayers' money. These values were still being embodied as late as the 1950s by independent, colourful, self-made MPs considerably more able and popular as constituency members than most on the benches opposite. But the party was drifting away from its origins. A new generation was not only duller, more conventional and more dutiful in following the line laid down in London, but also too full of landowners remote from urban or industrial problems. A grouse moor image imposed itself in Scotland just as it was fading in the South, and helped to undo a Unionism which till then had usually been able to get the better of Labour. It reckoned to have touched bottom in 1959, but its decline was to accelerate, first in the West, then even in the counties and especially in the Highlands.[1]

For a while all this lay hidden. John Maclay, retained as Secretary of State after the 1959 election, was an improvement on his predecessor, and active in transforming the Scottish Office into an agent of regional policy.[2] Whitehall's general interventionist framework, based mainly on a Local Employment Act (1960) giving grants to companies set up in specified areas, was supplemented by his own particular initiatives in Scotland. A modern steelworks was built at Ravenscraig, and an effort made to establish a motor industry with plants at Linwood and Bathgate. Grand designs were also much in fashion. Lord Fraser of Allander drew up one for the Highlands. On behalf of the Scottish Council, Sir John Toothill chaired a committee which reported in 1961 on the economy as a whole, showing how the latest theories of development could be applied to it. He proposed a systematic drive to stimulate expansion at 'growth points' through the attraction of new industries, rather than the endless propping up of the old. Meanwhile pits and shipyards were still closing, while crisis spread to other sectors such as locomotives, machine tools and textiles. With an industrial base far too narrow, Scotland fell behind the employment and living standards enjoyed by the rest of Britain. For a decade after 1955 she had the lowest growth rate in Europe.

Maclay had to shoulder the blame, and was axed in Macmillan's infamous Cabinet reshuffle of 1962. He was succeeded by Michael Noble, MP for Argyll, previously chairman of the Unionist party and Scottish whip, whose lack of ministerial experience and bland manner robbed him of much public confidence.[3] They disguised, however, the energy with which he went about putting the Toothill report into effect. The work was set in hand with a major administrative reform, the creation of the Scottish Development Department (SDD), to bring under one head the economic functions of St Andrew's House: thus policies for planning, local government, roads, housing and electricity could be better co-ordinated. To help with forecasting and the evaluation of progress the Scottish Office's first economists were recruited. The machinery had become sophisticated enough to produce in 1963 a Central Scotland Plan. Though more could thus be done than merely follow instructions from London, no quick or obvious improvement in the economy resulted. To a people now accustomed to the welfare state and content with official controls it was all quite inexplicable.

Against this background Unionist hopes of revival turned sour. Two seats were lost to Labour on the heavy swings against the Government at the ten Scottish by-elections of the Parliament—even at that in West Perthshire in 1963 when Sir Alec Douglas-Home, having renounced his peerage to become Prime Minister, re-entered the Commons. The General Election of 1964 showed a still more drastic decline. In Britain as a whole it was close-fought, but in Scotland the Unionists were humiliated by six more losses, reducing their number of MPs to a mere twenty-four. Even if their share of the poll, at 41 per cent, held up quite well, it was the worst reverse suffered by any Scottish party since the war. Two new Liberal members came from the Highlands to join Jo Grimond, while Labour's six net gains since 1959 gave it forty-four seats on nearly half the total vote. Since Harold Wilson's majority at Westminster was only three, the outcome had in effect been decided in Scotland.[4]

Unionists, thinking their record of the last five years rather good, were staggered by this awful performance. The blame was put, if a little too glibly, on organisational weakness. Still separate from its English sister, the party was certainly in a mess, badly off, burdened with an amateur and fractious machine, lacking facilities for research or policy-making and generally incapable of coherent action. It was all the same extremely loth to reform itself, as Lord Balerno had found in 1963 when he tried to persuade it to. Now, however, the case for change was unanswerable, and resistance to it collapsed. The most radical plan was merger with the English party, though London soon found that would be impossible to enforce. A milder scheme proposed by Fraser of Allander at least got rid of the more glaring defects. Power was vested in a chairman, appointed directly by the Tory leader, at the central office in Edinburgh, making it a real rather than merely nominal headquarters. It was to supervise the five regional associations into which, on the English pattern, the Scottish party was then sub-divided. The way was thus smoothed for eventual merger, though it could still only be carried out twelve years later. Already, however, the Scots had lost any true independence. They had devoted much energy to sustaining it but, with the withering of the native Right-wing tradition, their attitudes and organisation were unequal to the task. As if in token of that, the venerable title of Unionist was dropped in favour of Conservative.

More disgruntled Tories defected when Wilson sought a secure mandate in the General Election of 1966. Nowhere was it given with greater enthusiasm than in Scotland. Labour did better than ever before or since, getting forty-six MPs returned on just under 50 per cent of the poll. The advance was again at the expense of the hapless Conservatives, who besides lost another seat to the Liberal party and failed to recapture Roxburgh, Selkirk and Peebles, which David Steel had taken at the previous year's by-election. They were now reduced to twenty members, having seen a quarter of their vote disappear in a decade.[5]

That decline had two results: the establishment of Labour's dominance, never afterwards lost, and the emergence of a bloc of centrist voters leaning to what survived of the old non-socialist radicalism, of which Home Rule had been part. The first beneficiaries were the Liberals, among whom a new pragmatism was reversing half a century of decay. At their Scottish assembly of 1961 they had affirmed their commitment to a Parliament in Edinburgh with fiscal powers. But they had not developed this into a broader programme for Scotland. Nor were they in general taken seriously as a national force. Their revival, reflecting mainly the peculiar traditions and interests of the remote, atypical North, petered out before long. In fact the 1966 election—when the Liberal vote was actually smaller than in 1964—can be held to have marked its end. Though the leader, Jo Grimond, was a Scot, his party was seeking a future in the suburbs of English cities rather than on the Celtic fringe which had preserved it from extinction. That was only consistent with the line laid down by Sir Archibald Sinclair thirty years earlier. Home Rule was more a relic of the past sentimentally preserved than a policy Liberals realistically expected to pursue.

The revival had been notably weak in the Labour heartland, where much of the protest vote was picked up by an SNP now of soberly respectable and progressive outlook. Its share of the poll doubled in 1964 and again in 1966, though it was still far from winning any seat. But these were by its standards impressive advances, making it at least a minor party to be reckoned with. It was especially successful among groups, in the professions and the lower bourgeoisie, which had found no political role for themselves elsewhere. With this wider appeal it could progress in places where Liberals never would. Its main achievement so far, however, was simply to have attracted attention to itself.

For a time all this encouraged notions that the divided centre might unite as a more effective third force in Scottish politics.[6] As early as 1964 William Wolfe persuaded the Nationalists to offer the Liberals a pact. These responded cautiously despite the urgings of some prominent members, and nothing formal was concluded for that year's election. But the two parties found themselves opposed in only three of the forty-four seats which one or the other fought. Their combined poll rose considerably, for the SNP's relative strength in the burghs married with the Liberals' in the counties. The latter's interest in an accord quickened again after 1966, when they needed something to sustain their previous impetus. Grimond, after resigning the leadership, mounted a personal campaign for Home Rule. On his party's motion, the Commons debated it for the first time in forty years. At their assembly of 1968, the Scots Liberals approved a detailed federalist scheme for the four nations of the United Kingdom. The impression was somewhat spoiled when the English Liberals devised another defining Scotland as merely one among numerous regions. It had anyway become clear that there remained in both camps major figures averse to co-operation, let alone merger. The old guard of the SNP especially viewed with distaste any dilution of the purity which had allowed it to survive, and its victory at the Hamilton by-election seemed to render a pact superfluous.[7] The quest for unity thus proved fruitless.

Besides, the most important political development of the 1960s was the consolidation of class voting in central Scotland. Industrial decline robbed the Unionists of the support they had long enjoyed in the proletariat. It grew defensive, then militant in the face of painful economic change. Its tribal loyalties deepened to the point where the choice of any other party than Labour seemed inconceivable, an attitude which the odd Nationalist incursion did not in the long run alter.[8] The Scots began to believe the myths preached at them for fifty years: that since socialism was second nature to them, its supremacy was natural and inevitable.

The mythology was so powerful as to obscure the profound conservatism into which Labour had in fact fallen. It was unshaken by the defeat of Hugh Gaitskell's moderate leadership at the 1959 election, though that did allow more thoroughgoing doctrines to emerge from under the stifling weight of internal discipline in a way that had not been possible for a quarter of a century. This renascence of Labour's Left showed itself first in the growth of the Campaign for Nuclear Disarmament. In Scotland it sprang partly from an influx of disgusted Communists after the Soviet suppression of the Hungarian uprising in 1956. They assimilated easily, having all along retained through their strength among the miners a voice in the movement as a whole. Pacifism survived, too, from the old days in some of Labour's own more venerable figures, such as William Baxter, MP for West Stirlingshire, and Emrys Hughes, MP for South Ayrshire and Keir Hardie's son-in-law. The whip was withdrawn from both at one point for refusing to toe the Right-wing party line on defence.[9]

Even so, as late as 1974 the Left could claim no more than nine of the forty-one MPs then returned. On every other public issue the party stood still in the postures it had assumed after the war: the industrial structure was to be preserved, Home Rule to be forgotten, the permissive society to be resisted. Immobilism had its practical reasons. In the modern corporate state Labour had, by tailoring its policies and patronage to suit all electorally relevant groups, built a formidable institutional base. It naturally favoured the retention of power by those who had thus won it.

That power had struck deep root. It had done so as long ago as the 1920s among the Catholics.[10] They were held remarkably loyal through the influence the party offered to a sometimes still under-privileged minority, of which the symbol was commitment to its separate schooling. The power had been extended by a housing policy which deliberately served the interest of council tenants in low rents. This Labour had been able to pursue consistently as it took over the local authorities in the 1930s, and to turn into its main electoral ploy when it came to dominate them after 1945. Now the policy was proving its worth in widening the power base, as slum dwellers were shifted out into peripheral housing schemes, building up great blocs of Labour voters in old Unionist seats.

Recently the base had again been strengthened as Labour took up the causes which Scotland's accelerating economic decline presented to it. That naturally won support from workers anxious to preserve their jobs in the face of disappearing markets, and incidentally helped to secure the position of a conservative trade union movement entrenched in the older crafts. Scottish socialists were soon judging themselves by how much aid they could extract from London, and often by how much they could surpass their comrades from the English provinces in doing so. Subsidy seemed to offer such a perfect answer to the problems of the time that nobody asked whether it could have the ill-effect of tying up unproductively resources that might be used for profitable investments. The clamour for it concealed in truth an underlying pessimism, an assumption that Scotland had no choice but to live off hand-outs from the Exchequer. In any case, wider considerations were too easily excluded from politics defined as the direct satisfaction of sectional interests.[11]

Under Labour, all its MPs were to be brokers for them. The government of Scotland became in many respects merely local government writ large. That also favoured a special type of politician. His essential qualification was intimate knowledge of the network of power at the grassroots, among councillors and union officials. Without service as such, few could hope for a parliamentary candidature. Thus graduates and professionals were noticeably absent from the Labour benches. They were filled instead by backwoodsmen innocent of any concern with foreign or even with wider British affairs, outstanding only for their Scottishness, rather isolated from the rest of a party taking them at their own narrow valuation.

The system had come to rest on cliques of the orthodox. It inevitably fostered careerism, corruption and a positive aversion to anything smacking of public participation. Labour, long centralised and authoritarian enough, grew suspicious of all criticism and new ideas. That was especially true of the West, where the resemblance to a one-party state was closest. Even if the Tories had had something fresh to offer, they had been hounded thence by the collapse of their working-class vote. Labour commanded the centre of the stage, pontificating as the people's party on every Scottish issue.[12]

Its paladin was William Ross, MP for Kilmarnock and Labour's chief Scottish spokesman from 1963, starting then a reign over the party which was to last thirteen years. In the dying days of Unionist rule he was already a terrific antagonist, clearly outclassing the luckless Noble. Wilson had no hesitation in making him Secretary of State. He soon proved himself one of the great Scottish power-brokers. His good, if gruff, contact with the movement at home gave him a firm grip on the MPs, and neutralised those he did not like. He fought with prickly tenacity inside the official machine, which omitted at its peril to refer its business in Scotland to him and his civil servants. In Cabinet he constantly played the Scottish card, never letting it forget that he could deliver forty vital Labour seats, thus exerting an influence unusual in one who did not belong to the inner circle of decision-makers. Shaped to his own ends, the familiar methods of the devolved administration were turned into something approaching a policy for Scotland, and brought to a productive pitch they had otherwise attained only in the very different circumstances of war. In showing the Scots how in normal times, too, their demands could be articulated without alienating the sources of largesse in London, his achievement was second only to Johnston's. But in exactly the same way, that rendered Home Rule in his eyes otiose.[13]

On entering office he had found, of course, that matters were not so simple as he had been depicting them from opposition. His was, however, a genuinely progressive administration, by no means solely concerned with economics. The Scottish Law Reform Commission was instituted under Lord Kilbrandon, though there was trouble in finding time to legislate for its proposals. A Royal Commission was appointed under Lord Wheatley to bring up to date the creaking system of local government. Comprehensive education was enforced in state schools, four new universities were founded and a pioneering Act on social work was passed.

But Ross certainly devoted most of his energy to regional policy, and generally to getting and spending for Scotland as large a share as possible of the public purse.[14] One success came in the traditional area of greatest difficulty, when the Highlands and Islands Development Board was set up in 1965, with executive as well as planning powers over local industry, tourism and transport. It toyed with schemes for new cities, a university and much else, but more modest and useful work was done once this first flush of naive ambition faded.

Because of the need for co-ordination with grand designs drawn up in London, efforts in the rest of Scotland lagged behind. The first steps were to establish a planning board of civil servants, an auxiliary council of the usual economic interests and a regional development division inside St Andrew's House. In 1966 they produced a national plan. With the whole country, except Edinburgh, made into a development area, an all-round renovation of the economy could be attempted. Old jobs would be replaced by newly created ones, while social expenditure on housing, hospitals, schools and roads would make Scotland pleasant and prosperous enough to bring in the modern consumer and service industries long lacking.[15]

Public spending per head was soon 20 per cent above the British average. It still left unsolved some basic problems, notably in heavy industry: for the £600 million of aid in these years, 100,000 jobs were generated yet 150,000 lost. Fresh difficulties arose too. Firms remote from their markets were penalised by a growing prevalence of uniform national wage rates, to correct which a payroll subsidy, the regional employment premium, was given to manufacturers from 1967. But then native ownership was diluted by national-isation and by officially promoted mergers with companies from outside. In all, hopes were unrealistically raised through Labour's lack of sense of its own limitations. Many forecasts in the plans were absurd. They were anyway to be ruined by the sharp deflation immediately after the 1966 election.

This Government of change was thus in a position to change little. Hollow promises brought it a series of disastrous reverses at by-elections all over Britain. In Scotland that gave the impetus to the rise of the SNP, whose soaring vote first handed Pollok to the Tories and then took Hamilton.[16] As a new party without a baggage of compromise and failure it could compete with Labour in radicalism and sometimes win. While not markedly dissenting from the view that the state should run the economy, it did pledge a readier response to the problems than Whitehall could provide and, rather more dubiously, a greater flow of resources to solve them. But the glibness of these ideas counted for little when others' were not working anyway.

Free of class allegiances, the SNP could mobilise disillusioned groups so far left out of politics and release a great deal of frustrated idealism. It benefited, too, from the fact that they were not prepared to turn back to the Conservatives, whose policies were anyway similar to Labour's and whose unionism was just as strict. Scots jumped at a plausible alternative. Its advance was viewed with indulgence even in the establishment, prompting the Kirk, the STUC and much of the Press to come out for Home Rule.

Labour was astonished and horrified. Since the war it had treated only with contempt any suggestion that Scotland needed more than a devolved administration and special procedures in Parliament. The attitude was endorsed and encouraged from on high. In 1956 Gaitskell had told the Scottish conference why Home Rule was now an irrelevance: during the 1920s the free market had drained Scotland of vigour, but that had been cured by nationalisation and planning. Wilson was of the same mind, though his centralism was modified by the fashionable novelty of regional policy. Ross' dour persistence in exploiting it robbed him of any sympathy for more speculative schemes of reform. On the contrary, it fired him with extreme and abusive hostility towards them.

The bitterness of his reaction was deepened by the Nationalists' success in stealing Labour's thunder. He might rage in Cabinet, and his followers in the country, but they had no other remedy than to make their system yet more profligate—or, in their parlance, to give Scotland 'more socialism'—some-thing clearly precluded by the crisis in national finances.[17] In fighting back against the SNP's populism, they were hamstrung by the fact that their local organisation, always patchy, had in some places, notably in the safer seats, virtually ceased to exist. Ross contemplated resignation but even in this extremity refused to compromise. He engineered the rout of the Labour devolutionists, led by John Mackintosh, MP for Berwick and East Lothian, at the Scottish conference of 1968. His position was nonetheless weakening. His policy of no surrender was leaving his party as a helpless spectator of events. He had always been seen as the hard-headed realist, but now seemed to have got everything wrong.

Ross' own style of government was part of the problem, as Richard Crossman appreciated after forcing himself to stay away from an important Scottish debate:

> Just as we were going in we realised that the Scots would suspect some poisonous English conspiracy, so we would have to keep out, come what may. I quote this to show how deep is the separation which already exists between England and Scotland . . . Ross and his friends accuse the Scottish Nationalists of separatism but what . . . Ross himself actually likes is to keep Scottish business absolutely privy from English business. I am not sure that this system isn't one that gets the worst of both worlds, which is why I'm in favour of a Scottish Parliament.[18]

Crossman was almost alone among Ministers in his willingness to regard the problem not as a mere excrescence of economic crisis but as a deeper development demanding serious thought on the constitution. Others were torn between hostility and bemusement, Wilson dismissing the subject as 'boring and soporific'.[19]

With the failures of the Scottish party, the counter-moves had nevertheless to be left to London. The Government set up a Royal Commission on the Constitution chaired by Lord Crowther, later by Lord Kilbrandon.[20] It was, however, meant to bury the issue. The refusal to panic seemed justified when Labour held its seats in the remaining by-elections of the Parliament. Its morale rose with the approach of the General Election of 1970, just as the Nationalists' fell. At their most optimistic, they had hoped to turn it into a referendum on independence. But, though now as strong in the counties as in the burghs and able to campaign all over the country, they did not in the event sustain their challenge. On a high turnout, which they may have caused, they still secured a mere 11 per cent of the vote. The Western Isles were won but Hamilton was lost, and nowhere else were the big parties decisively shaken. The Tories, if unable to raise their share of the poll above 38 per cent, took twenty-three seats by recapturing two from the Liberals and one from Labour. The latter returned forty-four MPs on 45 per cent of the votes cast. Their distribution in Britain was almost the same as in 1955, but in Scotland there had meanwhile been a swing of 5 per cent against the Conservatives. It was the fourth consecutive election in which Labour had done much better than in England.[21]

In London a Tory Government was returned under Edward Heath. In Scotland his party thus found itself in a new and uncomfortable position—and with a growing crisis of identity. Before, it had always enjoyed wide support in the country, and sometimes a majority. Now it was in rather a small minority, at least in Parliament. The charge began to be heard that it merely imposed on the Scots measures they did not want. That demanded a more positive line on Scottish issues than had so far been deemed necessary. But the MPs and their leadership were increasingly ill-equipped to respond.

The Conservatives' decline had left them with two main constituencies.

One was rural, sturdily independent, little amenable to central control. But it loved a laird—the associations' selection procedures favoured men of high social standing, filling the benches at Westminster with aloof, well-born members remote from Scottish problems and anathema to the workers. They saddled the party with a feudal look that was almost a caricature of its English sister. They also frustrated aspirants from the central belt, often treated in the counties as presumptuous invaders. In this second constituency, the bourgeois districts of the Lowlands, Toryism continued to wither. With the extinction of the more independent type of self-made MP, Scotland's middle class lacked a representation after its own heart. Professional men could rarely get into Parliament because of the lack of winnable seats on their home ground. Lawyers, for example, prominent in the Conservative politics of the South, were conspicuous by their absence in Scotland: it was typical that Banff had actually turned down the Solicitor General in 1962. The party got less and less general support from business as the spring of native enterprise died, and was now almost entirely financed by the last two of the tycoons, Fraser of Allander and Hugh Stenhouse. With the aristocrats thus left in charge, the other voice most loudly heard was from the plebeian, populist Glaswegian Tories round Teddy Taylor, MP for Cathcart. But they opposed such cherished causes of the new Prime Minister's as Home Rule and the EEC, over which Taylor was to resign from the Government in 1971. In either case the Scottish party was out of tune with the dynamic, modernising image Heath had in mind to give it.[22]

He offered two answers. One was devolution. He had come in 1968 to the Scottish conference and made his Declaration of Perth, acknowledging the strength of national feeling and promising to respond to it. Sir Alec Douglas-Home was then put in charge of a committee to inquire into the possibilities. In March 1970 he proposed that an elected assembly of 125 members should meet in Edinburgh to vote on certain stages of Scottish legislation and thus act as a sort of third chamber of Parliament. While Home Rule sentiment was not absent from the party, this vague scheme seemed merely to provide its opponents with ammunition: the 1973 conference turned against devolution again. Heath had gone too far and too fast for most.

His second wish was to edge the Scottish party towards merger with the English one. But he could win over neither the aristocrats running it for the present nor the populists who might replace them in the future. Not till 1977 could this final reform be carried through, on proposals from Russell Fairgrieve, chairman of the party and MP for West Aberdeenshire. Integration was then sweetened by some sops to patriotism, such as the retention of a central office. But essentially it had been recognised that the only way to get a sound organisation was to make London pay for it. The quality of candidate rose, though not the number of MPs.

Heath's Secretary of State was Gordon Campbell, who had served as an Under-Secretary in 1963–4 and replaced Noble as chief Scottish spokesman in 1969.[23] His suave if hardly forceful manner was better suited to the embassy at Vienna, whence he had been plucked by James Stuart in 1959 as his personal choice to succeed him in Moray and Nairn. Diplomacy marked his style to the point where he struck some as being the United Kingdom Government's ambassador to Scotland. While able to speak for Westminster to the Scots and report back there on them, he could never comfortably have taken the same chauvinist position in Cabinet as the redoubtable Ross. Nor was he equipped by temperament or experience to enter the jungle of economic affairs which were the overriding pre-occupation of Heath and his senior Ministers. The immediate intention was broadly to reverse Labour's interventionism. When this failed to work fast enough, they impatiently returned to pursue it with even greater vigour, notably with the instruments to hand under the Industry Act (1971). The changes wrought in passing to regional policy could cause a good deal of disruption and annoyance. But that was the consequence of the major initiatives being taken in London.

Campbell accepted all this with equanimity. He could see Scottish experience offered little comfort to the notion that state aid might by itself save declining industries. He therefore found no great merit in special treatment for Scotland, which was anyway bound to be eroded by the extension of assistance in provincial England. The Scots would still have the advantage of a devolved administration at St Andrew's House. There another effort to improve policy-making was undertaken with the establishment in 1973 of the Scottish Economic Planning Department. A primarily bureaucratic response was also given to the controversy over North Sea oil, now working strongly to the profit of the SNP. Lord Polwarth, Campbell's Minister of State, was appointed head of an advisory oil development board for Scotland. This could not, however, quell the rising discontent with the facts that the direct benefits from the North Sea were not very visible and that the revenues were destined for the Treasury.

It was heavy industry that produced the Government's big crisis in Scotland, with the collapse of Upper Clyde Shipbuilders.[24] UCS had been formed with official funding in 1968 to rationalise the operations of several ailing yards, but labour relations remained poor and financial problems acute. In the summer of 1971 a liquidator was appointed. He quickly announced redundancies, to a furious reaction from the workforce. Under the leadership of two Communist shop stewards, Jimmy Reid and Jimmy Airlie, it occupied the yards. Reid's demagogic gifts made him a folk-hero (and soon Rector of Glasgow University) able to rouse wide support for the occupation. The Government was advised that public order on Clydeside could not be guaranteed, a threat accepted so gullibly that it reversed first its particular policy for shipbuilding and before long its entire economic strategy of forcing British industry to become more competitive. The yards were again saved by the Exchequer. Over the next four years £100 million were pumped into them, but no lasting solution to their difficulties was found. In Scotland at large, the affair powerfully reinforced the socialist myth that capitalism simply could not work there, so that state intervention would always be necessary.

In these matters the Government in London took the lead, the Scottish Office standing on the sidelines. It occupied itself meanwhile with the biggest reconstruction of the local authorities ever undertaken, based on the report of the Wheatley commission. That had followed clear, if by no means universally welcome, principles. But their translation into law was considerably mis-managed, not least because of the difficulty of devising a uniform structure for such a diverse country. What emerged was still a quintessential bureaucrats' measure catching the imagination neither of the public nor of the politicians. It remained, as it had been from the outset, a child of SDD, which wanted above all better means of enforcing its wishes.[25]

The aim was to break down the historic division between burghs and counties, replacing them with giant regions over which the planning of their major responsibilities could be consistently applied. A second tier of districts would take care of minor matters. This was radical enough to alarm many diverse interests, which joined in various combinations to force far-reaching amendments through. The original concepts were diluted when local patriotism in the Borders, Fife and the Isles managed to keep these as separate regions, even though the authorities ruling them might be too small to carry out all the appropriate functions. The administration of housing was transferred to districts so that Tory areas could escape Labour policies. On the same grounds, the richer peripheral burghs were removed from socialist Glasgow. In the end the Local Government Act, which came into force in 1975, still managed to displease nearly everyone. While the Conservative party now started contesting elections to the councils regularly, on the whole they just gave more power to Labour. The cities resented their diminished status. Strathclyde, containing half the population, was much too big. The regional authorities turned out in general to be remote and costly, enjoying neither the goodwill of their electorates nor the trust of central government. An alliance of Scottish Office bureaucrats and Westminster politicians had within ten years moved to control them so closely that little was left of Scottish local autonomy.

In retrospect, this was fiddling while Rome caught fire. Heath's Government had a last chance to respond rationally to the growing demand for devolution free of the panic which overtook its successor. But it chose to take refuge in a desire to get local government reform out of the way first and to wait on the Kilbrandon report—hoping no doubt that together they would dispel the need of every doing anything. For in view of Scotland's incurable penchant for voting Labour, the Conservatives were in any case having second thoughts. Now that they had steered Britain into the EEC, they could view yet another, Scottish, tier of government as all the more superfluous. When their conference rejected devolution in 1973, Campbell promised that there would be no further moves towards it during this Parliament.

But the new regional councils were too unpopular to be a substitute, and the Kilbrandon report made a more profound impact than anyone would ever have imagined. The Royal Commission had been set up with neutral terms of reference: 'to examine the present functions of the central legislature and government in relation to the several countries, nations and regions of the United Kingdom' and to consider 'whether any changes are desirable'. In itself it was an inconclusive document, suggesting four variations on a basic scheme in its main body, with a quite different fifth one in a memorandum of dissent. That enjoying the greatest support among the commission's members was for a legislative assembly and an executive controlling revenues awarded as a bloc grant by a mediating Exchequer Board. They would be sufficient to ensure that Scotland could maintain the same level of services as other parts of Britian, but the executive would be able to vary particular allocations and possibly raise a little more through minor taxing powers; it would have no other economic functions. The report also showed concern with questions of electoral equity bound to antagonise the big parties: it favoured proportional representation in the assembly and a reduction in the number of Scotland's MPs at Westminster to one commensurate with her population (at the time fifty-seven). This did nothing to commend the rest of the proposals to the evasive Tories or to the bitterly hostile Labour party. Little apparent excitement greeted publication of the report, which was generally expected to be shelved. Somehow, though, it managed to elevate devolution into a respectable political issue, no longer the prerogative of extremists and eccentrics.

The lull in the Nationalists' fortunes had been temporary, as they had been demonstrating at by-elections and especially in their victory at Govan in November 1973. That, with the high excitement of the Government's battle against the miners over the winter, threw the General Election of February 1974 wide open. Other parties found it hard to compete with the sudden access of energy and enthusiasm in the SNP, which burst into the Commons with seven seats and 22 per cent of the vote. Even so, Labour's Scottish majority was hardly dented—a fact remarkable in view of its low morale after setbacks at the by-elections, its organisational failings and its refusal of all concession to national sentiment but a tired old offer to see if the grand committee could meet in Edinburgh. Despite a 7 per cent fall in its share of the poll, it still returned forty MPs. The Conservatives' languor and ineptitude were rewarded with the reduction in their total of seats to twenty-one and their failure to retain the confidence of more than one-third of the electorate. Campbell suffered the ignominy of being beaten by Mrs Ewing, the former Nationalist victor in Hamilton. The Liberals had lost their impetus as an alternative, though their three members survived as personalities rather than partisans.[26]

Devolution had been hardly mentioned in the campaign, but the result placed it firmly on the political agenda. Not for decades had Scotland known such agitation, and many had real fears for the Union. In its increasingly fragile state, it might crumble under the force of one more big blow—and people dwelt with foreboding on how the economy might fail to recover or how, in Labour's promised referendum on the EEC, Scotland might vote in the opposite sense to the rest of Britain. The lack of deep popular support for separatism was on the whole ignored. Both major parties moved, if with scant enthusiasm, to harden up their commitments.

Labour's lack of a majority at Westminster meant another election was bound to follow soon, as it did in October. This time the specifically Scottish issues of devolution and oil were thrust to the forefront, assuming just as much importance as British ones. Competition for votes was exceptionally keen, since few constituencies were now dominated by the familiar battle of the two big parties and no MP was really safe. Labour, spurred into its strongest effort for years, weathered a serious erosion of support in many bastions, steadying its national vote at 36 per cent and managing one net gain for a total of forty-one seats. The three Liberals held on, but the Tories suffered another disaster. They had decided to give priority not to attacking the Government but to retrieving the counties lost to the Nationalists in February. The strategy entirely failed, for more of them fell. Only sixteen MPs survived, the lowest tally since the 1920s. In its share of the poll, a mere 24 per cent, their party was actually overtaken by the SNP, which won 30 per cent. Fighting all constituencies for the first time, it was inspired by others' belated conversion to devolution into another vigorous campaign, and rewarded with eleven seats. That was not as many as it hoped, but in thirty-five of those retained by Labour it came second, and in eleven was within 10 per cent of victory. Amid the more volatile swings to which Scotland was becoming used, the cumulative support for the Nationalists was ominous.[27]

This seemed not to bother Ross, back for his second term as Secretary of State and still denouncing them with his usual ferocity. But such intransigence was undermined by his own constant harping on the importance of Scottish questions. Insofar as his line was centralist, it had proved incapable of quelling the SNP; insofar as it was devolutionary, it vindicated the Nationalist case. His greatest mistake was to suppress objective discussion of it. Till 1970 he might fairly have claimed to be right in getting a serious response postponed, but his approach was inadequate thereafter.

Whatever else was to be done, Ross resolved to press on with his trusted policies for Scotland. On occasion he showed that he had lost little of his old touch. The finest example came in the crisis over the Chrysler car factory at Linwood, rescued from closure in 1976 at a cost of £600 million. On any other grounds than maintaining employment this was indefensible: over-capacity in the world motor industry was forecast and earlier in the year the Government had put £1,500 million into the rival firm, British Leyland, of which it was the majority shareholder. But the Scottish system of patronage could take such absurdity in its stride. To Ross the chance to bolster his territorial interest by asserting himself as an industrial Minister on a par with others was crucial. And he was ready to resign if he failed—something Labour simply could not afford while the devolution debate was raging. The Cabinet rode roughshod over objections in its ranks and gave him what he wanted.[28]

That also held generally true. Relative levels of public expenditure in Scotland were sustained. Ross won wider powers—not least, perhaps, because devolution might require new justifications for his post's existence. So that Scots could see more tangible evidence of the bounty from under the North Sea, the Offshore Supplies Office was sited in Aberdeen and the headquarters of the British National Oil Corporation in Glasgow. A further attempt at economic decentralisation came with the Scottish Development Agency (SDA), set up in 1975 to fund industrial ventures, restore derelict land and promote Scotland overseas; but despite an eagerness to impress which led it into some ill-judged projects, it could not spend all its budget. In 1976 St Andrew's House was given responsibility for making discretionary grants to companies, assuring it a long-term economic role as such selective aid replaced blanket subsidy. Control of the Manpower Services Commission in Scotland was transferred to the Secretary of State in 1977. Thus he had assumed a wide range of statutory powers in industry, and no longer had to rely solely on informal consultation or pressure behind the scenes. That was breaking the bounds of the Scottish Office's previously narrow scope for policy-making, largely coterminous with the existence of relevant Scots laws, and taking it beyond its old task of merely supervising the country's other institutions.

The system which Labour sought to reform had thus gone about as far as it could without a legislature—very little else might with advantage be administratively devolved.[29] St Andrew's House was now 'the real heart of executive government in Scotland, and there can be few governmental decisions affecting Scotland which do not involve it.'[30] According to the same authority, it had adapted happily to this wider role and proved one of the most successful Ministries, with a strong *esprit de corps*, good contact with the people and many achievements to its credit. Above all, as its evidence to the Kilbrandon commission declared, the Secretary of State was 'recognised as responsible for taking the lead in the preparation of plans for economic development in Scotland, and for co-ordinating the execution of those plans.'[31]

For their part, the English had indeed usually accepted the moral, if not legal, obligation to respect the parts of the Treaty of Union thought by Scotland essential to preserve her nationhood. Now, more than ever before, they were accepting an obligation, not enshrined in the Treaty, to create new means to the same end. Scots secured much of what they had wanted since 1832: the chance within a unitary state to resolve certain questions differently for themselves and to ensure that their interests were taken into account in central decisions affecting them. There might have been little room for doubt that the Union was healthy.

But big government in this Scottish guise was failing to satisfy the country even while finding favour. Scots assumed, when it failed to deliver on its promises, that they simply needed more of it. They ignored that it was not there just to please them: had it been, its development might not have been so piecemeal and productive of anomalies. It was equally there for London's convenience, to avoid burdening the central apparatus with the task of detailed attention to a distant country with its own laws and odd concerns. On any more general level of policy it had been relatively inflexible—St Andrew's House had remained in essence a Whitehall department which happened to be sitting on Calton Hill, and reluctant to depart from English precepts. Above all, it reflected the faults of the collectivism which had created it. It was inevitably bureaucratic, remote and unaccountable, responding invisibly to vested interests and pressure groups rather than visibly to public opinion. It thus rarely gratified a sense of national identity. Efforts at a remedy were being made, but there were limits to what any centralised state could do, especially one in chronic economic crisis.

The Secretary of State was not by himself in a position to provide it. Though usually held responsible for practically everything that happened in

Scotland, he still often had little formal control of it. Nor was his job necessarily one for an imaginative or ambitious type. True, there had been forceful incumbents of the post: but Johnston only succeeded because of the peculiar conditions of war and Ross, while largely getting his way, also misread much and released forces he was unable to control. Normal circumstances required rather an undemonstrative man able to wield effective influence behind the scenes, a combination in practice rare.[32]

The reasons for it lay in London. The Cabinet has seldom had time for Scotland as such. That could be fine for the Secretary of State, who thus avoided any awkward questions about his conduct of affairs. But it also meant that he could never step too far out of line with his English colleagues, for they were all members of the one Cabinet open to attack in Parliament if they discriminated in favour of Scotland. Above all spending priorities were not set, except at the margin, in accordance with Scottish needs, but had to be consistent with the conventions ensuring that the major powers of decision were in reality retained in Whitehall: a Government could not in the end be seen believing in different things at once. Arguments were therefore best suppressed in Cabinet, and relegated to committees of junior Ministers or resolved in direct negotiations with other Secretaries of State. This has been especially true for Tories in an era of high public spending, when policies different for Scotland, and costing more money, might require detailed justification. But Labour Governments have also preferred to keep their measures out of sight, legislating where possible through Scottish Bills, in which things might be slipped through that would not escape notice in one for the whole United Kingdom. Central political control has altogether brought strong pressure against Scottish deviations, even beneficial ones, except by nods and winks.[33]

Nor were the achievements such as could be bruited abroad. They came in administration rather than in high politics or even in law-making, and reinforced that colourless kind of leadership. By the same token they gave an uncommonly important role to the mandarins of St Andrew's House. This has been held to offer a better prospect of rational government: since they were used to tackling a wide range of individual, technical problems on their merits, they might develop an approach more flexible and pragmatic than Whitehall's. But there is little evidence that they have reacted quicker, with deeper wisdom or to greater effect than their English colleagues. That may be because the country expected of them not so much cool appraisal as a readiness to gratify organised interests. These had long been smoothly accommodated where they had a counterpart in a functional department, such as agriculture or education; there procedures handed down almost unaltered from an earlier era of loose political control frequently left the Secretary of State only to mediate rather than set priorities. As he assumed an economic role, the younger industrial pressure groups were waiting to follow suit.[34]

The Scottish Office became adept at exploiting the munificent British consensus to win extra resources for them. More strikingly, it even wrested from London its own powers of decision over industry. Here it had started with the least executive autonomy, yet often worked harder to get what it wanted than in those matters where it had a statutory responsibility. As state intervention grew, there was a logic in delegating to Edinburgh the tasks which the intensity of the lobbying showed to be of most concern to Scotland. Whether intent on innovation or preservation, St Andrew's House made itself a major influence on the pace of economic change, especially in the manufacturing sector. But in such work, once done by committees of benevolent capitalists, the mandarins had to start from scratch, not from a fund of business experience. Mistakes and delays were unavoidable, partly because of twists and turns in central policy, partly because the need to please all interests was often weightier than any commercial criterion. If they came into conflict, the temptation was the stronger to bury it in bureaucratic evasions. That also increased the chances of being wrong.[35]

The true accomplishment was to make Scotland herself the biggest pressure group in Britain. Reaching domestic consensus on an issue was easy because of the establishment's small compass and the countless channels through which its members regularly met. Once arrived at, it could be represented by the civil service as Scotland's national view, and carry much greater weight than was possible for any single sectional interest. At the same time, it could be done more discreetly, and effectively, than by a Secretary of State taking a political stance.

But the efforts were often misconstrued. When it worked behind closed doors, St Andrew's House was called a faceless juggernaut. When it took care to mend its forces in Whitehall, it was denounced as an agent of English imperialism. And this despite its being largely staffed by Scots, administering laws drawn up by other Scots in London and passed through Scottish parliamentary committees. The fact remained that the people thought themselves neglected rather than privileged, unable even to influence the administration much, let alone determine policy. For properly democratic pressure could only be brought to bear in two ways. One was through the local councils, but the attempt to improve their accountability and efficiency had largely failed. The other was by electing a small group of remote MPs. Fiercer competition in politics and lack of many really safe seats was making them more representative and active. That was still not enough to place them at the centre of the system.

The major innovation in Parliament, the development of the committees, was nevertheless important. Revamped after the war, they had since been further improved.[36] In 1963 a second standing committee was set up to take private members' Bills, for which facilities had been lacking. In 1968 a select committee was instituted to report independently on current issues of policy, but proved no great success and lapsed in 1972 (though it was revived in 1980). In any case the normal Scottish Bill now followed a unique, standard procedure of its own, giving wide scope for separate deliberation without affecting official control of business. Introduced by the Secretary of State, it had the equivalent of the general debate on second reading in the grand committee. The real legislative work of detailed scrutiny and amendment was carried out in the standing committee. The report stage went back to the grand committee, and only the largely formal third reading to the full chamber.

Originally the system had bristled with safeguards, but was working well enough for them to be relaxed. The objection procedure, permitting a handful of MPs to keep a measure before the whole House, was not used at all till 1961, when an attempt at licensing reform aroused old moral scruples. The Government was safe in the grand committee, its rules allowing for no more than a procedural vote rarely lost because of the presence of the makeweight English MPs. They became dispensable as it ceded its central role to the standing committees. There, too, the Ministry always had a majority and so could only be beaten by rebellion of its own supporters. When a Tory one was short of men to put on them, it did not—as had happened in the 1920s—abandon the arrangements, but just referred fewer Bills through them (referral not being automatic). In the case of the Local Government Bill of 1973 it did not even exploit its majority in the whole House to reverse amendments pushed through against it. Despite the snags it was now generally accepted that the committee stage should in any event go through the standing committee: a path followed by two-thirds of Scottish measures between 1958 and 1976.

The essential work on them was therefore being done by the Scots contingent, entirely if they were not controversial and frequently if they were. A fairly clear line was being drawn between English and Scottish proceedings—as Crossman noted, it was considered an affront for outsiders to attend the latter, let alone take part. This was for the Commons an innovation. Never had one set of members had delegated to them the oversight of a particular Minister and his department, for the constitutional doctrine was that all should attend to everything. The Scots began to stick out as a distinct group, though they themselves complained at the isolation from general business imposed on them by a time-consuming extra workload. Within the committees, too, there was still a problem of congestion. Despite the often technical and non-partisan nature of the measures, an individual MP could seldom leave his mark except on the most minor or routine points. Initiative lay even yet overwhelmingly on the side of the Government. The system was reasonably efficient, but had produced no shift between executive and legislature, merely a change of functions within the legislature. This in any case remained invisible to the Scottish public; and it hardly amounted to devolution.[39]

Means were then sought of getting at Governments more directly, at the points where policies were proposed.[40] It might be done, for example, through the pressure groups. Often of still greater influence were the executive and advisory bodies created by the state, yet in some sort autonomous, since dubbed quangos. They were much like the administrative boards which had regulated particular aspects of Scottish (though also of English) affairs in the nineteenth century, notably in being too inaccessible and unaccountable. They tended, too, to annul the reforms since. As Britain had evolved into a democracy, it was taken as axiomatic that major public decisions should be brought before her elected representatives (minor ones being safely left to local councils). The boards were then gathered together into or under single departments of state with heads in the Cabinet responsible to Parliament.

The Scottish Office had come into being through this process in 1885, though it took till the 1930s—much longer than in England—to complete. But almost at once, and especially under Johnston, it was put into reverse: a Ministry set up to eliminate the boards started creating new equivalents of them. The proliferation reached its peak in the 1970s. The aim was to distance Government or civil service from awkward decisions and neutralise opposition to them. Quangos were composed—with members from political parties, relevant interest groups, various regions and so on—in such a way that their advice could be presented in the guise of consensus. But in any serious democratic sense they represented nobody and, being usually of the establishment anyway, only made the procedure seem more remote.

The most obvious consequence was an administrative jungle—the quangos now numbered 600. They offered 5,000 jobs, approaching in aggregate the size of the Scottish Office, where appointment was strictly on merit. They thus also brought a vast extension of patronage—which ever since the Union had been at least as useful to Scotland's rulers as popular consent, efficient government or other worthy objects. It suited both the big parties, though perhaps fitting in especially well with Labour's more complex power structure. But at bottom the outlook was authoritarian: it not only devalued the process of democratic decision-making but doubted its very worth, taking administrative experience as the better basis for judgement. One purpose of devolution was to accomplish the work of enforcing political responsibility which had previously failed.

The piecemeal creation of distinct agencies and procedures had made the definition of a Scottish interest very untidy. It had all the same the cumulative effect of producing a body politic much more consciously Scottish. With its national identity reinforced, its debates were turned inwards and wider questions presented to it in some sort from its own point of view. That did not necessarily narrow its horizons: on the contrary, it gave the Scot as a political animal an extra perspective not available to other citizens of the United Kingdom. But the break was not clean, being commingled as much with party as with national differences.

A sure sign of that was the argument over the mandate. It arose out of the achievement of successive Secretaries of State in turning theirs into a territorial rather than functional Ministry, unique at least till the formation of (considerably weaker) counterparts in Wales and Northern Ireland. It arose, too, out of Scotland's deviation from the general voting pattern. Conservative administrations were thus not backed by a majority of Scots MPs. In its extreme form the doctrine of the mandate asserted that they should therefore abstain from proposals disagreeable to the majority. But was their Scottish programme simply to be given up, or the opposition's adopted? And would it work the other way, in forbidding a Labour party which seldom won in England to legislate there? It was worthy of note that no such conclusions were drawn in the other two small nations. And they were plainly incompatible with conventions such as the Cabinet's collective responsibility which were, to say the least, more widely accepted. The argument had real substance only as a Nationalist one. Yet its wide currency showed how deep, to quote Crossman again, the separation already was, if in no more than psychological terms. It struck home as a debating point and complicated the tasks of everyday political management, but in practice raised few issues of a deeper constitutional nature: whatever they said, Scots acted in accordance with the maxim that, while the United Kingdom existed, the mandate of its Government was mandate enough.

Without the SNP's descent on Westminster in 1974, these questions need never have become critical. No other party accordingly found, once spurred into action, that it had pondered them deeply. The Tories, in disarray, made neither now nor later a convincing response. The federalist plan which the Liberals had ready to hand did not, for all its theoretical virtues, address the problems of the moment. It thus fell to Labour, clinging to power without a majority, to decide in anxious haste what shape devolution ought to take.[41] But it proved itself the best fitted to stand up to the Nationalists. They had arrived set on rejecting all compromise over independence, and their support was to go on rising all through this hectic year and beyond. Yet at Westminster they could never press home that advantage. Labour did enough to make them in practice the most reliable allies of its legislation. Once it was on the table, they did not matter much.

Not that Labour sought the consensus which had been the key to Scottish constitutional progress in the past.[42] Consensus would be of little help to it in achieving one object of the exercise, the preservation of its own position in Scotland, without which its ability to form a Government in London would be permanently impaired. That hardly pointed to fundamental change of a system which had after all been largely set up to serve Labour's own interest. What was offered instead was better means of articulating and legitimising Scottish demands within it.

Those who then had most to lose were found not so much in the parliamentary opposition as in Labour's own ranks, or rather in the constituencies they represented. Its centralist tradition, though starting to dissolve in Scotland, was as strong as ever in England. Deep suspicions were at once aroused among the MPs from her poorer regions. Many had long disliked the Scots' favoured status, though with no hope of diminishing it. But their resentment was to prove decisive when an effort was made at reform. For them as for the rest of the party any real dilution of centralism was, on doctrinal grounds, out of the question; nor could they at heart consent to a lesser scheme which would still be bound to give the Scots more leverage at the centre. They were not to be mollified either by the appointment of one of them, Edward Short, Lord President of the Council, to produce a political deal.

The reservations on the back-benches were reflected in Cabinet. Some Ministers doubted whether anything much could be done and most believed it possible to fob off the demands with more economic promises. The strongest resistance came from the moderates who were gradually to impose their will on the general direction of policy. In the end the only ones at all committed were the repentant Ross, his Welsh counterpart and Short—they formed the political core of the minimalist school which was to emerge in Whitehall. The others' worries were overcome at least to the extent of their authorising the publication in June of an initial White Paper setting out alternatives for discussion.

That at once uncovered a further nest of opposition in the Labour party in Scotland. Perhaps people had assumed it was scared enough to accept any scheme from London—its history of defying central direction was not, after all, impressive. Its executive at any rate decided in July to reject all the options. This show of independence was not to be tolerated. The transport workers' boss, Alex. Kitson, was deputed to quell it. At a special conference in August, he swung the union's big battalions into reversing the decision. Even so, and despite continuous pressure from the devolutionists, the executive was for two more years to hold its line against any but the narrowest reform. From its own subordinate position, it could not put the Government off altogether, but certainly reinforced its wariness.

The conclusions of these hurried consultations came out in a second White Paper, *Democracy and Devolution*, in September.[43] To appease the Scots, it accepted that there should be a directly elected Assembly, financed by bloc grant to administer most of the functions of St Andrew's House. But it was to have no major economic powers, and the question of whether there should be some body that could be called a Scottish Government was left open. To appease the party, it provided that the elections should be held under the existing system, more or less ensuring a majority in Edinburgh for Labour. At the same time, its strength at Westminster was to be husbanded by retention of the full complement of seventy-one MPs. The Secretary of State was to stay too, with a veto over the Assembly's Acts. The document appeared the day before the October election was called, and served its purpose in averting further losses. Labour, whatever its misgivings, was now committed. Gratefully, it handed over the next stage of the task to the official machine.

In the new Parliament, Short continued his work with a 'devolution unit' of civil servants 'built for caution, not for speed', as Mackintosh acidly observed. It steered a minimalist course, judging that large concessions would merely produce demands for more, so that the least possible should be offered while Labour pressed on with reviving the economy. If an Assembly had to come, it should be quite unlike a Parliament, servicing a range of committees rather than a Government under a Prime Minister, and leave the main lines of policy to London.

The opposing, maximalist view was held by those in Scotland who actually believed in devolution, ranging from moderate Nationalists across the centre ground. Especially useful were converts among Labour MPs, reliable trade unionists of the traditional type—Jim Sillars from South Ayrshire, Alex. Eadie from Midlothian, Harry Ewing from the Stirling Burghs and John Robertson from Paisley. They added their voices in favour of a radical solution to that of the maverick Mackintosh. It meant an Assembly as much like a Parliament as possible, trusted with duties enough to divert it from grievances, able to arouse the public spirit of the disaffected. The minimalist scheme, they contended, would produce the worst of all worlds, satisfying nobody yet kindling the conflicts on which separatists set their hopes.

On the whole Whitehall prevailed against them. So much became clear when the definitive proposals were published in November 1975 in the White Paper, *Our Changing Democracy*.[44] The 142 Assemblymen who were to meet at the old Royal High School of Edinburgh would have no more functions than had been laid down a year previously, except for the cruel joke of being able to levy a surcharge on the rates in lieu of any wider taxing power. Worse was the illogical division between these and the responsibilities of a Secretary of State who had to be found something to do. He was to stay fully in charge of industrial policy, agriculture, law and order, and partly of housing, education, transport and local government. The main concession was that other affairs should be entrusted to a Scottish Executive, to consist of a Chief Executive and several subordinates (the terms Government, Prime Minister and Cabinet being scrupulously avoided). All were, however, to be appointed by the Secretary of State, acting as a sort of governor-general. He would besides approve their legislation and impose a veto if it was *ultra vires* or 'unacceptable on policy grounds'; nor was his veto to be subject to revision by the courts.

To be more minimalist would have been difficult, and the proposals were generally greeted by Scots public opinion as woefully inadequate.[45] The important question, however, was whether the Labour party could be held together on them.[46] In Scotland at first it seemed not. The recent converts to devolution tended towards the Left, and shared that faction's distaste for the EEC. In the previous summer's referendum on British membership they had fought their own Government and been defeated. Thus fears or hopes that Scotland would vote No while the rest of the United Kingdom voted Yes were unfulfilled (showing incidentally that a coalition at home of Labour and the SNP, the same forces as were to fight the referendum of 1979, could not be sure of sweeping the polls).[47] But for the moment it added an argument to the dissidents' quiver, the curious one that a Scotland in the EEC could safely have devolution—and indeed much more—because she could now never be fully separate from England. Sillars and Robertson in effect seceded in protest at the White Paper and were soon voting with the Nationalists on the question of greater economic powers for the Assembly. They acted against the background of a mounting sterling crisis and deep disquiet over its consequences on the back-benches, among the unions and in the electorate. The opinion polls showed a steady advance by the SNP at Labour's expense.

To the more impetuous rebels, all this heralded a collapse of the old dispensation—only some new form of nationalistic socialism could achieve anything for Scotland. In December 1975 they broke away to set up the Scottish Labour Party, consciously choosing the title adopted by Keir Hardie's following eighty-seven years before. As that suggests, it was at bottom a gesture of romantic frustration, too rash to win wide support. It appealed to the emotions of small circles of young enthusiasts, some of them Trotskyites. With those the leader, the authoritarian Sillars, was soon at odds, especially over his pro-European line. At a first traumatic congress in

Stirling the next year many were purged, and the party rapidly collapsed. The adventure was a mistake: it deepened Labour's suspicions of devolution and turned allies of the Government's plans into enemies.[48]

But it had the virtue of bringing home how badly they had been received. Early in 1976 Labour's Scottish executive at last demanded a much stronger measure and was backed by its conference. Something might have been extracted after Ross' retiral in April, following Wilson who concluded his own thoughts on a suitably inglorious note: 'For Parliament devolution has been a bore.'[49] The new Prime Minister, James Callaghan, was himself, however, a long-standing foe of the cause, if now grudgingly converted. To St Andrew's House he appointed Bruce Millan, MP for Craigton. As Minister of State he had been the architect of the latest extensions to its powers and in general had shown himself an able economic administrator of the old school. He too, though, saw devolution as no more than a necessary evil, and lacked the commitment or influence demanded by the circumstances. Michael Foot took charge of the Privy Council Office, where work on the project was proceeding, but being himself indifferent abandoned most of it to his gifted deputy, John Smith, MP for North Lanarkshire.

The scheme was thus not to be fundamentally altered. A supplementary White Paper in August set out some minor adjustments: the surcharge on the rates was dropped, leaving no taxation powers of any kind; the judgment of the *vires* of Assembly Acts was to be made by the judicial committee of the Privy Council rather than by the Secretary of State; and the Assembly was to have complete control of the SDA, rather than merely of its environmental functions. Labour had uttered its last word. The full policy was brought before the British party conference that autumn, there to be endorsed without amendment, and without much interest.

Finally, then, on 29 November, the Government published the Scotland and Wales Bill. Despite evasions and delays, the prospects of devolution being in the end won had so far seemed reasonably good. Only when it embarked on its progress through the Commons did they dim. The hostility of most MPs soon made itself felt, not least in their evident intention to block the legislation rather than find ways of making it work. It could not be dropped by a Government sensitive to electoral pressure and wishing to honour manifesto commitments. Nor, however, could it be saved in a Parliament jealous of a sovereignty it now felt to be threatened.

The Bill's faults were legion. Some arose out of tactical considerations, for example, out of the attempt to combine in it quite different proposals for the two nations. Some followed from the minimalist strategy: it was so cumbersome because, to preserve rather than transfer sovereignty, it delimited the Assembly's powers by the intricate device of abstracting them from existing legislation. Others were necessary contradictions in a Union to be decentralised without altering its basic nature: of these the focus was the so-called West Lothian question, the fact that henceforth Scots MPs would still be voting on purely English questions at Westminster, while English MPs would have no say on the purely Scottish ones decided by the Assembly. But at every other debatable point the bias was centralist, as observed by Enoch Powell in his dictum that 'power devolved is power retained'.[51]

The Bill had to go through on Labour's own precarious majority, for no concessions were made in it to other possible supporters, the SNP and the Liberals. Dissensions were soon obvious on the Government benches, offering the opposition the chance to exploit all these weaknesses. The immediate hurdle was the second reading, to be held on 16 December. Labour whips had good reason to worry, but in fact it was the other side which broke first. After ten years of the Nationalist challenge, the Tories at last decided what they wanted to be: the unionist party of Scotland. Within their shrunken popular base, the genuinely unionist forces, especially powerful in the business community, had anyway grown stronger. They also had the sympathy of the new leader, Mrs Margaret Thatcher, under whom the Conservatives were mounting a strong recovery by breaking with the politics of consensus. There was thus no embarrassment for her in ditching Heath's undertakings, which most of her followers had never liked. At home Taylor and Ian Sproat, MP for South Aberdeen, had launched an internal pressure group, Scotland is British, to resist devolution of any kind. At the conference in Perth in May 1976 their challenge to the official line, then still for devolution in principle, was only narrowly defeated. The unionist sentiment thus came right into the open.[52]

It was an unpleasant surprise for most of the MPs returned in 1974, and for at least a considerable minority of supporters in the country, who had committed themselves to reform. Their ascendency had apparently been confirmed when its strongest advocate in the party, Alick Buchanan-Smith, MP for North Angus and Mearns, was made shadow-Secretary of State after Campbell's defeat. Strict unionists still had to be reconciled, of course. That had been done, rather unhappily, with the peculiarly feeble scheme offered in the October manifesto, under which an Assembly would have been indirectly elected by regional councils. Afterwards there was every incentive to seek something more attractive, which had been found in a modified version of Home's old proposals.

But they, even as official policy, hardly incarnated the sort of Tory principles likely to restrain the Shadow Cabinet from doing Labour down. It voted to oppose the second reading. Buchanan-Smith promptly handed in his resignation, as did four other front-bench spokesmen, though only one of theirs was accepted. The most ardently populist unionist, Taylor, was then appointed shadow Secretary of State. Was it a disaster for Scottish Conservatism, as the dissidents maintained? Clearly Mrs Thatcher was gambling on the eventual defeat of devolution, in which case a temporary split could be taken in her party's stride. It was most of all significant that a major political force had turned against the very idea.

This was one reason for the Government's first big concession, that there should be a referendum in Scotland before the Bill became law. Announced for maximum effect on the day of the second reading, it ensured success on a whipped vote by 292 to 247. The manoeuvre was obviously aimed at English MPs, for the unanimity of the Scots was hardly dented. They were in favour by fifty-five to seven, the majority including all the Labour members but three, all the Liberals and Nationalists and three Tories, with six against and the other seven abstaining. It was nevertheless a hollow victory, for the Bill at once sank into a morass of 350 amendments in committee.[53]

The only way out was a guillotine motion, put to the vote on 22 February 1977. It was grossly mismanaged by Foot, Leader of the House. Approval of the Bill in principle had not overcome the deep reservations of many on the Labour side, most from the North of England, but egged on by Tam Dalyell, MP for West Lothian, and some others of his Scots colleagues. To Liberals hope was still denied of election to the Assembly by proportional representation. And moderate Conservatives were not prepared to help on a procedural rather than substantive motion. There was nobody in the Government capable of controlling the rebels or rallying support from across the floor. All the latent hostility to the Bill came boiling up, and the disparate forces united to defeat the guillotine.[54]

The disaster sent the SNP leaping ahead in the opinion polls: at the first electoral test, the district polls in May, Labour actually lost control of Glasgow. Callaghan, while refusing to make devolution a matter of confidence, was still in danger of being forced to go to the country. The one means of averting that was a pact with the Liberals, concluded in the spring and conditional on a new Bill being in due course brought forward.[55] This alone saved a project which the Cabinet would doubtless have preferred to drop. For some time the debate had been going into a degree of detail which inexorably wore down its emotional appeal to Scots voters, to the point where no-one could any longer be sure what, if anything, they wanted. Such conservative interests as business, the universities and the law had moved firmly into opposition. In Scotland generally, anger at the latest turn of events soon gave way to exhausted resignation. Even the strongest Home Rulers lost confidence and enthusiasm, while gloating unionists had all the less reason for reticence.

It was not a happy background to the introduction of the second, the Scotland Bill, in November 1977.[56] The redrafting by John Smith did not alter the basic aims, but made a few changes to appease the resistance. The proposals for each of the two nations were presented in separate measures, allaying the ill-will of most Welsh MPs. Because of the stubborn enmity among those from northern England, there was no point in seeking greater economic powers for the Assembly, though at Liberal prompting another review of tax-raising powers was promised.

While the Commons remained in a majority deeply antagonistic, this time honours were more evenly divided between the Government and its critics. Smith, in piloting the Bill through, played on general weariness with the issue. He repeatedly stressed that debate had to stop somewhere and practical proposals be made, since there was no such thing as devolution in principle. More to his advantage was the fact that the Ministry's position had meanwhile gravely deteriorated. The arms of Labour dissidents could be twisted under the threat that, if it failed again, there would have to be an election which it was likely to lose. They could scarcely resist when its need was so desperate.

With no coherent plan for altering the Bill's basic shape, and no other means of keeping Callaghan in power, they were prepared to pass up the chance of killing it and await their final chance in the referendum.

That chance could, after all, be rigged. On one bad night in January 1978, Labour rebels again combined with the Tories. They pushed through an amendment from George Cunningham, a Scot sitting for an English seat, stipulating that in the referendum a majority approving the Act should not suffice unless also exceeding 40 per cent of the electorate; otherwise the Government would be obliged to lay an order before the House repealing it. A second amendment proposed by Jo Grimond allowed Orkney and Shetland the chance to opt out of it if they voted No while the rest of the country voted Yes. That was the end of the opposition. Ill-disposed legislators had inflicted many wounds on the Bill, but only mangled rather than killed it. The anomalies they had created, as well as the inherent ones, were simply to be left as such. The Royal Assent was given in July, and the decks cleared for the referendum.[57]

The battle had been hard but, it seemed, not entirely in vain. Unusually, there were during 1978 three Scottish by-elections, at Garscadden in April, Hamilton in May and Berwick and East Lothian in October—this last after the death of John Mackintosh, a grievous loss to the cause of devolution. In the circumstances Labour might have been in danger of defeat. Yet it held all the seats comfortably. Even so, the Government was to be fatally weakened by the collapse of its economic policies and struggle with its own supporters in the unions during the following winter of discontent. The referendum delivered the *coup de grace*.

The mess of the Scotland Act was mirrored in confusion among the parties, none of which could lay claim to clear, unanimous purposes in the conflict over it. Luckily, they did not fight the referendum directly, but through umbrella organisations. Those on the No side were the stronger, especially in financial contributions from business. They also had the benefit of a largely united Tory party behind them. There many remaining waverers were won over when, just before the poll, Lord Home with his devolutionary record advised a No vote in the hope that a future Conservative Government would produce a better scheme. Moreover, dissident socialists were fortified by the half-dozen or so Labour MPs, with their friends in the unions and party apparatus, who had come down against the Act. The campaign tellingly concentrated on a few simple issues—the likely burden of extra government and taxation, the possibility of dominance by Strathclyde and the danger of conflict with London leading to separation.

The Yes campaign started off complacently enough in the expectation of victory, but soon descended into hopeless disarray. Inevitably, the question of devolution was linked with the fate of a now deeply unpopular Government, so that people were tempted to turn out against it on extraneous issues. Nor was opinion unanimous in those parties, Labour and the SNP, formally committed to an Assembly. There was not much compensation in the support from the Liberals and a handful of Tories. The different motives of these disparate groups often made their efforts and arguments contradictory. They had to prove conclusively that the Bill was wanted, and that was not at all clear. On the contrary, in its final state it commanded the positive enthusiasm of hardly anyone. The No side set the issues and the Yes campaign, dogged by tactical blunders, never got off the ground.

The outcome on referendum day, 1 March 1979, reflected all these failings. On a low poll of 64 per cent, the Yes majority was only 80,000 out of 1.4 million votes cast. Counting was by regions, and six—those in the central belt, together with the Highlands and the Western Isles—voted Yes. The four largely rural regions of the North-east and South voted No, as did Orkney and Shetland. Not a single one reached the 40 per cent threshold. The national result showed only 33 per cent in favour of the Act and 31 per cent against it.[58]

Clearly not even the Government could now be saved, let alone devolution. Callaghan hoped to sustain himself while postponing the vote on the order for repeal till after a General Election, due at the latest in the autumn—during which time the minor parties might support him. He offered talks on this procedure, but the Nationalists and Liberals insisted on his making devolution an issue of confidence. This he refused, for he had lost patience and would not now take risks for Scotland. It was the SNP which then pressed the no-confidence motion that felled him by one vote at the end of March.[59]

The election followed in May. It confirmed Labour's Scottish supremacy, bringing back forty-four MPs on 42 per cent of the vote. The Liberals kept their three. Taylor followed his predecessor as Tory leader by losing. But otherwise his party restored itself to about the position it had enjoyed before the rise of the Nationalists, regaining seven of their seats for a total of twenty-two and taking 31 per cent of the poll. The SNP suffered a catastrophe, holding just two constituencies on a vote very nearly halved. The new Secretary of State, George Younger, MP for Ayr, laid the order for repeal before the Commons on 20 June where it was duly passed by the Conservative majority.[60]

All this was difficult to interpret. Surveys of opinion still showed consistently a large degree of public support for Home Rule of some kind. Labour's negative achievement was to have divided it so far as to make it incapable of coherent action: there were many in the party who did not regret the fact. But the people's views were equivocal too—they wanted devolution, but only in a painless form. The Scotland Act could almost have fulfilled their wishes, as a cosmetic measure which would have left real power at Westminster and relieved them of unwelcome responsibility. Even so, given a political lever it was unlikely that they would have forborne to pull it at some stage, so that trouble undoubtedly lay in store. In any case they had not in the end been reassured by the Act. But it was hard to see how a different one could have been successfully framed in the conditions of the later 1970s. Labour, torn between its old unionist centralism and the new decentralising forces it had to harness to hold Scotland, found that the price of unity was a clumsy and unacceptable compromise.

If victory there was, then the Tories won it. They had got the Union affirmed and the Home Rule issue for the foreseeable future disposed of. Yet there was a cost, of which indulgence to the collectivism still pervading St Andrew's House after 1979 could not relieve them. Their posture of indifference to defects in the constitution inflicted lasting damage on their position in Scotland. But they had in effect deliberately sacrificed it in order to precipitate an election which they were bound to win and which in the event gave them their longest term in office since the 1950s.

For the Nationalists the outcome was indeed disastrous. Their exertions had created no coherent anti-unionist interest apart from themselves. No institution, no region of the country, no section of society was clearly converted to their cause. They had on the contrary been shown beyond doubt that, while many Scots saw them as a useful tool for securing reform, few actually shared their aspirations. Every previous upsurge of Nationalism had gleaned some benefit, extracted some concession. This, the biggest ever, achieved nothing but the intangible gain of a stronger national consciousness—though that might remain as diffuse and essentially apolitical as before.

On the other hand it had been demonstrated that there was much emotion behind the Union too. The challenge to it had put its champions on their mettle and revealed its latent strength. The widespread reluctance to risk its dissolution was, however, only rashly to be equated with blind defence of the status quo. After all, the Union could no longer be justified as in the old days, as a guarantee of prosperity in the bosom of a world power. For renewal, it needed fresh justifications. They are unlikely to be volunteered by the English who, because of their own nationalism, are more ignorant of the Celtic fringe than of some foreign countries. The onus therefore falls on a Scottish polity which, for all the dispiriting frustrations it suffers, has managed to survive. But whether the upheavals of the 1970s were the first stirring of rebirth or the final spasm before loss of consciousness is so far impossible to judge.

Chapter 10

'An Area Of Perpetual Friction'

The year of 1979, expected to mark a turning-point for Scotland, instead ushered in a period of despondency and dullness of the sort we have become accustomed to see succeed the cyclical upheavals. By contrast British politics, for a decade or more so tired and stale, found a new lease of life as the Prime Minister, Mrs Margaret Thatcher, overthrew the post-war consensus at home and adopted a stridently patriotic tone abroad. The extent of the break can be exaggerated—it was under the last Labour administration that monetarism, restraint of Government expenditure and market forces in the public sector had been introduced. They were nevertheless to be promoted now with much greater consistency and vigour.

The interesting question for Scotland was how she would respond. She was a notable beneficiary of the consensus. It had been taken as axiomatic that she deserved on account of her economic problems higher public spending than the rest of Britain. A smooth machinery embracing Government and Parliament, civil service and pressure groups ensured an unfailing supply of subsidy and patronage. It had been built by and for collectivism, for central planning of a welfare state. Even when the Conservatives were in charge they had been content to leave well alone, if indeed they were not embellishing the structure. Would they, in Scotland too, really dismantle a system unquestioned for forty years, with roots still older?

Owing little to the Scots, the new Ministry could not be expected to show any close interest in their affairs. So long as he did not step out of line with its general policies, the Secretary of State had on his own ground a fairly free hand. George Younger, great-grandson of the Unionist party boss in the 1920s whose viscountcy he would one day inherit, was true to his antecedents. His loyalty and paternalism were combined with a charm and good humour that disarmed all but the fiercest opponents. He saw his essential task as keeping Scotland quiet, on a shrewd assessment that excitation only risked reviving the passions of the preceding years. By the same logic, he had no time for the Right-wing radicalism of some among his Cabinet colleagues.

He managed to keep reactions to the worst recession since the 1930s surprisingly muted. Unemployment doubled and manufacturing industry

251

severely declined. The grandest monuments to interventionism collapsed, profligate prestige projects like the aluminium smelter at Invergordon, the paper mill at Corpach, the vehicle plants at Linwood and Bathgate—though frantic protests saved the steelworks at Ravenscraig. But the dreaded cuts in public spending never came to pass, and outlays per head still ran at 20 per cent above the average for the United Kingdom. A review of regional aid removed from its coverage only places manifestly in no need of it, such as Edinburgh and the North-east: Younger boasted yet that 70 per cent of the population lived in assisted areas, and 55 per cent in special development areas attracting the highest grants.[1] The SDA, too, survived sharp criticism, being merely turned to the novel task of making profits. New industries did quite well, micro-electronics with assistance, oil and finance without it. But most official effort was even now devoted, out of all proportion to their numbers, to that 2 per cent of the workforce employed in manual occupations in old, state-supported industries. The obvious reason was their weight inside the Labour movement, and thus inside the machinery by which Scotland was governed.

Rarely did Younger venture an attack on Labour's interests. He did, however, start in 1980 the sale of council houses to their tenants, with considerable success. By the latter half of the decade there was for the first time a majority of Scots families owning their homes. He also enforced strict control of local authorities. The Tories' ingenuous creation of an elaborate two-tier administrative structure had, without making the whole noticeably more efficient or popular, multiplied the number of Labour strongholds. It was necessary to set an example when the Lothian region and one or two districts defied the Secretary of State with their expenditures. But others, most crucially Strathclyde, opted for quiet co-operation. What Younger had failed to note in his quest for tranquillity was that many citizens still found the burdens imposed by the councils intolerable. It was a revolt in his own party that forced him to propose in 1985 a reform of local taxation, a nettle the Government had long hesitated to grasp. Even so, the emergence of a property-owning democracy worried about taxes rather than subsidies did not make it more willing to vote Conservative.

Elsewhere, parties of the Right in trouble can always play a nationalist card, but in Scotland that was impossible. If still supported in principle by a vast majority, devolution was no longer a burning issue. It did not, all the same, do the Tories any good. Till 1974 they never got much less than 40 per cent of the vote, and often rather more; afterwards they never got much more than 30 per cent, and often rather less. In the turmoils of the 1970s, they seemed to have forfeited a quarter of their support. But they remained unwilling to recognise the fact, even in internal debate. Younger had himself once been in favour of Home Rule. Experience had satisfied him, however, that it was not a serious proposition.

One hostage to fortune had been given before the referendum. The Government was committed to all-party talks, supposedly in search of a better scheme than Labour's. These, boycotted by the SNP, were convened in the spring of 1980. The outcome was to grant the grand committee yet ampler scope for discussion of Scottish affairs. It might also hold meetings in the elegant chamber built for the Assembly in Edinburgh. They took place regularly from 1981, and had a certain curiosity value. Meanwhile the Scottish select committee, abolished in 1972, was restored as part of the reform which equipped the Commons with a complete range of such committees to oversee the several departments of state, rather than being tied to legislation or other specific questions. In administration, Younger used the power acquired by the Secretary of State in 1978 to dispose of his expenditures as he wished, instead of being bound—as under the Goschen formula—to keep each allocation in strict proportion to its English counterpart. Without bringing dramatic variations, the extra discretion was useful.

Younger insisted that no other practicable improvements could be found. In any case, he claimed, Scots had lost interest in devolution. Since they were so strongly represented in central government and so generously treated in public spending, it was impossible to conceive of any new system, and especially to finance it, which would not 'either create an area of perpetual friction between Edinburgh and London, or an unacceptable and additional burden on the taxpayers of Scotland'.[2] But Scottish Conservatives were also notably reluctant to roll back the frontiers of the state. Though they never followed their argument to its conclusion, they were left implying still that Scotland was best served by central bureaucracy.

The consolidation of Labour's already commanding position in Scottish politics was surely not unconnected with these matters either. Its unionist faction shrank. Even former leaders of the No campaign were heard to announce their conversion to devolution, on the grounds that if the English working class refused to acknowledge the evils of Thatcherism, then it was time for Scotland, in some sense, to go it alone. In 1983 the party hardened its commitments, not only affirming the platform on which it had fought the referendum, but promising that an Assembly would have taxation powers too. It was all the same unclear how far the hostile English MPs had been reconciled, or how far centralism had really been renounced: Scottish policies were still to be pursued 'within the context of our overall national plan'.

The question naturally remained academic while Labour was out of power. Instead of seeking it, the party had given way to bitter internal strife as the faithful vented their wrath at the betrayals imputed to James Callaghan's Government. In the events which led to his resignation of the leadership, to the succession of Michael Foot and to the complete revision of the constitution, Scots played no prominent part. Among the MPs were few zealots. If they voted for candidates and causes of the Left, it was out of consideration not so much for their consciences as for their constituency activists. The prudence paid off, for none suffered the indignity of deselection, which was cutting swathes through the English members. Even so, in the 1979 Parliament only thirteen Scots Labour MPs out of forty-four joined the Tribune group, where the traditional Left mustered, and only five went on into the Campaign group, set up to accommodate the more extreme elements. The sober Bruce Millan remained throughout shadow Secretary of State. He was succeeded in 1983 by Donald Dewar, MP for Garscadden, an eloquent lawyer sprung from the Glasgow bourgeoisie. Cast in a similar mould was John Smith, the most powerful Scot in Labour's counsels. The party in Scotland remained much as it had been, moderate in outlook, seeking unity and stability.

Accordingly, it was little hurt by the splitting off of the Social Democratic Party (SDP). Only two Scots MPs joined it, Robert MacLennan, sitting for Caithness and Sutherland, and Dr Dickson Mabon, in Greenock and Port Glasgow. Nor from Labour at large did it lure many away, but rather brought into politics people who before had not been members of any party. All the same, one Scottish episode played a major part in its successful launch. The leader, Roy Jenkins, lacked a seat in Parliament after returning from the presidency of the EEC Commission. He found a haven at Hillhead, till then the Tories' last outpost in Glasgow, which he took off them at a by-election in March 1982. Jenkins was the biographer of Asquith and it was fashionable to compare this with the Paisley by-election of 1920, if not to note that the latter had no lasting results. The Alliance was already formed between the SDP and the Liberal party, whose own leader, David Steel, remained impregnable in his Borders constituency. For a while, then, there was the curious spectacle of both wings of the Alliance being headed from Scotland. This did not serve to avert its gaze from the English suburbs to the Celtic fringe. A sign of that was its hankering after the comfortable certainties of the old centralist collectivism, though now, of course, with a human face.

Yet it was more successful than its rival for support among Scots disaffected from the big parties. The SNP had escaped the quick demise which would have awaited a mere transient protest movement. On the contrary, its place in Scottish politics seemed assured. But with only two MPs, and little strength in large parts of the coutry, the place was very confined. It too was afflicted by internal disputes. The ineffable Jim Sillars came over to it, his third party in five years, and at once tried to press on it a socialist programme, contending that it could get nowhere without winning Labour's traditional vote. Its old guard, represented by the chairman, Gordon Wilson, MP for Dundee East, and Mrs Winifred Ewing, now a member of the European Parliament for the Highlands and Islands, resisted him. Some leading figures on the left were expelled, though soon re-admitted. In reaction to Thatcherism, the Nationalists were anyway moving to a position which, except on the constitutional question, hardly differed from that of Labour's mainstream. They certainly yielded to none in the vehemence of their calls for subsidies from London. It was hard to take seriously a party which preached independence yet practised dependence.

The striking thing about these years in Scottish politics was how little changed. Ever averse from the golden mean, they exchanged volatility for immobility. In Britain as a whole, Mrs Thatcher led the Conservatives at the General Election of 1983 to their greatest victory in half a century. In Scotland, however, she was soundly beaten. The Tories' vote actually dropped by 3 per cent to 28 per cent, and their total of seats, diminished to twenty-one since Hillhead, stayed the same. The SNP hung on to its two, with a share of the poll fallen from 17 to 12 per cent. The Alliance's reached an impressive 25 per cent, against 8 per cent for the Liberals alone in 1979. But the impact was blunted by failure to return more than eight MPs. The Liberals had five, after gaining Gordon and another constituency in the Borders to add to the three long held. The SDP kept Hillhead and Caithness and Sutherland, the loss of Dr Mabon being balanced by a victory in Ross, Cromarty and Skye. It was thought a dismal performance, and Jenkins at once resigned the leadership. Labour had followed the other parties down, retaining the confidence of only 35 per cent of the electorate. That did not, however, loosen its grip on forty-one seats.

The outcome, satisfying nobody, represented a fitting verdict on the Younger administration. He had done what he set out to do, generally defusing any conflicts, but had at the same time damped whatever spirit of innovation remained in the country. With a few inevitable shifts of emphasis, he was content to run the Scottish system as it stood, merely slotting in his own ministerial team above its collectivist cadres. They had no need to make life difficult for him because he did not make life difficult for them. Where he went against their interests, as in housing policy and local government spending, it was perhaps not so much from choice as in conformity with the policies laid down in London. In any event, he was early in 1986 swept on to higher things by the Westland crisis, leaving an uncertain legacy to his successor, Malcolm Rifkind, MP for Edinburgh Pentlands. This rising star of the Foreign Office thus reached the Cabinet before his fortieth birthday. An advocate by profession, highly intelligent and formidably articulate, he had the chance to show that, amid all these estimable political virtues, he possessed the crucial one, the ability to win votes.

The apparatus he took over had again been showing its ample capacity for stifling through institutional inertia all radical impulses, whether of Left or Right. The local oligarchies continued, as for the last 200 years, to mediate between central authority and a clamant populace with jovial venality. In this simple sharing of spoils the competition of parties was redundant. In Scotland it had anyway never done much demonstrable good. On the contrary, when their rivalry had been serious, as in the 1920s, or their discord deep, as in the 1970s, the result was only stalemate and failure, confirming Westminster in its preference for letting sleeping Scots dogs lie.

Hegemony, the establishment of something akin to a one-party state, had been found the better, because more efficient option. It suited the nation's penchant for hereditary political connections, originally of kinship, now of class. It could even be made compatible with democracy once the minor parties adopted in essentials the programme of the dominant one. Altogether, it provided the best conditions for building that united, non-partisan consensus which Thomas Johnston identified as the means by which London could be most easily bid.

If the Scots have thus gained more weight than their small numbers justify, they have also forgone some of the principal benefits of attachment to the English parliamentary constitution. Partisan spirit and alternation in power do, if rather self-consciously, foster constant critical scrutiny, diversity of opinion and efforts at reform. In Scotland, by contrast, government is conducted behind closed doors. Debates are predictable and lifeless. Policies are geared to institutions and interests either themselves adjuncts of the bureaucracy or else unconcerned with any but their own fixed demands. All this has been reflected, too, in the quality of those attracted to public life, marked by stolid orthodoxy rather than flamboyance or vision, the sort of people, moreover, who do not generally expect to be questioned or enjoy it if they are. The consensus, however well-meaning, inevitably turns inert, inflexible and hostile to novelty. Perpetual friction there may be, but it is of the sort which grinds down rather than produces bursts of flame. Against the power of patronage, principle stands little chance.

Notes

INTRODUCTION
1 My statement is still technically true. But it would be churlish to omit any note of I G C Hutchison's excellent Political History of Scotland 1832–1924, covering the first part of the period dealt with below. Had it appeared earlier, I would have regarded that portion of my own work as superfluous. But it was published when my already complete typescript was still being considered by the publisher. On reflection, I have retained the first chapters. In them I have often been able to take account of Dr Hutchison's views. Where we clearly disagree, however, I have preferred to let the differences stand.
2 Ferguson (1968).
3 A good survey of historiography in this period is given in Ash (1980).

CHAPTER 1
1 The political system before 1832 is fully described in Ferguson (1968). A summary is Pryde (1960). Many details can be teased from the tedious Porritts (1903). Matters were taken further by Mitchison and Phillipson (1970) and Murdoch (1980). Lenman (1981) gives a lively account incorporating this later research. Traditional views were again modified by Dwyer, Mason and Murdoch (1982)—the last of whom also wrote an excellent monograph on Edinburgh (1983)—and especially by Sunter (1986).
2 Church affairs will not be dealt with at any length till the next chapter, though the troubles which burst forth after 1832 were already brewing. They may be followed in the standard works, Mathieson (1912), Burleigh (1960), Bulloch and Drummond (1973).
3 The seminal account is J Fergusson (1947).
4 Omond (1883) gives a biography of each Lord Advocate with a survey of the main political and legal questions of his time. Some of what he wrote has now been superseded by the individual entries in Thorne (1986).
5 Parliamentary Debates, 22 June 1804.
6 Only recently have there been major advances on the work of Furber (1931) and Matheson (1933), the former dealing mainly with Scottish, the latter with imperial affairs. New directions are pointed in Dwyer, Mason and Murdoch, *op. cit.* A broader context is provided in Ehrman's progressing three-volume biography of the younger Pitt (1969 and 1982).
7 Ginter (1967) made available some important extracts from the Blair Adam Papers. *See also* in Thorne, *op. cit.*, the entries for Adam and Erskine.
8 Quoted, Furber, p 76.

9   Meikle's pioneering work (1912) remains invaluable, if overtaken in some respects.
10 H Cockburn (1856), p 73.
11 For Braxfield, *see* Lever (1974). Muir's subsequent, interesting fate is recounted in Bewley (1980).
12 There are inevitably great difficulties in arriving at estimates of parliamentary strength in this period. The figures here and below, on the exactitude of which one must always be cautious, are arrived at from Thorne, *op. cit.*
13 These fertile minds not only accounted for much of what happens in the rest of this chapter, but were also responsible for the Whig view of Scottish history alluded to in the Introduction. H Cockburn wrote (1874a and b) copiously about contemporary politics. His life of Jeffrey (1852) is less satisfactory. The Memorials, though less directly concerned with politics, make delightful reading. For Jeffrey, there is a more reliable but still sympathetic treatment in Clive (1957). Other members of the circle are covered in Aspinall (1939), Bell (1979), Brougham (1871), New (1961), Horner (1843) and Stewart (1985). Fontana (1986) places the *Edinburgh Review* in its widest context. Its development is, of course, best followed in its own volumes (1802–).
14 For contemporary comments, *see* Grierson (1932), Scott to George Ellis, 20 Feb 1806; H A Cockburn (1932), p 90.
15 A Fergusson (1882), p 439.
16 Patrick (1973), pp 157–8.
17 The main source for the following is Phillipson (1967). See also *Edinburgh Review*, ix, 1807, pp 468ff; Gray (1974), pp 26–43, 103–20.
18 The following is constructed from the articles on various members of the Dundas family, Thorne, *op. cit.*, vol iii, pp 635–55.
19 For the rise of radicalism, Saunders (1950) supplies the background, filled out by Logue (1979) and Murray (1978), especially ch 9, 'Radical Attitudes and Activities'.
20 A judgement contrary to the inflated claims made for this episode in Ellis and Mac A'Gobhainn (1970).
21 Letter to Horner, 26 Oct 1809, quoted Omond, *op. cit.*, p 195.
22 R Gourlay (1809), pp 11–12.
23 This social engineering still arouses passions, especially among people who favour more modern and efficient forms of it. A less partisan view is taken in Loch (1934) and Richards (1973).
24 An account of the Glasgow circle has to be gleaned from several, in themselves incomplete sources: Mackay (1866), Eyre-Todd (1934), J Gourlay (1942), Oakley (1980).
25 For Dundee, *see* Tennant (1970).
26 A full account is given in Cowan (1946).
27 For Scott's comments here and below, *see* Aspinall (1936), pp 539–43.
28 For Chalmers, *see* notes to the next chapter.
29 For a full account, *see* Muirhead (1974).
30 The basic study is Ferguson (1966).

CHAPTER 2
1   The lack of a full study of the Whigs after reform has now been remedied by Hutchison (1986), pp 33–53. *See also* Teviotdale (1963) and J C Williams (1972).
2   Brougham (1871), iii, p 336.

3   The best source is Pryde, *op. cit.*
4   Cockburn (1852), p 355.
5   Cockburn (1874b), Cockburn to Kennedy, 16 April 1833.
6   Cockburn (1874a), 19 Jan 1831.
7   For Murray, *see* Omond (1914), pp 1–50, together with Cockburn's comment (1874a), 12 Aug 1836.
8   *ibid.*, 27 Sept 1841.
9   We are again indebted to Hutchison, *op. cit.*, pp 1–25, for synthesising the material which has become available on Scottish Conservatism during these years. Many documents had previously been presented by Brash (1974). They were supplemented by monographs on particular constituencies from Broun-Lindsay (1960), Brash (1968) and Rosie (1978). Urwin (1965) had useful observations, though concerned mainly with later developments. Contemporary views can be drawn from Anon. (1837) and Alison (1883). Some reference to Scotland is found in works dealing with the party in Britain as a whole, Gash (1953), pp 42–3, 177–83, Stewart (1978), pp 93–6, Ward (1976), pp 147–51. Dyer (1983) again stresses the continuity before and after 1832.
10 *See* Ferguson (1968), *passim.*
11 Quoted in full by Brash (1974), pp 22–5.
12 House of Commons Papers (1837).
13 Quoted Mechie (1960), p 74.
14 Kitson Clark (1929), p 328.
15 Cockburn (1874a), 23 July 1841.
16 Another gap filled by Hutchison, *op. cit.*, pp 33–53, is in coverage of political activity by bourgeois radicals. Of the contemporary or Victorian sources, Mackenzie (1865–8) is entertaining but rambling, Anon. (1879) useful but brief, Mackie (1888) too reverent to its subject. Pinney (1977) necessarily shows only the exasperated reaction of a Whig. Ferguson brings out (1965) a particular example of how reform failed to quell Liberal squabbles, as does Montgomery (1982). Much can be gleaned from the wider studies of Hollis (1974), W H Marwick (1969), Saunders (1950) and Wilson (1970).
17 Machin (1977), pp 169–77.
18 Morley (1881), especially pp 153, 210, 357. For the origins of Scottish agitation against the Corn Laws, *see* Cameron (1979) and Montgomery (1979).
19 Cockburn (1874a), 23 April 1841.
20 Mackie (1888), i, p 235.
21 *See* Pinney (1977), especially letters from Macaulay to McLaren, 13 April 1842, 28 Dec 1842 and 12 Jan 1843; and to Black, 22 Feb 1843.
22 *ibid.*, quoted by Macaulay, 9 March 1843.
23 *See* Flinn (1977), pp 421ff. 'The demographic influence of the potato'.
24 Among contemporary sources for the trade unions are House of Commons Papers (1837–8) and Alison (1838), *passim*, (1883), pp 359ff; he is, of course, robustly hostile. The definitive account of the central episode, the cotton spinners' strike is Fraser (1976). It can be supplemented by Gray (1974), Lenman (1977), Saunders (1950) and Ward (1962). For the social background, *see* Levitt and Smout (1980).
25 With the works of the readable Wright (1953) and of the pedestrian Wilson (1959, 1970, 1971) the history of Scottish Chartism is essentially complete. McCalman (1970) and Troup (1981) provide regional perspectives. Scottish developments are placed in a British context by Briggs (1959), Jones (1975), Rowe (1969) and Ward (1973). Carlyle (1840) should not be missed.

26   Quoted Ward (1973), p 139.
27   General sources for the Church are Bulloch and Drummond (1973 and 1975),
     Cheyne (1983), Fleming (1937), Lyall (1980), Mathieson (1912) and Mechie
     (1960).
28   These were Melville's words to James VI himself when, in a famous incident, he
     importuned the King at Falkland Palace.
29   Cockburn (1874a), 30 May 1853.
30   A major re-assessment has been undertaken by S J Brown (1983), in which *see*
     especially pp 211–25 for the evangelicals' programme. He sees Chalmers' work
     as having been fundamentally a failure. McCaffrey (1981) has conceded the
     point, but presents redeeming considerations. Both are antidotes to the useful
     but pious official biography by Hanna (1852–4) and to the work of his hardly less
     reverent modern successor Watt (1943). On Chalmers as a political economist, *see*
     Nisbet (1964). The social background to his work is set out in McLaren (1964),
     especially chapter 3.
31   The lack of an account of the Disruption both all-embracing and objective is the
     most serious in modern Scottish historiography. Contemporary sources are all
     more or less partisan. The Free Church had the ablest champions in Bruce
     (1850), Buchanan (1852), T Brown (1877), Guthrie (1874) and Hanna (1852–4).
     In propaganda the Kirk could not compete and, of its defenders, only Turner
     (1859) is still worth consulting. The balance began to be restored by Mathieson
     (1912), and Henderson (1943) was the first to steer something like a successful
     middle course, followed in the later works cited under note 27. But all suffer
     from a narrowly ecclesiastical and legalistic focus. S J Brown provides a social
     background and Machin a political, both Scottish (1972) and British (1977). For
     London's point of view, usually ignored, it is worth seeing Erickson (1952) and
     Ward (1967). But a synthesis is badly needed.
32   Hanna, iii, p 549.
33   *ibid.*, iv, p 172.
34   *ibid.*, iii, pp 449ff.
35   Buchanan, i, pp 317ff.
36   Buchanan, i, pp 289ff; Bryce, pp 21–42.
37   Mackie, i, chapter 8; Hanna, iii, pp 461–2; iv, pp 19–20.
38   Hanna, iv, p 32.
39   Hanna, iii, pp 461ff.
40   Turner, pp 174–5.
41   Watt, pp 157ff; Buchanan, i, pp 398–491; ii, pp 1–15; Bruce, i, pp 42–72.
42   Omond, pp 54ff.
43   Cockburn (1874a), 19 March 1838.
44   Brown, pp 264–7; Buchanan, ii, pp 155–9.
45   This episode is very extensively documented, the whole correspondence having
     been published, Aberdeen (1840), on which later accounts of the Earl's role,
     Balfour (1922) and Stanmore (1893), are based. The most important parts of the
     correspondence are pp 22–4, 34–41, 49–50, 54–5. *See also* Bryce, i, 168–84;
     Buchanan, ii, 164–72; Turner, pp 224–32. A modern account is M E Chamberlain
     (1983), pp 290–2.
46   Cockburn (1874a), 6 April 1838.
47   Hanna, iv, 229; Argyll (1906), i, pp 169, 176–81.
48   Turner, pp 254–66.
49   Brown, pp 23–4; Bryce, i, pp 101–59, 195–217, ii, pp 53–172; Buchanan, ii,
     passim; Hanna, iv, pp 214–9; Watt, pp 206–21.

50   Bulloch and Drummond (1973), pp 39ff, 58–62.
51   Printed in full in Buchanan, ii, pp 633–47.
52   Buchanan, ii, p 564; Turner, pp 331–2; Machin (1977), p 141.
53   Buchanan, ii, pp 581–2; Hanna, iv, p 631.
54   Watt, pp 280–5.
55   *ibid.*, p 306.
56   There is again a glaring lack of any full account of the Disruption's consequences.
     This one is based on Campbell (1961), the Checklands (1984), Cheyne (1983),
     Ferguson (1948), Lenman (1977) and Mechie (1960) for the social and economic
     effects, on Machin (1977) and McIver (1979) for the political effects. Statistics
     are provided by McKay (1969).
57   The old Poor Law is dealt with, from contrasting points of view, by R Mitchison
     (1974 and 1979) and by Cage (1981). The new one is described in A Paterson
     (1976).
58   Checkland (1975) is exhaustive but quite misses the importance of the Scottish
     free banking system, which is better appreciated by Kerr (1926) and Fry (1985).
59   Hansard, 5 June 1845, cols 143.
60   For contemporary comments *see* Argyll (1906), p 276, and Cockburn (1874a),
     20 July 1852. Many important documents are again found in Brash (1974), pp
     179–219. The Peelites are dealt with in Black (1970), Conacher (1972), Jones and
     Erickson (1972), Stewart (1978).
61   For the hapless Macaulay's experiences and reactions, *see especially* Trevelyan
     (1876), pp 467ff.
62   Cockburn (1874a), 28 July 1846.

CHAPTER 3
1   The details are given in Omond, *op. cit.*, pp 105–9, 114. A useful comment comes
    in Craik (1901), p 605.
2   Hutchison, *op. cit.*, pp 59–70; Mackie, *op. cit.*, pp 287ff.
3   Gooch (1925), ii, pp 121–2.
4   Wemyss and March (1912), pp 260–6.
5   A modern study of this key figure who, off and on, headed the Scottish admin-
    istration for so long, would be extremely useful. As it is, we have still to rely
    mainly on Omond, *op. cit.*, pp 147–61, 163–202, 226–37.
6   The background to these educational disputes is sketched in Withrington (1964).
    See also Hutchison, *op. cit.*, pp 70–80. They were, of course, just one part of the
    great debate which Davie (1964) first delineated. His conclusions have been
    disputed by Anderson (1983), and the controversy continues. The view taken
    here tends towards Davie's.
7   This tangled story would benefit from a systematic treatment. This account is
    derived from scattered sources, Burleigh (1960), pp 363ff, Fleming (1937), pp
    176ff, MacEwen (1895), pp 498–507, T Smith (1888), ii, pp 494–513, W Wilson
    (1880), pp 565ff. *See also* Hutchison, *op. cit.*, p 70.
8   Victorian bourgeois radicalism has been grossly neglected. Application of the
    voluntary principle has to be followed in essentially non-political histories such
    as O Checkland (1980). Apart from the general works on British politics, Hanham
    (1959) and Vincent (1966), the patchy partisan Mackie (1888) is the only major
    source, Anon. (1879) a minor one. Hutchison, *op. cit.*, pp 132–41, adds something
    on organisation.
9   *ibid.*, pp 104–11 draws together the many fragmented sources on the land question
    in this period.

10   Even historians seem to have forgotten temperance, once a major political issue. Hamilton (1929) marked the centenary of the movement's foundation. The brief article by Paton (1981) covers the essential ground.
11   Mackie, *op. cit.*, pp 139ff is the only source.
12   Proletarian politics in the hiatus between the 1840s and the 1880s are no longer a closed book, especially since the publication of MacDougall's bibliography (1978b), in which *see especially* pp 112–3. In the Festschrift for W H Marwick by the same author (1978a), there are useful essays by W H Fraser and G M Wilson. Gray (1976) and Ward (1970) are valuable for the difficult area of rapprochement between the bourgeois radicals and the workers. Young (1979) is ridiculous. There is further material below, chapter 6.
13   The records of the Edinburgh trades council have been published by MacDougall (1968). Trades councils in the whole of Scotland are dealt with by Fraser (1967 and 1978). For the miners in particular we have Arnot (1955) and A B Campbell (1979).
14   Sources for the volunteer movement are Hanham (1973) and Cunningham (1975). The quotation is from the latter, p 29.
15   The following passages are based on the classic account in Hanham (1959), pp 155–91, supplemented by Vincent (1966), pp 84–90.
16   A list of the boards and their functions is given in Kellas (1973), p 123. Further detail is added by Gibson (1985), pp 15–18.
17   House of Commons Papers, 1870, vi, (115), p 55.
18   Letter to Sir John Cowan, 17 March 1894, quoted Morley (1903), p 353.
19   Taylor Innes in A Reid (1887), p 64.
20   For Palmerston in Scotland, *see* Omond, *op. cit.*, pp. 193ff. The General Election is covered in Hutchison, *op. cit.*, pp 81–3.
21   The whole process and Scotland's, admittedly minor, part within it are admirably covered in Vincent (1868).
22   Brash (1974), pp xxxix–xl.
23   Hutchison, *op. cit.*, pp 103–7.
24   Cowling (1967), pp 74–5.
25   The definitive article is Fraser (1971).
26   Elcho's own memoirs were posthumously published, Wemyss and March (1912). An an opponent of reform he finds a place in Cowling, *op. cit.*, p 11. The best account is Kauffman (1974), pp 183–208. For MacDonald *see* Challinor (1957) and G M Wilson (1982).
27   F B Smith (1966), pp 214–29.
28   Hutchison, *op. cit.*, pp. 103–9, 133–5.
29   House of Commons Papers, 1870, vi, (115), *loc. cit.*
30   Only a brief summary is attempted here. The reader should refer to chapter 9 and the accompanying notes.
31   House of Commons papers 1870 xviii, Cmnd 64, Civil Departments in Scotland.
32   Hansard 3rd series, vol ccix, 12 March 1872.
33   For this see in particular the special edition of Scottish Edicational Studies in 1872, notably the articles by Lenman and Stocks, which provides a good survey, by Myers, which discusses the aspect of anglicisation, and by Withrington.
34   Omond, *op. cit.*, pp 260–88.

CHAPTER 4
1   The best source for the Conservative revival is Crapster (1957) which has, however to be read in conjunction with Hutchison, *op. cit.*, 103–25. *See also* Urwin (1965) and Ward (1982).

2   Crapster, *op. cit.*, p 356.
3   Omond, *op. cit.*, pp 289–308.
4   *ibid.*, pp 308–14.
5   Wemyss Reid (1890), p 231.
6   The most comprehensive account of Liberal politics in the last quarter of the century is Kellas (1961), from which the only important omission is the land question outside the Highlands. Much of the material later appeared in learned articles, especially Kellas (1965); reference to the others will be made below. Hanham (1959), pp 158–65 and Hutchison, *op. cit.*, pp 132–93, are also most useful.
7   Gladstone, the dominating figure in Scottish politics during this period, is the subject of two classic political biographies, Morley (1903) and Magnus (1954). Except for the Midlothian campaign itself, however, neither has much material on Scotland. Better for our purposes are Barker (1975) and Cooke (1970), the latter showing how the Scottish adulation lavished on Gladstone was not always deserved. For Midlothian in particular, the speeches have been republished, Gladstone (1971). Kelley (1960–1) has competently summed up the whole episode. *See also* Lloyd (1968).
8   Speech at the Waverley Market, Edinburgh, 27 Nov 1879.
9   Speech at the Corn Exchange, Dalkeith, 26 Nov 1879.
10 Speech at the Foresters' Hall, Dalkeith, 26 Nov 1879.
11 Quoted Crewe (1931), i, p 132.
12 On disestablishment, the main source is Kellas (1964). *See also* Simon (1975). Among contemporary sources, there is Simpson (1909) on Principal Rainy for the disestablishers, Heuston (1964) and Lady F Balfour (1924) on two opponents, viz. George Finlay and Lord Balfour of Burleigh. *See also* Hutchison, *op. cit.*, 70–3, 143–9, 156–62.
13 Quoted Ward (1982), p 8.
14 *See especially* Kellas (1965), pp 1–5.
15 For working-class movements in this period, *see* the notes to chapter 7 below.
16 Checkland (1975), pp 469–81.
17 George (1880), especially book vii, 'Justice of the Remedy'. *See also* C A Barker (1982).
18 There is no separate study of the land question in Lowland Scotland, though something can be gleaned from the works by Dunbabin (1973) and Douglas (1976) on Britain as a whole. Important materials are presented in Hutchison, *op. cit.*, pp 148–9, 154–5, 170–1, 204–5, 209, 242–5.
19 True to the traditions of Scottish historiography, more has been written about the Highland problem during these years than about anything else. The originator of the modern current of interest was Crowley (1956), but his claims for the importance of the Crofters' party are excessive. Kellas (1962) is mainly narrative. Hanham (1969) writes admirably on the Scottish context but bases his article on the false question of why unrest burst out in the 1880s. Richards (1973 and 1974) shows that the protest was much older. The most balanced view is taken by Hunter (1974).

    Balfour was the Minister most concerned with the Highland disturbances. Some reference to his work is made in Dugdale (1936), Young (1973) and, at greater length, in Zebel (1973).

    For a contemporary source, *see* Blackie (1888).
20 Gladstone's difficulties with Rosebery may be followed in Crewe (1931), pp 148ff, Magnus (1954), pp 319ff.

21 Hanham (1965) covers all the ground very thoroughly. Milne (1957), historian of the Scottish Office, devotes considerable attention to its origins, as does the centenary study by Gibson (1985). A more general context is provided by Kellas (1973), pp 31ff.
22 For nationalism in this period *see especially* Hanham (1969), pp 90ff, as well as the detailed notes to chapter 8 below.
23 On claims for Scottish equality with Ireland *see* Hurst (1966), pp 41–2.
24 The Liberal schism enters in some form into most of the works cited so far. *See specifically* McCaffrey (1971) and Savage (1961).
25 On the Irish in Scotland, *see* Handley (1946), McCaffrey (1970), Walker (1972).
26 On the 1886 election, *see* Hutchison, *op. cit.*, pp 164–76.
27 On the continuing strength of the Gladstonians in Scotland, *see especially* Lady Aberdeen (1909), p 42; G M Trevelyan (1922), p 120.
28 For Glasgow, *see* Aspinwall (1977 and 1983). Contemporary sources are Smart (1894–5), Fisher (1895), Howe (1908). *See also* Best (1967–8).
29 Quoted, Checkland (1976), p 29.
30 Smart, *op. cit.*, p 36.
31 Hutchison, *op. cit.*, pp 193–212.
32 For relations between Conservatives and Unionists, *see* Hodgson (1883–4 and 1888).
33 Lady F Balfour (1895) and (1924), pp 68ff.
34 For the origins of the conflict between radicals and imperialists, *see especially* Hutchison, *op. cit.*, pp 175–9. Jenkins (1964), pp 40ff, Mathew (1973), pp 98–9. There is some information on Scotland in Douglas (1971), Searle (1971) and Semmel (1960). The older biographies or autobiographies of the participants, as Countess of Aberdeen (1909), Birrell (1937), Haldane (1929), Spender and Asquith (1923) are reticent. An exception to this tradition is J Wilson (1973), notably chapters 19–21.
35 Knight (1894), pp 302–3.

CHAPTER 5
1 The sources cited under note 34 to chapter 4 remain relevant to the narrative which follows.
2 *See especially* Searle (1971), pp 98ff.
3 Koss (1969), p 22.
4 Searle, *op. cit.*, p 112.
5 Wilson (1973), p 365.
6 *ibid.*, pp 342–356.
7 Letter to *The Times*, 21 Feb 1902.
8 Novar Papers, Scottish Record Office, letter to his wife, 27 Mar 1902.
9 *ibid.*, 3 July 1902.
10 Quoted, Hamer (1972), p 277. *See also* Carmichael (1929), pp 81ff.
11 Novar Papers, 30 March 1903.
12 Quoted James (1963), p 465.
13 Even in Hutchison, *op. cit.*, pp 221–7, treatment of the Unionist interlude is somewhat cursory. We must otherwise rely on biographies of A J Balfour—Dugdale (1936), Egremont (1980) and Zebel (1973)—and of Lord Balfour of Burleigh, Balfour (1924).
14 Quoted Ward (1982), p 19.
15 The standard account of the election is Russell (1973).

16 The land is the only Scottish political question of the 1906 Parliament to have been thoroughly explored, in J Brown (1968). R Douglas (1974 and 1976) is largely based on him.

17 For temperance, *see* Paton (1981) and Walker (1971).

18 The issue is again best followed in the standard histories of nationalism, such as Hanham (1969), pp 94–103. Campbell-Bannerman's view is set out in Wilson, *op. cit.*, p 551. Some last flickers of support for Home Rule among Unionists is noted in Sir J R M Butler (1960). But *see* the detailed notes to chapter 9 below.

19 House of Commons Papers, 1914, Cmnd 7338, xvi.

20 David (1977), pp 79–80.

21 Buchan (1940), p 146.

22 Blewett (1972) is the standard account of these elections.

23 Chamberlain (1936), p 198.

24 Except for another gushing volume by Lady F Balfour (1920), there is nothing on Scottish feminism but what can be found in general works. I have used Fulford (1957), Raeburn (1973) and Strachey (1928), but the choice is very wide.

25 The account here is only a summary. *See* the detailed notes to the next chapter.

26 The evidence for this, which contradicts some earlier studies, is from a memorandum by the Master of Elibank quoted by R Douglas (1971).

27 *ibid.*, p 80.

28 The pioneering work on the wartime economy by Scott and Cunnision (1924) has not in general been surpassed.

29 The best source for these complex disputes is the report of the Balfour of Burleigh Commission, Clyde Munition Workers, House of Commons Papers 1914–16, Cmnd 8136. For the capitalists in wartime, *see* Reader (1968 and 1971) and Geddes (1952).

30 The immense amount of material on the wartime labour movement will be dealt with in the notes to the next chapter. The most useful sources are Heaton (1971) and McLean (1975 and 1983).

31 Scott and Cunnision, p 212.

32 There is much uncertainty about who did or did not support the coalition. According to Craig (1971), candidates not possessing the coupon were elected for the Unionists in East Fife and Forfarshire; for the Liberals in Edinburgh East, Greenock, Leith, Paisley, Stirling Burghs, Western Isles, Midlothian South and Peebles, Kinross and West Perthshire; and for Labour in Aberdeen North, Dundee, Edinburgh Central, Govan, Ayrshire South, West Fife and Hamilton. The complexities are discussed in McEwen (1962) and T Wilson (1964). *See also* Sir George Younger's letters to the *Glasgow Herald*, 26 Nov and 14 Dec 1918.

33 War cabinet no. 523, 31 Jan 1919, CAB 23/9. Munro later had reason to rue his judgement, which is quoted against him in all the relevant sources. Many original documents and reports on this episode are reproduced in Anon. (1978).

34 House of Commons papers 1917–18, Cmnd 8731, The Housing of the Industrial Population of Scotland, rural and urban, p 234. *See also* Butt (1978).

35 Cooney (1982), pp 86–8.

36 On the Irish vote, *see* Walker (1972).

37 On Asquith at Paisley, *see* Kelley (1964) and Ball (1982).

38 For the Carlton Club episode, *see especially* Blake (1955) and Kinnear (1973). G Murray (1934) was a contemporary witness.

39 Quoted Jenkins (1964), p 496.

40 T Wilson (1966), p 339.

41   Boothby (1962), p 138.
42   Skelton, pp 24ff.
43   On the question of why after the war the Liberal party disintegrated and gave
      way to Labour as the main force on the Left, the principal protagonists are
      Pelling (1968) who ascribes the process to long-term social and economic changes,
      and R Douglas (1971) who sets out the case for regarding it as the product of
      the specific conditions of wartime. We are fortunate to have the matter considered
      also from the Scottish angle in Walker (1970) who on the whole tends to Douglas'
      side. Others have entered the fray, and the latest survey of the position is given
      in Hutchison, *op. cit.*, pp 285–92.

CHAPTER 6

1   For a comment on these points, *see* Paton (1936), pp 141–2.
2   The earliest origins of the Scottish labour movement were long obscure. Johnston
      (1920) was the first to try and penetrate the darkness, and more light was thrown
      by W H Marwick (1935, 1936, 1938 and 1948) and by MacDougall (1968). But
      full use has still to be made of the latter's monumental bibliography (1978).
3   Owen has been fully dealt with, not least in his autobiography (1957), but also
      by G D H Cole (1925 and 1927), M Cole (1953), Podmore (1969) and Butt (1971).
      His later influence is traced in the opening pages of Fraser (1967) and in Bulloch
      and Drummond (1973), pp 178–9.
4   *See* W H Marwick (1964), *passim.*
5   Marwick, *op. cit.*, also deals with trades councils, MacDougall has edited the
      records of Edinburgh's (1968). For their development in the whole of Scotland,
      see Fraser (1967 and 1978). For MacDonald *see also* note 26 to chapter 3 above.
6   Youngson Brown (1953–4), pp 35–50. MacDonald's comment was made to the
      Select Committee on Coal, 1873, x, question 4624.
7   Early attempts to elevate MacDonald into the socialist pantheon, G D H Cole
      (1948), Challinor (1967–8) did not really succeed. Kauffman (1974), indeed,
      connects him to 'anti-labour' history. Youngson Brown, *op. cit.*, takes the most
      balanced view, but *see* also G M Wilson (1982). Much of the discussion might
      have been redundant if note had been taken of Haddow (1888).
8   The story is tangled. The flavour of the times and of the people involved is best
      conveyed in L Thompson (1971).
9   Quoted W H Marwick (1948), p 14.
10   New unionism in Britain as a whole is summed up in Duffy (1962–3). The
      differences in Scotland are described by W H Marwick (1948).
11   Graham's wayward character is best conveyed in Tschiffely (1937). *See also*
      Davies and Watts (1979).
12   The early biographies, Lowe (1935), Stewart (1921) and Hughes (1956), are
      hagiographies. Since then interest has centred on when, and to what extent,
      Keir Hardie was converted from the advanced radical Liberal position to one
      approximating to the socialist. My own inclination is to place the conversion
      later rather than sooner, and to stress the continuity of old-fashioned radicalism
      in his thinking: at least up to the point, soon after 1900, when he ceased to have
      a close connection with Scottish affairs as such, and thus falls from my purview.
          Of other interpretations, Pelling (1965) is most inclined to find socialism in
      Keir Hardie, Reid (1971) hardly less so. Fraser (1967) places his definitive break
      with Liberalism in 1885, Morgan (1975) in the winter of 1886–7. McLean (1975)
      seems to me the most convincing.

Barker (1974), though writing about Ramsay MacDonald, demonstrates how ideas both socialist and radical in origin could continue to co-exist in minds disinclined to nice distinction.

13 Howell (1983), pp 143–9; Morgan, *op. cit.*, pp 24–31; Reid, *op. cit.*, pp 117–8.

14 Morgan, *op. cit.*, pp 35–6; Reid, *op. cit.*, pp 120–1.

15 Reid, *op. cit.*, pp 18–20.

16 Howell, *op. cit.*, pp. 160–2, 332–40, stressing the tentative, almost accidental nature of the events. McLean, *op. cit.*, pp 53ff, is the latest restatement of the previous point of view.

17 *See especially* R Q Gray (1976), pp 165–76, 182–3.

18 Lowe (1919), chapter 1, provides essential detail on socialist sectarianism. Paton (1935), pp 75ff, demonstrated the state of mind which produced it.

19 Levenson (1973) is not always accurate on Scottish detail, and Greaves (1961), pp 55ff is to be preferred.

20 For Barry, *see* Ward (1970b).

21 For Champion, *see* Buckley (1955), pp 141ff, whose material is placed in a wider context by Howell, *op. cit.*, pp 156–60.

22 Quoted, Cole and Drake (1948), p 33.

23 There are several accounts, of which the best are Bealey and Pelling (1958), pp 293–7, and McLean, *op. cit.*, pp 78ff. The latest summary is in Hutchison, *op. cit.*, pp 250ff.

24 On relations between Labour and Liberalism, *see especially* McKibbin (1974), pp 72–87.

25 For the independent mind of the miners, *see* Howell, *op. cit.*, pp 32–9. Smillie (1924), who counts as a primary source, explains much, pp 150ff.

26 *See especially* Walker (1979), pp 200–8.

27 In the standard work on these elections, Blewett (1972), *see especially* chapter 10.

28 Woods (1980), *passim*.

29 For the BSP, *see* the sympathetic witnesses, Bell (1941), Kendall (1969) and Milton (1973), and an antagonist, Shinwell (1963).

30 McKibbin (1974), admirably free of the labour historian's normal introversion, demonstrates the essential weakness of Scottish Labour before the First World War especially well, pp 43ff. There is a full discussion in Hutchison, *op. cit.*, pp 245–65.

31 McShane (1977), p 74.

32 As of general economic conditions, Scott and Cunnison (1924), pp 138–61, provide an admirably balanced account of the political developments which sprang from them.

Despite the vogue for revisionism on Red Clydeside, historians have never in fact taken the popular myths at face value. One interesting question is how they were ever established and perpetuated in the literature—surely it cannot all have been done by Gallacher (1936, 1947 and 1966) who is at many points demonstrably false. Only Kendall, *op. cit.*, has otherwise been able to see much that was revolutionary in the West of Scotland, though Pribicevic (1958), too, is indulgent to the posturing of the Left. But Hinton, who started (1971) by on the whole accepting a militant view of events, was soon (1973) modifying his position, and in particular stressing the CWC's narrow base. With Middlemas (1965), Wrigley (1975) and McLean (1983) it has become clear that the outlook of the Clydeside working class was very far from revolutionary.

33 With the end of the war, we encounter again the question which arose in the last

chapter, of why the masses switched from Liberalism to Labour. It is a question which in previous accounts has not always been squarely faced, except by Pelling (1961) and McKibbin, *op. cit.*, who agree with one another. That the extreme Left was isolated seems clear enough, and is indeed admitted by Gallacher (1966), p 146, and implicitly by Kendall, *op. cit.* This is not, however, the same as saying that the wartime events had next to no effect at all, a view represented by Harvie (1981), pp 31–2, and McLean (1983), pp 164–73. They are therefore forced to place the whole weight of reasons for the shift in political allegiance on the adventitious events of 1922. This appears to me not only inherently unlikely, but also belied by the electoral facts, as my own narrative seeks to make clear.

34   The shift to the ILP, *see especially* A Marwick, pp 11ff, and Howell, *op. cit.*, pp 338–9, can thus properly be seen as the outcome of much deeper forces, notably the collapse of the old Liberal values. For the odyssey of particular figures, *see* Challinor (1977), Graham (1947), Kirkwood (1935) and Shinwell (1963).

35   Thus it is possible to accept the view, given for example in Marwick (1968), pp 202ff, that the labour troubles in the war and the immediate aftermath were of profound importance. But this was of a nature different from that embodied in the older and more popular assumptions. Again, the introversion of Scottish Labour historiography has obscured it.

36   For the centralisation of the Labour party, Pelling (1961), pp 50ff is the best account.

37   For the ILP's resistance, *see* McKibbin, pp 166ff.

38   There are many variants on the Kirkwood story. This one follows Middlemas, *op. cit.*, p 113.

39   Shinwell (1963), p 124.

40   The impact of the Clydesiders on arrival at Westminster is discussed in Middlemas, *op. cit.*, pp 128–32.

41   The standard work on the first Labour government is Lyman (1958). *See also* the comments by Pelling (1961), pp 57ff.

42   For the ILP's growing antagonism to the Labour leadership, see especially McKibbin, pp 131–61.

43   For reactions in the Labour party, *see* Shinwell (1973), pp 66ff, McNair (1955), p 153, and especially Middlemas, pp 160ff.

44   Middlemas, *op. cit.*, pp 242ff.

45   *ibid.*, 274ff.

CHAPTER 7

1   *See* S Maxwell (1982).

2   For the economy in general, *see* Lenman (1977), pp 296–331, and for Clydeside in particular, Checkland (1976), pp 34–45.

3   Cook and Stevenson (1977), pp 145–65.

4   *See* the final chapter of Graham (1947). On Labour's resilience, there is Cole and Postgate (1938), p 595, and on the STUC in particular, J M Bell, in Cairncross (1954), pp 280–96.

5   Johnston (1952), p 66.

6   On the Communist party in Scotland during this period, Pelling (1958) and Gallacher (1966) are the most useful. An interesting study of its local bases, where they existed, is Macintyre (1980), which includes chapters on Lumphinnans and the Vale of Leven.

7   For the final stages of the ILP, *see* note 43 to chapter 6 above.
8   On this episode, *see* the chapter about Ramsay MacDonald in Williams (1965) and especially Wheeler-Bennet (1962), p 181.
9   R Douglas (1971), p 222.
10 Sinclair's position was described by me (1977) in an article based on his papers in Churchill College, Cambridge.
11 Quoted, Stannage (1980), p 109.
12 Sinclair Papers, Sinclair to Ranald Findlay, 27 May 1937.
13 *See* the detailed notes to chapter 8 below.
14 Of the works dealing with British Fascism, only Benewick (1969) makes so much as a passing reference to Scotland, p 67.
15 For the position in Edinburgh, *see* Mackintosh (1966). Harvie (1981) sums up the position there and elsewhere, p 100. The Kirk's Church and Nation Committee, Reports, 1938, pp 556–7, is quoted by Wood (1980), p 82.
16 *See* his Constructive Conservatism (1931), *especially* pp 22ff.
17 *See* Buchan himself (1940), and J Adam Smith (1965).
18 Boothby (1962) is rich with recollections of the period. The quote is on p 42.
19 The Duchess wrote her memoirs (1958).
20 For Lithgow, *see* J M Reid (1964) and Dickson (1980). *See also* C Weir (1953).
21 Pottinger (1979), pp 11ff.
22 Collins found a brief biographer in D Keir (1952). *See also* Pottinger, *op. cit.*, pp 54–62.
23 Best followed in the commissioner's annual reports. I give a list under House of Commons papers in the bibliography.
24 Stannage (1980) is a comprehensive study of the election.
25 Quoted, *ibid.*, p 77.
26 We owe Harvie a proper assessment of Elliot's work in Scotland. *See especially* his article in the Weekend Scotsman, 9 April 1983. Unfortunately, only the barest summary appears in his history (1981), pp 95–6 and 100–1. Coote (1965) has little on Scotland.
27 House of Commons Papers, 1937, Cmnd 5563. Hanham (in Wolfe, 1969), pp 63–9, is an excellent commentary on the prelude and result.
28 Cmnd 5563, p 680.
29 Pottinger, *op. cit.*, pp 74–8.
30 *ibid.*, pp 79–85.
31 Johnston made of himself another tenacious Scottish legend, though little of it can stem from his disappointing memoirs (1952). Harvie has done much to bring him into proper focus, his article (1981) being again much better than what appears in his history of the same date, pp 102–4. It will become clear that I differ in major respects from him.
32 Memories (1952), p 169.
33 W Ferguson (1968), p 384.
34 On the war economy, *see* Lenman (1977), pp 232–3 and A Marwick (1968), p 288. For the Clydebank blitz, *see* Harrisson (1976), pp 254ff.
35 Pimlott (1977), p 56.
36 Harrisson, *loc. cit.*
37 A Calder (1969).
38 C Stuart (1975), pp 300–1.
39 Harvie (1977), p 55. In later works he has modified his position.
40 R H Campbell (1981).
41 It is Pottinger who describes him as arrogant and insensitive, p 101. For the

contrary view *see* K Young (1974), pp 132–3. For the Liberals in general, *see* Douglas, p 257.

42 McCallum and Readman (1947) was the pioneering study of a General Election.

43 Harvie (1977) may be recommended on this immediate post-war period, pp 166ff.

44 Pottinger, *op. cit.*, pp 100–5.

45 *ibid.*, pp 106–16.

46 House of Commons Papers, 1948, Cmnd 7308. It has three pages.

47 The esoteric subject of Scottish committees is nevertheless well covered by J H Burns (1960), whom I follow, here and below.

48 Pottinger, *op. cit.*, pp 117–28.

49 For the 1950 General Election, we have Nicholas (1951) and Chrimes (1950), the latter dealing specifically with Glasgow. In his study of the 1951 General Election, Butler devotes a chapter to a Scottish constituency, which he coyly declines to name. From internal evidence, it is clearly Aberdeen North.

50 Stuart's memoirs (1967) are reticent. By far the best study of his administration is Seldon (1981) pp 130–40, who also gives the information about Elliot, p 78.

51 K Young (1970), p 82.

52 The pages of the Balfour report relevant to this account are pp 12, 95, 121.

CHAPTER 8

1 Nationalism is one of the few aspects of Scottish politics covered by useful general histories. The earliest was Coupland (1954), marred by some inaccuracies but still good for the end of the nineteenth century. Hanham (1969b) would have been the standard work had it not been so rapidly overtaken by events. Harvie (1978) has many ingenious ideas but suffers from having been written at the height of excitement over devolution. *See also* the bibliographies of K C Fraser.

2 *See* Cobban (1969), pp 154–9.

3 There is an excellent bibliography of Scotland in the age of the Enlightenment in R B Sher (1985).

4 For this episode *see* Hanham (1967).

5 Doomed to frustration and failure though it was, this Celtic strain of nationalism has nevertheless cast a certain spell. Hechter (1975) suffers from the delusion that Lowland Scotland is part of the Celtic fringe. O D Edwards (1968) is in some respects still more eccentric. By far the most sensible is Hunter (1975).

6 For what may be taken as the consensus view of the Union at the time, *see* Dicey and Rait (1920).

7 Both Pryde (1938) and A Marwick (1970) bring out well the essential difference in nationalism before and after the First World War.

8 The information in the general works can now be supplemented by the auto-biographies of some leading figures, J MacCormick (1955), Macdiarmid (1966), Sir C Mackenzie (1967).

9 For a view of the Union in this decade, *see* Pares (1954). Only a few years later, Paton (1968), is an example of the exasperation which was to be harnessed and transformed by the renewed rise of the SNP.

10 For developments in the 1960s, *see* the works of Brand (1978), Webb (1977) and Wolfe (1973), as well as the article by Grant and Preece (1968).

11 For premature predictions of the SNP's decline, *see* Begg and Stewart (1971), Bochel and Denver (1972), Cook (1970) and McLean (1970).

12 The first scholarly response was curious to hostile, *see* MacCrone (1969), N MacCormick (1970), J N Wolfe (1969).

13 The progression of the stimulus can be observed in such works as G Brown (1973), G Kennedy (1976), D I MacKay (1977 and 1979).

14 The equivocations of the Labour party may be followed in Keating and Bleiman (1979). The attitudes may or may not have been fostered by the differing conclusions of Marxist analysis, as in Dickson (1980), Nairn (1977).

15 Cmnd 5460, pp 345–6.

CHAPTER 9

1 See Seldon, *op. cit.*, pp 130–2, Kellas (1973), p 44 and, for a typical Unionist's relations with his constituency, Bealey & Sewell (1981), p 51.

2 Pottinger, pp 146–55.

3 Pottinger, pp 156–65.

4 Butler and Rose (1965).

5 Butler and King (1966).

6 W L Miller (1981), pp 47ff, tries to make too much of this. It is more accurately assessed by R Douglas (1971), p 272.

7 For the example of a particular constituency, *see* Bealey and Sewell, *op. cit.*, p 52.

8 Kellas and Fotheringham (1970).

9 W Thompson (1978), *passim*.

10 The distinctive behaviour of Catholic voters in Scotland was first noted by Budge and Urwin (1966), which can be supplemented by Harvie (1981), p 84. For the general background, *see* McRoberts (1978).

11 Lenman (1977), pp 243–4.

12 Kellas (1968), pp 198–9; Kinnear (1968), p 49; Bleiman & Keating (1979), pp 150–4.

13 Kellas (1973), pp 221, 223; Harvie (1981), p 44.

14 On regional problems as seen at the time, consult MacCrone (1969), and for a retrospect, R Saville (1986).

15 On the failure of planning, *see* Harvie (1977), pp 184–9, Keating & Midwinter (1983), pp 170–1.

16 *See* the detailed notes to chapter 8 above.

17 Bleiman and Keating, *op. cit.*, pp 154–9. *See also* the comment by Crossman (1975–7), vol ii, p 739.

18 *ibid.*, vol iii, p 48.

19 *Final Term*, p 46.

20 The views of the Royal Commission are best followed in the report itself, especially pp 350ff. As an analysis of and prescription for the constitution it has found little lasting favour, but *see* Birch (1977), Boyce (1975), Johnson (1976), Stacey (1975) and Stanyer (1974).

21 Bochel and Denver (1972), Cook (1970) and McLean (1970) were too confident in the conclusions they drew from this election. Kellas, pp 446–62, in the inevitable Butler and Pinto-Duschinsky (1971) is an essential antidote.

22 For these problems, *see especially* Urwin (1966) and Ward (1982), pp 39–43. Drucker (1979a) and Keating & Midwinter (1983), pp 63–6 offer a less sympathetic point of view.

23 *See especially* Pottinger, pp 177ff.

24 Checkland (1976), pp 50–1.

25 Drucker (1982a), pp 64–5.

26 Butler and Kavanagh (1974).

27 Butler and Kavanagh (1975).

28 *See especially* M Stewart (1977), p 220, and the comment in Castle (1980), p 579.
29 The standard history of the Scottish Office, Milne (1957), has now been supplemented for the latest period by Macdonald and Redpath (1980). W Ross (1978) adds little.
30 Bogdanor (1979), p 81.
31 Royal Commission on the Constitution, Cmnd 5460, 1973, written evidence, vol ii, memorandum by the Scottish Office, pars 15–16.
32 Keating & Midwinter (1983), p 5.
33 *See especially* Mackintosh (1964).
34 Kellas (1973), p 28.
35 Harvie (1981), p 113; Keating & Midwinter (1983), p 16.
36 Keating & Midwinter, p 10.
37 Keeton (1970), pp 173–4.
38 *See* Keating & Midwinter, pp 79–81, and for extensive details the articles by G E Edwards (1972) and Myers (1974).
39 For these dissatisfaction, *see* Edwards, *op. cit.*, p 319.
40 J P Mackintosh did most to draw attention to this problem, *see* for example, Drucker (1982), p 68. Keating and Midwinter also deal with it, pp 29ff. Elsewhere a whole paper has been devoted to it, Hogwood (1982).
41 Other items dealing with specific aspects of devolution will be referred to below, but for good general accounts *see* Brown & Drucker (1980)—a favourable view— and Dalyell (1977)—a hostile one.
42 Brown & Drucker and Bleiman & Keating are alike good on Labour's internal politics during these developments.
43 House of Commons Papers, 1974, Cmnd 5732, Democracy and Devolution.
44 House of Commons Papers, 1975, Cmnd 6348, Our Changing Democracy.
45 Drucker (1982), p 99. The distinction between minimalists and maximalists, which we owe to Mackintosh, is developed *ibid.*, pp 95–100.
46 For reactions, *see* Kellas (1976–7) and Drucker (1982), pp 102ff.
47 Butler and Kitzinger (1976).
48 Drucker (1978), *passim.*
49 Wilson (1979), pp 212–3.
50 House of Commons Papers, 1976, Cmnd 6585. For further comments, *see* Brown & Drucker, p 97.
51 For a good summary of the objections, *see* Gunn (1977).
52 J Kerr (1977).
53 *See* Bogdanor in Layton-Henry (1980).
54 There are numerous accounts of the second reading affair, among which may be mentioned Harvie (1981), pp 162–3, Bleiman & Keating, pp 186–7.
55 An account of this is given in D Steel (1980).
56 Naughtie (1979).
57 For the final state of the Bill, *see* Bradley & Christie (1979); Bochel, Denver & Macartney (1981). For the 40 per cent rule in particular (1980).
58 The campaign is covered in Perman (1980) and Bochel, Denver & Macartney, *op. cit.*
59 The fall of the government is charted in Naughtie (1980).
60 The election campaign is covered in the United Kingdom as a whole by Butler and Kavanagh (1979), in Scotland by Hetherington (1980).

CHAPTER 10
1 Scottish grand committee, 6 July 1982, col 53.
2 Speech to the Royal Institute of Public Administration, Edinburgh, 29 Oct 1982.

Bibliography

Abbreviations: *SHR   Scottish Historical Review*; *SLMSS   Scottish Labour History Society Journal*

Aberdeen, George Gordon, 4th Earl of, *Correspondence with the Rev Thomas Chalmers, 14 January–27 May 1840* (Edinburgh 1840)

Aberdeen, Ishbel, Countess of: *Lord Tweedmouth 1849–1909, Notes and Recollections* (London 1909)

Adam Smith, J, *John Buchan* (London 1965)

Adams, I H, *The Making of Urban Scotland* (London 1978)

Alison, Sir A, 'Trade Unions', *Blackwood's Edinburgh Magazine*, xliii (1838).

—— *Principles of Population* (Edinburgh 1840)

—— *Some Account of My Life and Writings* (Edinburgh and London 1883)

Anderson, R D, *Education and Opportunity in Victorian Scotland* (Oxford 1983)

Anon, 'A Word in Season to the Conservatives in Scotland', *Blackwood's Edinburgh Magazine*, xli (1837)

—— 'Why is Scotland so Radical?' *Quarterly Review*, cxlviii (1879)

—— 'Glasgow 1919' (Glasgow 1978)

—— 'The Scottish Socialists, a gallery of contemporary portraits' (London 1931)

Argyll, George Campbell, 8th Duke of, 'Land Reformers', *Contemporary Review*, xlviii (1885)

—— *The Unseen Foundations of Society* (London 1893)

—— *Autobiography and Memoirs* (London 1906)

Arnot, R P, *A History of the Scottish Miners* (London 1955)

A Scottish Conservative: 'Scottish Conservatism', *National Review*, xiii (1889)

—— 'The Growth of Conservatism in Scotland', *National Review*, xviii (1892)

—— 'The Decay of Scottish Radicalism', *National Review*, xx (1892)

Ash, M, *The Strange Death of Scottish History* (Edinburgh 1980)

Aspinall, A, *Lord Brougham and the Whig Party* (Manchester 1939)

—— (ed) *Letters of George IV* (London 1936)

Aspinwall, B, 'Glasgow Trams and American Politics', *SHR*, lvi (1977)

—— *Portable Utopia: Glasgow and the United States 1820–1920* (Aberdeen 1983)

Atholl, Katharine Murray, Duchess of, *Working Partnership* (London 1958)

Balfour, Lady Frances, 'The Election of 1895, some lessons from Scotland', *National Review*, xxvi (1895)

—— *Dr Elsie Inglis* (London 1920)

—— *Life of George Hamilton Gordon, 4th Earl of Aberdeen* (London 1922)

Balfour, Lady Frances, *Memoir of Lord Balfour of Burleigh* (London 1924)

Ball, S R, 'Asquith's Decline and the General Election of 1918', *SHR*, lxi (1982)

Balsom, D and McAllister, I, 'The Scottish and Welsh Devolution Referenda of 1979', *Parliamentary Affairs*, xxxii (1979)

Barker, A, *Quangos in Britain* (London 1982)

Barker, C A, *Henry George* (Oxford 1955)

Barker, M, *Gladstone and Radicalism* (London 1975)

Barker, R, 'Socialism and progressivism in the political thought of James Ramsey MacDonald', in Morris, *Edwardian Radicalism* (1974)

Barnes, G, *From Workshop to War Cabinet* (London 1924)

Barr, J, *Lang Syne* (Glasgow 1949)

Bartram, P, *David Steel* (London 1982)

Bealey, F and Pelling, H, *Labour and Politics 1900–1906* (London 1958)

——— and Sewell, J, *The Politics of Independence, a study of a Scottish town* (Aberdeen 1981)

Begg, H M and Stewart, J A, 'The Nationalist Movement in Scotland', *Journal of Contemporary History*, vi (1971)

Bell, A (ed), *Lord Cockburn* (Edinburgh 1979)

Bell, J D M, *The Trade Unions*, in Cairncross, *The Scottish Economy* (1954)

Bell, T, *Pioneering Days* (London 1941)

——— *John Maclean, Fighter for Freedom* (Glasgow 1944)

Beloff, M and Peake, G, *The Government of the United Kingdom* (London 1980)

Benewick, R, *The Fascist Movement in Britain* (London 1969)

Best, G, 'The Scottish Victorian City', *Victorian Studies*, xi (1967–8)

Bewley, C, *Thomas Muir of Huntershill* (London 1981)

Birch, A H, *Political integration and disintegration in the British Isles* (London 1977)

Birrell, A, *Things Past Redress* (London 1937)

Blackie, J S, *The Scottish Highlanders and the Land Laws* (London 1888)

Blackwood's Edinburgh Magazine (1817–   )

Blake, R, *The Unknown Prime Minister* (London 1955)

——— *The Conservative Party from Peel to Churchill* (London 1970)

Bleiman, D and Keating, M, *Labour and Scottish Nationalism* (London 1979)

Blewett, N, *The Peers, the Parties and the People, the General Elections of 1910* (London 1972)

Bochel, J M and Denver, D T, 'Religion and voting', *Political Studies*, xviii (1970)

——— ——— 'The Decline of the SNP, an alternative view', *Political Studies*, xx (1972)

——— ——— and Macartney, A (eds) *The Referendum Experience* (Aberdeen 1981)

Bogdanor, V, 'Devolution and the Constitution', *Parliamentary Affairs*, xxi (1978)

——— *Devolution* (London 1979)

——— 'Devolution', in Layton-Henry, *Conservative Party Politics* (1980)

——— 'The 40 per cent Rule', *Parliamentary Affairs*, xxxiii, 1980

Bonney, N, 'The Scottish Assembly', *Political Quarterly*, xlix (1978)

Boothby, R, *The New Economy* (London 1943)

——— *I Fight to Live* (London 1947)

——— *My Yesterday, Your Tomorrow* (London 1962)

——— *Recollections of a Rebel* (London 1978)

Boyce, D G, 'Dicey, Kilbrandon and Devolution', *Political Quarterly*, xlvi (1975)

Body Orr, J, *As I Recall* (London 1966)

Bradley, A W, 'The Devolution of Government in Britain', in Calvert, *Devolution* (1975)

——— and Christie, D J, *The Scotland Act 1978* (London 1979)

Brand, C, *The British Labour Party, a short history* (London 1968)

Brand, J, *The National Movement in Scotland* (London 1978)

Brash, J, The Conservatives in the Haddington District of Burghs 1832–1852, *Transactions of the East Lothian Antiquarian Society*, xi (1968)

—— *Papers on Scottish Electoral Politics 1832–1854* (Edinburgh 1974)

Briggs, A, *Chartist Studies* (London 1959)

—— and Saville, J (eds) *Essays in Labour History 1886–1923* (London 1971)

Bristow, E, 'The Liberty and Property Defence League and Individualism', *Historical Journal*, xviii (1975)

Brotherstone, T, 'The Suppression of the "Forward" ', *SLHSJ*, i (1969)

Brougham, Henry, Lord, *The Life and Times of Lord Brougham* (Edinburgh and London 1871)

Broun-Lindsay, E C, Electioneering in East Lothian 1836–7, *Transactions of the East Lothian Antiquarian Society*, viii (1966)

Brown, G (ed), *The Red Paper on Scotland* (Edinburgh 1975)

—— and Drucker, H, *The Politics of Nationalism and Devolution* (London 1980)

Brown, J, 'Scottish and English Land Legislation 1905–1911', *SHR*, xlvii (1968)

Brown, K D, *Essays in Anti-Labour History* (London 1974)

Brown, S J, *Thomas Chalmers and the Godly Commonwealth in Scotland* (Oxford 1983)

Brown, T, *Annals of the Disruption* (Edinburgh 1877)

Bruce, A B, *William Denny, Shipbuilder* (London 1888)

Buchan, J, *Memory Hold-the-Door* (London 1940)

Buchanan, R, *The Ten Years' Conflict* (Edinburgh 1852)

Buckley, K D, *Trade unionism in Aberdeen 1878–1900* (Edinburgh and London 1955)

Budge, I and Urwin, D W, *Scottish Political Behaviour* (Glasgow 1966)

Bulloch, J and Drummond, A L, *The Scottish Church 1688–1843* (Edinburgh 1973)

—— —— *The Church in Victorian Scotland 1843–1874* (Edinburgh 1975)

—— —— *The Church in Late Victorian Scotland 1874–1900* (Edinburgh 1978)

Burleigh, J H S, *Church History of Scotland* (London 1960)

Burns, J M, 'The Scottish Committees of the House of Commons 1948–1959', *Political Studies*, viii (1960)

Butler, D E, *The British General Election of 1951* (London 1952)

—— *The British General Election of 1955* (London 1956)

—— and Rose, R, *The British General Election of 1959* (London 1960)

—— —— *The British General Election of 1964* (London 1965)

—— and King, A, *The British General Election of 1966* (London 1966)

—— and Pinto-Duschinsky, M, *The British General Election of 1970* (London 1971)

—— and Kavanagh, D, *The British General Election of February 1974* (London 1974)

—— —— *The British General Election of October 1974* (London 1975)

—— —— *The British General Election of 1979* (London 1980)

—— and Kitzinger, U, *The 1975 Referendum* (London 1976)

Butler, Sir J R M, *Lord Lothian* (London 1960)

Butt, J (ed), *Robert Owen, Prince of Cotton Spinners* (Newton Abbot 1971)

—— 'Working Class Housing in Glasgow', in MacDougall, *Essays in Scottish Labour History* (1978)

—— and Ward, J T (eds), *Scottish Themes, Essays in honour of Professor S G E Lythe* (Glasgow 1976)

Cage, R A, *The Scottish Poor Law 1745–1845* (Edinburgh 1981)

Cairncross, Sir A, *The Scottish Economy* (Cambridge 1984)

Calder, A, *The People's War* (London 1969)

Calvert, H, *Devolution* (London 1975)

Cameron, K J, 'William Weir and the Origins of the "Manchester League" in Scotland 1833–1839', *SHR*, lviii (1979)

Campbell, A B, *The Lanarkshire Miners* (Edinburgh 1979)

Campbell, I, 'Carlyle and Secession, *Records of the Scottish Church History Society*', xviii (1963)

Campbell, R H, 'The Church and Scottish Social Reform', *Scottish Journal of Political Economy*, viii (1961)

—— 'The Committee of Ex-Secretaries of State for Scotland and Industrial Policy 1941–1945', *Scottish Industrial History*, ii (1981)

Carlyle, T, *Chartism* (London 1840)

Carmichael, Mary, Lady, *Lord Carmichael of Stirling* (London 1929)

Carney, J, Hudson, R and Lewis, J, *Regions in Crisis* (London 1980)

Castle, B, *The Castle Diaries 1974–1976* (London 1980)

Challinor, R, 'Alexander MacDonald and the Miners', *Our History*, pamphlet 48, (1957–8)

—— *John S Clarke* (London 1977)

Chamberlain, A, *Politics from the Inside* (London 1936)

Chamberlain, M E, *Lord Aberdeen, a biography* (London 1983)

Checkland, O, *Philanthropy in Victorian Scotland* (Edinburgh 1980)

—— and S G, *Industry and Ethos, Scotland 1832–1914* (London 1984)

Checkland, S G, *Scottish Banking, a History 1695–1973* (Glasgow and London 1975)

—— *The Upas Tree, Glasgow 1875–1975* (Glasgow 1976)

Cheyne, A A, *The Practical and the Pious, Thomas Chalmers 1780–1847* (Edinburgh 1983)

Chrimes, S B (ed), *The General Election in Glasgow, February 1950* (Glasgow 1950)

Clive, J, *Scotch Reviewers* (London 1957)

Clunie, J, *Literature of Labour* (Dunfermline 1967)

Cobban, A T, *The Nation State and National Self-Determination* (Glasgow and London 1969)

Cockburn, Henry, Lord, *Life of Francis Jeffrey* (Edinburgh 1852)

—— *Memorials of his Time* (Edinburgh 1856)

—— *Journal* (Edinburgh 1874a)

—— *Letters on the Affairs of Scotland* (London 1874b)

Cockburn, H A (ed), *Some Letters of Lord Cockburn* (Edinburgh 1932)

Cole, G D H, *Life of Robert Owen* (London 1925)

—— (ed), *Robert Owen—a New View of Society* (London 1927)

—— *British Working-Class Politics 1832–1914* (London 1941)

—— *A Short History of the British Working-Class Movement* (London 1947)

—— *History of the Labour Party from 1914* (London 1948)

—— and Postgate, R, *The Common People* (London 1938)

Cole, M, *Robert Owen and New Lanark* (London 1953)

——and Drake, B, *Our Partnership* (London 1948)

Conacher, J B, *The Aberdeen Coalition* (Cambridge 1968)

—— *The Peelites and the Party System* (Newton Abbot 1972)

Cook, C, *The Age of Alignment, Electoral Politics in Britain 1922–1929* (London 1975)

—— *The Liberal and Nationalist Revival* (in *Decade of Disillusion* . . . , see below)

—— and McKie, D (eds) *The Decade of Disillusion, British politics in the 1960s* (London 1970)

—— and Ramsden, J, *By-elections in British Politics* (London 1973)

Cook, C and Stevenson, J, *The Slump, Society and politics during the Depression* (London 1977)

Cooke, A, 'Gladstone's Election for the Leith District of Burghs', *SHR*, xlix (1970)

Cooney, J, *Scotland and the Papacy* (Edinburgh 1982)

Cooper, C, *An Editor's Retrospect* (London 1896)

Coote, C, *A Companion of Honour, The story of Walter Elliot* (London 1965)

Coupland, Sir R, *Welsh and Scottish Nationalism* (London 1954)

Cowan, C, *Reminiscences* (Edinburgh 1878)

Cowan, R, *The Newspaper in Scotland 1815–1860* (Glasgow 1947)

Cowling, M, *Gladstone, Disraeli and Revolution* (London 1967)

Craig, F W S, *British Parliamentary Election Statistics, 1918–1970* (Chichester 1971)

Craik, Sir H, *A Century of Scottish History* (Edinburgh 1901)

Crapster, B, 'Scotland and the Conservative Party in 1876', *Journal of Modern History*, xxix (1957)

Crathorne, N and Dugdale, L J, *Tennant's Stalk* (London 1973)

Crewe, Robert, Marquess of, *Lord Rosebery* (London 1931)

Crossman, R, *Diaries of a Cabinet Minister* (London 1975–7)

Crowley, D W, 'The Crofters' Party 1885–1892', *SHR*, xxv (1956)

Cunningham, H, *Volunteer Force* (London 1975)

Curry, K, *Sir Walter Scott's Edinburgh Annual Register* (Knoxville 1977)

Daiches, D, *A Companion to Scottish Culture* (Edinburgh 1981)

Dalyell, T, *Devolution, the End of Britain* (London 1977)

David, E, *Inside Asquith's Cabinet* (London 1977)

Davidson, R, 'Wartime Labour Politics 1914–1916', *SLSHJ*, viii (1974–5)

Davie, G E, *The Democratic Intellect* (Edinburgh 1964)

—— *The Crisis of the Democratic Intellect* (Edinburgh 1986)

Davies, F and Watts, C, *Cunninghame Graham, A Critical Biography* (Cambridge 1979)

Dewey, C, 'Celtic Agrarian Legislation and Celtic Revival', *Past and Present*, lxiv (1974)

Dicey, A V and Rait, R, *Thoughts on the Union between England and Scotland* (London 1920)

Dickson, T, 'Class and Nationalism in Scotland', *Scottish Journal of Sociology*, ii (1978)

—— *Scottish Capitalism* (London 1980)

Dod, C, *Electoral Facts 1832–1853* (new edn Hanham, H H, Brighton 1972)

Douglas, Sir G and Ramsay, Sir G (eds), *The Panmure Papers* (London 1908)

Douglas, R, *The History of the Liberal Party 1895–1970* (London 1971)

—— *God Gave the Land to the People*, in Morris, *Edwardian Radicalism* (1974)

—— *Land, Politics and People* (London 1976)

Douglas-Home, Sir A, *The Way the Wind Blows* (London 1976)

Dowse, R E, *Left in the Centre, the Independent Labour Party 1893–1940* (London 1966)

Drucker, H, 'Devolution and Corporatism', *Government and Opposition*, xii (1977)

—— *Breakaway, The Scottish Labour Party* (Edinburgh 1978)

—— 'The Political Parties' in MacKay, *Scotland, the Framework for Change* (1979)

—— *Multi-party Britain* (London 1979)

—— (ed), *John P Mackintosh on Scotland* (London 1982)

—— and Clarke, M G (eds), *Scottish Government Yearbook 1976– (Our Changing Scotland)* (Edinburgh 1976)

—— —— *Scottish Government Yearbook 1978* (Edinburgh 1977)

Drucker, H and N (eds), *Scottish Government Yearbook 1979* (Edinburgh 1978)
—— —— *Scottish Government Yearbook 1980* (Edinburgh 1979)
—— —— *Scottish Government Yearbook 1981* (Edinburgh 1982)
—— —— *Scottish Government Yearbook 1982* (Edinburgh 1983)
Duffy, A E P, 'The New Unionism in Britain 1889–1890', *Economic History Review*, xiv (1961)
—— 'The Origins of the Independent Labour Party', *Victorian Studies*, vi (1962–3)
Dugdale, B, *A J Balfour* (London 1936)
Dunbabin, J P D, *Rural Discontent in Nineteenth Century Britain* (London 1973)
Dwyer, J, Mason, R A and Murdoch, A, *New Perspectives on the Politics and Culture of Early Modern Scotland* (Edinburgh 1982)
Dyer, M, 'Mere Detail and Machinery'—the Great Reform Act and the effects of redistribution on Scottish representation 1832–1868, *SHR*, xii (1983)
Edinburgh Review (1802–   )
Edwards, G E, 'The Scottish Grand Committee 1968–70', *Parliamentary Affairs*, xxv (1972)
Edwards, O D, *Celtic Nationalism* (London 1968)
Egremont, M, *Balfour* (London 1980)
Ehrman, J, *The Younger Pitt, The Years of Acclaim* (London 1969)
—— *The Reluctant Transition* (London 1984)
Elliot, A E, *Life of George Joachim Goschen, First Viscount Goschen* (London 1911)
Elliot, B, McCrone, D and Skelton, V, *Property and Politics, Edinburgh 1875–1895*, in Garrard, *The Middle Class in Politics* (1978)
Elliot, W, *Toryism and the Twentieth Century* (London 1927)
Ellis, B and Mac A'Gobhainn, S, *The Scottish Insurrection of 1820* (London 1970)
Elton, Godfrey, Lord, *Life of James Ramsay MacDonald* (London 1939)
Erickson, A B, *The Public Career of Sir James Graham* (Oxford 1952)
Eyre-Todd, G, *History of Glasgow* (Glasgow 1934)
Ferguson, T, *The Dawn of Scottish Social Welfare* (Edinburgh 1948)
—— *Scottish Social Welfare 1864–1914* (Edinburgh and London 1958)
Ferguson, W, 'A Renfrewshire Election Account 1832', Miscellany X of the Scottish History Society (1965)
—— 'The Reform Act (Scotland) of 1832: intention and effect', *SHR*, xlv (1966)
—— *Scotland, 1689 to the Present* (Edinburgh 1968)
—— *Scotland's Relations with England, a survey to 1707* (Edinburgh 1977)
Fergusson, A, *The Hon Henry Erskine* (Edinburgh and London 1882)
Fergusson, J, ' "Making Interest" in Scottish County Elections', *SHR*, xxvi (1947)
Finer, S E, *The Changing British Party System* (Washington, DC 1980)
Fisher, G, 'Glasgow, a Model Municipality', *Fortnightly Review*, lvii (1895)
Fisher, H A L, *James Bryce* (London 1927)
Fleming, J R, *History of the Church in Scotland 1843–1929* (Edinburgh 1937)
Flinn, M (ed), *Scottish Population History* (Cambridge 1977)
Fontana, B M, *Rethinking the Politics of Commercial Society, the* Edinburgh Review *1802–1832*(Cambridge1986)
Foot, M R D, *War and Society* (London 1973)
Fraser, D (ed), *The New Poor Law in the Nineteenth Century* (London 1976)
Fraser, K C, 'A Bibliography of the Scottish National Movement 1844–1973', Scottish Nationalist Periodicals, *Bibliotheck*, vii (1974)
Fraser, P, *Joseph Chamberlain* (London 1966)
Fraser, W H, 'Trades Unions, Reform and the Election of 1868 in Scotland', *SHR*, l (1971)

Fraser, W H, 'Scottish Trades Councils in the Nineteenth Century', *Bulletin of the Society for the Study of Labour History*, xiv (1967)
—— 'Trades Councils in the Labour Movement in Nineteenth Century Scotland', in MacDougall, *Essays in Scottish Labour History* (1978)
—— 'The Glasgow Cotton Spinner, 1837', in Butt and Ward, *Scottish Themes . . .* (1976)
Fry, M R G, 'A Matter of Pact', *Weekend Scotsman*, 14 May 1977
—— *Banking Deregulation, the Scottish Example* (Edinburgh 1985)
Fulford, R, *Votes for Women* (London 1957)
Furber, H, *Henry Dundas, First Viscount Melville* (London 1931)
Fyfe, J, *Autobiography of John McAdam* (Edinburgh 1980)
Gallacher, W, *Revolt on the Clyde* (London 1936)
—— *The Rolling of the Thunder* (London 1947)
—— *Last Memoirs* (London 1966)
Gammie, A, *From Pit to Palace* (London 1931)
Garrard, J S, *The Middle Class in Politics* (Farnborough 1978)
Garvin, J L, *Joseph Chamberlain* (London 1933)
Gash, N, *Politics in the Age of Peel* (London 1953)
Geddes, A C, *Forging of a Family* (London 1952)
George, H, *Progress and Poverty* (London and New York 1880)
Gibson, J S, *The Thistle and the Crown, a history of the Scottish Office* (Edinburgh 1985)
Ginter, D E (ed), *Whig Organisation in the General Election of 1790*, Selections from the Blair Adam Papers (Berkeley and Los Angeles 1967)
Gladstone, W E, *Midlothian Speeches 1879* (Leicester 1971)
Gooch, G P, *The Later Correspondence of Lord John Russell* (London 1925)
Gourlay, J (ed), *The Provosts of Glasgow* (Glasgow 1942)
Gourlay, R, *A Specific Plan for Organising the People* (London 1809)
—— *The Village System* (Bath 1817)
Graham, T N, *Willie Graham* (London 1947)
Grant, W P and Preece, W, 'Welsh and Scottish Nationalism', *Parliamentary Affairs*, xxi (1968)
Gray, J L, 'The Law of Combination in Scotland', *Economica*, xxiv (1974)
Gray, R Q, *Labour Aristocracy in Victorian Edinburgh* (Oxford 1976)
Gray, W F, *East Lothian Biographies* (Haddington 1941)
Greaves, C D, *The Life and Times of James Connolly* (London 1961)
Gregory, R, *The Miners and British Politics 1906–1914* (Oxford 1968)
Grierson, H J C (ed), *The Letters of Sir Walter Scott* (London 1932)
Grigor, I F, *Mightier than a Lord* (Stornoway 1979)
Grimond, J, *The Common Welfare* (London 1978)
—— *Memoirs* (London 1979)
Gunn, L, 'Devolution', *Political Quarterly*, xlviii (1977)
—— and Lindley, P, 'Devolution', *Public Administration Bulletin*, iv (1977)
Guthrie, T, *Autobiography and Memoir* (London 1874)
Gutzke, D W, 'Rosebery and Campbell-Bannerman', *Bulletin of the Institute of Historical Research*, liv (1981)
Haddow, W M, *My Seventy Years* (Glasgow 1943)
Haddow, R, 'The Miners in Scotland', *Nineteenth Century*, xxiv (1888)
Haldane, Robert, Lord, *Autobiography* (London 1929)
Hamer, D L, *Liberal politics in the Age of Gladstone and Rosebery* (London 1972)
Hamilton, T, *The Temperance Reformation in Scotland* (Greenock 1929)

Handbook of Scottish Administration (Edinburgh 1953)

Handley, J, *The Irish in Modern Scotland* (Cork 1946)

Hanham, H J, *Elections and Party Management, Politics in the time of Gladstone and Disraeli* (London 1959)

—— *The Scottish Political Tradition*, an inaugural lecture at Edinburgh University (Edinburgh 1964)

—— 'The Creation of the Scottish Office 1881–1887', *Juridical Review*, new series, x (1965)

—— 'Mid-century Scottish Nationalism, Romantic and Radical', in Robson, *Ideas and Institutions . . .* (1967)

—— *The Nineteenth Century Constitution, documents and commentary* (Cambridge 1969a)

—— *Scottish Nationalism* (London 1969b)

—— 'The Problem of Highland Discontent 1880–1885', *Transactions of the Royal Historical Society*, 5th Series, xix (1969c)

—— 'The Development of the Scottish Office', in Wolfe, *Government and Nationalism in Scotland* (1969)

—— 'Religion and Nationality in the Mid-Victorian Army', in Foot, *War and Society* (1973)

Hanna, W, *Memoirs of Thomas Chalmers* (London 1852–4)

Hardcastle, M (ed), *Life of John, Lord Campbell* (London 1981)

Harrington, W and Young, P, *The 1945 Revolution* (London 1978)

Harris, W, *The Radical Party in Parliament* (London 1885)

Harrisson, T, *Living through the Blitz* (London 1976)

Hart, T, 'Urban Growth and Municipal Government, Glasgow in a comparative context', in Slaven and Aldcroft, *Business, Banking and Urban History* (1982)

Harvie, C, *Scotland and Nationalism* (London 1977)

—— *No Gods and Precious Few Heroes, Scotland 1914–1980* (London 1981)

—— 'Labour and Scottish Government, the age of Tom Johnston', *Bulletin of Scottish Politics*, ii (1981)

—— 'Elliot and the Politics of Adventure', *Weekend Scotsman*, 9 April 1983

Haseler, S, *The Death of British Democracy* (London 1976)

Hassan, J, 'The Landed Estate, Paternalism and the Coal Industry in Midlothian 1800–1880', *SHR*, lix (1980)

Hechter, M, *Internal Colonialism, the Celtic fringe in British national development* (London 1975)

Henderson, G D, *Heritage, a study of the Disruption* (Edinburgh 1943)

Hetherington, P, 'The 1979 General Election Campaign in Scotland', in Drucker, H and N, *Scottish Government Yearbook, 1981* (1980)

Heuston, R F V, *Lives of the Lord Chancellors 1885–1940* (London 1964)

Hobbs, S (ed), 'Historical Sources for Central Scotland', iii, *World War Two* (Stirling 1979)

Hodge, J, *From Workman's Cottage to Windsor Castle* (London 1931)

Hodgson, W E, 'Why Conservatism Fails in Scotland', *National Review*, ii (1883–4)

—— 'Conservatism in Scotland', *National Review*, xii (1888)

Hogwood, B, 'Quasi-government in Scotland', in Barker, A, *Quangos in Britain* (1982)

Hollis, P (ed), *Pressure from Without in Early Victorian England* (London 1974)

Hope, G, *A Sketch of the Life of George Hope of Fenton Barns* (Edinburgh 1879)

Horn, B (ed), *Letters of John Ramsay* (Edinburgh 1966)

Horner, L, *Memoirs and Correspondence of Francis Horner, MP* (London 1843)

House of Commons Papers, 1835, xxix, Cmnd 32, Municipal corporations in Scotland
—— 1837, xii, HC 215, Fictitious votes in Scotland
—— 1837–8, viii, Reports from the Select Committee on Combinations of Workers
—— 1867–8, xxix, Education Commission (Scotland) (Argyll)
—— 1870, xviii, 130, Report of the Commissioners . . . to inquire into certain Civil Departments in Scotland (Camperdown)
—— 1870, vi (115), Parliamentary and Municipal Elections (Hartington)
—— 1873, x, Select Committee on Coal
—— 1890–1, xlviii, HC 329, Financial relations (England, Scotland, Ireland)
—— 1907, Cmnd 3431, The Distress Committees in Scotland
—— 1908, Cmnd 3830, The Distress Committees in Scotland
—— 1909, Cmnd 4478, The Distress Committees in Scotland
—— 1914, Cmnd 7338, Royal Commission on the Civil Service, xii, The Scottish Departments
—— 1914–16, Cmnd 8136, Clyde Munitions Workers (Balfour of Burleigh)
—— 1917–18, Cmnd 8731, The Housing of the Industrial Population of Scotland, rural and urban (Bannatyne)
—— 1934–5, Cmnd 4958, Special Areas Report
—— 1935–6, Cmnd 5089, Special Areas Report
—— 1936–7, Cmnd 5245, Special Areas Report
—— 1937, Cmnd 5563, Committee on Scottish Administration (Gilmour)
—— 1937–8, Cmnd 5604, Special Areas Report
—— 1938–9, Cmnd 5905, Special Areas Report
—— 1945–6, HC 189-1, Third Report of the Select Committee on Procedure
—— 1948, Cmnd 7308, Scottish Affairs, a memorandum on the Government's proposals
—— 1952, Cmnd 8609, Scottish Financial and Trade Statistics (Catto)
—— 1954, Cmnd 9212, Royal Commission on Scottish Affairs (Balfour)
—— 1956–7, HC 211, Second Report of the Select Committee on Procedure
—— 1963, Cmnd 2188, Central Scotland Plan
—— 1964, Cmnd 2864, Scotland Plan
—— 1969, Cmnd 4150, Local Government in Scotland (Wheatley)
—— 1973, Cmnd 5460, Royal Commission on the Constitution (Kilbrandon)
—— 1974, Cmnd 5732, Democracy and Devolution
—— 1975, Cmnd 6348, Our Changing Democracy
—— 1975, Cmnd 6585, Devolution to Scotland and Wales
Howe, F C, *The British City* (London 1908)
Howell, D, *British Workers and the Independent Labour Party* (Manchester 1983)
Hughes, E, *Keir Hardie* (London 1956)
Hunter, J, 'The Politics of Highland Land Reform', *SHR*, liii (1974)
—— 'The Gaelic connection: the Highlands, Ireland and nationalism', *SHR*, liv (1975)
—— 'The Making of the Crofting Community', (Edinburgh 1976)
Hurst, M, *Joseph Chamberlain and Liberal Reunion* (London 1967)
Hutchison, I G, *A Political History of Scotland 1832–1924* (Edinburgh 1986)
Iremonger, L, *Lord Aberdeen* (London 1978)
Jacobson, P D, 'Rosebery and Liberal Imperialism', *Journal of British Studies*, xiii (1973)
James, R R, *Rosebery* (London 1963)
Johnson, D, 'Regionalism made Respectable', in Stankiewicz, *British Government in an Era of Reform* (1976)

Johnston, R J, 'Electoral Geography of the General Election of October 1974', *Scottish Geographical Magazine*, xciii (1977)
—— 'Regional variations in voting trends', *Regional Studies*, xv (1981)
Johnston, T, *The History of the Working Classes in Scotland* (Glasgow 1920)
—— *Memories* (London 1952)
Jenkins, R, *Asquith* (London 1964)
Jones, D, *Chartism and the Chartists* (London 1975)
Jones, J D and Erickson, R B, *The Peelites 1846–1857* (Ohio State University, 1972)
Jones, W R, 'England against the Celtic Fringe', *Journal of World History* (1971)
Judge, D and Finlayson, D A, 'Scottish MPs and Devolution', *Parliamentary Affairs*, xxviii (1975)
Kauffman, C J, 'Lord Elcho, trade unionism and democracy', in Brown, K D, *Essays in Anti-Labour History* (1974)
Keating, M, 'Administrative Devolution', *Public Administration*, liv (1976)
—— and Midwinter, A, *The Government of Scotland* (Edinburgh 1983)
Keeton, G W, *Government in Action in the United Kingdom* (London 1970)
Keir, D, *The House of Collins* (London 1952)
—— (ed), *The Third Statistical Account of Scotland* (Glasgow 1966)
Kellas, J G, 'The Scottish Liberal Party 1885–1895'. Unpublished PhD thesis, London University, 1961
—— 'The Crofters' War 1882–1888', *History Today*, xii (1962)
—— 'The Liberal Party and the Scottish Church Disestablishment Crisis', *English Historical Review*, lxxix (1964)
—— 'The Liberal Party in Scotland 1876–1895', *SHR*, xlv (1965)
—— 'The Mid-Lanark By-Election and the Scottish Labour Party 1888–1894', *Parliamentary Affairs*, xviii (1965)
—— 'Highland Migration to Glasgow and the Origin of the Scottish Labour Movement', *Bulletin of the Society for the Study of Labour History*, xii (1966)
—— *Modern Scotland, the Nation since 1870* (London 1968)
—— 'Scottish Nationalism', in Butler and Pinto-Duschinsky, *The British General Election of 1970* (1971)
—— *The Scottish Political System* (Cambridge 1973)
—— 'Reactions to the Devolution White Paper', in Drucker and Clarke, *Scottish Government Yearbook* (1976–7)
—— and Fotheringham, A T, 'The Political Behaviour of the Working Class', in MacLaren, *Religion and Social Class* (1974)
Kelley, R, 'Midlothian, a study in politics and ideas', *Victorian Studies*, iv (1960–1)
—— 'Asquith at Paisley, the content of British Liberalism at the end of its era', *Journal of British Studies*, iv (1964)
Kemp, B, 'The General Election of 1841', *History*, new series, xxxvii (1952)
Kendall, W, *The Revolutionary Movement in Britain 1900–1921* (London 1969)
Kendle, J E, 'The Round Table Movement and "Home Rule all round"', *Historical Journal*, xi (1968)
Kennedy, G, *The Radical Approach, papers on an independent Scotland* (Edinburgh 1976)
Kerr, A W, *History of Banking in Scotland* (London 1926)
Kerr, J, 'The Failure of the Scotland and Wales Bill', in Drucker and Clarke, *Scottish Government Yearbook* (1977)
Kinnear, M, *The Fall of Lloyd George* (London 1973)
—— *The British Voter* (London 1968)

Kirby, A M and Taylor, P J, 'A geographical analysis of voting patterns in the EEC referendum', *Regional Studies*, x (1976)

Kirkwood, D, *My Life of Revolt* (London 1955)

Kitson Clarke, G, *Peel and the Conservative Party* (London 1929)

Knight, W (ed), *Rectorial Addresses delivered at the University of St Andrews* (London 1894)

Knox, W, *Scottish Labour Leaders 1918–1939* (Edinburgh 1984)

Koss, S, *Asquith* (London 1985)

—— *Lord Haldane, Scapegoat for Liberalism* (London 1969)

Kramnick, J, *Is Britain Dying?* (London 1979)

Layton-Henry, Z, *Conservative Party Politics* (London 1980)

Lee, G W, 'North Sea oil and Scottish Nationalism', *Political Quarterly*, xlvii (1976)

Lee, J, *Tomorrow is a New Day* (London 1939)

Lee-Warner, Sir J, *Life of Lord Dalhousie* (London 1904)

Lees, J D and Kimber, R, *Political Parties in Modern Britain* (London 1972)

Lenman, B, *An Economic History of Modern Scotland* (London 1977)

—— *Integration, Enlightenment and Industrialisation, Scotland 1746–1832* (London 1981)

—— and Stocks, J, 'The Beginning of State Education in Scotland 1872–1875', *Scottish Educational Studies* (1972)

Levenson, S, *James Connolly, a biography* (London 1973)

Lever, T, 'Lord Braxfield', *History Today*, xxiii (1974)

Levitt, I and Smout, C, *The State of the Scottish Working Class in 1843* (Edinburgh 1980)

Lloyd, T, *The General Election of 1880* (Oxford 1968)

Loch, G, *The Family of Loch* (Edinburgh 1934)

Logue, K J, *Popular Disturbances in Scotland 1780–1815* (Edinburgh 1979)

Lowe, D, *Souvenirs of Scottish Labour* (Glasgow 1919)

—— *From Pit to Parliament, the story of the early life of Keir Hardie* (London 1935)

Lyall, F, *Of Presbyters and Kings* (Aberdeen 1980)

Lyman, W, *The First Labour Government* (London 1958)

McAllister, I and Ross, P, *United Kingdom Facts* (London 1982)

MacAllister, J M, *James Maxton, Portrait of a Rebel* (London 1935)

McCaffrey, J F, 'The Irish Vote in Glasgow in the later Nineteenth Century', *Innes Review*, xxi (1970)

—— 'The Origins of Liberal Unionism in the West of Scotland', *SHR*, l (1971)

—— 'Thomas Chalmers and Social Change', *SHR*, lx (1981)

MacCallum, R B and Readman, A, *The British General Election of 1945* (Oxford 1947)

McCalman, S D, 'Chartism in Aberdeen', *SLSHJ*, ii (1970)

McCalmont, F H, *Parliamentary Poll Book* (London 1910)

MacCormick, J, *The Flag in the Wind* (London 1955)

MacCormick, N (ed), *The Scottish Debate* (Oxford 1970)

McCrie, G, *The Church of Scotland, her divisions and reunions* (Edinburgh 1901)

McCrone, G, *Scotland's Future, the economics of nationalism* (Oxford 1969)

MacDiarmid, H, *Cunninghame Graham, a centenary study* (Glasgow 1952)

—— *The Company I've Kept* (London 1966)

—— 'Scottish Nationalism', in Edwards, *Celtic Nationalism* (1968)

Macdonald, M and Redpath, A, 'The Scottish Office 1954–1979', in Drucker, H and N, *The Scottish Government Yearbook* (1980)

MacDougall, I (ed), *Minutes of the Edinburgh Trades Council 1859–1873* (Edinburgh 1968)

—— *Labour Records in Scotland* (Edinburgh 1978a)

—— *Essays in Scottish Labour History* (Edinburgh 1978b)

—— 'Some Aspects of the 1926 General Strike in Scotland' (in the above)

MacEwen, A R, *Life and Letters of John Cairns* (Edinburgh 1895)

McEwen, J M, 'The Coupon Election and the Unionist Members of Parliament', *Journal of Modern History*, xxxiv (1962)

Macgeorge, A, *The Bairds of Gartsherrie* (Glasgow 1875)

McGovern, J, *Neither Fear nor Favour* (London 1960)

Machin, G I T, 'The Disruption and British Politics 1834–1843', *SHR*, li (1972)

—— *Politics and the Churches in Great Britain 1832–1868* (Oxford 1977)

Macintyre, S, *Little Moscows, Communism and working-class militancy in inter-war Britain* (London 1980)

McIver, I F, 'Cockburn and the Church', in Bell, A, *Lord Cockburn* (1979)

MacKay, D I (ed), *Scotland 1980, the economics of self-government* (Edinburgh 1977)

—— *Scotland, the Framework for Change* (Edinburgh 1979)

—— and Mackay, G A, *The Political Economy of North Sea Oil* (London 1975)

McKay, J R, 'The Disruption, an examination of some statistics', *Philosophical Journal*, vi (1969)

Mackay, M, *Memoir of James Ewing* (Glasgow 1866)

Mackenzie, Sir C, *My Life and Times, octave 6, 1923–30* (London 1967)

Mackenzie, P, *Reminiscences of Glasgow and the West of Scotland* (Glasgow 1865–8)

McKibbin, R, *The Evolution of the Labour Party 1906–1914* (Oxford 1974)

Mackie, J B, *Life and Work of Duncan McLaren* (Edinburgh 1888)

Mackintosh, J P, 'Regional Administration, has it worked in Scotland?' *Public Administration*, xlii (1964)

—— 'Devolution, Regionalism and the Reform of Local Government, the Scottish case', *Public Law*, xiii (1964)

—— 'The City's Politics', in Keir, *The Third Statistical Account of Scotland* (1966)

—— *The Devolution of Power* (London 1968)

—— 'Scottish Nationalism', *Political Quarterly*, xxxviii (1968)

—— 'The Kilbrandon Report', *Political Quarterly*, xlv (1974)

—— 'The Killing of the Scotland Bill', *Political Quarterly*, xlix (1978)

McLaren, A A, *Religion and Social Class* (London 1974)

MacLean, C (ed), *The Crown and the Thistle* (Edinburgh 1979)

McLean, I, 'The Rise and Fall of the Scottish National Party', *Political Studies*, xviii (1970)

—— 'The Ministry of Munitions, the Clyde Workers' Committee and the Suppression of "Forward"', *SLHSJ*, vi (1972)

—— 'Red Clydeside 1915–1919', in Quinault and Stevenson, *Popular Protest and Public Order* (1973)

—— *Keir Hardie* (London 1975)

—— 'The Politics of Nationalism and Devolution', *Political Studies*, xxv (1977)

—— *The Legend of Red Clydeside* (Edinburgh 1983)

Maclean, J, 'The 1926 General Strike in Lanarkshire', *Our History*, pamphlet 65 (1976)

Macmillan, H P, *A Man of Law's Tale* (London 1952)

McNair, T, *James Maxton, The Beloved Rebel* (London 1955)

MacRoberts, D, *Modern Scottish Catholicism* (Glasgow 1978)

McShane, H, *No Mean Fighter* (London 1977)

Magnus, Sir P, *Gladstone* (London 1954)

Magnusson, M (ed), *The Glorious Privilege* (London 1967)

Malcolm, C A, 'The Solicitor General for Scotland', *Juridical Review*, liv (1942)

Mansbach, R W, 'The Scottish National Party', *Comparative Politics* (1973)

Marquand, D, *Ramsay MacDonald* (London 1977)

Marwick, A, 'The Independent Labour Party 1918–1932'. Unpublished DPhil thesis, Oxford University, 1960

—— 'The Independent Labour Party in the 1920s', *Bulletin of the Institute of Historical Research*, xxxv (1962)

—— 'James Maxton, his place in Scottish labour history', *SHR*, xliii (1964)

—— *Britain in the Century of Total War* (London 1968)

—— 'Scottish Nationalism since 1918', in Miller, K, *Memoirs of a Modern Scotland* (1970)

Marwick, W H, 'Municipal Politics in Victorian Edinburgh', *Old Edinburgh Book*, xxxiii (1969)

—— 'Early Trade Unionism in Scotland', *Economic History Review*, v (1935)

—— *Economic Developments in Victorian Scotland* (London 1936)

—— 'The Beginnings of the Scottish Working-Class Movement in the Nineteenth Century', *International Review for Social History*, iii (1938)

—— *Labour in Scotland* (Glasgow 1948)

—— *Life of Alexander Campbell* (Glasgow 1964)

—— *Scotland in Modern Times* (Edinburgh and London 1964)

—— *Short History of Labour in Scotland* (1967)

Mason, J W, 'The Duke of Argyll and the Land Question in the Late Nineteenth Century', *Society for the Study of Labour History Bulletin*, xxiii (1976)

—— 'Political Economy and the Response to Socialism', *Historical Journal*, xxiii (1980)

Matheson, C, *Life of Henry Dundas, First Viscount Melville* (London 1933)

Mathieson, W L, *The Awakening of Scotland* (Glasgow 1910)

—— *Church and Reform in Scotland 1797–1843* (Glasgow 1912)

Matthew, H C G, *The Liberal Imperialists* (Oxford 1973)

Maxwell, S, 'The Secular Pulpit, presbyterian democracy in the twentieth century', in Drucker, H and N, *Scottish Government Yearbook* (1982)

Mbadinuju, I, 'Devolution', *Political Quarterly*, xlvii (1976)

Mechie, S, *The Church and Scottish Social Development* (London 1960)

Meikle, H W, *Scotland and the French Revolution* (Edinburgh 1912)

Middlemas, R E, *The Clydesiders* (London 1965)

Miller, K (ed), *Memoirs of a Modern Scotland* (London 1970)

—— *Cockburn's Millennium* (London 1975)

Miller, W L, 'The Connection between SNP voting and the demand for self-government', *European Journal of Political Research*, v (1975)

—— *Electoral Dynamics in Britain since 1918* (London 1977)

—— 'Class, region and strata at the British General Election of 1979', *Parliamentary Affairs*, xxxii (1979)

—— 'The Scottish Dimension', in Butler and Kavanagh, *British General Election of 1979* (1980)

—— *The End of British Politics?* (Oxford 1981)

Milne, Sir D, *The Scottish Office* (London 1957)

Milton, N, *John Maclean* (Bristol 1973)

Ministry of Munitions, History of (London 1920–4)

Mitchison, N and Phillipson, N T (eds), *Scotland in the Age of Improvement* (Edinburgh 1970)

Mitchison, R, *The Roots of Nationalism* (Edinburgh 1980)

—— 'The Making of the Old Scottish Poor Law', *Past and Present*, lxiii (1974)

—— 'The Creation of the Disablement Rule in the Scottish Poor Law', in Smout, *The Search for Wealth and Stability . . .* (1979)

Moffat, A, *My Life with the Miners* (London 1968)

Montgomery, F, Glasgow and the Movement for Corn Law repeal', *History*, lxiv (1979)

—— 'Glasgow and the struggle for parliamentary reform', *SHR*, lxi (1982)

Moody, T W, 'Michael Davitt and the British Labour Movement', *Transactions of the Royal Historical Society*, 5th series, iii (1983)

Moore, R, *The Emergence of the Labour Party* (London 1978)

Morgan, K O, *Keir Hardie, Radical and Socialist* (Oxford 1967)

Morley, J, *Life of Richard Cobden* (London 1881)

—— *Life of Gladstone* (London 1903)

—— *Recollections* (London 1917)

Morris, R J A, *Edwardian Radicalism* (London 1974)

Morton, A L and Tate, G, *The British Labour Movement 1770–1920* (London 1956)

Mowat, I, *Bibliography of Scotland* (Edinburgh, annually since 1976–7)

Muirhead, I A, 'Catholic Emancipation in Scotland, the debate and the aftermath', *Innes Review*, xxiv (1974)

Mullin, W A R, 'The Scottish National Party', in Drucker, *Multi-party Britain* (1979)

Munro, R, *Looking Back, Fugitive Writings and Sayings* (London 1930)

Murdoch, A, *The People Above* (Edinburgh 1980)

—— 'The Importance of Being Edinburgh—Management and Opposition in Edinburgh Politics 1746–1784', *SHR*, lxii (1983)

Murray, A C, *Master and Brother* (London 1945)

Murray, G, *A Man's Life* (London 1934)

Murray, N, *The Scottish Hand Loom Weavers, a social history* (Edinburgh 1979)

Myers, J D, 'Scottish Nationalism and the Antecedents of the 1872 Education Act', *Scottish Educational Studies*, ii (1972)

Myers, P, 'The Select Committee on Scottish Affairs', *Parliamentary Affairs*, xxvii (1974)

Nairn, T, *The Break-up of Britain* (London 1977)

Namier, Sir L and Brooke, J, *History of Parliament 1754–1790* (London 1964)

Naughtie, J, 'The Scotland Bill in the House of Commons', in Drucker, H and N, *Scottish Government Yearbook* (1978)

—— 'The Year at Westminster', in Drucker, H and N, *Scottish Government Yearbook* (1979)

Nevin, E (ed), *The Economics of Devolution* (Cardiff 1978)

New, C, *Life of Henry Brougham to 1830* (Oxford 1961)

Nicholas, H, *The British General Election of 1950* (London 1951)

Nicolson, A, *Memoirs of Adam Black* (Edinburgh 1885)

Nisbet, J, 'Thomas Chalmers and the Economic Order', *Scottish Journal of Political Economy*, xi (1964)

Norton, P, *Dissension in the House of Commons* (Oxford 1980)

Oakley, C, *Our Illustrious Forebears* (Glasgow 1980)

O'Connor, T P, *Sir Henry Campbell-Bannerman* (London 1908)

Omond, G, *The Lord Advocates of Scotland* (Edinburgh 1883)

—— *The Lord Advocates of Scotland* (second series, Edinburgh 1914)

Omond, G, *The Arniston Memoirs* (Edinburgh 1887)

Owen, R, *Life of Robert Owen* (London 1857)

Oxford and Asquith, H H Asquith, Earl of, *Memories and Reflections* (London 1928)

Pares, R, 'A Quarter-Millennium of Anglo-Scottish Union', *History*, new series, xxxix (1954)

Parker, C S, *Life and Letters of Sir James Graham 1792–1861* (London 1907)

Paterson, A, 'The Poor Law in Nineteenth Century Scotland', in Fraser, D, *The New Poor Law . . .* (1976)

Paterson, T A, *A Seat for Life* (Dundee 1980)

Paton, D W, 'Temperance', in Daiches, *A Companion to Scottish Culture* (1981)

Paton, H J, *The Claim of Scotland* (London 1968)

Paton, J, *Proletarian Pilgrimage* (London 1935)

—— *Left Turn* (London 1936)

Patrick, J, 'The 1806 Election in Aberdeenshire', *Northern Scotland*, ii (1974–5)

Pelling, H, *The British Communist Party, a historical profile* (London 1958)

—— *Short History of the Labour Party* (London 1961)

—— *Origins of the Labour Party* (Oxford 1965)

—— *Social Geography of British Elections 1885–1910* (London 1967)

—— *Popular Politics and Society in Late Victorian Britain* (London 1968)

Pentland, Marjory, Lady, *The Rt Hon John Sinclair, Lord Pentland, a memoir* (London 1928)

Perman, R, 'The Devolution Referendum Campaign of 1979', in Drucker, H and N, *Scottish Government Yearbook* (1979)

Petrie, Sir C, *The Victorians* (London 1960)

Phillipson, N T, 'The Scottish Whigs and the Reform of the Court of Session'. Unpublished PhD thesis, Cambridge University, 1967.

Pimlott, B, *Labour and the Left in the Thirties* (Cambridge 1977)

Pinney, T (ed), *The Letters of Thomas Babington Macaulay* (Cambridge 1977)

Pocock, J G A, 'British History', *Journal of Modern History*, xlvii (1975)

Podmore, F, *Robert Owen, a biography* (New York 1969)

Polsby, N W and Smith, G, *British Government and its Discontents* (London 1981)

Porritt, A M and E, *The Unreformed House of Commons* (Cambridge 1903)

Pottinger, G, *The Secretaries of State for Scotland 1926–1976* (Edinburgh 1979)

—— *The Winning Counter—Hugh Fraser and Harrods* (London 1971)

Pribicevic, B, *The Shop Stewards' Movement and Workers' Control* (Oxford 1958)

Prest, J, *Lord John Russell* (London 1972)

Proctor, J H, 'Party Interest and the Electoral System for the Projected Scottish Assembly', *Political Quarterly*, xlvii (1977)

Pryde, G, 'The Development of Nationalism in Scotland', *Sociological Review*, xxvii (1938)

—— 'Central and Local Government in Scotland since 1707', *Historical Association* pamphlet, general series no. 45 (1960)

—— and Rait, Sir R, *Scotland* (London 1954)

Pulzer, P, *Political Representation and Elections in Britain* (London 1967)

Quinault, R and Stevenson, J (eds), *Popular Protest and Public Order* (1974)

Raeburn, A, *The Militant Suffragettes* (London 1973)

Reader, W J, *Architect of Air Power, life of first Viscount Weir of Eastwood* (London 1968)

—— *The Weir Group* (London 1971)

Reid, A, *Why I am a Liberal* (London 1887)

Reid, F, 'Keir Hardie's Conversion to Socialism', in Briggs and Saville, *Essays in Labour History* . . . (1971)
—— *Keir Hardie, the making of a socialist* (London 1978)
Reid, J, *Reflections of a Clyde-built Man* (London 1976)
Reid, J M, *James Lithgow, Master of Work* (London 1964)
Richards, E, *The Leviathan of Wealth* (London 1973)
—— 'How Tame were the Highlands?' *Scottish Studies*, xvii (1973)
—— 'Patterns of Highland Discontent', in Quinault and Stevenson, *Popular Protest* . . . (1974)
Ridley, J, *Lord Palmerston* (London 1970)
Robson, R, *Ideas and Institutions of Victorian Britain, essays in honour of G Kitson Clark* (London 1967)
Rosie, I, *Thomas Balfour, MP for Orkney and Shetland, 1835–1837* (Stromness 1978)
Ross, W, 'Approaching the Archangelic?', in Drucker, H and N, *Scottish Government Yearbook* (1978)
Rowe, D H, 'The Chartist Convention and the Regions', *Economic History Review*, xxii (1969)
Russell, A K, *Liberal Landslide, the General Election of 1906* (Newton Abbot 1973)
Saunders, L J, *Scottish Democracy 1815–1840* (Edinburgh 1950)
Savage, D C, 'Scottish Politics 1885–1886', *SHR*, xl (1961)
Saville, J, 'Henry George and the British Labour Movement', *Bulletin of the Society for the Study of Labour History*, xix (1962)
Saville, R (ed), *The Economic Development of Modern Scotland 1950–1980* (Edinburgh 1985)
Schwarz, J E, 'The Scottish National Party, non-violent separation and theories of violence', *World Politics*, xxii (1969–70)
Scott, P H (ed), *Letters of Malachi Malagrowther* (Edinburgh 1981)
Scott, W E and Cunnison, J, *The Industries of the Clyde Valley during the War* (Oxford 1924)
Scottish Council (Development and Industry), *Inquiry into the Scottish Economy 1960–1961* (Edinburgh 1961)
Searle, G R, *The Quest for National Efficiency, a study in British political and social thought* (Oxford 1971)
Second Statistical Account of Scotland (Edinburgh 1841)
Seers, D (ed), *Underdeveloped Europe* (Hassocks 1979)
Seldon, A, *Churchill's Indian Summer, the Conservative Government 1951–1955* (London 1981)
Semmel, B, *Imperialism and Social Reform* (London 1960)
Shaw, A, 'Municipal Socialism in Scotland', *Juridical Review*, i (1889)
Shaw, T, *Letters to Isabel* (London 1921)
Sher, B, *Church and University in the Scottish Enlightenment, the moderate literati of Edinburgh* (Edinburgh 1985)
Shinwell, E, *Conflict without Malice* (London 1955)
—— *The Labour Story* (London 1963)
—— *I've Lived through it all* (London 1973)
—— *Lead with the Left* (London 1981)
Simon, A, 'Church Disestablishment as a Factor in the General Election of 1885', *Historical Journal*, xviii (1975)
Simpson, P C, *Life of Principal Rainy* (London 1909)
Skelley, J, *The General Strike* (London 1976)

Skelton, N, *Constructive Conservatism* (Edinburgh 1931)

Skidelsky, R, *Politicians and the Slump* (London 1967)

Slaven, A and Aldcroft, D H (eds), *Business, Banking and Urban History, essays in honour of S G Checkland* (Edinburgh 1982)

Smart, W, 'The Municipal Industries of Glasgow', *Proceedings of the Philosophical Society of Glasgow*, xxvi (1894–5)

Smillie, R, *My Life for Labour* (London 1924)

Smith, F B, *The Making of the Second Reform Bill* (Cambridge 1966)

Smith, T, *Memoirs of James Begg* (Edinburgh 1888)

Smout, T C, *History of the Scottish People 1560–1830* (Edinburgh 1967)

—— *The Search for Wealth and Stability, essays in economic and social history presented to M Flinn* (London 1979)

—— *A Century of the Scottish People* (London 1986)

Southgate, D, *The Passing of the Whigs* (London 1902)

Spender, J A and Asquith, C, *Life of the Rt Hon Sir Henry Campbell-Bannerman* (London 1923)

Stacey, F, *British Government 1966–1975, years of reform* (Oxford 1975)

Stankiewicz, W J, *British Government in an Era of Reform* (London 1976)

Stanmore, Sir A H Gordon, Lord, *The Earl of Aberdeen* (London 1893)

Stannage, T, *Baldwin Thwarts the Opposition, the General Election of 1935* (London 1980)

Stansky, P, *The Left and the War* (Oxford 1969)

Stanyer, T, 'Nationalism, Regionalism and the British System of Government', *Social and Economic Administration* (1974)

Steel, D, *A House Divided* (London 1980)

Stewart, M, *The Jekyll and Hyde Years, politics and economic policy since 1974* (London 1977)

Stewart, R, *The Foundation of the Conservative Party 1830–1867* (London 1978)

—— *Henry Brougham, his public career 1778–1868* (London 1986)

Stewart, W, *Keir Hardie* (London 1921)

Strachey, R, *The Cause* (London 1928)

Stuart, C (ed), *The Reith Diaries* (London 1975)

Stuart of Findhorn, James, Viscount, *Within the Fringe* (London 1967)

Sunter, R M, *Patronage and Politics in Scotland 1707–1832* (Edinburgh 1986)

Sutherland, George Leveson Gower 5th Duke of, *Looking Back* (London 1958)

Taylor, A H, 'The Electoral Geography of Welsh and Scottish Nationalism', *Scottish Geographical Magazine*, lxxxix (1973)

Tennant, C, *The Radical Laird, a biography of George Kinloch* (Kineton 1970)

Teviotdale, D A, 'The Glasgow Parliamentary Constituency 1832–1848'. Unpublished BLitt thesis, Glasgow University (1963)

Thomas, H, *John Strachey* (London 1973)

Thompson, A, 'Gladstone's Whips and the General Election of 1868', *English Historical Review*, lxiii (1948)

Thompson, L, *The Enthusiasts, a biography of John and Katherine Bruce Glasier* (London 1971)

Thompson, W, 'The New Left in Scotland', in MacDougall, *Essays in Scottish Labour History* (1978b)

Thorne, R G (ed), *The History of Parliament, 1790–1820* (London 1986)

Tilney Bassett, A (ed), *Gladstone's Speeches* (London 1916)

Trevelyan, G M, *Sir George Otto Trevelyan, a memoir* (London 1932)

Trevelyan, Sir G O, *Life and Letters of Lord Macaulay* (London 1876)

Troup, C, 'Chartism in Dumfries', *Dumfriesshire Transactions*, lvi (1981)
Tschiffely, A F, *Don Roberto* (London 1937)
Turner, A, *The Scottish Secession of 1843* (Edinburgh 1859)
Urwin, D W, 'The Development of the Conservative Party Organisation in Scotland until 1912', *SHR*, xliv (1965)
—— 'Scottish Conservatism, a party organisation in transition', *Political Studies*, xiv (1966)
Vaudry, R W, 'The Constitutional Party in the Church of Scotland 1834–1843', *SHR*, lxii (1983)
Vincent, J R, *The Formation of the British Liberal Party* (London 1966)
—— *Poll Books, how Victorians voted* (London 1967)
Walker, W M, 'Dundee's disenchantment with Churchill', *SHR*, xlix (1970)
—— 'The Scottish Prohibition Party and the Millennium', *International Review of Social History*, xviii (1971)
—— 'Irish immigrants in Scotland, their priests, politics and parochial life', *Historical Journal*, xv (1972)
—— *Juteopolis, Dundee and its textile workers 1885–1923* (Edinburgh 1979)
Ward, J T, 'The Factory Reform Movement in Scotland', *SHR*, xlvi (1962)
—— 'A Footnote on the First Reform Act', *SHR*, li (1967)
—— *Sir James Graham* (London 1967)
—— *Popular Movements 1830–1859* (London 1970a)
—— 'Tory Socialist, a preliminary note on Michael Maltman Barry 1842–1909', *SLHSJ*, ii (1970b)
—— *Chartism* (London 1970c)
—— 'Some Aspects of Working-class Conservatism in the Nineteenth Century', in Butt and Ward, *Scottish Themes . . .* (1976)
—— *The First Century, a history of Scottish Tory organisation 1882–1982* (Edinburgh 1982)
Watt, H, *Thomas Chalmers and the Disruption* (Edinburgh 1943)
Watt, J C, *John Inglis, a memoir* (Edinburgh 1893)
Webb, K, *The Growth of Scottish Nationalism* (Glasgow 1977)
Weir, Sir C M, *Civilian Assignment* (London 1953)
Wemyss and March, F Charteris, Earl of, *Memories 1818–1912* (Edinburgh 1912)
Wemyss Reid, Sir T, *Memoirs and Correspondence of Lyon Playfair* (London 1890)
West, F, *Cunninghame Graham* (London 1932)
Wheeler-Bennett, Sir J, *John Anderson, Viscount Waverley* (London 1962)
Williams, F, *A Pattern of Rulers* (London 1965)
Williams, J C, 'Edinburgh Politics 1832–1852'. Unpublished PhD thesis, Edinburgh University, 1972
Wilson, A, 'Chartism in Glasgow', in Briggs, *Chartist Studies* (1959)
—— *The Chartist Movement in Scotland* (Manchester 1970)
—— 'The Scottish Chartist Press', *SLHSJ*, iv (1971)
—— 'The Suffrage Movement', in Hollis, *Pressure from Without . . .* (1974)
Wilson, D, 'Party Bureaucracy in Britain', *British Journal of Political Science*, ii (1972)
Wilson, G M, 'The Strike Policy of the Miners in the West of Scotland 1842–1874', in MacDougall, *Essays in Scottish Labour History* (1978b)
—— *Alexander MacDonald, Leader of the Miners* (Aberdeen 1982)
Wilson, H, *The Labour Government, a personal record* (London 1972)
—— *Final Term* (London 1979)
Wilson, J, *CB, a life of Sir Henry Campbell-Bannerman* (London 1973)

Wilson, T, 'The Coupon and the British General Election of 1918', *Journal of Modern History*, xxxvi (1964)
—— *The Downfall of the Liberal Party* (London and Glasgow 1976)
Wilson, W, *Memorials of R S Candlish* (Edinburgh 1880)
Withington, D J, 'Towards a National System', *Scottish Educational Studies*, ii (1972)
—— 'The Free Church Educational Scheme 1843–1850', *Records of the Scottish Church History Society*, xv (1964)
Wolfe, J N, *Government and Nationalism in Scotland* (Edinburgh 1969)
Wolfe, W, *Scotland Lives* (Edinburgh 1973)
Wood, I S, 'Irish Immigrants and Scottish Radicalism 1880–1906', in MacDougall, *Essays in Scottish Labour History* (1978b)
—— 'John Wheatley, the Irish and the Labour Movement in Scotland', *Innes Review*, xxxi (1980)
Wright, L C, *Chartism in Scotland* (Edinburgh 1953)
Wrigley, C J, *David Lloyd George and the British Labour Movement* (Hassocks 1976)
Young, J D, 'The Rise of Scottish Socialism', in Brown, G, *The Red Paper on Scotland* (1975)
—— *The Rousing of the Scottish Working Class* (London 1979)
Young, K, *Arthur James Balfour* (London 1963)
—— *Sir Alec Douglas-Home* (London 1970)
—— *Harry, Lord Rosebery* (London 1974)
Youngson Brown, A J, 'Trades Union Policy in the Scottish Coalfields 1855–1885', *Economic History Review*, 2nd series, vi (1953–4)
Zebel, S H, *Balfour, a political biography* (Cambridge 1973)

Index